Sir Frederic Bartlett

BARTLETT, CULTURE AND COGNITION

Bartlett, Culture and Cognition

edited by
Akiko Saito
University of Cambridge, UK

Psychology Press
a member of the Taylor & Francis group

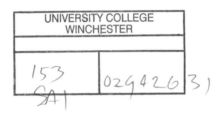

First published 2000 by Psychology Press

© 2000 Selection and editorial matter, Akiko Saito; individual chapters, the contributors

British Library Cataloguing in Publication Data

A catalogue record for this book is available from the British Library

*Front cover: Photograph of Sir Frederic Bartlett, reproduced by kind permission of the
Department of Experimental Psychology, University of Cambridge*

*Frontispiece: Oil painting of Sir Frederic Bartlett by Peter Greenham (1952), reproduced by kind
permission of the Department of Experimental Psychology, University of Cambridge*

ISBN 0-415-20172-1

Typeset by Graphicraft Limited, Hong Kong
Printed and bound in the UK by Biddles Ltd, Guildford and King's Lynn

Contents

Contributors

Alan Baddeley, Department of Experimental Psychology, University of Bristol, 8 Woodland Road, Bristol BS8 1TN, UK.

Hugh F. Bartlett, F.C. Bartlett's eldest son.

Erik T. Bergman, Department of Psychology, Washington University, One Brookings Drive, St. Louis, MO 63130-4899, USA.

Dorthe Berntsen, Institute of Psychology, University of Aarhus, Asylvej 4, 8240 Risskov, Denmark.

David Bloor, Science Studies Unit, Department of Sociology, University of Edinburgh, 21 Buccleuch Place, Edinburgh EH8 9LN, UK.

William F. Brewer, Department of Psychology, University of Illinois at Urbana-Champaign, 603 East Daniel St., Champaign, IL 61820, USA.

Jerome Bruner, New York University, Vanderbilt Hall, 40 Washington Place S., New York, NY 10012, USA.

Jennifer Cole, Department of Anthropology, Harvard University, Cambridge, MA 02138, USA.

Michael Cole, Laboratory of Comparative Human Cognition, University of California San Diego, La Jolla, California 92075, USA.

Mary Douglas, Department of Anthropology, University College London, Gower Street, London WC1E 6BT, UK.

Richard Gregory, Department of Experimental Psychology, University of Bristol, 8 Woodland Road, Bristol BS8 1TN, UK.

Steen F. Larsen, Institute of Psychology, University of Aarhus, Asylvej 4, 8240 Risskov, Denmark.

Michelle L. Meade, Department of Psychology, Washington University, One Brookings Drive, St. Louis, MO 63130-4899, USA.

Henry L. Roediger III, Department of Psychology, Washington University, One Brookings Drive, St. Louis, MO 63130-4899, USA.

Alberto Rosa, Departamento de Psicologia Basica, Facultad de Psicologia, Universidad Autonoma de Madrid, Cantoblanco, 28049 Madrid, Spain.

Akiko Saito, Faculty of Social and Political Sciences, University of Cambridge, Free School Lane, Cambridge, CB2 3RQ, UK.

Alan Welford, (1914–95).

Paul Whittle, Department of Experimental Psychology, University of Cambridge, Downing Street, Cambridge CB2 3EB, UK.

Figures and tables

Foreword

Sir Frederic Bartlett was plainly one of the great psychologists of his generation
—great in stature as a scholar, an extraordinarily appealing and charismatic
human being, gifted in the arts of getting people to work easily together, wonderfully generous in spirit, lucid in discourse. He was also one of the most British
Englishmen I have ever known, whether in carriage, habits, tastes or loyalties.
And he could never quite resist drawing his examples of everyday behaviour
from cricket, one of the least transparent forms of British life, at least to an outsider. Yet, I still cherish the memory of his describing to me with stunning acumen
the psychological (and indeed cultural complexities) of an umpire's call of 'leg
before wicket'—as a 'real' phenomenon, as the outcome of the umpire's decision
processes or as a 'cultural event' in the minds of spectators at a cricket match.
I was a visiting member of Bartlett's college, St. Johns, in the mid-1950s. Sir
Frederic, walking the college quads or chatting in Combination Room after
dinner, became for me as much a defining feature of Cambridge life as the
College bells striking the quarter hours.

Yet, for all that, he was an anomaly and remains one even today. Not a quaint
or eccentric anomaly, but one that seems to be virtually prototypical of the broad
field of scholarly inquiry to which he devoted his engaged life: the 'human
sciences', as we now call them, psychology, anthropology, neuropsychology and
the rest. His 1932 *Remembering* still stands today as a monument to his courage
and wisdom in trying to impose some unity on that vast domain. His later uncer-
tainties, 'unsteadinesses', even inconsistencies with regard to psychological
explanation seem, in retrospect, not so much personal anomalies as ones that are,
as it were, endemic to the human sciences and, most particularly, to psychology
itself. His intellectual life was so fraught with the very same puzzlingly deep
issues that we live with today that, indeed, even the authors of this volume in his

honour cannot agree on what he *really* stood for, what was the *true* outcome of his life's work.

Let me try to explain this a little, though it will be much clearer to the reader once into the body of the book that follows. To begin with, as several authors make vividly evident, Sir Frederic had two seemingly antithetical views of the nature of psychology. In one view, the major aim of psychology was to elucidate human meaning making; *effort after meaning* was the hallmark of human mental activity, and that the way to a successful psychology was through exploring the processes through which the effort after meaning achieved its ends—true meanings and illusory ones alike. These processes included such activities as schematisation, conventionalisation, assimilation to expectancies and the like, none of which were exclusively individual in nature. For all of them depended upon *cultural* givens, shared views of the world upon which individuals depended in *constructing* their schemata, their conventionalisations, and the like.

It is for these reason that several authors of chapters in this volume hail Bartlett as the 'founder' of *cultural psychology*, celebrating his kinship not only to his mentors and early models, W.H.R. Rivers and A.C. Haddon, but to such French thinkers as Durkheim, Halbwachs, Mauss and others. After all, Bartlett published a book in 1923 entitled *Psychology and Primitive Culture*, a book notable for its rejection and refutation of Lucien Lévy-Bruhl's conception of the pre-logical nature of primitive thought. For all his 'Englishness', the 38-year-old Bartlett had no qualms about crossing the Channel to enter the French debates about culture. But such issues were not to remain his chief preoccupation after the publication, nine years later, of *Remembering*.

Mary Douglas (see Chapter 11 in this volume) remarks that, in some deep sense, the life work of E.E. Evans-Pritchard, the gifted English anthropologist, represents a better extrapolation of Bartlett's early ideas than Bartlett's own later career. Indeed, the anthropologist, Clifford Geertz, remarks in his chapter on Evans-Pritchard in his *Works and lives: The anthropologist as author* (1988) that 'E-P' presents his observations on the Nuer as if to make it all clear to a fellow don in an Oxbridge common room. Perhaps it was Frederic Bartlett that Evans-Pritchard had in mind! In any case, I note from the Bibliography compiled by Hugh Frederic Bartlett that *Psychology and primitive culture* is 'in some sense a reflection of Bartlett's unrealised anthropological vocation'.

What about Bartlett's *other* view about the agenda for psychology? It might be said that if his first view was about 'how culture got into mind', the second was much more about mind itself, its capabilities, limits and properties. It was strongly linked to issues of what might best be called 'situated human skills', situated in the full sense of being related to the situations in which human beings actually *work* or operate. In this sense too it was 'cultural' in the sense of being 'situated'. But it was also *applied* psychology or, even more accurately, psychology linked to *engineering*. Yet it does not do to say merely that this was Bartlett's practical side, even though much of the work done under its aegis grew out of his involvement from very early on in defence-related research ranging from acoustic detection of aircraft in World War I to problems in using radar signals in World War II. For this line of work, centring on such matters as information-processing and its temporal limits and channel capacity, the conversion of input from short-term to long-term memory and so on, was also highly *theoretical.* Indeed, it provided a major conceptual base for what later came to be called the Cognitive Revolution. Certainly, the generation of students who worked under the sway of this second, 'applied' view of psychology are counted today among the stalwarts of that Revolution—Richard Gregory and Donald Broadbent, to mention only two. But 'applied' was no pejorative term to either Bartlett or his students. If I may be forgiven a personal anecdote, I can't help but recall an occasion during Donald Broadbent's extended visit to the Center for Cognitive Studies at Harvard in 1969 when he kindly agreed to give some lectures in 'Psychology 148', the course George Miller and I taught in the hope of under-mining the reigning 'eye-ear-nose-and-throat' psychology of that place and time. I introduced Donald to the class as 'one of the leading theoretical and experi-mental psychologists anywhere'. He then proceeded to give one of his usual stellar lectures. But as we were leaving Memorial Hall, where the class met, on our way to lunch at the Faculty Club he said to me, 'Jerry, you know that basically I'm *not* a theoretical psychologist but an *applied* one. That's what I really am and I wouldn't change it for anything.'

So what did 'applied' mean to Bartlett and to his students and why did they all cling so proudly to the word in the title of the Medical Research Council unit on Chaucer Road, 'The Applied Psychology Unit'. Well, doubtless Bartlett was proud of the pioneering work the Unit had done on military problems, on lessen-ing road deaths, on improving working conditions in British industry, on helping the deaf and blind and so on. Indeed, he was very caught up in it as a member of countless Government committees. And he was highly honoured for his part in it, and was made (as only the British can make you) one of the 'great and the good'—Fellow of the Royal Society, knighthood, honour upon honour. Increas-ingly, the 'applied' work became more sophisticated theoretically (and, of course, more powerful), but it moved further and further away from the concern with meaning making, conventionalisation, and schematisation of his earlier work toward an alternative model of human functioning, towards what might be called the 'human skills' or 'human factors' model.

Doubtless, both the exigencies and rewards of those times drew him in that direction. But there were other things as well. I'm of the view that Kenneth Craik's brilliant insights about explanation in man–machine systems were one factor. Another was the widening gap between those who thought of themselves as natural scientists and those who identified themselves as humanists—a chapter in intellectual history told compellingly in C.P. Snow's *The two cultures*, with Bartlett's Cambridge as its time and place. Perhaps too, the exotica of distant cultures lost their allure in the midst of a successful man's busy life.

Indeed, by 1958, when he published *Thinking: An experimental and social study*, there was very little left of the old 'cultural model' that had so intrigued him and his readers earlier. The model of thinking this time round was human skill. I was privileged to review it in the *British Journal of Psychology* (1958) when it appeared and expressed regret that, in dealing with the question of what led people to organise evidence in ways that led to 'gaps' and gap filling, gap filling being the aim of thinking in his view, he had said so little about such 'Bartlettian' matters as conventionalisation and schematisation and other matters relating to cultural shaping. But so it was to be for his remaining years. He had left his 'unrealised anthropological vocation' behind.

Yet, one chapter in the present volume makes quite plain that, earlier on, he had been just as interested in cultural or collective factors in problem solving and thinking as in the skill component. It is David Bloor's intriguing account (Chapter 12) of Bartlett's early work on group problem solving by different national teams engaged in designing acoustic devices for aircraft spotting and for directing anti-aircraft fire during World War I. In the 1920s, he was plainly interested in how national cultures might influence the kinds of solutions these national teams might achieve. Bloor concludes his fascinating chapter by reflecting on whether, historically considered, Bartlett's work might link 'the pioneers of the Torres Straits [W.H.R. Rivers and A.C. Haddon, who had lured the young Bartlett toward issues of cultural conventionalisation] to the controversial social constructivists of today'. It is an interesting if abstract historical hindsight, but it was not how things played out in real life over those years. For after World War II there developed an ever deeper separation between the 'human factors' skill-oriented Bartlett and his students and those who were interested in how culture formed mind and, in turn, was formed by it. The 'cultural programme', so to speak, was mostly realised by anthropologists and sociologists of knowledge who, if they knew mainline psychologists, knew them principally as dining companions in College.

But, as Bartlett put it, gaps attract problem solving and 'filling in'. Did this gap help stimulate the rebirth of cultural psychology? Why the revivification of interest in the cultural-historical views of Vygotsky; why a renewed Society of Psychological Anthropology in America? Why the revival of interest in the cultural psychology of Ignace Meyerson in France (cf. Parot, 1996)? What a special delight, then, to welcome the present volume.

For in its pages Bartlett's two approaches (considerably grown up) are back together again, at least together inside the pages of a single book! Not that all the authors are, as it were, talking to each other. Some have not quite been introduced, but it is good that they are at the same party. I suspect the time is ripe for a new mutual awareness. Mary Douglas (Chapter 11) queries—probably half jokingly but half in despair—why (allegedly) there is no theory of culture, and concludes that 'no one wants one. If they really wanted it they could have it.' It runs counter, she argues, to the individualist ethos of the West, where a 'collectivist theory of the construction of knowledge is unintelligible and unacceptable'. Perhaps so. I read the signs somewhat differently. There has never been such an upsurge of constructivism before. And never has it had such a variety of expressions—in history, in law, in anthropology, even at last in psychology. Psychologists are exploring concepts like schema and framing with a new freshness, as the reader will find in the chapters following. And there is a new appreciation of the supportive functions inherent in the 'situatedness' of human behaviour in institutional settings. So, this volume gives me hope—and informs me of developments of which I'd not been aware.

I think that the effect of all this activity will be to bring Bartlett's wonderfully fruitful life back into a single compass. And may this have the further effect, eventually, of bringing the various human sciences back under a single, communal tent!

Jerome Bruner
24 January 1999

Acknowledgements

Every effort has been made to trace all copyright holders, but if any have been inadvertently overlooked the publishers will be pleased to make the necessary arrangements at the first opportunity. Because of the nature of this volume, many excerpts from Bartlett's various works appear, especially those published by Cambridge University Press; thanks are due to Cambridge University Press for allowing these. Chapter 2 appears with the permission of the American Philosophical Society and Mrs. Ruth Welford; it originally appeared as 'Biographical Memoirs: Sir Frederic Charles Bartlett (1886–1969)' in the *Yearbook of the American Philosophical Society* (1970, pp. 109–114). Chapter 5 appears with the permission of Sage Publications Ltd; it originally appeared in *Culture & Psychology* (1996, 2(4), 355–378), and has been slightly revised for this volume.

I appreciate the support of all those people who made this work possible, especially the contributors and the British Academy who supported the preparatory research. I would also like to thank the helpful staff at the library of St. John's College, Cambridge. Special thanks are due to Simon Learmount, for his considerable support, encouragement and editorial assistance.

PART I

Introduction

CHAPTER ONE

Psychology as biological and social science

Akiko Saito

Frederic Charles Bartlett (1886–1969) is perhaps best known for his contributions within cognitive science. In particular his work on memory (e.g. 1932) is generally considered to have constituted an important foundation upon which memory research has subsequently been developed with the advent of the 'cognitive revolution' of the 1960s. Bartlett's emphasis on research using a naturalistic setting and 'ecologically valid' (i.e. true/close to real-life situations; also see Brewer, Chapter 6) experimental tasks led him to reject the classical Ebbinghaus approach to the study of memory, which centres on the memorising of nonsense syllables. Instead he conducted a series of experimental studies using a broader range of materials and methods (including his famous method of 'serial reproduction' of the story of the 'War of the Ghosts'), to analyse the manner and the matter of the changes made in the recalls, rather than the number of accurate recalls. This experimental method (i.e. stressing naturalistic settings and ecologically valid tasks) has been integrated into, for example, the 'ecological approach' in memory research (e.g. Neisser, 1967).

Beyond memory research, Bartlett's work is considered to have significantly influenced cognitive psychology and cognitive science with his theory of 'schema'. One of the chief findings from his studies was that human memory (and also other related cognitive processes that he studied, e.g. perceiving, recognising, imaging, thinking) is an active, selective and constructive process ('effort after meaning'), and not a passive reaction or a mechanical reproduction of the external information and stimuli. He also found that the range of human cognitive processes he studied is continually developing and adaptive, and is based upon affect, conation, images and the context. Bartlett developed his notion of schema in order to conceptualise this dynamic systems nature of memory and other

3

related cognitive processes. The notion of schema was rehabilitated in the 1970s in artificial intelligence research and computer science, especially with Minsky's frame theory (1975), although its dynamic systems nature was not fully captured at the time. Cognitive psychology was next, generating seminal works including Schank and Abelson's 'script' theory (1977) and Rumelhart and others' research on knowledge representation. The new schema ideas stimulated a variety of empirical research and further new theoretical interpretations of schema.

In addition to these classical applications in cognitive psychology and cognitive science (including memory research), there have recently emerged new types and areas of study that extend other aspects of Bartlett's work. For example, there is the study of 'reconstructive memory', which constitutes a strong and active research area originating from Bartlett's work on '(re)constructive memory' (e.g. Brewer & Hay, 1984; Thompson, Hermann, Bruce, Read, Payne & Toglia, 1998). Also Bartlett's study of 'expert memory', which was largely ignored until recently, along with his notion of '(re)constructive memory', is now attracting increasing attention in contemporary research on 'expert memory', 'false memory syndrome' and 'involuntary memories'. The full implication of Bartlett's finding that cognition is imbued with affect and conation has also begun to be scrutinised. For example, Bartlett's concepts of 'image' and 'attitude' are attracting attention, especially in relation to everyday and autobiographical memories (e.g. Larsen, 1998). Furthermore, an increasing number of researchers in cognitive science are becoming aware of the limitations of the classical information-processing form of schema theory, and are looking to Bartlett's original notion, which treats flexibility and context-sensitivity as intrinsic to human memory and other cognitive processes. One of the most exciting directions in which Bartlett's insight has been extended is the recent development of a dynamic systems approach to cognition and cognitive development (for a review see e.g. Saito, 1996b).

Besides the aforementioned specific cognitive science and memory research, however, Bartlett's work is also being studied by social and cultural psychologists. Although he produced a substantial body of relevant work, this has been largely neglected until very recently, but as the sub-discipline of cultural psychology has rapidly gained currency within psychology and cognitive science, it is being increasingly incorporated into various emerging approaches to the study of social and cultural bases of cognition and cognitive development. Examples include 'narrative approach' (e.g. Bruner, 1990), 'discourse analysis' (e.g. Middleton & Edwards, 1990a), 'cultural-historical approach' (e.g. Cole, 1996), 'social representation theory' (e.g. Saito, 1996a) and 'anthropological psychology' (e.g. Rosa, 1996).

Furthermore, Bartlett's work is also increasingly explored in the field of the history and philosophy of science. For example, some aspects of Bartlett's work are now being acknowledged as heralding the modern sociology of science and technology (e.g. Bloor, 1997). Also the fate of his sociocultural psychology is being re-examined, as it shows a similar trajectory to that of Wilhelm Wundt, the widely acknowledged founder of modern psychology, in that while their experimental psychology was celebrated, their sociocultural psychology was marginalised until very recently (e.g. Rosa, 1996; Saito, 1998). For example, reasons why British psychology developed almost exclusively as a natural science discipline under Bartlett, who is generally perceived as the founder of institutional British psychology, in spite of his sociocultural psychology, are being researched (e.g. Costall, 1991, 1992, 1998; Douglas, 1987). Such studies invariably originate from a wider concern with the conceptual foundations of the discipline of psychology, and Bartlett's work is examined as a case study to highlight the indiscerptibility of natural science and sociocultural science research in psychology.

Whilst the range of current interest in Bartlett's work is itself noteworthy, to date works that critically examine and extend various aspects of Bartlett's psychology have largely been carried out independently from one another. This volume brings together in one place a selection of these contemporary studies from a variety of fields (e.g. experimental psychology, cognitive science, cognitive psychology, social and cultural psychology, anthropology, the history and philosophy of science). It also provides the historical and theoretical background to the many of the ideas contained in these studies, by illuminating the intellectual and institutional contexts in which they were originally generated, i.e. Cambridge psychology in the first half of the 20th century. This volume therefore aims to make a first step in providing a comprehensive account of Bartlett's psychology and its contemporary applications. It is hoped that readers will not only gain new insights relevant to their own fields, but also catch a glimpse of Bartlett's particular vision of psychology, which can only be discerned by examining his work in its entirety.

Rather than outline Bartlett's life and work in this introductory chapter, I have left that to the following chapter, where it is far more ably done by Alan Welford (1914–95), a student and then colleague of Bartlett at Cambridge. This piece offers a succinct yet comprehensive overview of Bartlett's wide-ranging works (e.g. in cognitive science, applied and experimental psychology, sociocultural psychology). It is therefore apt as an opening to the rest of the volume, where some of these diverse aspects of Bartlett's work are examined and applied in various ways.

Moreover, it illuminates the thinking and intellectual style that underlie Bartlett's psychology as a whole, to an extent not covered by other accounts of his work, by providing perceptive insights from both private and public perspectives. Welford studied psychology under Bartlett between 1936 and 1937, and then became Chaplain of St. John's College, where Bartlett was a Fellow, in 1938. After returning from Princeton (1945–46), where he 'refreshed' (Mrs. Ruth Welford's letter to me, 7 August 1998) his psychology, Welford was invited by Bartlett to become Director of the Nuffield Unit for Research into the Problems of Ageing. In 1947, Welford became a University Lecturer in Experimental Psychology, and remained at the Nuffield Unit as Honorary Director. In 1956, he became a Fellow and Tutor at St. John's College, and remained there and also as a University Lecturer in Experimental Psychology until 1968. Welford is therefore extremely well placed to offer a candid and balanced biography of Bartlett, complementing the more widely known works by former students of Bartlett (such as Oldfield, Zangwill and Broadbent), which have until now constituted the main departure point for contemporary scholars examining Bartlett's life and work.

Having given the reader a broad outline and sense of Bartlett's life and work, the three chapters in Part II provide some more specific historical and theoretical accounts. The first chapter is by Paul Whittle (Chapter 3), and recounts the early development of psychology at Cambridge. The chapter focuses especially on the work of W.H.R. Rivers (1864–1922), one of Bartlett's most important mentors and one of the founding fathers of psychology at Cambridge. This chapter is based on a talk Whittle gave at the University of Cambridge in December 1997, to mark the centenary of the appointment of Rivers to the post of University Lecturer in Physiological and Experimental Psychology, the first University appointment in psychology at Cambridge. The chapter is not meant to be a systematic chronicle of the period, but retains the informal style of the talk, providing an engaging glimpse into the institutional setting in which Bartlett emerged and began his work.

In particular, the chapter sheds light on the thinking and styles of important figures such as Rivers, James Ward, Charles S. Myers and William McDougall, who were all central to the foundation of the discipline of psychology at Cambridge, and who had pivotal influences on Bartlett's subsequent work. Whittle discusses Rivers's practice of psychology as both biological and social science, Hughlings Jackson's hierarchical evolutionary theory of brain organisation, and Myers's flair for organisation, all of which were to be taken up later in Bartlett's work, and which are to varying extents explored in some of the following chapters in this volume. By tracing these ideas' intellectual lineage, Whittle's chapter offers a deeper insight into the conceptual foundations of Bartlett's psychology.

Chapter 4 comprises memoirs of Bartlett written by Alan Baddeley and Richard Gregory. Baddeley is a leading memory researcher, who worked with Bartlett at the Medical Research Council Applied Psychology Unit (renamed the Medical Research Council Cognition and Brain Sciences Unit in 1998) at Cambridge. Bartlett was instrumental in establishing the Unit in 1944, was made Honorary Director in 1945, and remained actively involved until his death in 1969. Baddeley joined the Unit in the late 1950s, initially for nine years as a research student and then as a research scientist. After a few years' break he returned as the Unit's Director between 1974 and 1995. Richard Gregory is another leading experimental psychologist, known for his work in a range of areas including vision and perception research, engineering psychology and artificial intelligence. Gregory was one of the last students of Bartlett at the Department of Experimental Psychology, University of Cambridge, where he subsequently held a lecturership.

Their memories of Bartlett are presented separately in this chapter: Baddeley focuses on Bartlett's significant contributions to applied psychology, while Gregory discusses the legacy of Bartlett in experimental psychology. Overall, the chapter complements Welford's chapter, by providing intimate recollections of Bartlett's work from the perspective of contemporary experimental psychologists who also knew Bartlett personally. They have themselves both had important influences on the subsequent development of psychology and its sub-disciplines, and demonstrate the enduring legacy of Bartlett's approach for psychology.

The chapter by Alberto Rosa that closes Part II (Chapter 5) acts as a bridge between historical and theoretical accounts of Bartlett's work and the contemporary applications of his work that follow in Part III of the volume. Rosa has long been interested in Bartlett's work and has written, for example, the introduction to the Spanish translation (1995b) of Bartlett's *Remembering*. In his own words, his chapter belongs to the realm of 'intellectual history', analysing Bartlett's earlier studies, which are devoted to the psychological study of anthropological questions, by placing them in the context of their production, that is Cambridge in the 1910s and 1920s. His analysis suggests that these earlier studies by Bartlett comprise important and enduring projects for cultural psychology.

Rosa's analysis includes Bartlett's work on feelings and affects, which are seen as biological responses that in turn rise into consciousness. The consciousness Bartlett considers is phenomenological consciousness, and Bartlett stresses the role it plays in behaviour, which is adaptive; here Rosa sees an affinity with Watt's notion of *Einstellung*. In Rosa's view, Bartlett's work elucidates intentional and experiential consciousness, where the effects of social institutions, practices and tools leave their mark via the composition of systems of functional processes. These processes produce conscious experiences that are instrumental for the orientation of behaviour, decision making and voluntary action. For Rosa, these aspects of Bartlett's work presage contemporary activity theory. A related analysis of Bartlett's work on phenomenological consciousness is presented in Larsen and Berntsen's chapter (Chapter 7).

Rosa's analysis touches upon an aspect of Bartlett's work that has wide implications, that is the practice of psychology as both biological and social science—studying human cognitive processes as generated in a social niche as well as being the outcome of actions of biological entities that have their own unique history. Rosa closes by pointing to the striking affinities between a number of scholars working around that time in very different geographical locations and with different backgrounds. He sees, for example, Bartlett in England, J.M. Baldwin and G.H. Mead in the United States, Pierre Janet in France and Lev Vygotsky in Russia all simultaneously addressing the question of the relation of the social and the cultural with the psychological, and with a similar sensitivity: Rosa counsels that contemporary researchers may well profit from the theoretical and methodological insights of scholars such as these who faced up to this difficult issue.

Part III consists of seven chapters on contemporary research carried out in a range of sub-disciplines of psychology and allied sciences that apply or extend certain aspects of Bartlett's work.

Chapter 6 is by William F. Brewer, who has published extensively on schema theory and the role of schema in memory and knowledge. As discussed earlier, this is an area in which Bartlett's contribution is perhaps best known; here, Brewer provides a critical reappraisal of Bartlett's schema theory, together with an extensive review of related modern empirical research. Brewer argues that recent work on knowledge representation has shown that generic knowledge, which is seen as Bartlett's notion of schema, is just one of many forms of human knowledge, and that other forms of mental representation such as mental models and naïve theories will be required for a full theory of the human mind.

Current research in cognitive science on how many different forms of mental representations are involved for the mind to represent the external world is based partly on this idea that information in different domains requires different forms of mental representation. This 'information-processing, representationist approach' (Varela, 1992) to cognition and mind is considered to be a strong tradition deriving from Bartlett's research programmes, as discussed in some of the chapters in this volume (e.g. Baddeley and Gregory, Chapter 4). Note, however, that other contributors to this volume (e.g. Rosa, Chapter 5; Larsen & Berntsen, Chapter 7; Cole & Cole, Chapter 9; Saito, Chapter 10) also discuss further dimensions of Bartlett's work, which recognise various other integral factors of cognition and mind, such as embodied experiential ('activity') or phenomenological aspects.

Although the concept of schema has become the centrepiece of constructivist theories of perception, memory and knowledge representation since Bartlett's work was 'rediscovered' in the 1970s, in Chapter 7 Larsen and Berntsen argue that Bartlett ascribed similar importance to two other concepts, namely 'attitude' and 'image', in his exposition of memory. Tracing Bartlett's concepts of image and attitude to the German introspectionist tradition in psychology, in particular the functionalist view of the Würzburg school, Larsen and Berntsen carefully reconstruct Bartlett's use of image and attitude as constraints to the possible range of memory reconstructions based purely on schemata; in today's terms, 'bottom-up' and 'top-down' constraints respectively.

Larsen and Berntsen's analysis also reveals that Bartlett took account of the phenomenal experience reported by his subjects, in explicit opposition to behaviourism, and went beyond pure description of introspective content by attempting to specify a functional role for mental images; in this sense Bartlett avoided an epiphenomenal view of consciousness, unlike subsequent work on mental imagery in cognitive psychology. Their analysis also shows the affinity of Bartlett's concept of attitude with Betz's (1910) notion of *Einstellung*. This develops Rosa's (Chapter 5) discussion of the parallels between Bartlett's work and Watt's (1905) notion of *Einstellung* (both Betz and Watt were affiliated to the Würzburg school). It also points to an important convergence between Bartlett's concept and Russell's (1921) concept of propositional attitude. Larsen and Berntsen round off their arguments by reporting findings from their own study on autobiographical memories, which applies Bartlett's concept of attitude, defining it operationally as a reflexive relation between the individual and the experienced or remembered content, i.e. 'autobiographical reference'.

In his introduction to the 1995 reissue of Bartlett's *Remembering*, Walter Kintsch discusses an aspect of Bartlett's experimental studies that has remained controversial to date. That is, Bartlett's 'curious and sad omission' of Ballard's study (1913) on reminiscence and hypermnesia, which appears to contradict sharply Bartlett's results and conclusions on memory. According to Kintsch, this omission has caused Bartlett's work to be ignored by experimentalists, in spite of the significant impact that his theoretical notions, such as schema, have had on memory research. Kintsch (1995, p. xiii) states that 'Bartlett's seminal work on reconstructive processes in repeated recall has never been successfully replicated', whilst there is a vigorous research area originating with Ballard's work on reminiscence and hypermnesia, in which studies conducted by Henry Roediger and his colleagues are cited as the foremost examples.

Partly as a sequence and partly as a rejoinder to Kintsch's claim, Chapter 8 is authored by Roediger, Bergman and Meade. The chapter critically examines Bartlett's repeated reproduction experiments, in terms of methods, results and conclusions. Although Bartlett's studies of repeated reproduction have become a staple of standard treatments of memory in textbooks and achieved legendary status in the field of cognitive psychology, Roediger, Bergman and Meade highlight his casual methods and the anecdotal presentation of his results. Worryingly, they point out that until recently the reliability and validity of his claims have not been scrutinised. After a careful, and tenacious, critical review of various studies in a similar vein to Bartlett's model of repeated memory testing, they report their own replication study of Bartlett's experiments, with notable results. These findings are important for an understanding of Bartlett's methodology and results, and for a better elucidation of memory; as they contend, because we repeatedly remember the important events from our lives, understanding how retention changes over repeated reproductions is critical to an adequate account of memory.

The chapter ends with preliminary findings from their ongoing research into the influence of one person's memory reports on another person's later recollections, which has potentially important implications for current research on false memories. Roediger, Bergman and Meade suggest that many of the research programmes and research ideas on memory outlined by Bartlett, including social aspects of remembering, have yet to see fruition in empirical research. The chapters that follow, where various aspects of Bartlett's work on social bases of cognition are scrutinised and applied, show that some progress is beginning to be made, though.

Jennifer Cole's and Michael Cole's interest in Bartlett's work stems from Bartlett's long-term effort to overcome the split between anthropological and psychological formulations of human thought processes that has dominated the 20th century social sciences. Their chapter (Chapter 9) focuses on the way in which Bartlett's concepts of schemas, conventionalisation and the social context of cognition make it possible to link sociocultural and psychological processes in a manner that is simultaneously relevant to psychologists concerned with the influence of culture on mind and anthropologists concerned with processes of cultural transformation that accompany cultural contact.

The chapter draws on two empirical examples that highlight the potential of Bartlett's approach to address these two levels of analysis. The first empirical example examined is Edwin Hutchins's (1995) influential study, which gives a clear and dramatic example of schema formation and conventionalisation in a small group. The second example is Jennifer Cole's study of colonial memory among the Betsimisaraka of Eastern Madagascar, which analyses how conventionalisation and schema formation are essential for the maintenance of identity among these formerly colonised people. These empirical examples have been chosen to highlight the pertinence of conventionalisation and schema formation in different forms of activity where psychological processes such as remembering and thinking are evoked, and to illustrate the usefulness of close ethnographic investigation as a source of evidence for such psychological processes occurring in context.

Cole and Cole's chapter is also important in demonstrating the relevance of Bartlett's work on remembering and thinking to modern cultural psychology, in enabling a synthesis of Vygotskian emphasis on remembering as a cultural instrument or tool with the contemporary concern (e.g. Middleton & Edwards, 1990a) on remembering as a discursive practice or discursive resource.

My own contribution in Chapter 10 continues to explore the relevance of Bartlett's ideas to contemporary cultural psychology. I distinguish several levels of analysis of cognition that Bartlett adopts in his work, which I expound upon as the individual, social–individual interactive, microgenetic, sociogenetic and phylogenetic levels of analysis. I then focus on Bartlett's sociogenetic analysis, that is, his work on 'conventionalisation', examining this in some detail both theoretically and empirically before discussing it in relation to social representation theory, a current research paradigm in social and cultural psychology.

Although Bartlett does not explicitly advance a multilevel methodology for the study of cognition, and moreover many of his analyses and notions require empirical scrutiny and theoretical elaboration, I suggest that his overall approach, as well as some specific elements of his analyses, do merit attention in contemporary cultural psychology. In particular, Bartlett's work suggests ways in which the interaction of three integral bases (i.e. social, individual psychology and biological) of cognition, as well as the relations amongst various multiplex social bases, might be empirically researched. This aspect of Bartlett's work can be seen as presaging some recently emerging approaches in cultural psychology and cognitive science, including the 'embodied mind', 'dynamic systems' and 'developmental science' approaches (e.g. Cairns, Elder & Costello, 1996; Edelman, 1992, 1998; Magnusson, 1996). It is also suggested to be compatible with the 'dialectic paradigm', which includes cultural psychological research programmes such as the Vygotskian sociocultural approach, Valsiner's co-constructivism and Nelson's cognitive development theory, which has been proposed as a more potent alternative to the extant, dominant 'Platonic/Cartesian paradigm' (Marková, 1982; Moscovici & Marková, 1998) in cognition research.

Chapter 11 is by the cultural anthropologist, Mary Douglas. In an influential publication (1987), Douglas claimed that Bartlett's work on social institutional influence on memory remains incomplete, as Bartlett 'forgot' his earlier interest in social bases of cognition as he became progressively more involved in the institutional framework of Cambridge psychology—this 'forgetting' is described by Douglas as providing support for his own theory. Subsequent publications (e.g. Costall, 1991, 1992) have suggested that it was not so much that he 'forgot'; he continued to believe in the importance of social bases of cognition throughout his lifetime, but this became increasingly marginalised in the later part of his career as he became more involved with institutionally developing British psychology. This intriguing and complex issue constitutes an issue for ongoing research in the history and philosophy of psychology (e.g. Costall, 1998), and again serves to highlight the difficulties of practising psychology as both a biological science and a social science at the same time.

Douglas explores ways in which Bartlett's work on social bases of cognition can be extended, and specifically focuses on developing the perspective and research methods advocated in Evans-Pritchard's works. She suggests a dual heritage of Evans-Pritchard's approach, in bringing together the English psychologists' (Bartlett, Rivers) interest in the institutional framework that sustains memory, and the French sociologists' (e.g. Durkheim, Mauss, Halbwachs) researches in the same direction. She also highlights the intellectual lineage of Evans-Pritchard's approach with other influential currents at the time, including the neurological views of H. Head, C.S. Sherrington and E. Rignano. By exploring these various related works, Douglas reveals a number of reasons, including political ones, why the development of a cultural theory of behaviour and cognition is so difficult. She draws attention to the need for a greater awareness amongst psychologists and anthropologists of these difficulties, and the need for more careful thought about what is required to advance Bartlett's and others' work concerned with social institutional influences on cognition. She concludes with some suggestions as to the best solutions.

The final chapter of Part III (Chapter 12) is authored by David Bloor, one of the founding quartet of the Edinburgh School of history and philosophy of science. Bloor's chapter discusses Bartlett's work as pioneering the sociology of science and technology—specifically it shows that Bartlett developed an approach which he called 'social constructiveness', which can be seen as a precursor to today's social constructivism. Bartlett elaborated some aspects of his constructivism (in Bartlett's own term 'social constructiveness') in detail: In particular, he developed his notion of conventionalisation to expound upon the operation of social constructivism involved in cultural transmission and transformation. In an earlier work (1997) Bloor has suggested that this notion of conventionalisation, which otherwise would be highly germane to the contemporary sociology of science and technology, has been selectively 'forgotten' by subsequent researchers, thereby somewhat ironically serving to provide empirical support for Bartlett's own theory of conventionalisation. In this chapter, Bloor investigates the design of aircraft detection systems developed during and after World War I, which, intriguingly, Bartlett seems to have had some knowledge of. Bloor analyses the different technologies that were developed in different countries, in order to assess the validity of Bartlett's thesis of 'social constructiveness' and to examine its more general application to the sociology of science and technology.

Through his account, Bloor shows that as early as the 1930s the work of Bartlett was presaging a movement that only began to flourish in the 1970s in the UK and the USA, with the emergence of the sociology of science and technology. In more or less developed forms, the main ingredients of today's sociology of scientific knowledge can all be found in Bartlett's work, including underdetermination, conventionalisation, the study of reception, the importance of conflict, the concern with practice, the role of metaphor, anti-individualism, methodological symmetry and reflexivity.

The book concludes with a bibliography of Bartlett's work, compiled by Hugh Bartlett, Frederic Bartlett's eldest son. It is partly based on Harris and Zangwill's (1973) well-known *The Writings of Sir Frederic Bartlett, CBE, FRS: An annotated handlist*, which has been generally considered the most comprehensive bibliography to date, but adds a significant number of works not recorded elsewhere. As well as extending the list of publications, Hugh Bartlett also records Bartlett's reports to government bodies, his book reviews, biographies and obituaries, public lectures, honours and awards. Not only does the bibliography provide an excellent research tool, it complements the preceding chapters by demonstrating the breadth of Bartlett's work; he published in biological and cognitive science, organisational and group psychology and sociocultural psychology, to name a few. Moreover it reminds us that, in spite of his many awards, the variety of his publications and so on, Bartlett maintained a balance in his life and remained a caring father.

PROSPECTS

Bartlett's work is, as this book demonstrates, multifaceted, and therefore different readers will probably focus on the aspects of his work relevant to their own interests. However, an important feature of Bartlett's work, which has not yet received the attention it is due, is its vision and its scope, in encompassing both biological/cognitive and socially oriented research. Several contributors discuss the continuities between Bartlett's earlier, socially oriented research and his later experimental and applied work, which becomes even clearer when his work is viewed in its entirety and in context. It is hoped that this book will encourage readers to explore the continuities Bartlett implicitly recognised, and follow up the implications both empirically and theoretically.

The various contributions in this volume show Bartlett's psychology to entail, in a more or less developed form, a framework that might help to address the emergent properties of the multilevelled (encompassing the biological/individual and social) bases of human cognition and action. Bartlett's tacit framework, which anticipates the current dynamic systems or developmental systems approach to cognition and action, is not entirely surprising, considering Bartlett's intellectual orientation, illustrated for example in the exchanges between Bartlett and Norbert Wiener (see e.g. Wiener, 1956), the originator of cybernetics. It is also the case that the idea of systems was already fairly current at the time (see e.g. Douglas, 1980).

Bartlett's scheme of psychology as a unified science composed of both bio-logical and social science is particularly pertinent for today's psychology and cognitive science. Some cognitive scientists are becoming increasingly aware of the integrality of social bases of cognition, yet lack the means to incorporate them into their empirical research (e.g. Damasio, 1994; Thelen & Smith, 1994), while the fast-growing band of cultural psychologists tend to be preoccupied with social and cultural bases of cognition, at the expense of the biological/individual. These states of affairs have been due largely to the lack of adequate theoretical and methodological frameworks to replace existing ones, which tend to treat the biological/individual and the social as alternative explanations. This dichotomous view might become increasingly outmoded though, as alternative but equally stringent frameworks are established. For example, various develop-mental systems approaches are currently being developed (e.g. Edelman, 1992, 1998; Johnson, 1987; Lakoff, 1987; Magnusson, 1996; Marková, 1982; Thelen and Smith, 1994) as a more potent alternative to the existing 'representationist' cognitivist or 'Cartesian disembodied' approach to the study of human action and cognition. Exploration of Bartlett's framework might play a useful role in this undertaking.

Bartlett's project is incomplete, but this volume shows the value of continu-ing to build on, rectify and refine where necessary, and expand his work. The following chapters serve to introduce readers to contemporary research that has drawn on selected dimensions of Bartlett's work. If the book as a whole serves to stimulate debate and encourage further critical scrutiny of Bartlett's psycho-logy and its relevance for contemporary research issues, its goal will have been achieved.

CHAPTER TWO

The life and work of Frederic C. Bartlett

Alan Welford

Frederic Charles Bartlett was born on 20 October 1886, at Stow-on-the-Wold in Gloucestershire. For many years before he died at Cambridge on 30 September 1969, he had been the most distinguished and influential psychologist Britain has ever produced. As a child his health had not been good and he was educated privately. He went, however, to London University where in 1909 he took his BA with First Class Honours in Philosophy, and two years later his MA with special distinction in Sociology and Ethics. He then went on to Cambridge where in 1914 he obtained First Class Honours in the Logic section of the Moral Sciences Tripos.[1] In the same year C.S. Myers, who was then director of the Cambridge Psychological Laboratory, took him on as assistant director, and when Myers went to London in 1922, Bartlett succeeded him. In 1931 he became the first professor of experimental psychology in Cambridge and a fellow of St. John's College. The next year he was elected to the Royal Society. He was made CBE in 1941 and knighted in 1948.

International recognition began early. He became a foreign associate member of the Société Française de Psychologie in 1930, and in 1937 the University of Athens made him an honorary PHD. His widespread international acclaim began, however, in 1945 when he was elected a member of the American Philosophical Society, whose members can thus congratulate themselves on their perspicacity. In the following year, at the invitation of his close friend, H.S. Langfeld, who was then chairman of the Psychology Department at Princeton, he went for the first time to America. During this visit he received the honorary degree of DSC from Princeton and was elected a foreign associate of the National Academy of Sciences.

After that, honours came thick and fast. He was given the honorary degrees of Doctor of Psychology by the University of Louvain, and of Doctor of Education by the University of Padua, became an honorary member of the American Academy of Arts and Science, of the Swedish, Spanish, Swiss, Turkish and Italian Psychological Societies, and of the International Association for Applied Psychology; and was given the Longacre Award of the Aero-Medical Association and the Gold Medal of the International Academy of Aviation and Space Medicine. In Britain he was awarded honorary degrees of DSC from London and Oxford Universities, and of LLD from Edinburgh University; and he was made an honorary fellow of the British Psychological Society, and an honorary member of the Ergonomics Research Society and of the Experimental Psychology Society. He was also invited to give a number of distinguished lectures [see Bibliography].

In 1952, the year in which he retired from his Chair, the Royal Society awarded him a Royal Medal. The citation for this included the statement: 'The School which he founded at Cambridge ... became under his leadership the dominant school in Britain and one of the most famous and respected in the world.' Bartlett regarded this medal as marking the high point in his career. What, we may ask, had brought him to it?

First and foremost was undoubtedly his quality of scientific thought. His early training in logic, combined with a profound intuitive insight into complex problems, enabled him to see quickly what was important in experimental results, and gave his thinking a constructive character and originality which made him an unusually stimulating teacher and research director. In the discussion classes he held for final-year students he would talk for a few minutes upon some topic of current research interest, and would then suddenly pick on one member of the class to say what he or she thought. Bartlett would listen carefully, seize upon anything worthwhile in what the student had said, enlarge on it and take the discussion on from there. As with many original thinkers, his ideas were not always accurate, but, in the light of subsequent events, they almost invariably seemed to have been on the right lines. He himself once remarked: 'You will never say anything sensible if you don't risk saying something foolish', and he was not afraid to act on his belief. Anyone who did research in the Cambridge Laboratory during the years just after the war will remember how Bartlett would burst into the room after a brief knock, introduce a visitor and at once plunge into an account of the research one was doing. The account was often surprising as it seemed at first sight to bear little relation to what was actually being done, yet on reflection one came to realise that it was by no means far from the mark, and was in fact what *ought* to be done—an indication of what could be achieved if the problem was viewed correctly. It was an enlivening experience, which made it seem urgent to think the problem out more thoroughly, and to get to work on it at full speed without delay.

Coupled with this adventurous quality in his thought was a determination not to get caught up in trivialities. As a colleague once put it: 'All the problems Bartlett studied were *real*.' His research fell into three periods. During the first, between 1914 and 1939, he was concerned to look at perception and memory under controlled conditions, but to see them more as they occur in real life than is possible with the highly artificial situations commonly used in laboratory studies. These researches are described in his best-known book *Remembering* published in 1932. When they appeared they were heavily criticised, and they have not been followed up to the extent they deserve. The reason is that they were far ahead of their time: The ideas they set out anticipated by a quarter of a century those to which the general run of experimental psychology is now laboriously making its way.

Remembering broke new ground not only as a study of cognitive functions for their own sake, but also in its attempt to link these to biological ideas, as James Ward, who was one of Bartlett's heroes, had urged, and to social behaviour following the encouragement of his close friend W.H.R. Rivers. On the biological side, Bartlett viewed perception and memory in terms of the continuously evolving 'plastic' model postulated by Sir Henry Head to account for the body schema in terms of which posture and action are co-ordinated. On the social side he insisted that the individual cannot be fully understood except in his social setting. He not only concerned himself with social influences on individual performance but, long before his time, tried to work out some of the ways in which individual capacities and characteristics account for social behaviour. Interest in social studies, especially social anthropology, continued throughout his career. It showed in two of his early books, *Psychology and Primitive Culture* published in 1923, and *Psychology and the Soldier*, which appeared in 1927; and by his joining in the editorship of the unpretentious but highly influential book *The Study of Society*, published in 1939. His attainment in this area was recognised by the Royal Anthropological Institute, which appointed him to deliver its Huxley Memorial Lecture in 1943.

Bartlett will probably, however, be remembered best for his second period of research, from the beginning of the Second World War until his retirement. It was a time of active development for many types of complex equipment such as anti-aircraft and other gun-laying systems, radar, asdic [an early form of sonar] and ground-to-air control. He quickly saw that the effective operation of these could not be secured solely by the selection and training of personnel: The equipment and the methods of operating it needed to be designed with due regard for fundamental human capacities and limitations. This meant studying and analysing the operational skills involved. Bartlett's characteristic contribution was his insistence that it was not enough to look at simple sensory and motor requirements and measure these in isolation. On the one hand, the components of the skill have to be studied without destroying the performance as a whole; and on the other, it is necessary to go beyond the study of achievement to an examination of the way in which it is attained. These were difficult tasks which required new methods of analysis, and the erection of a broad new theoretical structure. The tasks appealed strongly to Bartlett, no doubt in part because of his life-long interest in the skills of cricket and tennis. He and his colleagues at the Laboratory undertook research for all three military services, and its long-term importance was recognised by the British Medical Research Council, which established its Applied Psychology Research Unit there in 1944 with the late K.J.W. Craik as director. The work continued after the war and was extended by a Unit on Research into Problems of Ageing set up by the Nuffield Foundation in 1946. Research on skill was being actively pursued at the same time on a large scale in America, but it is fair to claim that the Cambridge Laboratory under Bartlett led the world to an extent that no British university department of psychology has done before or since. His best-known statements emanating from this period are his Royal Society Ferrier Lecture 'Fatigue Following Highly Skilled Work' published in 1943 and his Oliver Sharpey Lectures 'The Measurement of Human Skill' to the Royal College of Physicians, London in 1947.

Bartlett's third period of research overlapped the second and continued after his retirement. Both the previous periods had shown the need for studies of thinking, and it is therefore not surprising that Bartlett turned his attention in this direction. In 1950 he published a paper outlining a programme of experiments on thinking, and in 1958 a book, *Thinking: An experimental and social study*. The experiments which were reported examined the processes of thinking as analogous to the skilled sensory-motor performances that he and his colleagues had studied earlier. It opened up a new and promising approach to an area which has hitherto been one of those most elusive of scientific study.

Bartlett's ideas would not, however, have brought him to the position he occupied in British psychology if they had not been backed by the personal qualities needed to make them effective. He was an able negotiator, he fought hard for the kind of psychology he regarded as right, he was a severe but constructive critic, and he had a facility for expressing complex ideas elegantly in simple language without losing their force or talking down to his audience. This last shows especially in his book *The Mind at Work and Play* (1951), based on the Royal Institution's 1948 Christmas Lectures for Children. He had something of a flair for committee meetings, which he treated as though they were cricket matches, disposing his forces to outwit the other side and win the day, although always strictly by fair means—he could be formidable but never devious. In closer view, he was a complex person who combined genuine humility with clear-headed confidence, great kindness with occasional ruthlessness, sensitivity with robust attitudes to life, a rapid mind with the deliberate speech of the West Country, loyalty and trust with difficulty in distinguishing some enemies from friends, a cheerful ease of manner with a touch of sadness. He worked hard, but believed in keeping his work in perspective: Each Wednesday morning he claimed that he could accept no engagements because of an important meeting—it was for golf.

Looking back, what was Bartlett's essential achievement? It was, surely, that he guided the main stream of British psychology away from the speculations of the psychoanalysts, and from the assessment of differences between individuals by means of mental tests, towards the task of understanding the broad principles of human capacity and behaviour. Further, he severed the links that had in the earlier years of the century held the main stream of psychology to associationist philosophy, and established it clearly as one of the biological sciences, close to physiology. Perhaps most important of all in the long run, he suffused those who worked under him at Cambridge with the characteristic outlook of British biology: an outlook which is not concerned with grand theories or panacea principles, but which tries to view things as they are, and to answer in direct and simple terms the fundamental questions of 'What is it?' and of 'How does it work, and why?'

NOTE

1   The undergraduate examination at Cambridge.

PART II

Historical and theoretical issues

CHAPTER THREE

W.H.R. Rivers and the early·history of psychology at Cambridge[1]

Paul Whittle

INTRODUCTION

A hundred years ago, the *Cambridge University Reporter* announced the appointment of William Halse Rivers Rivers as University Lecturer in Physiological and Experimental Psychology. This was the first university appointment in psychology in Cambridge. During the next 25 years, until his premature death in 1922, Rivers made remarkable contributions to psychology, neurology, anthropology and psychotherapy. A century later, he is much better remembered by anthropologists than by psychologists. But he was very much a psychologist throughout his life. Of Bartlett's teachers, Rivers and his pupil C.S. Myers had the most influence on him.

Although there is currently something of a Rivers revival, in psychology Rivers was pretty firmly forgotten.[2] I looked through the indices of seven standard fat psychology textbooks from the 1930s to the 1960s, mostly American, but not all; only one mentioned Rivers. Even when his famous experiment with Henry Head was mentioned, it was attributed only to Head, ignoring the original account of which Rivers was first author. Yet Rivers did so much in so many fields and at such a pivotal transitional time that interesting stories and reflections branch off from every bit of his life and work—both intellectual stories within particular disciplines, and grander narratives situating him in 20th-century culture and history.

One general reflection at the start, on a theme that kept recurring: Rivers and his contemporaries were in the business of founding disciplines. Academic disciplines both facilitate and impede. They facilitate the work done within them, but put up boundaries around themselves which impede communication. It is remarkable how many of the people I shall mention refused to stay within the disciplines they were creating. They demonstrated it with their lives, Rivers in particular, and often were quite explicit about how irksome they found the restrictions. I came to feel it was appropriate that the oldest meaning of 'discipline' in English, according to the *Oxford English Dictionary*, is 'chastisement'.

Before getting on to dates and events, I want to try to give you some feeling for Rivers the man, as seen by his contemporaries.

RIVERS REMEMBERED BY HIS CONTEMPORARIES

People who knew Rivers fell under his spell. It's easy to believe, because those who study him now find the same thing happening to them. You can feel it in Pat Barker's novels. To show you what I mean, consider this note made by Norman Buck, the Assistant Librarian of Rivers's old college, St. John's. I found it hard at first to read with dry eyes:

> W. Arnold Middlebrook, of Downsway, Kirk Ella, East Yorks, called in the College Library in July 1963. He was treated for shellshock by Rivers at Craiglockhart Hospital in September 1917. He visited the Library on at least two occasions. Each time he asked to see the portrait of Rivers. He would stand, at the salute, and thank Rivers for all he did for him. On his last visit he was obviously in poor health and finished with the words 'goodbye my friend I don't suppose we shall ever meet again.'
>
> (Buck, 1963, p. 1)

That is 46 years after he was Rivers's patient. Put it together with the moving poems written to Rivers by Siegfried Sassoon, another of his World War I patients. Sassoon, a man so fearless in battle that he was known as 'Mad Jack', collapsed at Rivers's funeral. Put it also with Bartlett's expressions of devotion, at Rivers's death and repeated 15 and 45 years later. Here is Bartlett writing in the St. John's magazine just after Rivers died:

> Rivers was intolerant and sympathetic . . . He was once compared to Moses laying down the law. The comparison was an apt one, and one side of the truth. The other side of him was his sympathy. There is really no word for this. Sympathy is not good enough. It was a sort of power of getting into another man's life and treating it as if it were his own. And yet all the time he made you feel that your life was your own to guide, and above everything else that you could if you cared make something important out of it.
>
> It is no good. I cannot say what I want. What I want to say will not go down in ink and be made public.
>
> (Bartlett, 1923, p. 14)

My reading is that Bartlett couldn't bring himself to use the word 'love'. For it is clear that Rivers, like the other founding father William in the other Cambridge —William James, with whom many comparisons spring to mind—was loved by many people.

Here is Bartlett on Rivers 15 years later, in the *American Journal of Psychology*:

> He was a great man. We met him and had no doubt of it. He needed contact to communicate his greatness, which lived in him, and would not wholly go into any form other than himself.
>
> (Bartlett, 1937, p. 107)

There was Rivers I and Rivers II. Rivers I, before the Great War, was a diffident scholar. Here is Walter Langdon-Brown, in the St. Bartholomew's Hospital Journal, looking back over 40 years to the Rivers of the 1890s:

> In those days he was very reserved in mixed company, and was hampered by a stammer which he had not yet entirely overcome. But if among two or three friends his conversation was full of interest and illumination. He was always out to elicit the truth, entirely sincere, and disdainful of mere dialectic. In the laboratory he devoted himself to experimental psychology of the Wundt type. In 1897 I got him to come and address the Abernethian Society. The occasion was not an unqualified success. He chose 'Fatigue' as his subject, and before he had finished his title was writ large on the faces of his audience.
>
> (Langdon-Brown, 1936, p. 29)

He was at this time, according to Bartlett:

> Very much of a recluse, almost entirely wrapped up in his sociological and anthropological studies, and sailing off whenever he could to his beloved Melanesian islands and people. He warned me rigorously against getting entangled in any College or University affairs: 'they will take your mind off research' . . . Sometimes he asked me to tea and produced little slices of dry bread and butter and even drier Madeira cake. I do not remember anyone else at any of these tea parties.
>
> (Bartlett, 1967, p. 157)

But after the War 'he became another and far happier man', C.S. Myers tells us. 'Diffidence gave place to confidence, reticence to outspokenness, a somewhat laboured literary style to one remarkable for ease and charm' (1923, p. 168). Every one else confirms this: 'I have finished my serious work,' he said to Bartlett, 'and I shall just let myself go.'

> He moved into larger rooms in the New Court and there he entertained all sorts of notable people, in literature, in politics and in Society. He flung aside completely

all his dislike for practical affairs in College and University . . . His Sunday breakfasts became famous. He formed a club for discussion known as *The Socratics*, and he brought to it all sorts of influential visitors—H.G. Wells, Arnold Bennett, Siegfried Sassoon and lots more.

At the High Table he talked more than he had ever done in the old days and about far more topics . . . He was enormously active. He lectured often both in and out of Cambridge . . . In those days you never quite knew where Rivers would break out next . . . He came rushing round to my room one morning early, only partially dressed, and he put on my desk a piece of paper written over in his queer, almost illegible handwriting and said 'Look I want you to sign *this*.' It recorded that when he woke up that morning he had a strong impression that a distant friend of his was trying to communicate with him . . .

Sometimes when I dropped in to see him I would find him sitting still, apparently doing nothing, and looking desperately tired. He would take off his steel rimmed spectacles and pass his hand over his eyes. And then he would jump up and be active again. He wrote, talked, read, dashed about, took on new things and kept on old ones all in a terrific hurry as if he thought he wouldn't have time to finish.

(Bartlett, 1967, pp. 158–159)

One of the new things he was taking on was being a Labour candidate for parliament. 'Because the times are so ominous, the outlook for our own country and the world so black, that if others think I can be of service in political life, I cannot refuse' (Rivers, 1923b, p. v). He died before the election.

I hope that puts the man before us. Now to the history lesson.

CHRONOLOGY

I organise the history around a simple chronological table of events. I put the headings in bold so that you can, if you like, skim rapidly through it to get a sketchy cognitive framework. (I am indebted to Hearnshaw, 1964, Richards, 1998, Slobodin, 1978, and Smith, 1997, and the autobiographies of Myers, Bartlett and McDougall in *The History of Psychology in Autobiography*, for much of this background).

1864   Rivers born.

1875   Ward's fellowship dissertation on psychophysics.   This is James Ward, who became Professor of Philosophy at Cambridge. Early in his career he did experimental work on frog nerves, and his fellowship dissertation at Trinity College, Cambridge, *The Relation of Physiology and Psychology*, was a study of Weber's and Fechner's psychophysics. Later, he propounded a systematic philosophical psychology that allowed only a modest role for experimental psychology. Nevertheless, it was he who started the ball rolling, and kept it rolling, to establish the subject in Cambridge. In this same year William James first offers a course in physiological psychology at Harvard.

1879   Wundt founds the first psychological laboratory in Leipzig.   German universities were at this time benefiting from reforms in the 18th and early 19th centuries, and were decades ahead of the British in many respects. The *Cambridge University Reporter* for these years, in which the total university teaching staff occupies less than two pages, devotes large numbers of pages each year to comprehensive lists of the courses given in several German universities. Even though we were not providing the education ourselves, we knew where to go and get it. Publishing the information so prominently in the *Reporter* shows an admirable pragmatic realism. It is also a reminder of what a tragic rupture in European culture was caused by the world wars.

Another event in this year was the arrival of G.F. Stout at St. John's. He became a Fellow in 1894. Stout was in Cambridge for 17 years, and his *Manual of Psychology* was the dominant British text for decades (last printed in 1938). In spite of that, he seems to have made less impression on Cambridge psychology than Ward, Rivers or Myers, perhaps because he was a philosopher, and even less a biologist than Ward. But let him be a reminder that the Department of Experimental Psychology was not the whole of Cambridge psychology, then as now.

1886   Ward and Venn ask the General Board for psychophysical apparatus. The department has an origin myth that is rather different from this. According to both Myers and Bartlett, in several accounts, Ward and Venn, the logician, in 1877, nine years earlier, 'proposed to the University that there should be established in Cambridge a laboratory of psychophysics' (Bartlett, 1937, p. 98). The proposal is said to have been attacked in a Senate discussion by 'a certain theologically minded mathematician' who asserted that it would 'insult religion by putting the soul in a pair of scales'.

However, what is in the *Reporter* is a Report of the General Board (the principal executive committee of the university) in 1891, when they finally granted some money, which also reviews earlier requests. The first was this, in 1886, followed by a second in 1888. Bartlett describes the double request, but places it nine years earlier. This has the advantage of suggesting that Cambridge could have had the world's first psychological laboratory, if only the university hadn't been so conservative (Bartlett, 1937).

Nor could I find the famous discussion. There is some entertaining obscurantist protest in 1897, when Rivers's lectureship is proposed, but I could find no discussion of anything to do with these earlier requests. It may well be lurking in sources that I have not searched, but I am left with a distinct suspicion that Myers and Bartlett were demonstrating Bartlett's later thesis on the constructive nature of memory. Though, to be fair, in one account Bartlett admits 'I have never seen the actual report of the proceedings' (Bartlett, 1937, p. 98).

1886   Rivers qualifies at St. Bartholomew's Hospital; takes many voyages as ship's surgeon.   He is already showing his love of travel (he came from a naval family). On one voyage, he spends a month in the company of George Bernard Shaw: 'many hours every day talking . . . "the greatest treat of my life" ' (Kingsley Martin, 1966, p. 97).

1889   1st International Congress of Psychology; Charcot is President.   Its early occurrence in our story can remind us that we are talking about the founding not of psychology, but of some of its institutions; the word 'psychology' was coined in the 16th century, and there was a course in 'empirical psychology' at Göttingen by the mid-18th century (McClelland, 1980, p. 43). When Helmholtz published his *Handbook of Physiological Optics*, starting in the 1860s, he was already summarising a century or more of experimental psychophysical work on vision. Psychology is not a young subject.

1890   Rivers at Queen Square (Hughlings Jackson, Horsley).   Hughlings Jackson's hierarchical evolutionary theory of brain organisation was perhaps the dominant intellectual influence on Rivers, throughout his life. It emphasises the phylogenetically recent nature of the cerebral cortex, and sees a prime function of cortex as refining, keeping control of and inhibiting the more primitive processes of the older mid-brain. This is one of those theories which contains a good deal of truth, but may be too powerful and attractive for its own good. In this case, glib metaphorical versions of it appear in psychiatry, social science and politics.

Victor Horsley was developing newly precise techniques for brain surgery. Rivers assisted him, which is comparable to a young medical researcher a few years ago getting hands-on experience of the just emerging techniques of brain imaging.

1890   William James's "Principles of Psychology".   The opening chapter of this is also a Jacksonian account of the brain.

1891   University grants Ward £50 'for apparatus'.   Venn and Ward had asked for £50 in 1886, and then in 1888 for '£100 urgently required for the purchase of psychophysical apparatus; and the Special Board for Biology and Geology [which meant in effect the Physiological Laboratory] joined with the Special Board for Moral Science [Philosophy] in urging the appointment of a University Lecturer in the Physiology of the Senses (including Psychophysics)' (*Reporter*, 1891). The response to this urgent request is to allocate £50 for apparatus after a three-year delay. The lectureship is not mentioned.

1892   Rivers in Jena; resolves 'to devote his life to psychology, and especially to its morbid manifestations'; post at Bethlem Hospital.   2nd International Congress of Psychology, in London. Sully and F.W.H. Myers (no relation to C.S. Myers) are joint secretaries.

1893   Works with Kraepelin in Heidelberg.

1894   Rivers visiting lecturer on Special Senses (Foster).   Sir Michael Foster, the professor of Physiology, was engaged in rejuvenating Cambridge medical studies. An external examiner had complained of the weakness of Cambridge students' knowledge of the senses, and Foster appointed Rivers to remedy this.

1895   Breuer and Freud's **"Studies in Hysteria".**

1897   Rivers appointed University Lecturer.   By Cambridge standards, this innovation was relatively painless and prompt. Compare it with degrees for women, which were recommended by a lengthy report in this same year, 1897. They were not granted until 1948. Or with sociology: It too was thriving in Germany in the late 19th century, but the first Cambridge post was not till 1970. In hindsight, we might say it that was correctly perceived that psychology was not so subversive after all. I do not mean that entirely as a compliment.

I should like at this point to introduce two more dramatis personae: Charles S. Myers and William McDougall. By 1897, Myers 'had already published in physical anthropology and had become a Fellow of the Royal Anthropological Institute in 1896, four years before Rivers was elected' (Slobodin, 1978, p. 21). Myers was an organiser who created institutions. I have not managed to get a strong impression of him intellectually, but Bartlett credits him with 'the scientific temper, the sanity, the breadth, the clarity, the insight possessed to the same degree by no other living English psychologist . . . Psychology in Cambridge was built by all these three (Ward, Rivers, Myers), and by others; but if I had to say upon whom its present position and its future possibilities most of all depended, I would, without hesitation, declare: upon C.S. Myers' (1937, p. 98).

McDougall passes through this story like a comet. He was academically precocious, entered Manchester University at the age of 14, obtained a first-class science degree, and then came to Cambridge and read medicine. He was a pupil of Rivers, but a Fellow of St. Johns some years before his teacher. His *Introduction to Social Psychology* (1908) is said to have been the most widely used psychology text ever. He moved to Harvard in 1920, but found himself the wrong man in the wrong place. Behaviourism had swept into American psychology, and McDougall had no sympathy with it.[3]

1898   Torres Straits expedition: Haddon, Rivers, McDougall and Myers.   The main scientific motive behind the psychological work of the expedition was to test the 'fairly unanimous' attribution 'to savage and semi-civilized races [of] a higher degree of acuteness of sense than is found among Europeans' (Rivers, 1901b, p. 12). The three psychologists measured thresholds and

performed other tests in all five sensory modalities. They found little difference between Torres Strait islanders and Europeans, and in spite of subsequent
criticisms of their methods (see Richards, 1998), this conclusion has by and
large held.

Rivers also started to collect genealogies (see later). This not only led to his
steadily increasing involvement in anthropology, but can also be seen as the start
of the strong concern with kinship systems in British Social Anthropology.

This expedition has been described both as the founding moment of British
anthropology, and a turning point in British psychology. For example, Richards
(1998, p. 136) says: 'The expedition was thus a pivotal moment in psychology's
metamorphosis from a discipline dominated by philosophical agendas and *a
prioristic* Spencerian evolutionary theorising into its post-1900 Modernist forms'
(only a few years later—1907—Picasso will paint *Les Demoiselles d'Avignon*,
the icon of modernism).

One of the surprises of the expedition was how friendly, welcoming and
co-operative the islanders were, belying their earlier reputation for hostility and
even cannibalism. Pat Barker portrays suggestively how relationships made here
started a process of change in Rivers. It also started a relationship which is still,
100 years later, of great importance for the islanders. The published reports
of the expedition are still well known, having supported successful land rights
claims against the Australian government. In 1998–99 islanders visited Cambridge
in connection with the centennial exhibition. This is living history (Herle &
Rouse, 1998).

1900   Rivers's chapter on 'Vision' in Schäfer's "Textbook of Physiology".
'Until 1898 he was immersed in the task of mastering the entire literature of past
experimental work on vision. . . . This exhaustive article of 123 pages . . . is still
regarded as the most accurate and careful account of the whole subject in the
English language' (Myers, 1923, p. 154).

1901   'a room acquired in a dark and uncomfortable cottage'.

1901   British Psychological Society founded by Sully, Rivers and McDougall.

1901   Rivers in India with the Todas for five months.   Volume 2 (psychophysics etc., mostly written by Rivers) of the Torres Straits Reports is published.
Rivers is efficient: Haddon did not get Volume 1 published until 1935!

1902   Studies regeneration in Head's arm.   A surgeon was engaged to sever
a cutaneous nerve in Head's arm. This rendered a largish area of skin on the
hand and lower arm anaesthetic. They studied the slow return of sensation. 'For

five happy years,' says Head, 'we worked together on weekends and holidays in
the quiet atmosphere of his rooms in St. John's College' (Head, 1923, p. iii).

Rivers interpreted the results in terms of a Jacksonian distinction between 'protopathic' and 'epicritic'. The more discriminative, epicritic, mode of
response,

> has been superimposed on one of a primitive character, which, under normal condi-
> tions, is in part inhibited and in part utilised in the final sensation. The excessive
> reaction to certain stimuli, apparent during recovery of sensibility, is due to the escape
> of 'protopathic' impulses from the control normally exercised by the 'epicritic'
> system. This conception had a profound influence on Rivers' psychological views
> and subsequently formed the basis of *Instinct and the Unconscious* (1920), the
> most far-reaching and popular of his writings.
>
> (Head, 1923, p. iii)

Rivers later extrapolated the distinction also to the interaction between cultures.

1903   Psychology acquires 'a whole house' in Mill Lane.   There are by this
time more than 40 psychological laboratories in the United States.

1904   Ward and Rivers found the "British Journal of Psychology".   They
are helped by Myers, McDougall and Sherrington. Myers becomes University
Demonstrator in Experimental Psychology at Cambridge. He holds this in parallel
with a professorship at King's London (whose psychology department later
moved to Birkbeck) until 1909 (Myers, 1936).

1906   "The Todas".   Here Rivers developed further his genealogical method,
generating kinship diagrams. Bartlett recalled years later how when he first
visited Rivers, as a new undergraduate, the conversation sprang into life when
Rivers found a pretext to show him these diagrams.

The method, as I crudely understand it, consisted of asking every informant
to name as many of his or her relatives as possible, stating the relationship. This
allowed to him to place every member of the community (there were about
800 Todas) on a vast grid of relationships. It provided internal checks on the
reliability of informants, because each relationship is described by more than
one person. You can see it would appeal to an experimental psychologist. It is
quantifying culture, or at any rate social organisation. Its attraction diminishes
slightly when one reflects that it was all carried out through an interpreter, and
that the meanings of the relationship terms were the end product, not the start.
The book, however, contains much more than genealogical charts, and is described by Mandelbaum, in an essay on the book in 1980, as being for 50 years
'a standard of ethnography'.

1908   Rivers in Melanesia.

1909   Myers becomes the first full-time University Lecturer in Experimental Psychology in Cambridge.

1912   Psychological Laboratory opened: The result of four years' work by Myers, plus a good deal of his own money.   In the Easter term, Wittgenstein (who arrived in 1911) and Myers experiment on musical rhythm (Monk, 1990). A tenuous link to another sub-culture.

1914   **"Kinship and Social Organisation"** *and* **"The History of Melanesian Society".**   The former (1914a) was reprinted as recently as 1968. Rivers regarded *The History of Melanesian Society* (1914b) as his most important contribution to science. It is now little read. 'In 1914, a Tripos[4] in Anthropology was established, which I likewise initiated' (Myers, 1936, p. 221).

1915   'Shell-shock' in World War I.   World War I produced an enormous and totally unforeseen epidemic of what came to be called 'shell-shock'. This was Myers' term, and caught on immediately, to his later regret. It is certainly more catchy than 'Post traumatic stress disorder'. It affected, it has been estimated, 7–10% of officers, and 3–4% of other ranks and led to 200,000 discharges (Stone, 1985).

Myers, too old for the army, went to France as a civilian volunteer but was soon commissioned in the Royal Army Medical Corps (RAMC) and 'instructed to supervise the treatment of functional nervous and mental disorders in the British Expeditionary Force' (i.e. he was in charge of shell-shock cases for the whole British army in France). 'I must have been, I suppose, the first to recognize . . . the essentially psychological nature of this condition' (Myers, 1936, p. 223). He was not always successful in preventing the military authorities from shooting his patients for cowardice.

Back in England, the Medical Research Council set up a Military Hospital at Maghull, near Liverpool, under the charge of Ronald Rows. Rows had read Janet and Freud and saw the relevance of their ideas about dissociated states following traumatic experiences. Maghull became a college of psychotherapy, such as has never been seen before or since. Among those passing through were Rivers, Pear, Hart, MacCurdy, Seligman, Myers, McDougall and William Brown. (Costall, 1996). So this, after Torres Straits, was the second dramatic formative experience linking the lives of our main characters.

'By the end of the war . . . At Maghull . . . squads of 50 RAMC officers were being given 3-month courses on the techniques of "abreactive" psychotherapy— including dream analysis' (Stone, 1985, p. 243). Rivers was posted from Maghull to Craiglockhart hospital, near Edinburgh. His post-war books on psychodynamics, and Pat Barker's novels, are based on his experiences there.

1920 **"Instinct and the Unconscious".**   This is Rivers's theoretical reflection on his War experience as a therapist. *Conflict and Dream* (1923a), published posthumously, continues the discussion.

1922 Rivers dies.   He dies without warning, of a strangulated hernia. It was a weekend, he was alone in his college rooms and not found until too late. He died in the Evelyn Nursing Home, after an emergency operation. He was given an elaborate college funeral according to his own detailed instructions: Funerary rites were one of his specialities. His ashes are buried in what was St. Giles's churchyard, which contains many famous Cambridge figures.

Both Bartlett and Sassoon give moving testimony to their intense grief at Rivers's death, and both describe dreams in which he came back to them.

1922 Myers leaves Cambridge.

> On demobilization I returned to Cambridge, fired with the desire to apply psycho-logy to medicine, industry, and education and becoming increasingly disgusted, after my very practical experience during the War, with the old academic atmos-phere of conservatism and opposition to psychology. I found that the wild rise of psychoanalysis had estranged the Regius Professor of Physic; I received little encouragement from the Professor of Physiology; and the Professor of Mental Philosophy, to my surprise, publicly opposed the suggested exclusion of the word 'experimental' in the title, now about to be conferred on me by the University, of Reader in Experimental Psychology. Thus medicine, physiology and philosophy had little use then at Cambridge for the experimental psychologist.
>
> (Myers, 1936, p. 224)

He stayed for four years, however, until he could hand over to Bartlett. Then he left to found the Institute of Industrial Psychology in London, which, with no government support, reached a staff of 50 within a few years.

1922 Bartlett becomes Director of the Psychological Laboratory, a position he is to hold for 30 years.

1926 The Royal Commission on the Universities of Oxford and Cambridge leads to the Psychological Laboratory being placed in the biological sciences
...   This was part of a reorganisation of departments into faculties. 'Very nearly all the subsequent changes have grown out of this one' wrote Bartlett in 1937 (p. 108). One side of him was clear that this was right: 'Psychology is a biolo-gical science. This means that it definitely restricts its study to the conditions by which any type of animal and human response to stimuli and organisation of stimuli is determined. We agree to give up asking *what* a sensation, or an image, or an idea, or an emotion actually is and we ask under what conditions responses

involving these occur' (Bartlett, 1936, p. 42). And yet in the same article he wrote that the Torres Straits 'expedition did another thing. It put a social and ethnological stamp upon Cambridge psychology and this has perhaps done more than anything else to make Cambridge psychology human as well as scientific' (Bartlett, 1936, p. 41).

Bartlett was aware both of the benefits that would accrue from establishing the department in a biology faculty, and also the drawbacks. He seems to have put a barrier in place while at the same time wanting not to.

1931   Bartlett appointed to a new chair established in Experimental Psychology.

DISCUSSION

How do we now evaluate Rivers? He carried out work of considerable influence in three quite separate fields: sensory psychophysiology, ethnology and psychiatry. And his work in all these fields is still very much worth reading, even if one has to reframe it a little, which is inevitable. However, none of the current evaluations are uncontroversial.

'Protopathic' vs. 'epicritic'   Zangwill, in the *Oxford Companion to the Mind* (1987, p. 686) remarks: 'Although raising much interest at the time, this theory has now been wholly discarded.' But Sherrick and Cholewiak, in a lengthy and authoritative review on cutaneous sensitivity, are much less dismissive and conclude (1986, chap. 12, p. 37) that 'certain aspects of Head's duality theory have found support from electrophysiological evidence'. However, it will hardly surprise any expert on sensory processes that a duplicity theory still finds some supporters.

Todas   I cited Mandelbaum; but Adam Kuper, in *The Social Science Encyclopaedia* (Kuper & Kuper, 1985, p. 712), says: 'his ethnographies are not among classics of their time'. Anthropologists will be able to place these authors in their corresponding tribe.

Psychodynamic work   Ellenberger, in his major history of psychoanalysis (1970, p. 827), says: 'In England [1918] psychoanalysis became increasingly popular, mainly through the work of Rivers.' But what strikes me is how he disappears from sight so soon after his death, and is ignored by the up and coming true Freudians. Karin Stephen's Cambridge lectures, given only a few years later, make no mention of him. Ernest Jones mentions Rivers two or three times in his biography of Freud, but only as 'the distinguished anthropologist' called upon to grace some committee or occasion. There is no mention that he was a psychotherapist even though Jones had reviewed *Instinct and the Unconscious*, not entirely unfavourably, in 1920.

A major cause of these contrary evaluations is the turbulence of the professional landscapes since Rivers, particularly in the decade after his death. In anthropology, the Malinowskian revolution with its emphasis on extended fieldwork made Rivers look amateurish, and its theoretical stress on the autonomy of cultures was inhospitable to Rivers's diffusionism. In psychiatry, the aforementioned 'wild rise of psychoanalysis', that is, the rise of the psychoanalytic *profession*, produced a polarisation with respect to Freud's ideas, from which we still suffer. Rivers's critical acceptance of some Freudian ideas, together with an attempt to place them in a biological context, survived only as a rather tenuous minority position.

As I have learnt more about Rivers and his contemporaries I have been repeatedly struck by the contrast between their enthusiastic founding of disciplines and their impatience with the consequent restrictions. Rivers showed it by his restless life. And in 1914 he wrote:

> specialisation has . . . in recent years reached such a pitch that it has become a serious evil. There is even a tendency to regard with suspicion one who betrays the possession of knowledge and attainments outside a narrow circle of interests.
>
> (Rivers, 1914c, p. 184)

We saw earlier how Myers reacted against the restrictions of academic experimental psychology after his war experience. William James (1920, p. 2) expressed it even more strongly in a letter: 'Psychology is a nasty little subject—all one cares to know lies outside.'

One feature of this ambivalence is perhaps peculiar to experimental psychology. That is, the tension between a high estimate of the importance of laboratory methods, on the one hand, and a certain impatience with practising them, on the other. Rivers, Myers and Bartlett all repeatedly insist—it recurs like a mantra—on the importance of a sound grounding in the psychophysical methods in the formation of a psychologist, and they did all perform lengthy studies using them.[5] But here is Bartlett describing his experience, when he was a student, around 1909, of James Ward:

> He was . . . alternatively a little amusing and terribly irritating in the laboratory. He prowled about, up and down, ill at ease, a bit envious maybe, but far more than a bit disgusted, and inclined to rate all our problems as trivialities.
>
> (Bartlett, 1937, p. 100)

Twenty years later he describes it from his point of view:

> I doubt if we can have been a very rewarding class. Privately we grumbled and groused like anything. We vowed we would lift no more weights, learn no more nonsense syllables, strike no more tuning forks, cross out no more e's . . . Everything that could be was in a strict pattern of psychological method, and now I

know it was greatly to our good. [But] when we left the laboratory we promptly dropped it all. What had it to do with our daily life? It was indeed just a laboratory game, boring in parts, engrossing in others, but just a game.

(Bartlett, 1956, pp. 82–83)

And here is Bartlett described by one of his own students:

in 1929, in my last year in his laboratory, I chided Bartlett on the infrequency of his appearances when we were doing our practical work. The occasion was, I think, the first on which I had ever seen him in the room; and I had the temerity to ask why. He smiled in his Bartlettian way; his bushy eyebrows shot up, his brow furrowed and his cheeks puffed out. 'I suppose,' he said, 'it is because I think most of the things you do here are dull and rather trivial.'

(Rodger, 1971, p. 178)

In contrast to this, Bartlett's own experimental techniques in *Remembering* (1932) are, as has often been pointed out, remarkably free and innovative.

These founding fathers were thus highly ambivalent. They set up disciplines of training and boundaries, and then belittled the former and cut across the latter. Rivers's work in particular cut across boundaries over which academic wars have been fought in the past century. I am thinking of: individual versus collective explanations, interpretative versus natural science. He was also at the start of the trend to increasing reflexivity in human science (which is the right catch-all term for him). His pointing to these large issues is one reason why he is of great interest now.

The subject that Rivers sketched out by his restless life as a psychologist (and he was always that, whatever else he also was) seems to me more attractive, more lovable you might say (like the man himself), than any institutionalisation of it that we have yet achieved. Try to hold in your mind at once, if you will, the young medic studying in Germany and returning full of excitement at the latest ideas about the nervous system, about colour vision and about insanity, the anthropologist spending months with an exotic south Indian hill tribe, the careful experimental neurologist observing over years the regeneration of sensitivity in Henry Head's arm, the psychotherapist earning the undying gratitude of his patients by helping them to live with the terrible memories of trench warfare. All this and more from a man who sometimes could work no more than four hours a day. And these were not just random scraps in a patchwork quilt. For Rivers they were unified within a framework based equally on Jacksonian ideas about the evolution of the nervous system, and on painstaking attention to his own experience (compare the other Will in the other Cambridge). It is the *spaciousness* of the subject that his life sketches out that seems to me of enormous and lasting appeal, and a standing reproach to us when we allow the specialist disciplines that he helped found to restrict our vision rather than to facilitate our research.

ACKNOWLEDGEMENTS

For help of various kinds I should like to thank Alan Costall, Jack Goody, Keith Hart, Anita Herle, Graham Richards, Paul Ries and Simon Schaffer.

NOTES

1 This chapter originated as a talk to the Department of Experimental Psychology, University of Cambridge in December 1997 to mark the centenary of Rivers's appointment. It gives some of the background to Bartlett's work, but it is not systematic history. I have deliberately retained the informality of the talk.

2 The revival started with Elaine Showalter's chapter on him in *The Female Malady* (1985). In 1991, 1993 and 1995 a trilogy of novels by Pat Barker appeared in which Rivers is a central character. The third of those won the Booker prize, and a successful film, *Regeneration*, has been made of the first (1991). The main biography of Rivers, by Richard Slobodin, has been reissued as a paperback. And in 1998 a book (by Herle and Rouse), an exhibition and a conference marked the centenary of the Torres Strait expedition, in which Rivers was one of the most important participants. It has again become true that 'you never quite know where Rivers will break out next', as Bartlett said of him.

3 Knowing little about McDougall, I was surprised to find when I read his autobiography (McDougall, 1930) that he jumped out of the page at me more vividly than any of our other characters. Immensely intelligent, self-assured, even arrogant, in charge of his life, and romantic. He describes rising at 4a.m. when he was a clinical medical student in London, to catch the mail train to Cornwall and watch the sea breaking on the rocks. In the second half of his life he slowly lost faith in his work. He remarks sadly that whereas when William James published one of his lesser-known works he received 500 letters within two weeks, he, McDougall, was lucky to receive half a dozen postcards in response to the many copies he sent out. Hearnshaw ends his chapter on McDougall (a chapter, note, where Rivers does not even appear in the Contents) 'McDougall had nearly all the ingredients for the making of a scientific psychologist except the scientific attitude'.

4 The undergraduate examination at Cambridge.

5 The 'psychophysical methods' are techniques for obtaining reliable measures of sensory thresholds. One of their origins was the realisation of 'observer error' in astronomical observations in the late 18th century (see, for example, Mollon & Perkins, 1996). These methods have since been generalised to other cognitive functions.

CHAPTER FOUR

Remembering Bartlett

Alan Baddeley and Richard Gregory

BARTLETT AND APPLIED PSYCHOLOGY

Alan Baddeley

When I first joined the MRC Applied Psychology Unit in Cambridge in the late 1950s, Bartlett had retired from his joint post as Professor of Psychology and Director of the Unit, but still had a room at the APU which he would use from time to time. I remember him as a tall distinguished grandfather figure known affectionately as 'Sir Fred', who would occasionally attend tea or coffee, and from time to time would bring visitors around. I was working with nonsense syllables at the time, which given his views on the Ebbinghaus approach to psychology cannot have been the material closest to his heart. He was always very genial however; perhaps the fact that I was attempting to apply the recent developments in information theory that had stemmed from his department, and that I was concerned with the practical problem of developing better postal codes was enough to compensate!

My last memory of Bartlett was at the presentation of the first Bartlett lecture, at which I remember Bartlett being present, a rather unusual occurrence since such events are usually posthumous. I remember Bartlett treating the whole thing with a wry good humour. As a young research student, comparatively unfamiliar with the Cambridge scene, I can remember feeling somewhat overwhelmed by the throng of the great and the good that attended the reception at St. John's College afterwards, and I remember with affection Bartlett's grandfatherly way of ensuring that I felt included.

So my personal memories of Bartlett are limited but very positive; I can understand why he was held in such esteem and affection by his students, who formed a large part of the generation that preceded mine in British psychology.

I went on to spend a total of some 30 years of my research career at the Applied Psychology Unit (APU)—an initial 9 years as research student and scientist, and after a few years' break, a further 21 as Director between 1974 and 1995. The APU was very much Bartlett's creation; after the tragic death of its first Director, Kenneth Craik, Bartlett himself directed the Unit, which was in turn directed by his students Norman Mackworth, and subsequently Donald Broadbent.

The Unit was created on the basis of a wide-ranging programme of applied research going on at the Experimental Psychology Laboratory in Cambridge during World War II. Its underlying philosophy was that basic and applied research should go hand in hand. Bartlett appreciated that the application of scientific psychological principles to important real-world problems could both enrich theory and facilitate practice. The most brilliant exponent of this philosophy was Kenneth Craik, whose book *The Nature of Explanation* (1943) outlined the value of physical models as a basis for scientific explanation, and whose work on anti-aircraft gun control was probably the first empirical application of a computer model to a psychological problem (Craik, 1948). This blend of pure and applied work characterised the wide range of work carried out by Bartlett and his group, some of it described in the contribution by Richard Gregory which follows this. The approach was continued by Bartlett's students, some of them such as Broadbent, Conrad and Poulton, at the Applied Psychology Unit, with others such as Richard Gregory and Alan Welford moving from the Unit to academic teaching posts.

When I myself became Director of the APU many years later, I tried to continue this spirit. I resisted any temptation to change what could have been regarded as a slightly old-fashioned title, which probably failed to reflect the amount of theoretical work that was done at the Unit, because I too believe in the importance of blending pure and applied research. The APU has been fortunate over its first 50 years, since for the whole of that period it has been both possible and fruitful to combine pure and applied work. I suspect this is often not the case in other subjects, and perhaps will not be true of psychology in the future. However, because of Bartlett's influence both directly and through his students, British psychology has, over the last half century, been highly sympathetic to the attempt to blend pure and applied research.

The information-processing tradition that has strongly influenced cognitive psychology gained much of its impetus from applied problems that began in Bartlett's laboratory. Selective attention, which had, during the 1930s and 1940s, been regarded as a concept reminiscent of introspectionism, was linked by Broadbent (1958) to the practical problem of a pilot attempting to select the appropriate call sign from the air traffic control tower. By refining this insight, he was able to formulate one of the first and most influential information-processing models forming the foundations for the study of selective attention, which is now one of the most well-established areas of cognitive psychology. Problems of optimally manning telephone exchanges fitted in neatly with Conrad's laboratory-based research on measuring mental load, allowing him to produce a solution to an important practical question (Conrad, 1955). This in turn led him to consider other problems facing the telephone services, including that of the telephonist required to remember and key long sequences of numbers and letters, leading to some of the earliest and most influential work on short-term memory (Conrad, 1964). Once again, some of the concepts of information theory, originating from collaboration between psychologists and engineers, led to the formulation of new approaches to human memory, approaches that are still with us and which continue to be fruitful.

Not all of Bartlett's influence of course emanated from the APU. Arguably, the greatest impact on the development of cognitive psychology that has come from British psychology has been through the development of cognitive neuropsychology. This reflected the application of the methods of cognitive psychology to the study of carefully selected single cases. Although Bartlett himself did not, to my knowledge, engage in neuropsychology, he clearly was strongly influenced by his contact with physiologists, and notably with the neurologist, Sir Henry Head. It may be recalled that Head developed the concept of a schema in order to account for the way in which we maintain a representation of where our body and limbs are in space over time, automatically adjusting it as our limbs move, and adapting it to include, for example, a hat we might be wearing or a vehicle we might be driving. As Bartlett (1932) acknowledges, this was the basis for his concept of a memory schema, a concept whose impact is recorded elsewhere in this volume.

The direct application of cognitive concepts to neuropsychological cases came from two of Bartlett's students, namely Oliver Zangwill, who succeeded Bartlett to the Chair of Psychology at Cambridge, and Carolus Oldfield, who held the first Chair in Experimental Psychology at Oxford. Zangwill's principal clinical links were with the National Hospital for Nervous Diseases in Queens Square, London, where he established a new graduate, Elizabeth Warrington, whose subsequent career has had a huge impact on the development of cognitive neuropsychology. Elizabeth's work has been important, not only because of the remarkable number of theoretically important cases she has investigated, making major contributions to the psychology of memory, perception and language, but also through her impact on cognitive psychology. By convincing colleagues such as Shallice, Weiskrantz and myself of the value of the neuropsychological approach, she greatly increased the degree of contact between mainstream experimental psychology and neuropsychology.

Britain is not of course the only place that combines pure and applied psychological research. During World War II, many North American psychologists began to tackle practical problems, and during the early years of the development of cognitive psychology at least, these influences continued through scientists such as George Miller, Ulrich Neisser and most notably Paul Fitts. Sadly, Fitts died a young man, certainly having had more time to establish himself than Kenneth Craik, but by no means having rivalled Bartlett's influence on the field.

On the whole, US scientists who left their military laboratories tended to move away from applied questions, seeking the increased level of experimental control that is possible in a highly constrained laboratory.

At the same time, North American psychologists concerned with applied questions seem to have opted for practical answers to practical questions, often developing highly sophisticated psychometric methods, but typically not linking their work to the issues being tackled in the laboratories of their more theoretically inclined colleagues. Such elegant psychometric methods provide very powerful ways of improving test design, for example, by systematically weeding out sub-tests that have little predictive value. They are, however, essentially based on correlational approaches, that is on *association* rather than *dissociation*. We have argued elsewhere that, despite the short-term practical gains from such approaches, they are much less theoretically incisive than single case neuropsychological studies that focus on dissociation of theoretically targeted processes (Baddeley & Gathercole, 1999).

In conclusion, I would suggest that Bartlett's breadth of interest and willingness to apply theoretical concepts to rich and complex practical problems has been one of his major contributions to psychology. In contrast to his contribution to the psychology of memory, this aspect of his impact is not reflected by any one book or series of papers. Its long-term impact comes from the sustained influence of his ideas and commitment on his students, and through them on the development of experimental psychology in Britain, and in the longer term through its impact on the way in which psychology is conducted internationally.

BARTLETT AND EXPERIMENTAL PSYCHOLOGY

Richard Gregory

Remembering Bartlett goes back half a century. I became one of his last students at Cambridge in 1949. This was just before Bartlett succeeded in moving Experimental Psychology from the Moral Sciences Tripos (Philosophy) in the Arts Faculty, to the Natural Sciences, which pleased him greatly. In spite of his early training in logic, he found philosophical debate more irritating than helpful, and for him psychology was an empirical science, though, as for other basic sciences, dependent on theoretical concepts for deriving meaning from experiments.

At the special occasion of his Weekly Lecture, he would share with us ideas that were interesting him at the time; especially the importance of prediction in skills, his favourite example being from cricket—the batsman reading the present from his past knowledge, to predict the immediate future within his 'range of anticipation'. Such ideas countered the stimulus–response accounts of Behaviourism that still dominated American psychology at that time. This was the year of Sir Frederic Bartlett's Royal Institution Christmas Lectures,[1] which became the book *The Mind at Work and Play* (1951), with chapters on the mind as a

The Mushroom Race you have to seek
In weeds about the Root,
Who scarce dare at the Oak to peep
Or at its Princely fruit.

FIG. 4.1   The Royal Allied Oak and self-created mushroom kings (1815). Reproduced in F.C. Bartlett's *The Mind at Work and Play* (1951, p. 68).

measuring instrument, controlling, observing, connecting things, remembering and thinking. His essential interest in mind as actively going beyond the available evidence, to seek or create meaning, is evident in his use of the picture, shown in Fig. 4.1, which was popular in England in 1815 after the Battle of Waterloo. The faces are suggested by the tree but produced by the mind.

The ideas in these lectures, as indeed in all his work, were largely supported by familiar experiences. Thus, reading continuing though parts are missing shows that the mind creates what 'should' be there, in its continual effort after meaning. He applied such concepts to the design of displays for controlling machines, especially for flying. The 'Cambridge Cockpit' made a significant contribution to the war. This was perhaps the first research simulator for evaluating pilots' skills—or lack of them. Bartlett continued to chair high-level military committees after the war, and was very proud of his speech-scrambling red telephone, presumably connected to the War Office. He was clearly sad when it was taken away. Actually his hearing was greatly impaired at that time, though miraculously improved by a wax-removing operation.

He was an awesome figure to his students. He had his favourites, with rather clear signs of acceptance. In my own case, I had the honour of looking after Lady Bartlett at the Royal Society when he received a Royal Medal. I went to his house frequently, with very formal tea—Lady Bartlett wearing white gloves— and played tennis with the sons Hugh and Dennis. Sir Fred was a much-loved father figure to many of us at that time.

It is well known that Bartlett was much influenced by Kenneth Craik's engineering concepts—presented in his short book *The Nature of Explanation* (1943)—seeing Craik as his natural successor. Kenneth Craik's premature death by an accident in 1945 was a major tragedy; yet his inspiration continued, and remains with us now. Notable were the concepts of servo-control and predicting, developed for anti-aircraft guns during the war, and Craik's notion of the brain as *representing* by physical states—allowing anticipation and gap filling, though with errors that could be suggestive. It is interesting that Bartlett supported and took a great interest in technical ideas, especially from engineering. Although he was not himself an engineer or a mathematician, he respected people who were, and regarded these ideas as essential for developing theories in psychology. He saw the importance of the newly developing Information Theory, and the concept of limited channel capacity of the human operator. In particular, he supported W.E. Hick, who carried out his celebrated experiments on 'rate of gain of information' in the Department (Hick, 1952), finding that reaction time increases with the number of alternative stimuli and responses (small lights and keys). So skilled behaviour is not simply responding to what is happening—but also to possibilities of what might happen. There were only two subjects, William Hick and myself. He did not actually complete the testing, so Hick's Law is based on my nervous system. The experiments required an hour a day for three months, so this was quite onerous.

There was a conflict in Bartlett's thinking—as indeed in the fabric of the whole study of psychology—between the significance of individual experiences and the need for averaged data and smooth curves for publishable results. I remember him saying of the learning curves of Ebbinghaus, that the more respectably smooth the experimental curves are, the less their meaning. The point being that Ebbinghaus only got such lawful physics-like results by avoiding meaning in the material to be learned. As Bartlett's prime interest was in meaning, he dismissed Ebbinghaus's approach, though he conceded that it did look scientifically respectable. In his celebrated book *Remembering* (1932), Bartlett describes individual results with little or no statistics. Perhaps there is something of a return to this approach with current 'qualitative psychology'. There was a serious conflict here for Bartlett, for although he found individual observations most interesting he was also concerned with generalisations—especially for skills in industry and the military—essential for predictions to new situations. He was concerned both with selection of individuals for specific skills and responsibilities, and also to discover generalisations for appreciating the nature of skills, which should apply to just about everyone.

Bartlett seconded me to the Navy for a year to work on escaping from submarines. This followed the *Affray* disaster, where two crews, the normal crew and a training crew, were lost when the submarine sank without warning. There were several issues, especially the engineering of the escape equipment and also physiological and psychological questions for improving escape procedures. It turned out that surprisingly frequently crews would not attempt to escape, even after some hours awaiting rescue. This was especially so for the escape method in which their living compartment had to be flooded, to equalise the internal atmosphere with the external pressure of the sea. Then crew members escaped individually through the 'twill trunk', bobbing up to the surface in a bubble of air as they breathed out during the ascent. Better psychologically is the gun tower escape method, in which each crew member escapes via a special chamber in the gun turret; but this involves some 44 operations for each escape. Mistakes can occur, especially as the oxygen level falls, which may incapacitate or kill the escaping crew member, blocking it for the rest. Bartlett got me to work on this problem, carrying out experiments at the Royal Naval Physiological Laboratory at Portsmouth. It was just this kind of mixture of engineering and psychology that appealed to him. No doubt he inspired it in me, as one of his students.

It was possible to do just about anything in the Cambridge of that time. I hope this is still true. The freedom was wonderful, though it should be confessed that perhaps the students sometimes came off second best. Compared with the present, teaching was quite casual in the Department and the library was not well organised. Bartlett thought that only a very few psychology books were worth the trouble of reading. Certainly, combining research with teaching is vitally important, and students gain greatly from the excitement of ongoing research, but it is hard to keep the balance right. In perhaps all universities at present, teaching surely over-dominates—making playing with risky ideas too difficult—which takes the fun out of research and teaching and may indeed drain science of its creativity. Bartlett, and later Oliver Zangwill, who succeeded as Head of the Department, allowed infinite freedom to their protégés, for which I and no doubt many others are deeply grateful.

Certainly the Craik–Bartlett philosophy of combining engineering with more traditional psychology, though with an emphasis on meaning rather than stimulus response, was taken seriously by many students at that time. In my own case it led to applying a cognitive idea to the design of an instrument: a disturbance-rejecting telescope camera, involving a Craikian 'internal model'. Briefly the method was, first, to take a long photographic exposure of, for example, the moon, through the annoying image-disturbing turbulence of the atmosphere. The positions of the moon's contours were correctly placed, though blurred, in this photographic 'Internal Model' taken over a minute or more. Second, after rapid processing, the photographic plate was replaced in precisely the same position in the camera—so the dynamically disturbed image fell on to its own averaged negative picture. When the image most nearly matched the negative 'internal model', the least light passed through. This provided an auto-correlation signal, from a photo-multiplier receiving the light from the fluctuating image sitting on its own negative. This signal opened the shutter of a second camera, which received the image directly—but only at moments when the disturbance was minimal—when the auto-correlation was high. Then the disturbed present was improved by the averaged past, as disturbances were rejected (Gregory, 1964, 1974).

This idea (which occurred to me while making positive–negative difference pictures for showing stereoscopic disparity from the eyes) followed rather directly from the prevailing Bartlett–Craik philosophy of that time, with its emphasis on enhancing limited present sensory data by using knowledge stored in memory from the past. The camera was developed with the talented engineer, famous for extracting power from waves in the sea, Stephen Salter. He built the final version which we tested on a century-old telescope at the Cambridge Observatory, and then on large telescopes on mountains in New Mexico and Arizona. This was perhaps an early example of Artificial Intelligence, before the use of digital computers, and based on psychological principles that may apply to brain processes of perception.

Bartlett's general approach made me see a lucky chance through his eyes. It was my colleague for many years, Jean Wallace, who saw in a Midlands local paper that a man, SB, blind all his life, was to receive corneal transplants at the age of 52. This was very rare, and might be of great interest for studying the development of vision. It presented a quandary, as immediate action was essential but we were very busy at the time with teaching and other duties. Within an hour we packed every imaginable visual experiment into the car and set off for the hospital to see SB. It was the best decision I ever made, and I don't think the students suffered.

Whatever we may have found of benefit to others, it was this investigation that set my path to vision and illusion as the most fascinating topics in psychology. For it suggested how one might think about the nature of perception, and pointed to how much is innately given from birth and what has to be learned. In brief, we found that he could see almost immediately objects already familiar to him, especially through touch; but he remained effectively blind for a long time to objects he knew nothing about. Most striking, he could read upper case letters, which he had been taught to read by touch in the blind school; but not lower case letters, which (according to the blind school records and the practice of the time) the children were not taught. Further, he could tell the time visually without any help or practice. Here his previous touch experience was from a large pocket watch with no glass: He could unhesitatingly tell the time by touch from its hands. Evidently this early knowledge from exploring by touch was available for his new-found vision. Lastly, the well-known distortion illusions had little effect. And he did not experience the 'flipping' ambiguity of Necker Cube drawings. The general conclusion was that object vision depends on a vast knowledge of the world of objects—largely derived from active exploration—giving meaning to the ghostly images in the eyes. It also showed, more technically, the importance of cross-modal transfer—knowledge from one sense being available to other senses—though the transfer could be 'negative' to produce illusion from false or misapplied knowledge. Perhaps Jean Wallace and I would not have looked at SB in this kind of way if we had not been 'Bartlettian'. Our findings were surprising at that time (cf. Hebb, 1949), though there is now confirming evidence from other cases (Valvo, 1971). It is now clear that babies have far more innate visual capacity than believed at that time, though one does have to be cautious in generalising from newly gained vision in adults, who have many years of experience by other senses, to development of vision in babies.

This emphasis on the importance of knowledge for perception was very different from, for example, J.J. Gibson's approach (1950), which was then highly influential and indeed still is, though now generally modified. Our more cognitive 'Bartlettian' view suggested that many phenomena of illusions could be due to 'negative transfer' of previous knowledge (of objects or of general rules) when knowledge is accepted inappropriately for reading sensory signals. This is a 'psychological' rather than a 'physiological' theory. More generally, this approach suggests that perceptions are *hypotheses* of the external world (Gregory, 1980, 1997).

There are practical implications of this view of perception, which surfaced in the 1960s, for anticipating dangerous illusions of astronauts soon to be engaged in moon landing and docking. The American Air Force supported experiments (undertaken in the then top floor of the Cambridge Department, before the present top floor was added) involving an electric carriage running along the darkened corridor, and a large parallelogram swing. Both had linked dynamic displays. The essential idea was to measure Size Constancy during motion, with controlled information provided of the observer's motion. It was measured by making the display shrink as it was approached—until it appeared to remain the same size, although the image in the eye was expanding. This 'nulling' technique related perception to the observer's motion through terrestrial or (simulated) astronomical space. The question is whether Perceptual Hypotheses (perceptions) would remain appropriate in bizarre conditions that were unfamiliar to the observer, or the astronaut. This is just the kind of thing that Bartlett found interesting. Indeed, one day he brought six young nuns who were visiting the Department to see these experiments. They were entranced by playing on the large swing and the electric railway, becoming quite un-nunnish. Bartlett was extremely amused.

Bartlett's Department was in the same building as Physiology. Physiology was extremely distinguished, with such luminaries as Lord Adrian, Sir Brian Matthews, William Rushton, Horace Barlow, and later Fergus Campbell and many other top-flight physiologists. Unfortunately psychologists—though Bartlett himself was the great exception—were looked down upon as second-class citizens. This came to a curious conflict over explanations of illusory phenomena of vision (which were my major interest) as the physiologists, if implicitly, wanted to 'own' the phenomena, though (especially following the experience with SB) I believed that many are cognitive and so psychological. If indeed they are due to 'negative transfer' of object knowledge (and also inappropriate rules), rather than to physiological upset of neural signalling, they have a quite different status and 'belong' to psychology rather than physiology. Since then I have tried to categorise phenomena of illusions, and some—though not all—do belong to the physiologists!

Later the Craik Laboratory was founded, which very effectively combined the ideas and work of physiologists and experimental psychologists. The situation is now far more equitable and mutually creative. The fact is, of course, we all have to learn from each other and no science is an island.

This approach to visual phenomena stemmed from the still growing influence of Kenneth Craik's engineering approach to the brain and the effort-after-meaning of Sir Frederic Bartlett who drew truths even from errors. He inspired the thinking of many of us to this day and no doubt into the future. He will be remembered with affection and respect for a very long time to come.

NOTE

1 The longest running series of lectures in the world, started by Michael Faraday over 150 years ago. They are now televised, as an annual event.

CHAPTER FIVE

Bartlett's psycho-anthropological project

Alberto Rosa

INTRODUCTION

This chapter examines the early work of F.C. Bartlett, which was devoted to the psychological study of anthropological questions. It is striking to find that in very different geographical locations scholars with different backgrounds (e.g. Bartlett in England, G.H. Mead in the United States, Pierre Janet in France and Lev Vygotsky in Russia) were simultaneously addressing the question of the relation of the social and the cultural with the psychological, with quite a similar sensitivity. This chapter aims to 'recover' this facet of Bartlett's work and as such perhaps belongs to the realm of intellectual history.

It is a truism to note that history is written for the consumption of contemporaries, and therefore carries with it judgements of the time in which it is written. It is hardly a surprise, then, that our picture of the past carries the weight of the values of our current symbolic market (Bourdieu, 1991). Vygotsky's work was recovered in the West at the beginning of the so-called 'cognitive revolution' and soon became a valuable commodity in some sectors of the intellectual market. Other figures of the past, such as Wilhelm Wundt, Henri Wallon, John Dewey or Heinz Werner are also emerging from the pages of the history books (when they were considered relevant enough to be inscribed into them) and now merit attention beyond simple antiquarian curiosity.

THE 'SYMBOLIC MARKET' OF IDEAS AND BARTLETT'S HERITAGE

Goods on a market stall have a tag attached to them, which lists their components, provides instructions for use and, often, presents the value given for their inter-exchange. Epistemic products are no exception. Voices from the past are sometimes introduced into the current symbolic market by specialists in a field or by historians. Whatever the case, such 'recoverings' share the characteristic of highlighting particular features of past contributions which are of use for current interests. One of the side effects of such recoverings is the schematising of complex ideas into sets of simple utterances. What appears in the marketplace therefore is not only voices from the past, but echoes ventriloquated (Bakhtin, 1981; Wertsch, 1991) for current purposes, also with a tag and instructions. Consumers frequently do not pay very much attention to the advice of the merchant, which, fortunately, allows for novel uses, new readings and a myriad of understandings. Consumption of utterances, in addition, has many other uses, from tying knots of alliance to showing allegiance, passing through attempts to add value to one's own contribution by borrowing from quotations and references (Latour, 1987).

Appreciation of Bartlett's work has had many ups and downs following the meanders of the mainstreams of psychological thought. His most praised contribution has been his borrowing of Head's (1926) concept of *schema* in a theory of remembering (Bartlett, 1932; see Lachman, Lachman, & Butterfield, 1979, p. 450). Schema is an important construct, but it has not been valued unanimously; indeed it has been described as a 'theory that never seemed plausible to me, which perhaps it is better to forget' (Zangwill, 1972a, p. 168), or as Broadbent (Broadbent, 1970, p. 4) put it, 'Theoretical concepts of this kind, without public definitions, are almost bound to be self-defeating. Like others of its breed, schema expired unregretted among mutual misunderstanding.' This premature burial of a healthy corpse contrasts with some of the current uses of the construct (Rumelhart, Smolensky, McClelland, & Hinton, 1986, p. 20).

Bartlett has been also considered a forerunner of cognitive psychology before the arrival of computers (Neisser, 1967, p. 19), and, rather epically, as 'a solitary psychologist working in Britain [who] was also keeping the cognitive faith' (Gardner, 1985, p. 115). There is no doubt this view is justified if his contributions, in collaboration with Kenneth Craik, to the early works of the Applied Psychological Unit of Cambridge are taken into account (Grande & Rosa, 1993). But Bartlett's interests were not limited to the realm of what today is called cognitive psychology. His best-known book *Remembering* (1932) bears the subtitle *A Study in Experimental and Social Psychology*. As Jones (1985) notes, the links Bartlett showed between individual remembering and social factors are quite significant in the development of Social Psychology (see Sherif, 1936).

More recently, Bartlett's ideas have been reinterpreted as a means for studying collective remembering, rather than individual memory (Edwards & Middleton, 1986; Middleton & Edwards, 1990a). Shotter (1990), contrasting two contributions of the early Bartlett (1923, 1932), has offered a picture of how social institutions and practices have a decisive role in individual remembering.

It seems to me that if Bartlett was ever a cognitive psychologist, he was of the type that would agree with many of Bruner's arguments in *Acts of Meaning*

(1990) concerning current cognitive psychology. I will try to show in this article that Bartlett is among those intellectuals at the beginning of the 20th century who could not think of psychology as something different from cultural psychology. In order to do so, we should not take for granted the current fragmentation of disciplines, but attempt to understand the intellectual landscape of that time.

There is a side of Bartlett's biography that I want to highlight here, since I believe it is significant for the understanding of his work. Bartlett enrolled in St. John's College, Cambridge, in 1912, as he himself explained:

> largely because [W.H.R.] Rivers was there and my interests were turning strongly toward anthropology. However I decided to read moral science first, and that is how I came into the Cambridge Psychological Laboratory.
>
> (Bartlett, 1936, p. 39)

It was Rivers who 'told me that if I wanted to be an anthropologist I must be a psychologist first, and especially I must know the psychological methods' (Bartlett, 1937, p. 105). It is my belief that Bartlett, for a time, was torn between these two disciplines. The final outcome, his becoming a professor of psychology, was the result of a set of circumstances that developed over a period of 15 years. This span of time was long enough for him to develop a set of ideas about the relationship between culture and individual action, which is the main focus of this chapter.

The Bartlett I want to highlight here is the early one. Undoubtedly, I am going to prepare a tag to attach to his early production; this is unavoidable when presenting a particular reading of texts. I am not going to try simply to report his work, but to offer a particular interpretation *vis-à-vis* current interests concerning the relationship between culture, social life and individual action. In particular, the connections among social practices, cultural materials, meaning and affect are sketched. Only some aspects of Bartlett's contribution are considered here, while others, which I judge to be of lesser interest, or which have become casualties of the passage of time, are excluded. I am going to follow a historicist strategy for the preparation of my tag; that is, I am going to present Bartlett's ideas within my understanding of the context of their production—Cambridge in the 1910s and 1920s.

THE ANTHROPOLOGICAL BACKGROUND OF THE CAMBRIDGE PSYCHOLOGICAL LABORATORY

When Bartlett enrolled in Cambridge, the psychological laboratory had only existed for a short period, and its founders were still lecturing the courses he followed. The laboratory was largely the outcome of James Ward's (1843–1925) efforts. Ward was a philosopher who spent some time in the 1860s in Germany with Ludwig and Lotze, and was very interested in psychophysics, as a pro-paedeutic discipline for metaphysics. He was also the author of an influential programmatic work on psychology (Ward, 1886), which presented a functionalist view, as well as a demolishing critique of associationism and the psychology of faculties. The Cambridge laboratory was founded in 1897, the same year that Ward was promoted to a chair in Mental Philosophy and Logic. It was Sir Michael Foster, then director of the Physiological Laboratory, who managed to persuade the university to establish a lecturership in Experimental Psychology and Physiology of the Special Senses, which was offered to W.H.R. Rivers who had been teaching courses on the physiology of the senses in Cambridge since 1893. He was the first person to offer a course on Experimental Psychology in Britain (Bartlett, 1936).

William Halse Rivers (1864–1922) had a medical training and a wide range of interests. He spent a period in the National Hospital for the Paralysed and Epileptic under the direction of John Hughlings Jackson, participating in some of his famous brain operations (Ackernecht, 1942). There, he developed a long-lasting friendship with another disciple of Jackson's—Henry Head, which also resulted in joint research (e.g. Rivers & Head, 1908). It was Rivers who intro-duced Head to Bartlett, and also it was he who introduced William McDougall and Charles S. Myers, both medical trainees at the time, to experimental work in psychology.

When A.C. Haddon organised an anthropological expedition to the Torres Straits (1898–99), he wanted to have psychologists with his team, and he con-vinced Rivers to join. Rivers, in turn, enrolled two of his students: McDougall and Myers. The experiments carried out by the psychologists were mainly on sensation, perceptual illusions and reaction time. However, Rivers had had—up to that time—no interests in anthropology. He was a nephew of James Hunt, the founder of the British Anthropological Society. Not long before going to the Torres Straits, Rivers had rejected the library of his deceased uncle, claiming that it was of no use to him (Ackernecht, 1942). Nevertheless, Rivers became an anthropologist, embarking on long expeditions to Melanesia and India.

Rivers at first held a classic evolutionary view of anthropology, stressing the role of physiological factors in cultural differences. For example, in his psycho-logical experiments in the Murray Islands, he believed that hypermetropia was more common among the 'savages'. This required a more extensive use of visual accommodation, and predominant attention to sense objects, thus leaving less attention for the more serious aspects of life. That was interpreted as an obstacle to higher mental development (Rivers, 1901a; quoted from Jahoda, 1982, pp. 19–20). But the closer the acquaintance to 'savages' he developed over time, the more respect he developed for their mental abilities. Around 1911 he shifted his theoretical view from 'evolutionism', and its naïve idea of 'psychic unity', to 'diffusionism' of cultural materials. This new view led him to consider a new role for psychology in relation to anthropology. According to his view, cultural material is carried about in the world in the psychological form of sentiments, beliefs and ideas. From his point of view, psychological factors are 'interpolated as links in a chain of causation connecting social antecedents with social consequences' (Rivers, 1926; quoted by Jahoda, 1982, p. 20). This does not mean that social relationships have to be explained psychologically, but rather they could be referenced to antecedent social conditions. This insight Rivers gave to Bartlett when the latter enrolled in the moral sciences programme of Cambridge (Jahoda, 1982).

Rivers resigned from his readership in 1909, and Myers took his place. The laboratory expanded under Myers's direction, and was moved to a new building in 1913. Bartlett graduated in 1914 and immediately became Assistant Director of the Laboratory. The same year he started a series of experiments on perceiving and imaging that opened a line of research which first resulted in his fellowship thesis at St. John's, entitled *Transformations Arising from Repeated Presentations: A contribution towards an experimental study of the process of conventionalisation* (Bartlett, 1916c). This set of experiments spanned the 1920s and forms the backbone around which *Remembering* (Bartlett, 1932) was written (see Rosa, 1995a).

These experiments show Bartlett's mixed interests in anthropology and psychology, over which Rivers (1912) had no little influence. Bartlett attempted a psychological study of the way in which a particular cultural form (figurative or narrative) is transformed when passing from a cultural group to another. In this process, the borrowed material loses its initial representative character, moving into a final arbitrary or conventional status within the group that borrows it, as in the case of alphabetical writing. Olson (1995) retraces the process of construction of syllabaries and alphabets, interpreting these to be the result of a culture borrowing symbols developed by another and changing their use. It is the change of use of a graphic sign that gives it an arbitrary meaning in a conventionalised process of communication. Although Olson does not mention Bartlett, Haddon or Rivers, it seems to me that there is a similarity in treatment with Bartlett's idea of conventionalisation. The purpose of this series of experiments was precisely to retrace this process, working first with individuals and then with groups. Some of these experiments were published immediately (Bartlett, 1916a), whereas others appeared later (1920a, 1921). The empirical material gathered there was subjected to theoretical interpretation in other articles (1920b, 1924, 1925) and finally reinterpreted in *Remembering* (1932).

There is another text of Bartlett's in which he examines the relationship of psychology and anthropology: *Psychology and Primitive Culture* (1923). This was an outcome of a course he taught, following the advice of Rivers, at the Bedford College for Women, London University, in 1922. During these years Bartlett worked on an essay entitled 'Contribution to the Experimental Study of the Processes of Conventionalisation'. He even reached an agreement with Cambridge University Press to publish a book on this issue, but he reports (Bartlett, 1958) that he was unsatisfied with the results of his writing and destroyed the manuscript. However the 16th chapter of *Remembering* (1932) bears the title of 'Conventionalisation'. Following the conclusions of his studies on remembering, I think it is not an error to consider the account he offers in 1958 as an attempt to justify his early work from the much broader context of his total production.

It seems to me that the late Bartlett underestimated the value of his seminal insights regarding conventionalisation, while regarding his later work on experimental psychology as most important. It is interesting, in this respect, to contrast the autobiographical reports Bartlett offers at different moments of his life (1936, 1937, 1958). It seems that the events in Cambridge following the beginning of World War I prevented Bartlett from following the advice Rivers gave him when they first met:

> Whatever you do don't let Cambridge get hold of you. They'll try to. But don't get muddled up with administration.
>
> (Bartlett, 1937, p. 105)

Bartlett was charged with the responsibilities of the laboratory when Myers joined the Royal Medical Corps, and became director of the laboratory and lecturer in experimental psychology in 1922, the same year that Rivers died. Two years later (1924) Bartlett became editor of the *British Journal of Psychology*, and was promoted to a Chair in 1931. It is very risky to speculate whether Bartlett's interests in anthropology were surpassed by his career as a psychologist. It is not my purpose here to embark on a biographical study of Bartlett's life. What is important to note is that during these years he developed a series of ideas concerning the relationship of culture and psychological action that merits further attention.

THE SOCIAL AND THE INDIVIDUAL IN BARTLETT'S EARLY WORK

One of the leitmotivs that runs throughout all of Bartlett's production is his insistence on a molar approach. He explicitly argues against any type of reduction to simplicity, be it either individual, social or a mixture of both. This point of view is clearly stated in his first book (Bartlett, 1923) where he criticised the reduction of the individual to a set of psychological 'processes' (e.g. 'It is possible to know a large amount about the particular response, and at the same time to know strikingly little about the man as he makes the particular response'; Bartlett, 1923, p. 19). Likewise, one can attempt to treat social explanations as a consequence of the beliefs and attitudes of individuals. The question, he wrote, is how to connect individual actions with social antecedents and consequences:

> it is frequently necessary to take established social conventions and institutions as facts determining the character and relations of individual response. Such

institutions and conventions are legitimately regarded as group responses. They are social facts, but they exercise a direct and important determining influence upon varied series of individual reactions. If we refuse to admit the *psychological* signific-ance of this determination, we have to resolve all such group responses into their individual components. Theoretically, no doubt, this might be regarded as possible, but it would in practice resolve itself into an endless, and indeed in many instances a hopeless, task.

(Bartlett, 1923, p. 25)

This is the case not only in social psychology or anthropology, but also in the psychological study of individuals. The individual is an 'individual-in-the-laboratory', an 'individual-in-his-everyday-working-environment' or an 'individual-in-a-given-social-group', never a pure and simple individual (1923, p. 11). Thus:

It is only if we interpret individual to mean pre-social that we can take psychology to be pre-historic. The truth is that there are some individual responses which simply do not occur outside a social group.

(Bartlett, 1923, pp. 12–13)

When one attempts to explain behavioural differences among individuals belonging to different cultures, one should not look for differences in isolated psychological processes, but consider the individual who acts. The reason is that the process in the end is the same; it is the material the process deals with that is different. The task then is:

1   to identify the uses of the cultural material in a culture
2   to study the relationship between the different types of 'responses'
3   to attempt an understanding of the interrelation of responses in a particular 'cultural stage'
4   to localise which are dominant and why
5   to analyse what happens when they are in conflict and when they collaborate
6   to study the lines along which they change their interrelationships along history.

In sum, a whole programme of cultural psychology was outlined. Bartlett's terminology looks shocking to the contemporary eye. The use of terms such as 'primitive' or 'cultural stage' seem to reveal a notion of cultural evolutionism; that is, a ranking of cultures from the more primitive to the most advanced is implied, with the correlate of more or less advanced cognitive processes in individuals belonging to them. However, I do not think this is the appropriate interpretation of Bartlett's view. A closer examination of his argumentation shows the use of the anthropological terminology of the time, while he follows a diffusionist view inherited from Rivers. As Bartlett views it, the psychological study of 'primitive' and 'modern' social life should not be treated differently, since both require the analysis of social life. He is critical of Lévy-Bruhl (1910, 1922) for his limited analysis of mental processes without consideration of the conditions in which they were used. He also criticised the comparison of the behaviour of 'primitives' with that of the 'scientist working on his own field' instead of with that of the 'ordinary member of a modern social group'.

> The error here, as in much recent social and abnormal psychology, is not that the primitive or the abnormal are wrongly observed, but that the modern and normal are hardly observed at all.
>
> (Bartlett, 1923, p. 284)

As Bartlett viewed it, the main difference between primitive and modern individuals is in the organisation of the 'tendencies of action', which derive from culture. That is why the first step is to determine which tendencies are dominant in a particular 'stage' and, especially, the way they operate in the more complex modern social life. The 'savage', like any of us, attempts to offer explanations and rationalisations, which are evident when their adaptation to their environment and their creations are observed. Like the modern individual, he or she produces rationalisations beyond ordinary observation (e.g. magic and religion). In other words, human individuals are not essentially different, but 'primitive' culture is less complex than modern culture, and this is what makes its study of interest.

Bartlett's objective was to identify the 'agencies' which determine human action which have a mental nature or have a direct relationship with mental conditions. Among them are the innate tendencies for action mentioned by McDougall (1908, 1920), which, according to Bartlett, take a particular form in each particular group and become interrelated in a particular way. These 'tendencies for action' show themselves in the subject as an 'affection', which take a particular form in each culture as a result of its institutions, habits and customs. These 'tendencies' are not only apparent when studying a remote social group, but are also to be taken into account in the experimental work in the laboratory. What is more, the appropriate way of exploring these tendencies is through psychological experimentation, since this will prevent useless speculations with respect to the realms of social history or psychology.

> By tendency, then, I mean an active prompting towards a given mode of response— whether cognitive, affective, or expressed in definite bodily movement—which arises when an individual is brought in touch with a situation and attends to it. The tendency must have material to work upon, there must be some situation apprehended; while for its part the material must be met by a tendency if it is to provoke response. The tendency is to be regarded definitely as a mental factor, but it by no means follows that it is a conscious factor. Generally indeed the subject is wholly

unaware, at the time at which he makes them, of the part of which it is playing in his adjustments. It is a factor which he himself must be regarded as contributing, while the specific situation to which response is made must be regarded as something supplied from without. Consequently tendencies, though mental in their character, can, as I have urged, be treated in a perfectly objective manner if we so please. Just as we say that a given series of responses was conditioned by a definite set of external conditions, in precisely the same sense we may say that it was also conditioned by a given set of tendencies.

(Bartlett, 1923, p. 274)

Immediately he clarifies his position further:

the notion of tendency, as it may be arrived at by an analysis of a subject's experimental responses in a laboratory, is always of something *in operation*. That is, it requires, as a correlative notion, the idea of a situation which is in some way being attended or reacted to. . . . Properly speaking a tendency not in operation, whatever it may be, is not a tendency.

(Bartlett, 1923, p. 274)

It seems that Bartlett's conception of tendency bears a great resemblance to Watt's (1905) *Einstellung* (determinant tendency towards the task—*Aufgabe*), as well as an emphasis on situatedness, via the use of the term 'situation':

'Situation' is no doubt a term which is much in need of a definition. From my point of view a 'situation' is all the cognitive, affective and reactive factors which are, at a given time, the limits of which must be determined empirically, organised by a common interest.

(Bartlett, 1925, p. 17, note 1)

It seems to me that Bartlett here is on the threshold of developing a theory of activity which links together cultural practices and individual cognitive and affective processes in order to explain human behaviour. From this general point of view, Bartlett goes on further in specifying a method of inquiry:

Our first step, then, in the search for the psychological conditions of primitive human responses, is to elaborate a basic scheme of the main tendencies that are operative in helping to shape the course of behaviour in the group, and to see how, in general, such tendencies are related one to another. Our next step is to apply this scheme, so as to discover how it actually works in reference to this or that type of concrete material or problem.

(Bartlett, 1923, pp. 276–277)

His idea was to proceed to the study of special problems, mainly those concerned with 'the maintenance of elements of culture within a community, and their consequent elaboration and simplification' (Bartlett, 1923, p. 277); namely the question of 'conventionalisation'. Conventionalisation, as mentioned before, was the subject matter of his research from 1914 to the mid-1920s. He approached its study with a set of experiments carried out with individuals. It has to be remembered that Bartlett, following Rivers, viewed laboratory and field work not as separate realms.

FEELING, EMOTION AND COGNITION AS THE SUBJECTIVE SIDE OF ACTION

The method Bartlett chose to study conventionalisation is well known. It was the repeated remembering of a series of perceptual presentations (ink-blots, geometrical figures, human faces) and folk stories, which were presented only once. As he found, repeated remembering showed a transformation of the representation of the materials. This methodological approach seems to have come to his mind from different sources. For example, he reports having been shocked by the wide range of responses he found when performing a set of experimental demonstrations to the public during the inauguration of the new building of the Cambridge Psychological Laboratory in 1913. He also pays tribute to Ward's recommendation of Jean Philippe's (1897) method of serial repetition, and acknowledges Norbert Wiener (then a student at Cambridge) for offering some suggestions which geared him towards the use of this method (Bartlett, 1932, 1958).

These experiments are well known, since they are reported and extensively analysed in *Remembering* (1932). However, the articles Bartlett published during the 1910s and 1920s, although they form the backbone of this book, are not concerned with remembering; rather, they focus on perceiving and imaging. It should be noted here that Bartlett consistently uses the gerund (perceiv*ing*, imag*ing*, remember*ing*, think*ing*) and practically never nouns such as perception, imagery, memory or thought. I think this is intentional, serving the purpose of emphasising the active character of psychological processes that results from his functionalist approach. There was one occasion when he explicitly referred to the use of this grammatical form, at a symposium in Oxford where he criticised John Watson for his use of the term 'thought' instead of 'thinking', pointing out that:

> in this way the distinction between response and expression appears to be slurred over. It may very well to be the case that whenever we think, we employ language in one form or another, but obviously this does not prove that the act of thinking and the language movement are the same.
>
> (Bartlett & Smith, 1920, p. 62)

My purpose here will be to restrict myself to the interpretations Bartlett makes of his data before the composition of *Remembering* (1932), which I believe marks the beginning of his gradual shift towards an increasingly disciplined psychology. This shift is understandable in that his new appointments in the mid-1920s and early 1930s mark a shift in his activity setting, from cultural-psychological concerns to others closer to mainstream psychology, especially those related to applied psychology. In *Remembering* he reinterpreted many of the same data already collected, but with a different frame of mind (Rosa, 1995a, 1995b). Bartlett's first article of this series, 'An Experimental Study of Some Problems of Perceiving and Imaging' (1916a), shows the importance he attributed to 'effort after meaning' as the tendency around which all the processes involved in the act of perceiving find their justification; without such a tendency 'we cannot speak of perceiving at all' (Bartlett, 1916a, p. 261). But,

> meaning may be attributed either in a very vague or in a very definite manner. In the former case there is the tendency to speak of the experience as a 'feeling' of something. . . . when meaning is vaguely attributed, there is a tendency to speak of it as feeling.
>
> (Bartlett, 1916a, p. 262)

Bartlett's inference is that the situation is understood as a whole by the subject, who tends to consider it as an instantiation of something, whether the material presentation has a definite form and can be named (such as a geometrical figure), or whether it is something shapeless (such as an ink-blot). Even in this second case the individual cannot resist the tendency to give it a name or to consider it as an instance of something. For Bartlett,

> it is the feeling which, upon the repetition of the same general situation, plays a leading part in tending to reinstantiate the content. But, at first, since the feeling qualifies the act as a whole, it is the whole content in all its particularity that tends to be reinstantiated.
>
> (Bartlett, 1916a, p. 263)

He insisted on this view later: 'the function of affection in reproduction was to reinstate a *situation* rather than a specific object' (Bartlett, 1921, p. 324, italics in original). This becomes clearer when subjects focused on an outstanding detail of the material which arouses a particular feeling have no problem in rein-stantiating the material. However, when the feeling is vague, the material is not likely to be reproduced in a very definite way.

The role of feelings in cognition was a persisting interest for Bartlett, and later he dedicated an article ('Feeling, Imaging and Thinking', 1925) to it. This article begins with a discussion of the conditions in which feelings appear, and the terms which he chooses to use are worth noting: He mentions feelings, affect and sentiments. For him feelings form a continuum with emotions and affect, being emotion on the strong side and affect on the weak extreme. They are viewed as biological responses, which rise into consciousness and so have an adaptive function. It should also be noted that 'feeling' is a word with some history in British psychology (e.g. Spencer), being sometimes considered synonymous with sensation.

In Bartlett's view, affects are apparent when there is a conflict of tendencies. Affects are biological reactions, and since behaviour is adaptive, one has to ask what role affects play in adaptation. This takes Bartlett into a detailed analysis of the interrelation of tendencies, the way in which they hinder each other, or get reinforced or composed in a system. His view is that the facilitation of an isolated tendency does not have to produce affect, since the more isolated and facilitated the tendency is, the more easily behaviour becomes a habit free of affect. However, when affect appears, it is not because of the exercise of a tendency or a group of tendencies, but because of the simultaneous exercise of more than one response or a group of responses.

> According to this view, then, it is incorrect to say that affect is a way in which blurred, ill-discriminated, repressed and fragmentary material is *known*. Affect is not, in fact, the inadequate *knowing* of any sort of material whatsoever but is a matter of the balance of reaction tendencies which are called into operation when a given situation is presented.
>
> (Bartlett, 1925, p. 22, italics in original)

Affection and feelings then act as markers in consciousness to orient action when different courses appear open or in conflict. This gives them not only a functional, but also a cognitive role. Feeling accompanies the apprehension of material, but it is not an appendage fastened to particular cognitive material. However, there is a peculiar characteristic of feeling as an experience:

> For affect possesses a remarkable readiness of diffusion. Itself aroused by a shock or by a balance of tendencies it runs over the whole situation, including the cognitive details in which these tendencies are expressed with the very greatest ease.
>
> (Bartlett, 1925, p. 23)

This characteristic gives feelings a somewhat dangerous property:

> The feeling which properly arises in one situation, and is then diffused over the cognitive content defining that situation, gets easily transferred to another which is in some way connected with the first. It is now attached, in a derivative manner, to images, ideas and trains of thought depicting or describing this second situation. In our normal reactions in these instances we can detect no clash and no balances of tendencies. We can say that the feeling is the 'natural' addendum of the images, ideas or thoughts. In a strictly analytical sense we are right, but from a point of view of how the affect was actually determined we are definitely wrong.
>
> (Bartlett, 1925, pp. 21–22)

This readiness of diffusion and transference that characterises affect makes feeling an extraordinarily inefficient way of solving problems, since on the basis of affect, there is no safe way of distinguishing two situations. This problem can be solved by calling cognition into play; that is resorting to the use of images or by thinking. Images are a result of evolution; 'it is the beginning of the growing dominance of cognitive reactions' (Bartlett, 1925, p. 26). But images also have drawbacks: they are too definite, they are too rigid and therefore may be of no use in a novel situation. We find a better way of solving conflicts when we think:

> We find our solution by a careful analysis of the situation which provokes the conflict. The analysis proceeds by isolating and generalising the elements which gave rise to the check, and the solution secured is on the whole a more adequate one because it gets farther away from the accidents of a particular environment. ... Hence thinking, imaging and feeling, all springing out from a conflict between reactive tendencies in behaviour, and the last two defining and determining the conflict, persist side by side. It is in fact as leading a principle of mental development as it is of biological evolution that real advance is dependent upon the fact that the acquisition of new specialisations does not of necessity shut us out completely from the older and more primitive modes of response.
>
> (Bartlett, 1925, pp. 26–27)

This is not the only occasion on which Bartlett discussed imagining and thinking as different methods for solving problems (Bartlett uses the term 'method' here to denote something similar to what currently is termed 'strategy'). In an earlier paper (Bartlett, 1921), he classified his subjects as 'visualisers' and 'vocalisers', as a result of their preferred tendencies in using either images or words for solving the tasks. It is worth noting that Bartlett pointed out that the use of words allows the selection of a particular feature of the material from which divergent associations can be formed. This may result in an attitude of uncertainty in the subjects, but nevertheless 'the employment of words in reproduction leads away from the reinstatement of material in close relation to emotions' (Bartlett, 1921, p. 335). There is another favourable consequence of the use of words:

> words are able to maintain the advantages of sensory imagery, while in addition their ease of communication, and the greater range of situation with which they can adequately deal, make them capable of rendering further development more ready and certain.
>
> (Bartlett, 1921, p. 336)

The consideration of these three processes (feeling, imaging and thinking), and the instrumental use he acknowledges for words in thinking, seems to suggest an idea of composition of functions. This was, perhaps, an idea not foreign to Bartlett, as someone familiar with the teaching of Hughlings Jackson through close contact with some of his most distinguished disciples, namely Rivers, Myers and Head.

CONVENTIONALISATION AND MEANING:
A STUDY ON SYMBOLISM

Bartlett's main preoccupation in this period, we must keep in mind, was the experimental study of conventionalisation. His interest was to study not methods of problem-solving, but how individuals and groups borrow, modify and adapt foreign materials. His work on matters apparently so far apart as perceiving and imaging, on the one hand, and cultural anthropology, on the other, are linked together in two issues usually divorced from one another: feeling and meaning. These, in turn, are considered jointly via the study of the cultural use of symbols. Bartlett's aim was to examine the way in which materials foreign to a culture are employed; taking into account how these new materials gather tendencies of action, produce emotions, are used in a particular way and become assimilated by a group that has an organisation and tendencies for action already well established. In sum, he was interested in how the introductions of new materials acquire a new symbolic value.

Bartlett dedicated an article also to this issue ('Symbolism in Folk Lore', 1924). One should point out, however, that here he centres on symbolism, without going into any depth on the issue of meaning:

> Now whatever else is true about meaning, it is certain that meaning is very largely dependent upon tendency. What a thing indicates, or whether it indicates anything at all, is not a matter, to an important degree, of the external characteristics of the thing, but of the tendency and attitude with which it is met.
>
> (Bartlett, 1924, pp. 287–288)

Since the subject matter of his study is the conventionalisation of cultural symbols, his first task is to characterise what he understands as a symbol. So he begins by pointing out that all signs are symbols, but not every symbol is a sign. He goes on to say that a symbol is something that at once has a double, or even a multiple significance:

> A symbol may thus be characterised as a sign which carries, at one and the same time, a double or a multiple significance, one part of what is indicated being obvious, and constituting the 'face value' of the symbol, and another part producing an effect without being definitely or purposively attended to, this part constituting the 'hidden value' of the symbol. Furthermore, all symbols possess a picture character. They may no doubt be conventionalised, and their directly concrete derivation may be far from obvious at the first glance. But if they become so far conventionalised that they lose altogether their pictorial character, they cease to be symbols, though they may continue to be signs.
>
> (Bartlett, 1924, p. 278)

The fact that a symbol has a double or multiple significance has an easy psychological foundation, which is that the same cognitive material appeals to more than one interest, calling for the operation of two or more reaction tendencies. This is no surprise, since there is 'no tendency in actual human life that is not already itself a group of tendencies, a system, an organisation, having its own peculiar quality and characteristics' (Bartlett, 1924, p. 280). If we look at the development of symbols in individual life, there are always some tendencies or group of tendencies that take a dominant role over others and determine the direction of individual symbolism:

> But the mechanism of the production of the symbol is always the same. Material arouses a given tendency, is attended to, and put into relation with other material to help to form a particular mental system. At the same time another tendency comes into play, and by it the same material gains different relations and a place in a different mental system. Mental systems, however, are not normally isolated. They are linked together, first because they share common materials, and secondly because among all tendencies which take a share in their formation, one or two are always masterful. The masterful tendencies set the systems migrating, so to speak, and the watchword of the growth of symbols in the individual mental life is the 'contact of mental systems'.
>
> (Bartlett, 1924, p. 281)

Bartlett goes on to refer to how symbols appear in the cultural lore, pointing out that many are a contribution of individuals; people who create a particular symbolic significance in their own mental life, and, because of their position within the group, make the symbol become commonly used. The contact between cultural groups is another possible alley. Every group has conventions and all conventions are symbols. When two groups get in contact, there is an interplay of conventions; many of the symbols that can be found in the folk lore of a particular people have entered by this route:

> Just as, in the case of the individual, it is the contact of mental systems that produces the symbol, and gives it its double or multiple significance, in the case of the community it is the contact of groups.
>
> (Bartlett, 1924, p. 283)

The way in which symbols become social products is a question for the study of a psychology concerned with intercultural contact. Bartlett discards any idea of universal symbols residing in any type of universal mind—a critique of Jung's collective unconscious, without naming him (Bartlett, 1920b).

Bartlett's next move is to refer to the persistence of popular lore symbols. Tendencies and feelings are again in play:

> It is almost an essential condition of the long persistence of a symbol that it should become attached to some sentiment, or sentiments, instead of to direct

representative pictures. ... Sentiments are stabilising factors which help con-
servation. Moreover, they are remarkably easily stabilised by education, and soon
become deeply rooted. A community which develops a common lore must, by its
constitution, display considerable homogeneity of character. It is precisely the type
of group in which sentiments, once stabilised, can be most readily transmitted from
person to person, generation after generation. To this the persistence of symbols is
largely due.

(Bartlett, 1924, p. 284)

It is to the 'hidden' value of the symbol that its persistence is largely due. And
that 'hidden' value can get diffused throughout a community in a most secret and
subtle manner. Round about certain cultural materials stable sentiments are formed.
Then comes the conflict of groups. New material replaces the old; but the sentiments
remain, and with them the old interpretations. The new material constantly stirs up
the old interpretations, preserves them, but at the same time prevents them from
gaining overt expression. The persistence of the old interpretations is directly
dependent upon the fact that in any community that is sufficiently homogeneous to
develop a common lore, a very strong social bond of comradeship exists, by virtue
of which it is possible for one member of a group to catch at once at the significance of slight marks in the behaviour of another.

(Bartlett, 1924, pp. 285–286)

In these quotations we can again hear echoes of McDougall (1908). Furthermore, the role of symbols in keeping social harmony deserves comment. Symbols
have a pictorial character that helps sentiments to avoid losing contact with
concrete affairs. Symbols also are an instrument for the preservation of the
group. When a stronger ('higher') group comes into contact with another, the latter
seems to be swept away, but there is usually an increase in the use of symbols
subsequently, in which the old group is, in a way, perpetuated.

The old lives still in the new, and the social situation has simply become more
complex. Then, if some social storm and stress appears, there is reversion. The
'hidden' value once more becomes the 'face' value. The old group lives again for
all to see, and we say that history repeats itself. To such regressions those groups
are most of all prone where symbols most vigorously flourish.

(Bartlett, 1924, p. 289)

The new material, irrespective of whether it has been developed inside the
group, or borrowed from a different culture, derives its significance from the
sentiments of the individuals. These, in turn, depend on the form tendencies take
in the group and the use these materials receive in the activities of the group. It
seems, then, that feelings play not a negligible role in semiosis and cultural
development.

There is another aspect of the material which Bartlett considers in his study
of conventionalisation: he uses folk stories. He dedicated two articles to their

examination (Bartlett, 1920a, 1920b). One of these articles (Bartlett, 1920a) reports empirical results obtained from the repeated reproduction of two stories ('The War of the Ghosts' and 'The Son who Tried to Outwit his Father') that later on he also presented in *Remembering* (1932).

Bartlett treats folk stories as a social product to be psychologically studied. Stories are used for communication and this leads him to take a rhetorical approach. He notes two steps in dealing with this type of psychological study: first, impulses and tendencies that carry a role in the formation, expression, retention, transmission and transformations of folk stories and, second, the processes through which these impulses and tendencies use the materials that appear in myths, legends and fairy tales. In order to do this, he points out the need to distinguish between the *matter* and the *form* of the story.

When examining the tendencies that shape a folk story, Bartlett noted that since folk stories are a form of social intercourse, their matter must appeal to a group of listeners, while their form will be particularly determined by the impulses which come into operation when an individual becomes the centre of attention in a social group. Bartlett also pays attention to the connection between the moral and the rhetorical:

> The outstanding social characteristic of the tales is, in fact, reaction against a grinding constraint, whether of the law, or of any other authority of the powerful. If he should, in his stories, deal with the real world, man waxes satirical at the expense of laws and judges, and often gets the better out of them by all kinds of successful trickery; but in the realm wherein his fancy freely roams, he envisages a world where all his social tendencies find unrestrained expression. Yet when love intrudes into the folk tale, as it often does, the social relations of equality disappear, and are replaced by those of superiority on the one side, and of inferiority of the other.
>
> (Bartlett, 1920b, pp. 285–286)

He also emphasises the fact that a particular tale told is an individual expression, as well as a social product. This leads him to carry out some experiments on the repeated reproduction of folk stories. These experiments had the goal of studying the mental processes (tendencies, impulses, desires) which are involved in production and reproduction, and are affected by, as much as they affect, the material they work upon.

> My own experiments on the reproduction of folk tales illustrate this fact very clearly. They show how the reproductions in question bring into operation various specific tendencies towards dramatisation, condensation, rationalisation, and so on; but at the same time they make it clear that the function of those tendencies, and also the moment at which they come into play, are determined in part by differences in the character of the material employed. . . . But whether any given material *does*

produce such an affective accompaniment depends very largely upon its relations
to the customs and beliefs prevalent in the community to which the subjects belong.
... We need to know not only the psychological processes which are operative in
a given case, but also everything that can be discovered concerning the history and
nature of the material upon which they operate. For there is a constant interplay
between the material and the processes.

(Bartlett, 1920b, p. 290, italics in original)

It seems to me that Bartlett, in this excerpt, is not very far from the consideration
of narratives as mediational means which are at the service of (but also set
constraints on) individual action (see also Wertsch, 1994).

FROM BARTLETT TO OUR TIMES:
ELABORATIONS

So far I have offered a summary of my understanding of Bartlett's work concerning the psychological explanation of cultural change. This last section is a
commentary on some of the aspects which I believe are worth further consideration. At first glance, Bartlett's psychological approach appears outdated. He may
be considered as an analytic psychologist, not far from the continental psychology of his time, with the addition of McDougall's functionalist view. Bartlett's
dependency on the latter can easily be viewed as a psychology which carries
with it the curse of an extensive use of instincts under the cover term 'tendency'.
There is some truth in this view, but I believe there is more to the heritage of
Bartlett than such easy labelling. I think Bartlett's work has merit in having
created a set of categories which allow us to connect social practices and cultural
materials with psychological processes and personal experience, while keeping
psychology a biological science, and using the experimental method.

The use Bartlett makes of the concept 'tendency' merits further discussion.
Tendencies are viewed by him as the raw material for individual action. To ignore
the fact that human beings are biological entities can only lead to mechanistic
views which consider humans either as mechanisms that respond to stimuli, or
as machines that process information according to their physical properties,
never as entities acting with purpose. This does not mean that psychology has to
abandon the idea of looking for the determinants of behaviour; rather, it has to
look for them both inside and outside the skin, in the physical and in the social
and cultural environment. Bartlett was not naïve—behaviour for him is not a
result of the work of consciousness. But this does not mean that consciousness
plays no role in behaviour. The consciousness he considers in the writings here
reviewed is the phenomenological consciousness.

Bartlett's treatment of intentional consciousness, although rather evasive, can
be found under the heading of 'A Theory of Remembering' in the 10th chapter
of *Remembering* (1932), which is experiential in its focus. It is in this realm that
the effects of social institutions, practices and tools leave their mark, via the

composition of systems of functional processes (processes that produce conscious experiences which are instrumental for the orientation of behaviour, decision making and, eventually, voluntary action). This does not mean that psychology cannot proceed beyond cultural boundaries; rather, its task is to explain how psychological functions and human behaviour are shaped (and explained) when society, culture and their evolution are taken into account. The marks biological evolution has left in the very structure of humans, and that human ethology is exploring, also cannot be ignored.

In Bartlett's view, laboratory and field work are not to be divorced from each other; he employs categories that allow the researcher to bridge the gap between these two settings. This is possible when human action, wherever it appears, is taken as social action, not as a 'pure, simple behaviour'. This is where his use of the concept of 'masterful tendency', which I have interpreted as derived from Watt's *Einstellung*, comes into play. The individual-in-the-laboratory is not a subject who is expected to perform the task the experimenter dictates, but is an individual who has an understanding of the situation, someone for whom the experimenter has to gain his or her 'good will', to create a disposition to 'play the game' (Bartlett, 1923, p. 270).

Bartlett here echoed the ideas widespread in psychology before his times. Danziger (1985) discusses the various ways in which social relations in the laboratory have been dealt with at different moments in the history of psychology. From this point of view it seems that the subjects' misunderstanding of experimental task demands results from ignoring the social situation in the laboratory, and cannot be 'solved' just by refining procedures. If this social character is acknowledged, the laboratory situation can then be treated as a setting which does not leave aside the situatedness of human action.

The way in which Bartlett views the parallelism of individual and society can be useful in our contemporary discussions on cultural psychologies. If Bartlett's ideas were to be considered together with Vygotsky's first law of cultural formation (Vygotsky, 1979), the process of internalisation would go beyond the realm of cognition, including also feelings, values, a sense of belonging and so on. Barclay and Smith (1992) have advanced a model which borrows from these two scholars, as well as presenting useful insights and a current reinterpretation of conventionalisation applied both to individual growth and to cultural change.

There is another legacy of Bartlett's which I believe is worthy of being highlighted. Bartlett always insisted that Psychology is also a biological science; his use of Head's concept of schema is evidence of this. It might be thought that Bartlett's applied experimental work was a diversion from his cultural and social preoccupations, but I do not believe this. As Gruber (1989) points out, scientists organise their knowledge, purposes and affects in a *network of enterprises*. Even when two enterprises seems to be far apart, there may be an internal connection between them. I think this is the case with Bartlett's two enterprises, and I believe that even his early work contained the seeds of this connection. Bartlett reconciled in his work an analytical study of psychological processes, a sensitivity for taking into account the experiences of the individual, a preoccupation for the practical outcomes of his work and, often, tolerance for dissent when he saw a value in the dissent. All these features could be covered under the title of a functionalist approach, a label which I think also applies to Vygotsky and Luria.

I believe that Bartlett's pledge to keep these facets of psychology together is a part of his legacy that we may profit by; otherwise we may fall into the Scylla of idealism when trying to escape the Charybdis of positivist mechanicism. It may be comfortable and satisfying to retreat to academic games of language, pointing out the political uses of applied psychology and its messy and irrelevant outcomes, but this option may result in leaving the field only to those who offer useful marketable products. Psychology may profit enormously from discourse analysis; however, I think it would be better not to lose sight of the fact that discourses are not something given, but are to be explained within the social niche in which they appear. Discourses are also the outcome of actions of biological entities that have their own history, and reflexivity also applies to this. Psychology is in the difficult position of being at once social and biological; it has to understand social processes, but also cannot refrain from the attempt to explain them as the result of actions of living organisms. Bartlett, Baldwin, Janet, Luria, Wallon or Vygotsky placed themselves in that difficult position; I think we may profit from their theoretical and methodological insights.

Finally, I cannot resist making a historical comment. Some of Bartlett's ideas bear a striking resemblance to those presented by the early work of Luria (1932). Both of them resort to the idea of systems and acknowledge the common influence of Henry Head (Bartlett, 1926a, 1926b, 1932; Luria, 1932, p. 370), and, through him, Hughlings Jackson's view of the nervous system. As the reader has surely noticed, this is not the only resemblance between some of Bartlett's ideas, and those developed by the early cultural-historical tradition of Vygotsky and Luria (see Van der Veer, 1996).

Bartlett—similarly to the Vygotsky–Luria tradition—also mentioned the resemblance of his early work to that of Pierre Janet. However, he acknowledged that each of them had reached their ideas independently (Bartlett, 1932).

CONCLUSION: A NEW LOOK AT FUNCTIONALISM

It may very well be the case that a fresh look into the varieties of functionalist thought of the early 20th century would allow us to imagine a history of psychology, not yet written, in which certain contributions, such as those of Baldwin, G.H. Mead, Bartlett, Janet or Vygotsky, are regarded not just as interesting works authored by dissident figures outside the mainstream of psychology. It may be that the construction of a master narrative which links together functional and sociogenetic views of human action would be more helpful for the orientation of the psychologists' research, rather than the worn-out tale or narrative of the evolution of 'schools' of psychological thought (structuralism, functionalism, behaviourism, cognitivism and their successors). I hope that our construction of a future will cast some light on the records of the past, and the landscape so illuminated will empower us in our choices.

PART III

Contemporary research

Bartlett's concept of the schema and its impact on theories of knowledge representation in contemporary cognitive psychology

William F. Brewer

INTRODUCTION

The purpose of this chapter is to provide a critical analysis of Bartlett's concept of the schema, to show the influence of this theoretical construct on the development of cognitive psychology, and to place the schema construct in the context of contemporary theories of knowledge representation in cognitive psychology and cognitive science.

Bartlett as time traveller

Bartlett developed the schema construct in the 1920s, yet the idea had its main impact on cognitive psychology and cognitive science in the 1970s and 1980s. What was the cause of this 50-year lag? In developing the schema construct Bartlett was essentially proposing a completely new form of mental representation. Unfortunately for him, he made the proposal during the period when behaviourism was becoming the dominant intellectual framework in psychology, and a core component of the behaviourist framework was that mental entities were to be excluded from scientific psychology. In addition, Bartlett's experimental work on memory took an approach quite at odds with the dominant atomistic/reductionist approach deriving from the important early work of Ebbinghaus. The first sections of this chapter will describe Bartlett's schema proposal and give an account of how he came to be so far out of phrase with mainstream psychological thought.

BARTLETT'S EMPIRICAL STUDIES OF HUMAN MEMORY

Ecological validity

Bartlett's schema construct was developed to account for memory data that he gathered around the time of World War I. The unique nature of these findings was driven by a set of metatheoretical assumptions that Bartlett held. The most common laboratory approach to memory at the time was derived from the work of Hermann Ebbinghaus (1885–1964). Ebbinghaus developed the nonsense syllable as the material to use in memory experiments. He argued that the use of this type of material would reduce or eliminate confounding variables and allow the study of a relatively 'pure' form of memory. He and those in his research tradition implicitly assumed that the laws of memory uncovered with these simple materials could be used to account for more complex forms of memory.

Bartlett rejected the Ebbinghaus approach early in his professional career (Bartlett, 1958, p. 142). Bartlett argued that the experimental tasks used by psychologists should reflect the characteristics of the real-world phenomena that the researcher is interested in understanding. In modern terminology Bartlett was arguing for the research strategy of using 'ecologically valid' tasks (cf. Neisser, 1978). In one autobiographical account Bartlett says that after carrying out a standard series of laboratory experiments in psychophysics he thought to himself, 'What had it to do with our daily life?' (Bartlett, 1956, p. 83).

Bartlett made a wide range of arguments against the Ebbinghaus approach (Bartlett, 1932, chap. 1); however, one particularly powerful line of attack was the argument for emergent properties. Bartlett was aware that laboratory simplification had played an important role in the development of other sciences, but he argued that the simplification of materials in memory experiments gave rise to severe problems. He stated, 'if a psychologist who is concerned with relatively high-level responses like recall endeavors to isolate the response *by simplifying the stimulus* he has performed a very different operation. This has been the traditional method, as, for example, in the use of so-called meaningless material in the bulk of memory experiments' (Bartlett, 1936, p. 44, italics in original). Essentially, Bartlett was arguing that complex memory material had emergent properties and that in simplifying the material the experimenter was losing the ability to study those properties (cf. Brewer & Nakamura, 1984 for a more detailed analysis of this issue). Bartlett made a similar argument against the assumption that simple laws of memory could be scaled up to account for complex forms of memory. He used an analogy with chemistry and argued that, as with chemical combination, the 'combinations or organizations of "mental elements" may have different properties from the elements themselves' (Bartlett, 1936, p. 49). Finally, on a somewhat narrower issue, Bartlett argued that the Ebbinghaus approach focused almost exclusively on the number of correct responses and ignored the rich data that can be obtained by examining the qualitative nature of errors made in recall (cf. Koriat & Goldsmith, 1996 for a contemporary discussion of this issue).

Given his belief in the need for ecologically valid materials, Bartlett rejected the use of nonsense syllables and chose to use pictures, figures and prose passages as his experimental materials. In particular, he focused much attention on data that he gathered on the recall of a Native American folk story titled, 'The War of the Ghosts'. In retrospect, one might argue that having participants read a difficult Kathlamet folk story twice and then asking them to recall it 15 minutes or 10 years later does not exactly fit his own arguments for ecological validity. However, as will become obvious later in this chapter, the change from nonsense syllables to text passages was enough of a shift in methodology to lead to very important new experimental findings that eventually forced Bartlett to develop the construct of the schema.

Bartlett's core empirical results

Bartlett gathered many of his data on human memory during the period around World War I. He published some of them (e.g. Bartlett, 1920a) without an overall theoretical framework. In the early 1920s he was very frustrated by his inability to work out a theoretical account of his data. He stated (1958, p. 144) that during this period he wrote up several chapters for a book describing his memory research, but eventually destroyed them. However, during the early 1920s he spent much time interacting with the neurologist Henry Head and he reports that these discussions led to the development of the schema construct. Finally, in 1932 he published his famous book, *Remembering*, which contained a more detailed account of his empirical studies of memory and a theory of the schema to explain his findings. In this section of this chapter I will outline Bartlett's core empirical findings; in the sections that follow I will sketch out Bartlett's schema theory; then I will explore the ability of his theory to account for his data.

It requires a bit of work to summarise Bartlett's findings. Even by the standards of his times Bartlett's presentation was not quantitative and very informal. For the most part, he presented a number of recall protocols, gave an account of several prominent features of the protocols, and then made some verbal statements about the general nature of selected findings. Nevertheless, it is usually possible to gain a fair idea of the overall nature of his results. There have been some recent debates about the details of his work (e.g. Wheeler & Roediger, 1992); however, most of his core findings have been replicated in experiments that use more modern standards of methodology and data presentation (see Brewer & Nakamura, 1984 for a review).

Changes in recall

The most general finding that Bartlett noted was that the information in the recalls he obtained was changed in many ways from the information originally presented. He stated that in his data 'accuracy of reproduction, in a literal sense, is the rare exception and not the rule' (1932, p. 93).

Summarisation processes

He noted that the recall protocols were typically much shorter than the input material. In what way was the material shortened? First, Bartlett noted that the underlying structure of the text tended to be retained. He stated, 'the form, plan, type, or scheme of a story seems, in fact, for the ordinary, educated adult to be the most dominant and persistent factor in this kind of material' (1932, p. 83). The converse of this was omission of the irrelevant. He noted that there was 'much general simplification, due to the omission of material that appears irrelevant' (p. 138). For example, in the 'War of the Ghosts' the main character comes home after being wounded in battle and the text states that he 'made a fire'. This event was not crucial to the overall plot or structure of the story and was frequently forgotten in the sample recalls presented by Bartlett.

It appears that Bartlett also thought two other classes of items tended to be omitted in recall—unfamiliar material and inconsistent material. For example, on the issue of unfamiliar material he stated, 'any element of imported culture which finds very little background in the culture to which it comes must fail to be assimilated' (1932, p. 125). On the issue of inconsistent material he stated, 'whenever anything appeared incomprehensible, or "queer", it was either omitted or explained' (p. 68). It is not completely clear that Bartlett was attempting to make a distinction between these two classes of material; however, in a section of his book when he was discussing the changes in the drawings of designs in recall he refers to a type of design which is 'not readily assimilated—on account of its oddity or unfamiliarity' (p. 182). This text does suggest he considered these to be two different classes of material—both of which tended to be omitted in recall.

There was, however, a discrepancy in this overall account of his data in terms of a summarisation process. In addition to the general finding that irrelevant material is omitted, he noted that there were occasionally clear examples of the 'curious preservation of the trivial' (1932, p. 184). For example, the 'War of the Ghosts' text mentions that there were five warriors in a canoe. This fact plays no role in the underlying plot, yet was very frequently recalled in the protocols presented by Bartlett.

Transformations to the familiar

Another important phenomenon noted by Bartlett was what I will call transformation to the familiar. Bartlett stated that one class of transformations of the input material consisted of 'changing the relatively unfamiliar into the relatively familiar' (1932, p. 89). In another place in a discussion of the recall of unfamiliar designs he stated that when one of the designs was visually similar to 'some common object, but contains certain features which are unfamiliar to the community to which the material is introduced, these features invariably suffer transformation in the direction of the familiar' (p. 178). Examples of this type of transformation given by Bartlett include the shift of the relatively unfamiliar 'peanut' to the more familiar 'acorn'. For example, in the 'War of the Ghosts', right before the main character dies the text included the somewhat puzzling statement that 'something black came out of his mouth'. Bartlett noted that one participant recalled that phrase as he 'foamed at the mouth' (p. 72); another participant recalled it as 'his soul passed out from his mouth' (p. 127).

Inferences in recall

Another class of changes that occurred in the recalls consisted of the addition of information that went beyond that explicitly given in the text. Bartlett tended to refer to these as 'rationalisations'; I will refer to them as inferences. I will sub-divide them into gap-filling inferences and pragmatic inferences. With respect to gap-filling inferences, Bartlett noted that the text of the 'War of the Ghosts' is relatively episodic, with events following one another without explicit connections. In discussing the recall of this material Bartlett stated that 'reasons were definitely and explicitly formulated and introduced into reproductions to account for material which had been presented without explanation' (1932, p. 84). Bartlett gives many examples of gap-filling inferences. For example, in the 'War of the Ghosts' one of the men declines to go off to battle by stating ' "I will not go along. I might be killed. My relatives do not know where I have gone. But you", he said, turning to the other, "may go with them" ' (p. 65). One participant recalled the last section of this text as 'But you have no one to expect you' (p. 71). Another participant recalled it as 'You have no parents' (p. 120). In each case the participant has provided an explanation (not given in the original text) for why it would be all right for the second man to go off to battle.

Ironically it turns out that in discussing recall errors in his book Bartlett himself made a classic memory inference. He stated that participants frequently shifted the word 'paddling' to 'rowing' (1932, pp. 82, 88). However a careful examination of the original text of the 'War of the Ghosts' (p. 65) shows that the word 'paddling' never appears! The text mentions that the warriors were in canoes and that the two men heard the noise of paddles. But when the canoes move along the river the text uses terms such as 'went on up the river' and 'went back to Egulac'. Clearly, Bartlett made the inference that the warriors 'paddled' up the river and then back home. And to add icing to the cake and show that Bartlett's own error was lawful and predictable it turns out that at least one of his participants produced the same inference in recall that Bartlett made in writing his book. In recalling the 'War of the Ghosts' participant H's protocol includes the sentence that 'The party paddled up the river' (p. 66).

Pragmatic inferences have been defined as inferences that 'lead the hearer to expect something that is neither explicitly stated nor necessarily implied by the original sentence' (Brewer, 1977, p. 673). Bartlett does not give an explicit discussion of this class of inferences; however, his protocols are full of clear examples. For example, in the 'War of the Ghosts' the original text describing the battle included the phrase 'that Indian has been hit' (1932, p. 65). This text was recalled by different participants as: 'An Indian is killed' (p. 68); 'the Indian has fallen' (p. 70); 'he had been wounded by an arrow' (p. 72); and 'you are wounded by an arrow' (p. 120).

These results are very similar to those that I gathered 45 years later. In fact, one of the items I used in my study of pragmatic inferences was conceptually quite close to the specific examples from Bartlett given earlier. In my experiment the sentence 'The Titanic hit an iceberg' was presented to participants and was occasionally recalled as 'The Titanic sank'. My notes for the 1977 study show that my interest in pragmatic implications in recall derived out a concern with distinguishing logical inferences from pragmatic inferences and so was independent of Bartlett's work. However, there is a reference to Bartlett in that paper, so there may have been some direct influence from Bartlett's data.

Style shifts and other memory findings

Bartlett reported a number of other memory findings (e.g. recall of humour was good, and recall of the direction of face profiles was poor). These seem only tangentially relevant to the schema theory. There is one final class of memory transformations that Bartlett discussed in moderate detail—style shifts. These do not seem as directly related to the schema issues as the other findings described previously and so will only be discussed briefly. Bartlett stated that linguistic style was rarely recalled correctly (1932, p. 81). He noted that if the original text was written in some non-standard style it tended to be recalled in more ordinary modern style (p. 68). He also noted that some of his participants attempted (unsuccessfully) to style match in recall (p. 81). All of these findings were replicated by Brewer and Hay (1984).

A brief autobiographical note

The Brewer and Hay study (1984) was designed and carried out as part of a programme of research on literature and psychology and is a completely independent replication of Bartlett. I do recall the intellectual history of this one because I can still remember how surprised I was when I accidentally ran across Bartlett's section on style just before we were ready to submit that manuscript for publication—it had not been obvious to me at that time that Bartlett's work was a place to look for data on literary variables in recall—clearly I was wrong.

Unconscious shifts in recall

One final finding that is relevant to Bartlett's construct of the schema is the issue of conscious awareness. In his discussions of the various types of omissions and transformations discussed previously, Bartlett repeatedly asserted that these memory processes operated outside of conscious awareness (e.g. 1932, pp. 52, 68, 86, 87, 89, 126). Bartlett typically used the term 'unwitting' to make the point (e.g. 'the . . . process of rationalisation . . . was unwitting from start to finish'; p. 87), but it is quite clear that this was intended to mean unconscious.

THE SCHEMA THEORY

In this section I will describe Bartlett's schema theory. Bartlett's basic intellectual achievement was to realise that a theory of the human mind requires an account of human knowledge and to propose a specific solution to this problem— the schema. Bartlett's discussion of this issue is quite difficult, and over the years it is clear that this section of his book has served as a Rorschach test for his readers. Therefore, I will tend to quote his actual text rather than describe his view, in order to try to keep us as close as possible to *his* version of schema theory.

Influences leading to Bartlett's schema theory

Conventionalisation

Before launching into the discussion of schema theory, I will give a brief account of Bartlett's earlier attempts to provide a framework for his empirical results. In his early years at Cambridge, Bartlett was quite influenced by work in anthropology (cf. Bartlett, 1936; Brewer, in press a; Oldfield, 1972; Zangwill, 1970). He was particularly taken with discussions by anthropologists of the process of conventionalisation seen in decorative art and in the design of human artefacts (e.g. in Western culture the conventional drawing of stars with points or the fact that pencils are conventionally orange/yellow). Bartlett saw conventions as culturally stable patterns and was particularly interested in anthropological descriptions of the results of cross-cultural contact. He stated, 'Conventionalisation is a process by which cultural materials coming into a group from outside are gradually worked into a pattern of a relatively stable kind distinctive of that group. The new material is assimilated to the persistent past of the group to which it comes' (1932, p. 280).

Bartlett saw the obvious connection between these ideas and his data showing that after repeated recalls the recall protocols reached a fairly stable fixed form and that the changes in recall frequently showed the impact of old information on new information. Bartlett stated that he intended his first research programme to be 'an all out experimental attack upon conventionalizing' (Bartlett, 1958, p. 143). In his first write-up of his data on recall of the 'War of the Ghosts' Bartlett (1920a) made explicit use of the construct of conventionalisation.

However, he eventually became disenchanted with this approach (cf. Bartlett, 1958, pp. 143–144). In retrospect, I think the problem was that conventionalisation was not an *explanatory* concept—instead it was a label for an interesting similarity between two different domains. If, in fact, there was going be explanatory power here, it was probably that the processes of human memory (as found in the laboratory by Bartlett) were likely to explain the cultural data rather than vice versa. Thus, Bartlett was left without an explanatory theory to account for his memory data.

Head's concept of the schema

In all of his accounts of the schema construct Bartlett gave much credit to the work of the neurologist Henry Head. The impact of Head's ideas on Bartlett is a story that has been told in some detail (Bartlett, 1932, pp. 198–202; 1958, pp. 146–147; Oldfield & Zangwill, 1942a, 1942b, 1943) and so will not be repeated in detail here. Head needed a construct to account for disorders of body position and orientation. He postulated a physiological structure he called the 'postural schema' to explain how the past information about the location of the body influences current actions. In retrospect, it seems to me that Bartlett was too generous in giving Head credit. It is a long way from a physiological structure to account for body position to an understanding that psychology must provide an account of human knowledge and the proposal of a new form of mental structure. It is clear from Bartlett's autobiographical accounts that discussions with Head helped start Bartlett's thinking along new lines, but there is only modest transfer of specific details from one schema theory to the other.

Trace theory

In thinking about how to represent human knowledge, the psychological approach to that issue that Bartlett was most familiar with was the work of the British Empiricist philosophers, in which knowledge is represented in terms of specific mental images (see Brewer, 1993 for a discussion of these philosophical positions as psychological theories of representation). Bartlett summarises these positions as follows: 'when any specific event occurs some trace, or some group of traces, is made and stored up in the organism or in the mind' (1932, p. 197). He goes on to note that 'the traces are generally supposed to be of individual and specific events. Hence, every normal individual must carry about with him an incalculable number of individual traces' (p. 197). Contemporary versions of these positions (with the images removed) are known as instance theories (e.g. Medin & Ross, 1989). Bartlett thought these instance views ('trace' views in his terminology) were obviously wrong and incompatible with his memory data. In recent years it has become apparent that instance views are much more flexible than they were once thought to be, and they have been adopted by a number of researchers in the area of knowledge representation and human memory (e.g. Hintzman, 1986). I will take up this issue again when I deal with the issue of the representation of specific information in Bartlett's schema theory.

Pure schema theory

In trying to explicate Bartlett's views, I will argue that he has two somewhat different views. First I will describe what I refer to as the 'pure schema theory'. This theory is his 'up-front' view with the clearest explicit textual support. However, I will argue that there is also textual evidence for a somewhat less extreme form of theory that I will refer to as 'schema plus instance theory'.

Ontology

First, what did Bartlett take schemata to be? There is no explicit discussion of this fundamental issue in *Remembering* (1932), but in his autobiography Bartlett (1936) describes a case where someone is using a schema and stated, 'He is not able to describe this scheme as something that he can find by introspection, but it has a character theoretically the same as other things, e.g., images, sensory patterns, ideas, and so on, that he is able to find in this way' (p. 47). I think it is clear that Bartlett conceived of schemata as mental entities like images, but unconscious.

Abstraction

Bartlett took a very uncompromising view on the issue of abstraction. He argued that all individual experiences are abstracted (schematised) to produce schemata. He stated, 'the past operates as an organised mass rather than as a group of elements each of which retains its specific character' (1932, p. 197). In another place he stated, 'there is not the slightest reason, however, to suppose that each set of incoming impulses, each new group of experiences persists as an isolated member of some passive patchwork' (p. 201).

Turning round on one's schema

Bartlett was aware that his extreme view on abstraction led to a very difficult problem—how could one ever recall a specific episodic event? Bartlett stated, 'we have to find a way of individualising some of the characteristics of the total functioning mass of the moment' (1932, p. 208). Bartlett's solution to this problem is the famous operation in which individuals 'turn round on their schema'. This aspect of Bartlett's theory has consistently been considered to be the most incomprehensible part of the theory. Broadbent in his obituary of Bartlett even went so far as to imply that even Bartlett did not know what the term meant (1970, p. 4).

Bartlett discussed the issue of 'turning round on one's schema' in several places. He stated, 'An organism which has discovered how to [turn round on its schemata] might be able not exactly to analyse the settings, for the individual details that have built them up have disappeared, but somehow to construct or to infer from what is present the probable constituents and their order which went to build them up' (1932, p. 202). In another place, he stated that in order to find the specific information needed in a particular situation the 'organism has somehow to acquire the capacity to turn round upon its own "schemata" and to construct them afresh' (p. 206). In reading these accounts it seems to me that the difficulty is that they do a better job of stating the problem than in offering a solution. In current cognitive science it might be possible to give an account of the type Bartlett wanted with some form of holographic metaphor or some form of connectionist model, but this seems an unfair anachronism. Given the theoretical machinery Bartlett had available, my best interpretation is that 'turning round on one's schema' would consist of constructing a specific representation by taking the modal schema properties of the relevant schemata. Thus, in trying to recall a specific room one had seen in the past, one would not recall the sum of all previous rooms one had experienced but a particular room with a ceiling consisting of the modal room ceiling material (say plaster), a door of the modal door type (say a wooden door), etc. This interpretation retains Bartlett's extreme abstractionism and produces a particular room, but it does have the severe problem that it does not provide for the successful recall of the episodic details of a given non-modal room.

Images

Another aspect of Bartlett's theory that has been difficult for people to understand is his discussion of the relationship between schema and images. He stated, 'one of the great functions of images in mental life [is] to pick items out of "schemata"' (1932, p. 209). In a longer account he stated, 'images are, then, literally details picked out of "schemes" and used to facilitate some necessary response to immediate environmental conditions. They are essentially individual and concrete in their character' (p. 303). More recent commentators on Bartlett have found this aspect of schema theory difficult to understand. The solution here is to take into account Bartlett's early training in philosophy and introspective psychology. Bartlett assumes that specific memories of the past are recalled in terms of recollective memory. By recollective memory I mean the form of memory that consists of 'memory for a specific episode from an individual's past. It typically appears to be a "reliving" of the individual's phenomenal experience during that earlier moment . . . The information in this form of memory is expressed as a mental image' (Brewer, 1996, p. 60). Thus Bartlett discusses images because he considers them part of the recollective recall process.

Schema plus instance theory

In the previous sub-section I have done my best to sketch out Bartlett's 'official' theory—the pure schema theory. However, it is obvious from the paragraphs on turning round on one's schema that Bartlett was acutely aware of the problems with his extreme form of abstractionism in terms of the recall of specific information. In addition, one must take into account that the whole point of the schema theory was to explain Bartlett's empirical findings about human memory, and it is obvious in reading the recall protocols that the participants recall much specific and non-schematic information from the original texts that they read.

Thus, I think, in practice, Bartlett often took a somewhat more moderate view in which recall included schema information plus some specific episodic information. There is some textual support for this interpretation in *Remembering* (1932). For example, Bartlett stated that in the recall of pictures 'it may well be that inferences ... are mingled unwittingly with the actual recall of perceptual material or patterns' (p. 52). He stated that in the recall process 'the need to remember becomes active, an attitude is set up; in the form of sensory images, or, just as often, of isolated words, some part of the event which has to be remembered recurs, and the event is then reconstructed on the basis of the relation of this specific bit of material to the general mass of relevant past experience or reaction' (p. 209). In another place Bartlett stated that remembering is 'built out of the relation of our attitude towards a whole active mass of organised past reactions or experience, and to a little outstanding detail which commonly appears in image or in language form' (p. 213). Although this schema plus instance theory does allow for some retained specific episodic information (e.g. outstanding details), it still has major problems that will be discussed later in this chapter.

Active nature of schema

Many recent commentators on Bartlett's construct of the schema have emphasised his discussion of the active nature of schema. (We clearly did this to some degree in Brewer & Nakamura, 1984.) There is certainly considerable support for this characteristic of schemata in Bartlett's writings. For example, he stated:

> The connecting of the given pattern with a special setting is obviously an active process, for, speaking in an abstract sense, the setting used is only one of a large number, any of which might be brought into play. But though it is active it is not conscious, for the observer is not aware of a search and a subsequent match. I shall call this fundamental process of connecting a given pattern with some setting or scheme: *effort after meaning.*
>
> (Bartlett, 1932, p. 20)

In what is perhaps Bartlett's strongest statement of the view he stated:

> the process is emphatically not merely a question of relating the newly presented
> material to old acquirements of knowledge. . . . To speak as if what is accepted and
> given a place in mental life is always simply a question of what fits into already
> formed apperception systems is to miss the obvious point that the process of fitting
> is an active process, depending directly upon the pre-formed tendencies and bias
> which the subject brings to the task.
>
> (Bartlett, 1932, p. 85)

If these extracts are taken to suggest that schemata are dynamic entities
that undergo flexible reorganisation to deal with specific situations, then it seems
to me that there is a real conflict with Bartlett's clear statements (see the previous sub-section on the pure schema theory) that schemata are the mental
representations of generic knowledge in long-term memory. Another line of
evidence against attributing too much activity and flexibility to Bartlett's schemata is to consider that his first attempt to account for his memory data was
to relate them to the anthropological concept of conventionalisation. It seems to
me that among anthropological constructs the idea of conventionalisation is one
dealing with relatively static aspects of culture that change relatively slowly
over time.

So what did Bartlett mean when he said schemata were active processes? I
think a close reading of Bartlett shows that he was trying to make the point that
in interacting with the world human beings are not merely passively making
responses determined by the current physical environment. In the terminology of
modern cognitive psychology (Lindsay & Norman, 1977) Bartlett was saying
that in interacting with the world there is a large *top-down* contribution to the
interaction that comes from the individual. More specifically, the generic knowledge represented in schemata is brought to bear on the processes of perception
and memory. This interpretation of Bartlett's position seems strongly supported
by the extracts given previously. The first of the two extracts is taken from
Bartlett's analysis of his data showing top-down effects in visual perception (see
Palmer, 1975 for a classic treatment of the same issue in modern cognitive
psychology). What Bartlett meant by 'effort after meaning' in that extract is that
the participants were not merely responding to the physical stimuli being shown
to them but were using top-down schema information to interpret the stimuli.
The second extract is taken from Bartlett's discussion of his memory data, and
there he is making the point that the participants did not just passively accept the
text they read, since the inferences they made in recall are evidence of the
activity of 'pre-formed tendencies and bias' (i.e. generic schema knowledge).
Thus, it seems to me that Bartlett's discussions of the active nature of the
schema are not in conflict with his proposals that schemata are the repository of
generic knowledge in long-term memory.

BARTLETT'S DATA AND BARTLETT'S THEORY

It is clear that Bartlett developed schema theory to give an account of his experimental data on perception and memory. In fact, however, he never gives an explicit account of how the schema construct would explain his data! The problem is that he gathered most of his experimental data 15–20 years before he wrote the book, *Remembering* (1932), in which he presented the fully worked out schema theory. He had already published many of the data (Bartlett, 1916a, 1920a, 1921, 1928a) before he developed the schema theory and in *Remembering* he reports many of the data as he had previously presented them and then, in chap. 10, he lays out his new schema theory. Thus, the actual application of the schema theory is left, for the most part, as an exercise for the reader. In this section of this chapter I will attempt to carry out this exercise.

Pure schema model

First, I will use the pure schema model and explore the degree to which it can explain Bartlett's data as outlined earlier in this chapter. Bartlett's general finding that recall in his experiments was rarely accurate can be explained. As I understand the pure schema model the only type of information that would be recalled accurately as presented would be examples of pure generic schemata. All other types of information would be changed by virtue of their interaction with the relevant schema. Thus, a text that stated, 'there was a room, it had walls, a door, a ceiling and windows' would be expected to be recalled as given because it maps the schema for rooms. Any other type of text would likely contain transformations to the familiar or inferential changes.

The theory does a good job of explaining the basic summarisation findings. Unlike most previous work (and much later work!) Bartlett's schema theory provided a way to talk about the underlying structure of a piece of text. Thus, for example, the schema theory provided a motivated way to define what was irrelevant (not part of the current schema), unfamiliar (not part of any schema), or inconsistent (not compatible with the current schema). If we assume that, in a memory task, participants recall the schema and omit things that are not part of the schema, then the theory predicts that participants will recall schema-related material but will tend not to recall irrelevant, unfamiliar and inconsistent material.

The theory also does a good job of explaining the various transformations in recall. Thus, to use Bartlett's example, if someone reads a text that mentions an uncommon type of nut (in World War I England) such as a peanut, then the theory would predict a shift in recall to the most common form of nut (acorn). If participants are given a text that omits parts of a schema then one might predict that, in recall, the participants will insert the missing material, thus accounting for gap-filling inferences and pragmatic inferences.

It should be clear now why Bartlett's theory was destined to play an import-ant role in later developments in cognitive psychology and cognitive science. The theory gives an explanatory account of a wide range of puzzling memory data. However, there are serious problems: (1) The theory cannot account for the recall of schema-related material that is not the modal information (i.e. it cannot account for the correct recall of a text that included the statement that the 'pecan fell from the tree' if we assume that acorns are the most common form of nuts that grow on trees); (2) The theory cannot account for the correct recall of any non-schema episodic information. In particular, the theory cannot account for Bartlett's finding of the 'curious preservation of the trivial' (1932, p. 184); (3) The theory assumes that all memory structure consists of generic knowledge.

Schema plus instance theory

The schema plus instance theory retains all of the properties of the pure schema theory so it can explain all of those aspects of summarisation and inferences in recall that can be explained by the pure schema theory. In addition, the schema plus instance theory allows for some episodic recall. For example, in trying to recall a specific room one had seen in the past, one might be able to recall 'outstanding detail' such as that the door to the room was a sliding door or that there was a platypus in a cage in the room. However, the theory could not account for successful recall of schema-related information (e.g. that there were two incandescent lights and a rocking chair in the room) or for ordinary non-schematic episodic information (e.g. that there was a brick on the rocking chair). In addition, this interpretation of Bartlett's schema theory also assumes that all memory structure consists of generic schema information; the problems with this assumption will be discussed later in this chapter. So again with the modified schema theory we find an impressive theory that can account for a wide variety of data, but a theory that has some severe flaws.

THE RECEPTION OF BARTLETT'S SCHEMA THEORY

In England, where behaviourism had made only modest inroads, Bartlett's schema theory was initially received very favourably, and there were a number of attempts to explicate and extend the theory (Oldfield & Zangwill, 1942a, 1942b, 1943). In a review of *Remembering*, Burt (1933, p. 187) stated that this 'volume is by far the most important contribution to psychology that has appeared in this country during recent years'. Oldfield and Zangwill (1942a, p. 268) stated that the schema construct 'in the hands of Bartlett especially, has led to the provisional establish-ment of what we believe to constitute a truly novel approach to some of the fundamental problems of psychology'.

In the United States, where behaviourism had already become the dominant theoretical perspective, the book was received much less favourably. For example,

Jenkins (1935, p. 715) stated that 'the book will find a place upon the shelves of those who study remembering, but it will not be in the special section reserved for those investigators whose writings have become landmarks in the advance towards the comprehension of this important problem'.

As time went on and behaviourist and reductivist approaches came to have a greater influence in English psychology, opinion turned strongly against Bartlett's construct of the schema. Bartlett died in 1969, and his obituary writers were quite critical of this aspect of his work. Zangwill (1970, p. 78) stated that the schema concept 'seemed to many to do little more than re-describe the data which it was designed to explain and to lack a theoretical basis of sufficient precision for genuine advance'. Oldfield (1972, p. 136) stated that 'efforts to clarify the essential elements of the theory so as to make it applicable to further use in empirical investigation and experiment were unsuccessful'. Broadbent (1970, p. 4) stated, 'These concepts provoked enormous discussion . . . It is fair to say, however, that this discussion is now dead and that the term "schema" appears to have become completely disused.' In a retrospective review of *Remembering* originally given as the 1971 Bartlett Lecture, Zangwill (1972b, p. 127) con-cluded that '[schema] theory, in my view never very plausible, is perhaps best forgotten'. Clearly, things did not look good for the schema concept some 40 years after it was published. However, the world changed and by the 1980s a citation study (White, 1983) showed that *Remembering* was the second most cited work in the area of human memory. (The story told in this section should be good for the morale of all researchers. Even if your contemporaries have rejected one of your pet ideas, it is possible that it may yet turn to gold!)

MODERN SCHEMA THEORY

Schema theory made its way back into mainstream psychology via a detour through the field of computer science. In the early days of the development of the field of artificial intelligence, researchers were attempting to develop machines that would show human-like intelligence. It was (and still is) very difficult to develop computer programs that allowed machines to perceive, talk and learn. The computer scientist Marvin Minsky considered human beings to be an exist-ence proof of the ability of organisms to carry out these tasks and therefore spent some time thinking about how humans achieve them. In the course of these deliberations Minsky read Bartlett's *Remembering*, and it helped him see that in tasks such as perceiving the world humans were 'cheating' and using top-down knowledge about the world to help solve the perception problem (Minsky, 1975). Minsky then argued that if machines were to carry out higher-level tasks such as perception, language understanding and learning, they too would have to be provided with large amounts of knowledge. Minsky's general arguments had an enormous influence on the early development of the field of artificial intelli-gence (Brewer, in press b; Dyer, Cullingford & Alvarado, 1990; Maida, 1990).

Frames

Minsky went on to make a specific proposal about how knowledge could be represented in machines. He introduced the construct of 'frames' to represent knowledge of the world (Minsky, 1975). For our purposes frames can just be considered another name for schemata. Minsky proposed that frames were knowledge structures that contained fixed structural information. Frames have slots that accept a range of variables. Each slot has a default value which is used if no value has been provided by bottom-up information from the outside world. For example, if a machine (or person) is trying to represent a particular university classroom, the generic classroom frame will contain fixed information (e.g. rooms have walls, rooms have ceilings, rooms have doors, rooms have lighting). The room frame will have a slot for door and if no information is provided from the world (e.g. through a TV camera scan of the room) then the frame fills the slot with a default value (i.e. the most common type of door for classrooms). In essence, Minsky's frame construct is an explicit proposal for how to represent generic knowledge. The frame construct as just outlined is able to explain all of Bartlett's memory data dealing with summarisation and inferential recall.

Schema instantiation

In addition to inheriting the advantages that are obtained from having a theory that represents generic knowledge, Minsky's theory overcomes one of the major shortcomings with Bartlett's theory—the extreme form of abstractionism that left the theory with no mechanism to deal with specific schema-related information. Minsky's frame proposal represents generic knowledge (in the fixed frames and in the default values), but it also includes a mechanism (using episodic information to fill slots) that produces a specific schema representation for a particular instance in the world.

By the 1970s, the behaviourist approach had faded from psychology and the cognitive revolution was well under way (see Brewer & Nakamura, 1984 for a discussion of how these changes led the way to the re-emergence of schema theory). Minsky's ideas were rapidly taken up by cognitive psychologists (e.g. Rumelhart & Ortony, 1977; Schank & Abelson, 1977), and this work forms the basis for modern schema theory. In a very influential paper, Rumelhart (1980, p. 36) described the general notion of schema instantiation as follows: 'a schema is *instantiated* whenever a particular configuration of values is bound to a particular configuration of variables at a particular moment in time'. Researchers (e.g. Bower, Black & Turner, 1979) postulated that there was generic schema information in long-term memory and that when an individual was exposed to a particular instance of schema-related information the exposure gave rise to a specific instantiated schema representation (e.g. a memory representation of a particular room that had fluorescent lights, a green wooden door, etc.).

Abstractionism

Recent discussions of the relationship of specific knowledge and generic know-ledge (Barsalou, 1990; Hintzman, 1986; Medin & Ross, 1989) have made it clear that Bartlett's decision to abstract across the instances and then discard the instances was simply one of a number of options one could choose to account for the impact of old knowledge on memory performance. For example, Hintzman (1986) has argued that one could store all the instances and then carry out the abstraction process at the time of recall. One could also have a theory in which the instances were abstracted to form the schema but *also* retain all the instances in memory. These are very difficult issues and, in fact, Barsalou (1990) has argued that it may never to be possible to distinguish some of the alternative accounts. However, it should be noted that all of these proposals retain Bartlett's focus on the impact of old knowledge on new knowledge and would predict results much like those found by Bartlett.

Modern empirical research

The new schema ideas led to a wide variety of new experimental studies that followed directly in the intellectual tradition set by Bartlett. For example, Bower, Black and Turner (1979) carried out experiments on scripts (the sub-class of schemata dealing with the domain of human actions) and found high rates of script-based intrusions in the recall of script texts. Brewer and Treyens (1981) found schema-based intrusions in the recall of visual scenes (e.g. of an office). (See Brewer and Nakamura, 1984 for a full review of this experimental literature.)

PROBLEMS WITH SCHEMA THEORY AND NEW DIRECTIONS

Irrelevant and inconsistent information

One area where modern schema theories face problems is in their treatment of schema-irrelevant information and schema-inconsistent information. Several critics of schema theory (Alba & Hasher, 1983; Thorndyke & Yekovich, 1980) have pointed out that the theories have trouble dealing with schema-inconsistent information. For example, most schema theories would predict schema-inconsistent information should show poor recall, whereas some studies (e.g. Davidson & Hoe, 1993) have found superior recall for this type of information.

Brewer and Tenpenny (1998) have attempted to articulate schema theory to deal with these problems. We gathered memory data from texts such as: 'Gordon decided to make some fresh coffee for supper. He emptied out the old coffee grounds. He took the coffee out of the cabinet. He got out a new filter. He put the coffee in the filter. He rode the horse along the trail. He put the filter under the coffee maker. He got some cold water from the sink.' (Brewer & Tenpenny, 1998). In texts such as these the recall of schema-inconsistent sentences (e.g. 'He rode the horse along the trail.') was quite high.

First, we pointed out that a schema theory of some type is required to make sense of the terms 'irrelevant' and 'inconsistent' as applied to generic knowledge (i.e. for something to be inconsistent there has to be a mental structure against which the inconsistency is defined). In the example given previously there is nothing intrinsically odd about the sentence dealing with riding the horse down the trail; it is only in the context of the making coffee script that it is inconsistent.

Second, we proposed that the high recall of schema-inconsistent material was due to attention being drawn to the schema-inconsistent material. We argued that the participant's attentional resources are used to elaborate new episodic links between the inconsistent material and the underlying script structure and this gives rise to the high recall for this type of item. Although Brewer and Tenpenny (1998) made considerable progress in dealing with these issues, there is still work to be done. It is still not clear if any current schema theory can provide a natural account of Bartlett's 'curious preservation of the trivial'.

Conflating generic knowledge with all knowledge

It now seems obvious that a major problem with Bartlett's schema theory and modern schema theories is that, in their initial enthusiasm for this new form of mental structure, schema theorists (the present writer included) tended to state or imply that schemata were the form of mental representation for all complex forms of knowledge. For example, Rumelhart (1980, p. 34) stated that a schema was 'a data structure for representing the generic concepts stored in memory'. Yet he then went on to say that schemata represent 'our knowledge about all concepts, those underlying objects, situations, events, sequences of events, actions and sequences of actions' (p. 34). In a similar fashion Brewer and Nakamura (1984, pp. 140–141) stated, 'schemas are the unconscious mental structures and processes that underlie the molar aspects of human knowledge and skill. They contain abstract generic knowledge that has been organised to form qualitative new structures.'

Non-generic knowledge

The problem with the attempt to have schemata deal with all forms of human knowledge is that human beings use many forms of structured knowledge that are not generic in nature. For example, consider narrative fiction. If generic knowledge were the only form of structure available then narrative fiction would resemble American 'Dick and Jane' reading primers of the 1940s and 1950s in which a typical 'plot' might consist of Jane's mother giving her a quarter and asking her to go to the store and buy a loaf of bread. Jane then goes to the store, picks out the bread, pays for it and takes it home to her mother. Schema theory could easily provide an account of the structure of narratives of this type.

However, narratives based on this type of structure are very rare. Currently, American primers no longer use this type of script structure. One of the few current genres that comes close to this type of generic structure are American daytime soap operas which make use of relatively scripted plots involving car accidents, amnesia, extra-marital love affairs, etc. Nevertheless, the vast majority of entertainment narrative fiction is organised with non-generic knowledge structures in which the reader typically cannot predict the events that occur, but can see, after the fact, that there were plausible causal links between the events. Finally, to see that there is structure to the plot of standard entertainment fiction one can contrast it with examples of post-modern fiction, in which the author frequently has deliberately removed most forms of underlying structure.

Another domain in which one can see the contrast between generic and non-generic knowledge is the domain of human action. Generic knowledge structures such as scripts do a good job of accounting for the fact that even very young children can describe how a birthday party is structured or how one orders a meal at McDonald's™. However, generic knowledge cannot provide an account of the structure of a novel planned action. Thus, if you were asked to (rapidly) find a copy of Ebbinghaus's book, *Memory*, and cover it with whipped cream you could set up an appropriate plan and carry it out. Clearly, this would involve a unique sequence of acts and so cannot involve running off a pre-stored generic script. Yet, the novel plan definitely has structure since it would be much more efficient than a non-structured approach (e.g. wandering around randomly until one happened across the book and some whipped cream). Solutions to the problems of representing non-generic knowledge are still a work in progress for cognitive psychology and cognitive science; however, there have been some important proposals.

Mental models

Johnson-Laird (1980, 1983) has made convincing arguments for a form of mental representation that he refers to as 'mental models'. He states, 'A model *represents* a state of affairs and accordingly its structure is not arbitrary like that of a propositional representation, but plays a direct representational or analogical role. Its structure mirrors the relevant aspects of the corresponding state of affairs in the world' (1980, p. 98). If someone who knows the geography of the United States hears a text describing a drive from Maine to Boston to New York City to Florida the spatial information is presumably represented in generic form (i.e. a mental map). Thus, recall of this information could probably be accounted for in terms of a schema plus instance version of schema theory. However, Johnson-Laird has pointed out that, if one hears a new text describing a new spatial array (e.g. the layout of a town one has never visited), one can form a non-linguistic mental model of the spatial information expressed in the text and that the mental model then has a variety of effects in comprehension and memory similar to those outlined above for schemata. For example, if one reads the text 'Frederic is to the right of Phil and Phil is to the right of David' one can construct a mental model of the spatial relationships among these three individuals. With this mental model one can make model-based inferences (e.g. David is to the left of Frederic) that go beyond the information given explicitly in the text. An experimental demonstration of this point can be found in Perrig and Kintsch (1985). These researchers showed that participants given a text describing a fictitious town could rapidly answer questions about the spatial position of various objects (e.g. True or False: 'The general store is to the north of the church.') that were not given explicitly in the text. See Brewer (1987) for a more detailed account of the differences between schemata and mental models.

Once one grasps the differences between schemata and mental models, it is possible to go back to Bartlett's data and see that there are clear examples of mental models in his experimental materials. For example, one of the texts used by Bartlett is a 'cumulative' story from Africa. In this story a peanut is swallowed by a bird, the bird eaten by a bush-cat, the bush-cat eaten by a dog, and the dog eaten by a python (Bartlett, 1932, p. 129). I think it is extremely unlikely that Bartlett's participants had ever heard this sequence of events before, yet it is quite easy to build a new mental model to represent this information, and, interestingly, Bartlett reports that this cumulative structure was among the best retained information in his memory experiments (p. 188).

Naïve theories

Another important class of mental representations is naïve theories. There is a large literature (cf. Driver, Guesne & Tiberghien, 1985) showing that children and adults have a wide variety of naïve beliefs about the natural world (e.g. the germ theory of diseases, the belief that heat is a mobile substance). Gopnik and Wellman (1992) made strong arguments that this type of information must be represented in terms of naïve theories. In a recent discussion of these issues (Brewer, in press c), I have stated that naïve theories 'are mental structures that include theoretical entities (usually non-observable), relationships among the theoretical entities, and relationship of the theoretical entities to the phenomena of some domain'.

In a recently completed study Mishra and Brewer (1998) have shown that, if adults are given theoretical explanations for a set of data, the resulting theory facilitates recall in ways similar to that seen in the schema literature. For example, in this study some participants were given passages containing facts about Hawaii such as: 'Kauai, the westernmost island, is approximately 40 million years old. It is highly eroded by the weather. To the west of Kauai are a chain of underwater mountains. . . . Hawaii, the easternmost island, has two active volcanoes. The mountains on the island of Hawaii are not very eroded' (Mishra & Brewer, 1998). Before reading these facts one group (the theory group) was given text which contained a theory of the development of island chains in terms of oceanic plates moving over a hot spot in the earth's mantle. The group given the hot spot theory showed much better recall of theory-relevant information from the fact passage than did a control group. The participants who took part in this experiment were screened to eliminate those who already knew about the hot spot theory, so the knowledge structure that facilitated memory in this experiment must have been a non-generic theory derived from the hot spot theory passage.

Other forms of knowledge representation

The examples of non-generic knowledge discussed earlier suggest that information in different domains requires different forms of mental representation. Thus, arrays of objects require a knowledge representation that can capture new spatial relationships, whereas human actions require a knowledge representation that captures novel intentional plans.

One obvious domain not discussed yet is logical argument. It seems clear that we need some form of representation to capture the information contained in a new logical argument. Johnson-Laird has argued (1980, 1983) that many forms of logical argument can be accounted for in terms of mental models; however, it is probably the case that some more algebraic logico-semantic mental structures will also be needed. At this point in the development of cognitive psychology and cognitive science it is not clear how many different forms of mental representation will be needed for a full account of how the external world is represented in the mind. It is obvious that there is much work remaining to be done.

CONCLUSIONS

From the vantage point of 65 years, it appears that Bartlett's major intellectual achievement was to have seen the need for a form of mental representation to explain how human beings deal with complex structural knowledge. The analysis of Bartlett's schema theory given in this chapter shows that, although his theory was able to capture certain aspects of generic knowledge, his specific proposal also contained a number of crucial flaws. Nevertheless, aspects of his theory remain core components of contemporary schema theories.

Recent work on theories of knowledge representation has shown that generic knowledge is just one of a number of important forms of human knowledge. It now seems clear that other forms of mental representation such as mental models and naïve theories will be required for a full theory of the human mind.

CHAPTER SEVEN

Bartlett's trilogy of memory: Reconstructing the concept of attitude

Steen F. Larsen and Dorthe Berntsen

INTRODUCTION

In the richly detailed account of human memory developed in Bartlett's *Remembering* (1932), three concepts played the key roles: schemata, images and attitudes. Later researchers have focused almost exclusively on the schema concept that became the centrepiece of constructivist theories of perception, memory and knowledge representation when Bartlett's work was rediscovered in the 1970s (see Brewer & Nakamura, 1984). Compared to the spectacular career of the schema, the concepts of attitude and image as used by Bartlett have led a quiet life and generated no succeeding research to speak of. This is hardly because these concepts were any less precisely described than the schema. It has been a common complaint that Bartlett's memory theory was generally too vague, even to the extent that his students Broadbent (1970) and Zangwill (1972b) concluded, shortly after Bartlett had died, that this was the reason the entire theory had failed. The schema was soon revived, but not image and attitude. It is a likely reason for their continued neglect that these concepts are too mentalistic, too closely associated with conscious introspection—that is, with the phenomenal aspects of remembering—to be seen as relevant or even comprehensible in the behaviourist and information-processing eras. Bartlett's notion of memory images most obviously bears evidence of his original interest in introspectionist psychology (see Zangwill, 1972b) and his continuing conviction that introspective observations should not be ignored (Bartlett, 1936; see also Brewer, 1986; Larsen, 1998). The notion of attitude is also concerned with conscious experience. Image and attitude may in fact be seen as descendants of the two opposing sides in the introspectionist debate early in this century between the Leipzig school and the

Würzburg school on the content and function of consciousness (Boring, 1950), as we discuss later.

We shall have occasion to comment only briefly on Bartlett's view of images and its relation to work on mental imagery since the rise of cognitive psychology. The main aim of the chapter is to examine if there might be insights in Bartlett's memory theory that have been overlooked by failing to consider seriously his concept of attitude. We shall distinguish a purposive and a cognitive side of attitude, corresponding to the Würzburg notions of 'determining tendency' and 'imageless thought', respectively. The cognitive side has some affinity with the notion of 'propositional attitude' introduced by Russell (1921) and it points to questions of personal perspective and self-relevance in autobiographical memories. We illustrate the usefulness of this interpretation of attitude by an empirical study of how people organise their memories.

IMAGES: THE LEIPZIG HERITAGE

Bartlett's (1932) summary section of the chapter 'A theory of remembering' opens by asserting in one sentence that the process of remembering involves schema, details and attitude:

> Remembering is not the re-excitation of innumerable fixed, lifeless and fragmentary traces. It is an imaginative reconstruction, or construction, built out of the relation of our attitude towards a whole active mass of organised past reactions and experience [i.e. a schema], and to a little outstanding detail which commonly appears in image or in language form.
>
> (Bartlett, 1932, p. 213)

If only the schema were taken into account, Bartlett's theory of memory would be purely reconstructive: New information is organised by an existing schema, which is itself modified to some extent by the new information; at recall, the individual infers from the modified schema what information in the past is likely to have resulted in the present state of that schema. This reconstructive view is undoubtedly the core of Bartlett's theory of how the process of remembering proceeds. As he intended, the theory represents a fundamental break with the notion of mechanical reproduction of associated traces that was the rock bottom of all classical memory theory.

The pure reconstructive theory is a common interpretation of Bartlett's position and has been developed further by theorists such as Neisser (1976, 1984). However, we do not find the interpretation entirely adequate. Schematic reconstruction was Bartlett's first principle, not his full theory—not even his 'official theory' as Brewer and Nakamura (1984) put it. The previous extract succinctly expresses a theory that holds recall to depend on both schemata and specific episodic material, that is, what Brewer and Nakamura called a *partially reconstructive view*.

Bartlett clearly recognised that a pure schema theory was incomplete since it did not account for recall of non-schematic information, and it did not allow for reconstructions that were specific to one particular remote incident in the history of the schema (1932, p. 208). In discussing the experiments, he noted that it was common for some outstanding or striking details to dominate in perception and to come to mind again early in the process of remembering, usually in the form of mental images but occasionally as isolated words or phrases (e.g. the strange names Egulac and Kalama in 'The War of the Ghosts'). The return of such details 'certainly looks very much like the direct re-excitation of certain traces', Bartlett admitted (p. 209). He went on to argue, however, that the details are not mechanically impressed, stored and re-excited but rather selected, organised and recovered by virtue of the relatively permanent interests of the individual. Consequently, 'The traces that our evidence allows us to speak of are interest-determined, interest-carried traces. They live with our interests and with them they change' (p. 212). Still, Bartlett concluded this summary section by saying that though the image and word traces may change, 'without them no genuine long-distance remembering would be possible' (p. 214).

In other words, remembering relies on schemata but also on specific traces, and the latter are usually represented by images. This is not a minor point in the theory. Bartlett devoted the entire succeeding chapter to a more detailed discussion of 'Images and their Functions', seeing images in general as 'a device for picking bits out of schemes' (1932, p. 219). Images thus allowed the generic schemata to be individualised and provided the outstanding details around which the reconstructive process would build recall of a particular incident. Furthermore, he assumed that, initially, schemata were rigidly ordered in chronological sequence but that images allowed the individual to overcome the force of this order and 'turn round upon its own schemata' (p. 208), for instance, by jumping at will to particular points in time. The *schema + image* theory is evidently a partial reconstructive theory, and it is equivalent to later, more detailed, proposals of this type, such as the *script pointer + tag* theory of Graesser (1981).

By using the notion of images to perform the job of memory traces, Bartlett retained a concept central to Wundt's Leipzig school of introspection, or 'descriptive psychology'. The Leipzig view—based on British Empiricist philosophy—was that the contents of consciousness were either sensations (*Empfindungen* or *Wahrnehmungen*) arising from sense impressions or images (*Vorstellungen*) derived from sensations; memories had to consist of memory images. Bartlett wanted to take account of the phenomenal experience reported by his subjects, in explicit opposition to the doctrine of the blooming school of behaviourism. However, he went well beyond pure description of introspective content by attempting to specify a functional role for mental images; he wanted to 'give to consciousness a definite function other than the mere fact of being aware' (1932, p. 214), that is, to avoid epiphenomenalism (cf. Larsen, 1998). In contrast to the plentiful later work on mental imagery in cognitive psychology (e.g. Kosslyn,

Pinker, Smith & Shwartz, 1979), Bartlett confronted the issue of function—what images are good for—however preliminary the ideas of 'picking bits out of schemes' and 'turning round upon one's schemata' might be.

ATTITUDES: THE WÜRZBURG HERITAGE

Unlike later memory theories, Bartlett ascribed great importance to one more concept, attitude, as our first quotation indicated. Just before introducing the schema concept in the beginning of that chapter, he even made the sweeping statement that:

> very probably the outstanding characteristics of remembering all follow from a *change of attitude* towards those masses of organised past experiences and reactions [i.e. schemata] which function in all high-level mental processes.
>
> (Bartlett, 1932, pp. 197–198, our italics)

What was the motivation for introducing this additional concept, one for which later theorists have seen no need? One motive might be to furnish the *schema + image* theory with a device for selecting the outstanding details that are represented in images. As pointed out earlier, Bartlett assumed that the perceptual processes performed such selection according to the individual's 'interests and ideals', which he conceived to be represented as configurations of schemata. However, this selection is mechanical, based on the congruence or incongruence of new material with the particular schema. We shall argue that the attitude concept aimed at something different, namely, the purposive and intentional aspects of remembering.

Bartlett on attitude

Bartlett summarised his experiments on perceiving and describing—in more current terms, *encoding*—of simple drawings and ink-blots by saying that the subject first tries to form a 'general impression of the whole':

> Ask the observer to characterise this general impression psychologically, and the word that is always cropping up is 'attitude'. I have shown how this 'attitude' factor came into nearly every series of experiments that was carried out. The construction that is effected is the sort of construction that would justify the observer's 'attitude'.
>
> (Bartlett, 1932, p. 206)

Here, attitude is apparently a kind of Gestalt formation, an abstract level of grasping the material, in a story maybe the gist or the genre (cf. Spiro, 1980). When summarising his observations of the course of *recall*, Bartlett also put the attitude at the very beginning of the process:

when a subject is being asked to remember, very often the first thing that emerges is something of the nature of attitude. The recall is then a construction, made largely on the basis of this attitude, and its general effect is that of a justification of the attitude.

(Bartlett, 1932, p. 207)

Thus, the attitude not only initiates remembering, it is also seen as determining the goal of and guiding the reconstructive process that ensues. Whereas this functional importance of the attitude for both encoding and recall is asserted with great confidence, its *phenomenology* is described somewhat confusingly:

Attitude names a complex psychological state or process which is hard to describe in more elementary psychological terms. It is, however, as I have often indicated, very largely a matter of feeling, or affect. We say that it is characterised by doubt, hesitation, surprise, astonishment, confidence, dislike, repulsion and so on.

(Bartlett, 1932, pp. 206–207)

These examples seem to concern mostly the subject's evaluation of his recall performance, but also his personal reactions to the materials, such as the ghost story. Further examples in Bartlett's next paragraph rather seem to characterise the material itself, although in personal terms: Subjects in the perception experiments 'felt the material presented to be *regular*, or *exciting*, or *familiar*' and in the memory experiments 'the stories or other material were first characterised as "*exciting*", "*adventurous*", "*like what I read when I was a boy*"' (1932, p. 207, our italics).

What is the basis of attitudes? On p. 21, attitude is classed with temperament as one factor that influences perceiving and remembering, and on p. 307 'attitudes, orientation, appetitive and instinctive tendencies and interests' are all classed as 'persistent reaction tendencies' that organise psychological material. However, on p. 193, it is said that attitudes may also be created by objective stimulus conditions and experimental instructions. In still another vein, Bartlett suggested that attitudes emerge from one's schemata when consciousness is directed at them (p. 208).

This by no means exhausts the different ways Bartlett talked about attitudes. Let us pause before the reader is exhausted and ask what made Bartlett put together under the one term attitude such diverse things as doubt and confidence, feelings of familiarity and excitement, perceptions of regularity or adventurousness in a story, and its similarity to particular other stories? And what made him state that all this is 'largely a matter of feeling or affect'?

The Leipzig–Würzburg debate

Zangwill (1972b) traced the use of the term attitude to the concept *Einstellung* of the German psychologist Betz (1910) whose work Bartlett discussed in his Fellowship dissertation (1916c).[1] Betz was affiliated with the Würzburg introspectionist school that emphasised the *intentional* character of consciousness, in contrast to the emphasis on the *content* of consciousness in the Leipzig school. With the notion of attitude, it thus seems that Bartlett wanted to preserve and develop insights of the Würzburgers which he deemed important. As we will explain, Zangwill's statement that *Einstellung* 'broadly signifies mental posture or set' (1972b, p. 126) only captures part of Bartlett's idea.

When Bartlett in 1913 began the work that culminated in *Remembering* (1932), the fierce debate between the Leipzig school and the Würzburg school was coming to an end—although not to a clear conclusion (see Boring, 1950, and Rapaport, 1941/1971, for details). Rather, both groups were being overtaken by the development of Gestalt psychology and behaviourism. Bartlett was thoroughly acquainted with the Leipzig–Würzburg feud from his seniors at Cambridge, Myers and Ward, who seem to have adopted opposing sides in the battle (see Boring, 1950).

Attitude was at the centre of the debate, along with a number of related concepts, such as mental set, mental orientation and mental posture, determining tendency and task orientation. These concepts were used with varying definitions, however, and there was considerable uncertainty about the translation of terms between English and German. To keep in mind today the breadth of meaning of these concepts, it is important to realise that the current use of attitude as a narrowly social-psychological concept was not yet established (Rokeach, 1968). A closer examination of the issues discussed around the turn of the century in psychology—and in parts of philosophy—may help to dissect the meaning Bartlett intended.

On the surface, the Leipzig–Würzburg debate was about the contents of consciousness, specifically whether, as the Würzburgers claimed, there existed in consciousness *imageless thoughts* and *determining tendencies* in addition to sensations and images. At a deeper level, the issue was nothing less than the nature of mental life and its relation to material reality. On the one hand, Humean empiricist theories, such as those of Wundt and Ebbinghaus, saw mental life as essentially passive, its content reflecting sense impressions and associations determined by contiguity or similarity. On the other hand, Kantian rationalist theories ascribed an active role to the mind. In particular, the philosopher Brentano found the essence of mind in *mental acts* that are intentional, that is, directed at and referring to, physical phenomena, not to some purely mental content. As Boring (1950, p. 360) put it, 'When one sees a color, the color itself is not mental. It is the seeing, the act, that is mental.'

Modern philosophy of mind and cognitive psychology have embraced Brentano's notion of intentionality as meaning mental representation. However, contemporary psychology seized on intentionality as meaning purposiveness. For a short time in the 1870s, Brentano was a professor at Würzburg. Among his students were not only the phenomenological philosopher Husserl, but also several psychologists whose influence came to fruition at Würzburg just after the turn of the century, directed by Külpe. These psychologists accepted introspection, but they assumed consciousness to be motivated and governed by goals and purposes, just like external acts.

A famous demonstration of the power of such purposes over mechanical association strength was given by Ach and Watt in 1904 (Boring, 1950, pp. 403–405). Ach and Watt showed that people, when instructed to do so, could readily give synonyms or superordinates in response to words instead of 'strongly associated' words. Moreover, in the introspection of the subjects, the operations they had presumably applied to the task materials, such as rules of semantics or logic, were almost never reported; the operations of thought did not seem conscious at all. Instead, subjects described aspects of the task (*Aufgabe*) they were told to perform, the goal to be achieved, and the response to be given. These thoughts of the task did not appear to consciousness as images, and they appeared prior to the task materials, as if to prepare for the task performance, similar to Bartlett's description of the appearance of the attitude. During performance, subjects also reported no images but rather experiences of doubt and hesitation, belief and confidence, effort and boredom, in short, reactions to the progress of the task. Some of Bartlett's examples of attitudes in the previous section are strikingly similar.

This conscious but imageless task orientation, or preparedness, and response monitoring was initially called *Bewusstseinslage*, which Boring (1950) translates as 'conscious attitude'. Under *Bewusstseinslage* were included a number of other contents of consciousness that seemed to escape Wundt's rigid dichotomy of sensations and images: inner feelings and affects, James's (1890) fringe of consciousness and Høffding's (1885/1891) quality of familiarity—in Boring's words (1950, p. 403), 'obscure, intangible, unanalyzable, indescribable contents'. This phrase echoes Bartlett's general description of attitude, as well as his examples of how subjects 'felt'. Notice also that the Würzburg notion was intended as a supplement to Wundt's images, not as a replacement, just as Bartlett employed images as well as attitudes in his memory theory.

In subsequent work of the Würzburg school, somewhat more specific terms were introduced. To denote the purposive or motivational aspect of thinking in the Ach–Watt experiments, the term *determining tendency* was coined. On the other hand, the various imageless experiential qualities, cognitive as well as affective, that subjects reported to accompany thinking—Boring's 'indescribable contents'—were subsumed under the term *Einstellung* by Betz (1910). Later researchers have emphasised identification of the purposive aspects of thinking as the major contribution of the Würzburgers. Interpretations of Bartlett's attitude notion have had a similar emphasis on the purposive side, conceiving attitude either as emotional factors (Rapaport, 1941/1971) or as mental set (Zangwill, 1972b). However, Bartlett (1932) apparently had both aspects in mind, that is, he conceived of attitude as close to the vague and ambiguous concept *Bewusstseinslage*. We discuss the purposive and the cognitive interpretations of attitude in turn.

The purposive side of attitudes

Bartlett's phrase that an attitude 'is very largely a matter of feeling, or affect' has suggested to many readers an interpretation in terms of emotions. However, this is only partly justified. It is clear from Bartlett's examples that 'feeling or affect' are not limited to basic emotions in the modern sense, such as the anger caused by being slighted or the sorrow caused by unexpected loss. Rather, feelings denoted all conscious sensations assumed to arise from inside the organism; they could have qualities as pleasant/unpleasant and excited/bored and they could be associated with external sensations (cf. Rapaport's, 1941/1971 survey of early theories of emotion and memory). Emotions further required that overt bodily reactions occurred, such as trembling or blushing. Attitudes were felt, that is, conscious phenomena, but they did not need to be emotional. This may be the reason that the attitude concept does not show up in current research on the effect of emotions on memory which is primarily concerned with states involving autonomic arousal (see Christianson, 1992).

A basic problem in memory theory according to anti-associationists, such as the Würzburgers and Bartlett, was that the emergence of particular ideas in consciousness—for instance, particular memories—could not be explained solely by associations derived from contiguity or similarity. To complement the passive, mechanical operation of associations, other, more active and dynamic, 'selective forces' were needed, in Rapaport's (1941/1971) words. The notion of determining tendency was concerned with the selective effects of accepting a particular task: purposiveness, goal-directedness. It was assumed to be a temporary and specific readiness, confined to the stimuli and reactions required by the task. In this sense, determining tendency was soon replaced by the term *mental set*. Mental set became an important topic in pre-World War II research on perception and problem solving, in particular in Gestalt psychology (see Woodworth & Schlosberg, 1954). Some studies were concerned with the preservation of mental set across several tasks, for instance, Rubin's (1921) study of the transfer from presentation to recognition of a set towards seeing a reversible drawing in a particular way (cited by Bartlett, 1932, p. 192). The perseverance of unfinished tasks (the Zeigarnik effect) and undue adherence to old methods in problem solving (functional fixation) could also be seen as caused by the stability of sets across time. Such examples seem to be part of what provided Bartlett with the idea of applying the notion of set—or attitude—to the explanation of memory.

Still, mental sets seemed relatively short-lived and context-dependent; to use them for explaining memory begged the question of how they were preserved. However, some theorists assumed that associationist principles were subordinate to enduring 'reaction tendencies' deriving from individual differences in *temperament and character* (e.g. a habitual 'feeling-tone', called attitude by Müller-Freienfels, cf. Rapaport, 1941/1971). In Bartlett's (1936) autobiographical account published shortly after *Remembering* (1932), he actually seems to endorse this quasi-biological view entirely. There, he talks of attitudes only in terms of enduring, 'extremely persistent . . . determined tendencies' (p. 44) linked to personality differences, although modified by individual and social learning.[2]

Whether attitudes are interpreted as persistent sets or as enduring individual reaction tendencies, we think that this considerably detracts from the interest of Bartlett's (1932) memory theory. The similarity of experience at encoding and recall that a memory theory must explain is the similarity specific to the experienced situation, not the similarity contributed by properties of the person or the organism. Memory accuracy cannot be explained by individual 'reaction tendencies'. However, consistent inaccuracies may. Bartlett (1936) was undoubtedly eager to address the problem of individual differences in memory. It is worth keeping in mind that this may have been part of his motivation for using the attitude concept in *Remembering*.

The cognitive side of attitudes

Betz (1910) proposed the concept *Einstellung* as a complement to Wundt's *Vorstellung* (image, i.e. memory image). He was speculating about recognition, in particular the curiously modern problem of how confidence in recognising certain items could arise, for instance, a smell or a face. Høffding (1889) had argued that previous encounters with an item establish a trace that facilitates present perception of the item, and that this results in an immediate and confident feeling of familiarity (cf. Jacoby's, 1988 perceptual fluency explanation of the feeling of familiarity). Betz considered cases where recognition was difficult and uncertain, in which it was assumed that the present percept was mentally compared to a memory image of a particular previous encounter. He noted that smells could hardly be recognised by comparison to an image because they are almost impossible to imagine, and so are familiar faces to many people. More generally, Betz claimed, particular images only arise *after* recognition has taken place. On the basis of introspection, he proposed that the first thing to occur was a reproduction of the internally felt effects that an earlier encounter of the same or a similar percept had exerted on the person. This largely unconscious *internal setting*, as we might say, he named *Einstellung*. Recognition, he suggested, then follows to the extent that the present percept fits into the context of the reproduced *Einstellung*. Since the *Einstellung* itself is mostly unconscious, it is difficult to pin down by the person unless it subsequently elicits a conscious memory image that 'delivers the key' to and explains the state of the *Einstellung*. This is obviously very similar to Bartlett's idea that explicit remembering serves to justify the prior attitude.

Betz's (1910) theory might appear pretty esoteric, in particular because he tried to describe *Einstellung* in terms of somatic reactions, such as changes in respiration, posture, eye muscles, affective reactions and other 'minimal bodily changes . . . to which the James–Lange theory and most recently Herrn von Osten's horse have drawn attention' (p. 270, our translation). However, if the then customary focus on peripheral sources of sensation is disregarded, the theory is not far from current explanations of the 'recollective experience' that sometimes accompany recognition in terms of memory of the external and internal context of the item (cf. Gardiner & Java, 1993; Johnson, 1988; Tulving, 1985).

Apart from the peripheralist bias, this description of *Einstellung* is also close to Bartlett's (1932) account of attitude and makes it understandable why he frequently referred to affective components of attitudes. Affect was not conceived as a special system of somatic reactions but only as sensations with an internal origin, along with 'cognitive feelings' of familiarity, confidence or well-formedness of a story. Personal evaluation might be a better term than affect. Betz (1910) already underlined that the impression made by a present situation is *eine gefühlsbetonte Einstellung*, that is, a state of the person that includes a feeling tone but is much more than a feeling (*Gefühl*). On the other hand, he specifically excluded the intentional character inherent in concepts such as determining tendency and mental set; his view was clearly cognitive rather than conative.

The most radical claim made by Betz (1910) was that *Einstellungen* 'can be reproduced with great exactness. It may even be assumed that this exactness of reproduction is greater than for images (*Vorstellungen*)' (p. 278, our translation). Bartlett (1932) did not explicitly make similar claims. But he noted that an attitude often persists and that in remembering it is the same at both encoding and recall, which suggests that he entertained an analogous idea of attitudes as easily and accurately reinstated. This is also suggested by his later (Bartlett, 1936) anchoring of attitude to enduring personality characteristics.[3] Furthermore, he never explored the consequences of seeing attitudes as temporary, for instance, determined by the circumstances at any given time (i.e. a retrieval context theory). We therefore consider it likely that Bartlett agreed with Betz on the notion that attitudes serve to enhance the accuracy of remembering: They put top-down constraints on the process of schematic reconstruction, so to speak, at the same time as images provide bottom-up constraints. This view also conferred a definite function on the vague experiences and 'feelings' reported by his subjects. However, Bartlett could not admit to the trace-like theory of the reproduction of attitudes espoused by Betz, which may have induced him to think in terms of temperament and personality as the causes of attitudes.

Among later theorists, Spiro (1980) is to our knowledge the only one who has interpreted attitude in a manner reminiscent of Betz (1910). Spiro proposed that attitude as used by Bartlett denotes the 'summary feeling' of what it is like to hold a particular schema in mind—'the quality of the experience's existential feel . . . textural, Gestalt-like properties that can only be felt' (1980, p. 272), in analogy with what it feels like to hold a ball in the hand. The assumption is that schemata and other complex knowledge structures have holistic, experiential aspects that cannot be analytically examined or verbally described. Spiro's examples of the phenomenology and function of attitudes echo Bartlett's, but it is hard to see the benefit of introducing another vague metaphor where clarification is needed.

PROPOSITIONAL ATTITUDES AND REMEMBERING

Russell on propositional attitude

Whereas Bartlett's use of the term attitude in psychology became almost extinct, a not too different use of the term was introduced in philosophy at about the same time and has flourished ever since. Furthermore, this use of attitude grew out of the same scientific soil in Cambridge and was presented by Bertrand Russell (1921) in the book *The Analysis of Mind*. Russell here advanced the concept of *propositional attitude*. The paradigm propositional attitude is the mental state of 'belief'. Beliefs can be represented in language (or other symbols) by expressions of the form 'Person believes that Proposition', where the proposition refers to a possible state of affairs in the world. The proposition is now usually called the content of the belief (see Crane, 1995). For example, if I believe that there is wine in the cupboard, the content of this belief is that 'there is wine in the cupboard'. I may also hope, or expect, or wish, or fear, or see, or remember that there is wine in the cupboard. These mental verbs express different attitudes to one and the same proposition, or content, that refers to a state of the world.

Russell's (1921) interest was mainly in the logical status of these mental terms and their implications for a theory of knowledge. Propositional attitudes posed a problem for the correspondence view of truth and knowledge that he had been developing for more than a decade. The truth value of a content proposition can be decided by its correspondence to the observable world; the truth or falsehood of the proposition 'there is wine in the cupboard' is easily checked. But the attitude taken to the content escapes this criterion. A belief may be shown to be false, an expectation may turn out to be in vain, a memory may be found to be in error, depending on the correspondence of their content to the world; but the phenomenological fact that it is believed, is expected, or is remembered may still be true and is thus logically independent of the truth value of the content. Propositional attitudes can therefore be sharply divided into a part that belongs to logic and the theory of knowledge and a part that belongs to psychology. In this way, the analysis supported the general enterprise of Russell (and his colleagues G.E. Moore, Whitehead and Wittgenstein) against 'psychologism' in logic and philosophy.

For our present purpose, the interesting thing to notice is that Russell offers a very precise, bare-bones conception of attitude: It is *a psychological relation of a person to some content*, and the veracity of this content is immaterial. The attitude is experienced as a 'feeling', a term that Russell uses in a purely cognitive sense—such as a feeling of belief, a feeling of familiarity, a feeling of remembering, all of which can be held with different degrees of certainty: confidence, hesitation, doubt and so forth. In the chapter he devoted to memory, Russell (1921, p. 186) concluded that the psychological essence of 'remembering in its pure form' resides in a particular attitude to the content, namely, a belief that 'I have experienced this in the past'. It is this 'element of belief that is the distinctive thing in memory' (p. 176) as opposed to pure imagination.

Relations between Russell and Bartlett

Bartlett's treatment of memory and attitude is cognate to Russell's in several respects: The emphasis on the attitude as central to remembering, the view of attitude as a feeling that refers to the remembered content, even the view that memory accuracy is irrelevant to the psychological analysis. In other respects, their views are clearly opposed. Russell's (1921) psychology, as distinct from his theory of knowledge, was largely a Wundtian associationism. He followed Wundt in claiming that only sensations and images furnish the materials of the mind. He agreed with the behaviourists that consciousness was functionally unimportant. And the main object of his epistemological criticism was Brentano, whose position:

> is one I shall be concerned to combat. Like Brentano, I am interested in psychology, not so much for its own sake, as for the light that it may throw on the problem of knowledge. Until very lately I believed, as he did, that mental phenomena have essential reference to objects . . . Now I no longer believe this, even in the case of knowledge.
>
> (Russell, 1921, p. 15)[4]

Despite the differences, it is puzzling that Bartlett never seems to have made reference to Russell's work; the lack of references on Russell's side is less surprising, perhaps, since Bartlett was 14 years his junior and did not publish on psychology until 1916, the year Russell lost his fellowship at Cambridge. Also, no correspondence between the two men is known (Hugh Bartlett, personal communication, May 1998).

Nevertheless, it is reasonable to assume that Bartlett was well acquainted with Russell's ideas. Bartlett's first publications were a textbook and a book of exercises on logic in 1913–14 (see Harris & Zangwill, 1973), a topic on which Russell was an undisputed authority. Furthermore, Bartlett's very first publication in psychology was a discussion paper for a symposium in the Aristotelian Society (Bartlett, 1916b), where Russell was a vice-president—and Wundt was among the seven foreign members. In that symposium, the target paper was a philosophical critique of Russell's account of recognition. Bartlett advanced some psychological arguments favourable to Russell (who was not present).[5] The entire proceedings suggest an atmosphere of hostile polemics quite different from Bartlett's style of thinking.[6] Over the next two years he presented a couple more papers to the society, but then he seems to have stopped affiliating with the philosophers. Still, we consider it likely that he read Russell's *The Analysis of Mind* (1921), which attracted great attention and was reprinted twice in three years.

By these remarks we do not want to imply that Bartlett's use of the term attitude was directly influenced by Russell. First, the term attitude had been common currency for a long time and both men knew the tradition well. Russell cited Wundt, Brentano and particularly James, as well as the most prominent critic of the tradition, Watson (who was even acknowledged for reading a draft of *The Analysis of Mind*). Second, we suspect that Russell's stripped-down version of traditional psychology provided Bartlett with a clear example of what he did *not* consider a satisfactory psychological theory. Russell's work may have convinced Bartlett that a concept of attitude simplified to its logical marrow would not do. At any rate, as he expressed several times in *Remembering* (1932), Bartlett had reached an opinion that dove-tailed with Russell's anti-psychologism, namely, that psychology should avoid getting entangled in philosophical disputes.

Whichever is the true story concerning Bartlett and Russell, we believe that Russell's use of attitude as 'a psychological relation of a person to some content' comes close to being the common denominator of the variety of meanings Bartlett intended by the term. Russell's notion of attitude is conceptually simple and general, to a large extent because it ignores the intricacies of separating cognitive, conative and emotional aspects, temporary and enduring attitudes, and so forth. Is it also operational? In the case of story memory, it should be relatively easy to distinguish the subject's personal evaluations and reactions, that is, attitudinal material, from the story content recalled. Most of Bartlett's examples fit this sense of attitude, for instance, seeing a story as familiar, as exciting, as surprising, like what I read as a boy. Some of his other examples clearly denote the certainty with which an attitude is held (doubt, hesitation, confidence). Only a few of the examples given by Bartlett do not fit Russell's criterion for an attitude, but they serve to illustrate the stringency of that criterion. Thus, calling a story 'regular' or 'adventurous' does not characterise the person's attitude but rather the structure and genre of the story itself. The same would hold for Gestalt-like summaries or abstractions of the story.

In the remainder of the present chapter, we will attempt to apply this basic meaning of attitude to autobiographical memory research.

ATTITUDES IN AUTOBIOGRAPHICAL MEMORY

Autobiographical reference as an attitude

In the final chapter of *Remembering*, Bartlett (1932, p. 308) briefly discusses the fact that 'Most psychologists who have written about recall have pointed out that memory, in its full sense, always contains a peculiarly personal reference.' For instance, James stated that memories are experienced as belonging to '*my* past' and have the quality of 'warmth and intimacy' that characterises everything 'owned' by the self (James, 1890, p. 650). Claparède (1911/1951) talked of the feeling of 'me-ness' that distinguishes real memories from habitual associations. More recently, in Tulving's (1972) distinction between episodic and semantic memory, one of the defining features of episodic memory is 'autobiographical reference'. Though he cited James, Tulving was not concerned with experiential qualities or relations to the self, only with spatio-temporal specificity. His notion of autobiographical reference is therefore even weaker than Russell's minimal definition of the attitude of memory-belief.

Both Brewer (1986) and Nelson (1993a) attempt to define autobiographical memory, as distinct from plain episodic memory, in terms of self-relevance of the memory content. Brewer simply stated that autobiographical memory concerns 'information related to the self' (Brewer, 1986, p. 26); Nelson proposed the stronger criterion that the content should be of significance to the person's life-story. However, self-relevance is not a property of the memory content, it is a relation between self and content. This relation could properly be called autobiographical reference. According to the present terminology, the relation of autobiographical reference will phenomenologically appear to the person as a particular attitude towards the memory content, an attitude richer than the plain 'I remember X'. The point is not that autobiographical reference causally generates attitudes, or vice versa. Autobiographical reference simply presents itself to the rememberer as an attitude towards the remembered material, on top of just believing that one remembers it. Even the memory of reading a folk story or a novel might acquire autobiographical reference and be remembered with 'me-ness, warmth and intimacy', depending upon how the person relates to the story (Berntsen & Larsen, 1996; Larsen, 1996).

Earlier, Berntsen and Kennedy (1994, p. 206) suggested that attitude be defined as 'the meaning ascribed to an event by an individual's present understanding of his or her self', that is, an interpretation of the event from the particular perspective of the individual. In a very similar vein, Robinson (1996) argued that the individual's perspective is centrally important to autobiographical memory, indeed noting Bartlett's concept of attitude as a precursor of this view. Robinson saw perspective as 'the integrated operation of both stable and transient factors that shape a person's state of mind moment by moment' (1996, p. 199). Although we prefer to use attitude in a more restricted, and perhaps old-fashioned, phenomenological sense, we agree with Robinson (1996) that attitude and perspective are closely related: An attitude presupposes the perspective of a particular individual.

Viewed in this manner, the attitude of autobiographical reference should come in many forms, depending on exactly which kind of relation the person perceives between the self and the remembered event. An important type of autobiographical attitude is often called theme or life theme in everyday speech (cf. Conway, 1996). This alludes to long-standing interests or concerns reflecting one's personal perspective on life, or a period of life—at times even conflicting perspectives, such as 'overcoming being ashamed of myself' or 'being street-smart' (Bruner, 1990). In our usage, personal themes always contain a component of evaluation, or appraisal, to borrow a term from Lazarus (1991). Personal themes are concerned with personal well-being and ideals, not just with facts about events or periods in one's life. 'Going to school' would not be considered a personal theme, whereas 'striving to learn my profession' would. The evaluative component renders the theme attitudinal. Obviously, different participants will usually relate quite differently to a shared event since the attitude emerges from the perspective of the particular person. However, in cases where people realise that they share not only an experience but also the attitude towards the experience, there is typically a feeling of relatedness deeper than the coincidence of joint presence.

A consideration of such autobiographical attitudes should thus be useful or even indispensable for understanding the way people think about and organise their memories. An emphasis on attitudes differs from extant theories of autobiographical memory, which focus heavily on memory content to account for the organisation of memories. Consider a few examples. Some theories stress the importance of event order or *temporal* structures, such as lifetime periods (e.g. Anderson & Conway, 1993; Barsalou, 1988; Conway & Rubin, 1993). Time is clearly independent of the subject's personal perspective, and lifetime periods are similarly conceived in factual terms, for instance, defined by 'Working at X' or 'Married to Y' (Conway, 1996). Instead of time, Neisser (1988) suggested that the *place* of events might be the basic dimension for memory organisation. The content feature of *action* is assumed to be crucial for memory organisation in Schank and Abelson's (1977) theory of scripts as well as in Schank's (1982) elaboration of it. And, finally, some clinical theories take *participant* to be a critical category in autobiographical memory because good relationships with significant others are assumed to be crucial for the healthy development of individuals (e.g. Horowitz, 1988).

Theories that view *emotions* or emotional colouring as the basis for memory organisation do go beyond the factual content of memories. For instance, Tomkins (1979) assumed that intense emotional scenes—so-called nuclear scenes—constitute powerful reference points for the organisation of other personal experiences. Here, however, it is important to keep in mind that attitude is a broader conception than emotion. Since attitude is concerned with an individual's personal perspective on the content of a memory, it may of course sometimes be emotional. It often *is* affective—as Bartlett stated—but it need not be. Clearly, an emotion (such as anger) implies an attitude (usually a thwarting of one's goals or ideals), but with the same perceived relation, one's reaction might be entirely cool.

A study of the organisation of autobiographical memories

We explored the occurrence of attitudes in autobiographical remembering by conducting a study of how people subjectively organise their memories. A corpus of each subject's specific memories was used to probe their conceptual organisation of memories. This is in a sense the reverse of the common strategy of using generic questions or prompt words to trigger specific memories (such as 'tell me about events you were involved with this past summer', Barsalou, 1988, p. 199). Subjects' task was first to categorise a set of personal recollections. This was followed by an interview inquiring about membership criteria for the categories they had formed. For each memory category, it was examined whether the critical attribute for category membership was a feature of the content of the memories—such as participant, activity, place or time—or whether the critical feature was to be found in the perspective that the subject applied to the memory content (e.g. 'these are the boring parts of my life'). More specifically, organisation via attitudes would be displayed if: (1) the subject explicitly referred to an attitude towards the remembered events when accounting for the category during the interview *and* (2) category membership could not, by independent judges, be accounted for via the propositional content of the memories, that is, by features denoted by the subject's memory description.

Method

Seven males and seven females (average age 23 years) were asked to categorise 50 of their own personal recollections according to whatever principles they preferred. The memories were recorded during a previous diary study (Berntsen, 1996, 1998) of involuntary memories, that is, memories emerging spontaneously in the person's everyday activities. In that study, subjects were instructed to record 50 involuntary autobiographical memories during an open-ended time period. They were to record no more than the first two involuntary memories that occurred each day. An involuntary memory was defined as a memory of a past situation that comes to mind without preceding attempts at retrieving this memory. This definition did not exclude that, retrospectively, the memory might appear as having been cued by the present surroundings or by current thoughts. The subject made a preliminary record of the involuntary memory and the current context promptly when an involuntary memory had occurred. Later the same day, he or she answered a more extensive questionnaire about each memory, assisted by the preliminary record. As it turned out, the memories were spread throughout the life-span of each individual though events from recent years dominated. Memories were more often emotionally positive than negative, and fairly unusual experiences were common. Before the present categorisation task, the subject's description of each memory was printed separately on index cards.

Instructions for the categorisation task were framed in everyday terms: 'Your task is to arrange these memories according to the way you think they fit together'. It was stressed that: (1) the subject could use any principle he or she found relevant; (2) the same principle did not have to be used for every category; (3) not all of the 50 memories had to be organised, only as many as possible. Adhesive labels were provided to write short titles for the memory categories if that was considered helpful. The requirement to explain the categories afterwards was not mentioned. The task was self-paced with an average duration around 30 minutes.

When the categorisation task was finished, an interview was conducted to detect the membership criteria for each memory category. The subject could decide the order in which categories were considered. For each category, the interviewer asked why the memories were grouped. When the subject suggested a defining attribute (e.g. 'Because they all deal with my time in Greenland'), the interviewer asked whether every memory in the group shared the attribute and whether these were the only memories in the sample possessing that attribute. If not, possible reasons for the exceptions were discussed. To further clarify and challenge the subject's account, the interviewer routinely suggested alternative interpretations to each category (e.g. 'Could it also be the same life period?' 'Do the memories deal with the same participants?'). When a membership criterion was established, it was classified as dealing with any one or a combination of the following: Place; Activity; Lifetime Period; Participants; Sensory Experience; Other Content; a common Personal Theme or a common Feeling (i.e. Attitude). The interviewer made sure that the subject fully agreed with the final classification. The proceedings were tape recorded.

However, this subjective assessment might be misleading since categorisation could be governed by content criteria to an extent which subjects did not fully acknowledge. Therefore, the second author and an independent judge examined, for each memory category, whether a criterion for membership could be adequately defined in terms of content features of the memories (i.e. Participant, Place, Activity, Extended Event,[7] or Lifetime Period[8]). To accept such an explanation for a category, the two judges were required to make sure that the critical attribute (such as a specific kind of Activity) was present in every memory in the category and that no memories with that attribute were found in any other of the subject's categories. Thus, if the critical attribute was the game of football, all memories in the category should be concerned with football and no football memories should be present in other categories. The two judges agreed in 86% of the cases; disagreements were decided by discussion.

Results

The average number of categories formed by each subject was 12 (disregarding a few superordinate categories), and the average number of memories in each category was 4. Most of the subjects had a few memories that could not be categorised (the average number of such leftovers was three). Eleven of the fourteen subjects wrote brief titles for some or all of their categories.

According to some theories of autobiographical memory we should expect a hierarchical or narrative organisation to dominate. For example, Conway (1996) argues that information about specific episodes is nested in a hierarchical structure with concrete details at the bottom of the hierarchy and lifetime periods at the top (for a similar view, see Barsalou, 1988; Conway & Rubin, 1993). However, only one of the subjects in the present study employed a consistent division between superordinate and subordinate categories. According to another popular view, personal experiences are organised narratively (Barclay, 1996; Bruner, 1990). Again, only one of the subjects wanted to account for her categories in a specific narrative ('life-story') order, beginning with her childhood and ending with her present life situation. Thus, the organisation was generally found to be low in structure—that is, each group of memories was typically treated in isolation.

A simple count of the subjects' category explanations showed that attitudes were associated with the categorisation of 416 memories, or 64% of the total sample of 655 memories (excluding leftovers). This dominance of attitudinal categories in the subjects' own accounts was substantiated by results from the two independent judges, which showed that only a small minority of 36 out of the 416 memories that subjects claimed to be organised by attitudinal criteria might alternatively be classified by content. Thus, it is apparent that almost two-thirds of the memories in the sample were organised in terms of attitudinal criteria rather than by straightforward features of their content.

Table 7.1 illustrates the two types of criteria by a selection of the titles or labels that subjects attached to the memory groups during the categorisation task. Since the study is exploratory, we have not attempted to establish an exhaustive classification or to assess the rate of occurrence of the various subtypes. Instead, we next present examples more fully to give an impression of the variety of attitudes the subjects cited to justify their memory categories. These examples are organised according to the classification suggested by Bartlett (1932), namely, attitudes based on affect, interests, and ideals and values.

Examples of attitudinal memory organisation

Emotions as criteria

In our study, attitudinal criteria for memory categories were frequently expressed in terms of the emotions associated with events. In this sense, it is understandable that Bartlett's (1932) characterisation of attitude as 'largely a matter of feeling, or affect' is often interpreted as pointing to emotions. As a way of example, one subject (male, 22 years) divided his memories into three superordinate groups according to the valence of his present emotions:

TABLE 7.1
Category labels associated with each of the five content criteria compared with
labels associated with attitudes

Critical attribute	Examples
Participant	'Mum' 'My friendship with John'
Place	'Australia' 'The clinic'
Activity	'To travel and work outside Denmark' 'School and beer'
Lifetime period	'My time in Cambridge' 'When I was very small'
Extended event	'Holiday experiences in Spain' 'To begin a new life—breaking up'
Attitude	'My relation to school—Laziness' 'Bad experiences with my family' 'Light childhood' 'Fun, extremely positive, more recent' 'Others laughing at me—shame' 'Aspects I was satisfied with' 'Nostalgia' 'Vulnerable' 'Social memories' 'Dull work'

These are all happy, exciting and positive ones. They fill me with happiness when I read them, really. I am filled with happiness by going through them again. And that's basically what they mean for me. The next group is an intermediate one, more flat, it does not mean a lot to me. And the third group is more sad, but not insignificant. It's just the most negative ones—for example, the one about my friend's funeral, it's not insignificant, but it's sad—sorrowful, may be a better term.

Likewise, a female subject (aged 23 years) grouped six memories together because they were all associated with negative feelings: 'It's bad feelings. They differ a little but are anyway united by the fact that I haven't felt comfortable about them.' One was about an inflammation of her throat as a child at which occasion she had been forced to drink tea which was 'just the worst thing I have ever tasted or smelled'. Another dealt with a clerk with a 'dreadfully bad breath', and yet another memory was about a frustrating meeting in her tutorial group at the university.

In some cases, more distinct emotions, such as embarrassment or annoyance, were given as the rationale. A subject (male, 26 years) clustered seven of his memories because they all referred to episodes in which somebody had annoyed him: 'They all deal with episodes where I have been together with people that have annoyed me one way or other.' The remembered events spanned 16 years and involved different persons, locations and activities. In one memory, he is in a minibus:

> I was very annoyed by a small talk discussion about which amounts of snow are usual and unusual in Denmark. Apart from being stubborn, the bus driver has a very loathsome voice.

Another memory takes place in the reading room at the university library:

> It's a late afternoon in the reading room. A girl has just entered and taken a seat right behind me. We are the only persons in the room. She is underlining *every single line* in her book, and the noise gets on my nerves.

Ideals and values as criteria

Some memory categories were less explicitly emotional and rather emphasised ideals and values held by the person. For example, a male subject (aged 25) grouped seven memories under the informative heading: 'Challenging experiences in relation to establishing contact with others. Good and bad experiences. Afraid of doing the wrong things. Contact holds its obligations.' The majority of memories dealt with his relations with his girlfriend's friends, two referred to his role as a participant in a therapy group and one was about a meeting with a possible new employer. As another example, a female subject (aged 20) grouped five memories under the heading 'The core family'. These memories dealt with experiences that she had had with her parents and siblings in her childhood, such as seeing her newborn younger brother in the hospital when she was 3 years old, buying smelling salts at a vacation at the sea as a 3-year-old, and eating applecake with cream at age 12. There were several other childhood memories in her sample, but these five were clustered because now (as a young adult) they represented an ideal for her:

> I can see now that many values and norms were established for me at that time in my family. And it means a lot to me now . . . The family is sacred to me. To me it's the goal of life to live the way a small family does.

Finally, a male subject (aged 21) categorised three memories under the title 'Relaxing sport-activities' and explained: 'It's just the fun, not the big competition, but just the pleasure of skiing down the mountain or sliding through the water.' This category was contrasted with another group of memories of sport-events associated with competition.

Interests as criteria

Memory categories could also be united by self-reflection in a rather cold or detached manner, with no apparent emotion involved. Rather, each memory was seen as self-attributive by exemplifying a long-lasting interest. For instance, a 28-year-old male subject clustered six memories because 'they are very representative for some aspects of myself'. The memories dealt with very different situations: exploring the shelves in a second-hand bookstore, going fly-fishing along a small river, skiing in the mountains, playing his guitar, listening to rock music, meeting a good friend. More straightforwardly, another male subject (aged 21) clustered three memories under the heading 'The skirt-chaser':

> I guess it's me, or rather it *is* me . . . The reason why these three memories are grouped together is that they all deal with the act of looking after girls or talking about girls as boys do, as everybody does. It's the theme, a little filthy: 'Oh, she is good-looking. Have you seen her?'

Very similarly, a 23-year-old female labelled a group of three memories 'My appearance at parties'. She explained: 'I mean my own appearance . . . the way I look from the point of view of others, how other people consider me . . .'. The memories dealt with episodes in which she had been especially reflective about the way she was looking, including this one:

> I am dancing, observing my clothes and my legs (how they are moving) . . . A guy that I know a little passes me while he says: 'You look good today.'

A different type of interest is exemplified by a male subject (aged 25) who clustered nine memories under the heading 'What it was like to be a ten- to thirteen-years-old boy'. Eight of the memories did in fact stem from that period. However, one memory from the past year was also included. It dealt with a successful attempt at solving a technical problem. When asked to explain this deviation, he said:

> It's because it was about technology which is an interest that I very much had as a young boy. And it was so great to be allowed to play that part again . . . much the same atmosphere as while I was sitting alone in my room as a boy, soldering tiny things together.

Combination of content and attitude criteria

In many cases, content and attitude criteria were combined, with the content criterion being secondary to the attitude. For example, memories belonging to one and the same lifetime period were often divided into two or more groups according to distinct attitudes. The male subject from the previous example divided memories of his later teen-years into two groups, one comprising the 'nostalgic' aspects and another containing 'the more negative sides'. Also, his category of 'what it was like to be a ten- to thirteen-years-old boy' shows that subjects sometimes, on closer scrutiny, revised their description of the criterion they had used for organising their memories from content to attitude features. This is reminiscent of Bartlett's (1932) phrase that the attitude enables the organism 'to turn round upon its own "schemata" and to construct them afresh' (p. 206). Such revisions occurred quite frequently, often when exceptions from the criterion the subject had initially stated were pointed out. For example, a 28-year-old male categorised six memories under the heading 'parties'. However, the interviewer noticed that he had at least two other party memories in the sample that were not included in the category. When confronted with this, the subject elaborated:

> It was decisive but it has to be a *good* party. And the one with the rowdies I don't characterise as such, neither the schoolparty where I am talking with my school-teacher. It's ambivalent too. It's not a real party.

Thus, the actual criterion was not the activity of 'party' but whether he had enjoyed it. Similarly, a female subject (aged 24) put all memories about her father in a group, except from one. When confronted with this deviation, she explained:

> Yes, I have a whole group of memories about my dad, but this one did not fit into it, because it refers to a good experience, whereas the other memories about my dad are associated with some negative emotions.

Discussion

In summary, most of the memories in our sample were organised in terms of attitudinal criteria rather than by features of their content, such as activity, location, participants or chronological order. Why did subjects employ a strategy that required constant considerations of such subtle ideas as 'feelings' or personal 'themes'? It is unlikely that organisation by memory content did not occur to them or was impossible with this sample of memories. Many subjects did employ content-addressing categories for some of their memories, and others acknowledged that such criteria could have been used. Thus, the relevant question is not whether subjects were able to use a content-oriented strategy, but rather why they generally preferred an alternative one, governed by attitudes? We suggest that this is because the individual's attitude towards the remembered event—the way it relates to the self—is a highly salient feature in consciousness. As we have shown, subjects often considered it inappropriate to cluster memories similar in content if they were associated with opposing attitudes. Thus, attitudes put constraints on the arrangement that can be formed. This appears in harmony with Bartlett's overall claim that remembering is a constructive justification of an attitude. However, we have no grounds for claiming that the attitude component determines an underlying, relatively permanent, organisation of memories. What the study shows is that, once events are remembered, the present attitudes exert a powerful effect on how people find it natural and appropriate to group those events.

CONCLUSIONS

This chapter has argued that Bartlett's (1932) concepts of image and attitude both reflect his indebtedness to the German introspectionist tradition in psychology and, at the same time, his opposition to behaviourism. 'Image' harks back to Wundt's Leipzig school of introspection, which was a direct descendant of British Empiricist philosophy, 'attitude' to the Würzburg school, which took its inspiration from Brentano's philosophy of intentional acts. When *Remembering* was published, Bartlett's approach, focusing on conscious experience, as well as his concepts, may therefore have seemed outdated, belonging to a period that was already well into the past. Gestalt psychology had replaced the atomistic introspection of Wundt, behaviourism had replaced the Würzburgers' interest in conduct.

Evidently, Bartlett's heart was with the functional view of the Würzburgers, not the passive associationism of Wundt. Accordingly, his use of images in the memory theory emphasised their functional properties, namely, that they served the retention of specific details which provided materials for the process of schematic reconstruction. Similarly, Bartlett emphasised the functional role of attitudes, although his presentation is marred by the difficulty of just describing the phenomenology of this notion. First, it seems that he wanted preservation of attitudes from encoding to remembering to account for the overall stability of recall. He was probably leaning on Betz's (1910) claim that an *Einstellung* is reproduced with greater accuracy than perceptual details. Second, Bartlett also used attitude to explain consistent individual differences in remembering, and therefore tended towards seeing attitudes as determined by the person's basic personality traits, character and temperament.

An important conclusion from this discussion is that Bartlett's (1932) theory of memory was only partially reconstructive. When read in its entirety and in its context, his account indicates that image and attitude both were meant to constrain the possible range of reconstructions based purely on schemata—in modern terms, bottom-up and top-down constraints, respectively. Though the notion of schematic reconstruction was his original contribution, a purely reconstructive theory was not his intention, and certainly no radical, social constructivism. Of course, this is not to deny the importance he ascribed to social patterning of schematic structures, as shown by his emphasis on conventionalisation, for instance.

Finally, Bartlett used attitude to capture the 'peculiarly personal reference' that may adhere to memories in consciousness. We contend that there is an underlying sense to the various ways in which Bartlett employed attitude, and that this sense is close to Russell's (1921) concept of propositional attitude: a psychological relation of a person to an instance of mental content—here, to the content of a memory. Russell's concept was dissected for the purpose of his epistemology from the same scientific tradition as Bartlett was drawing upon. We suggest that Bartlett knew Russell's views on attitudes and memory, but their respective conceptualisations of what an adequate psychology was like were widely divergent. Moreover, Bartlett wanted to keep clear of philosophical polemics.

Since memory attitudes are relations of the self to particular, remembered situations, they are often emotional, but their defining feature is not emotionality. They embody the perspective of the person towards the remembered event, its 'autobiographical reference'. The findings of a study in which subjects organised a sample of their memories into coherent categories showed that the organisation they arrived at was most often based on commonalities of attitude rather than factual memory content. We therefore propose that theories of autobiographical memory, in particular, need to take the attitudinal aspect of remembering into account as a principle of memory organisation.

Returning to the functional role of remembering, the hypothesis of Betz (1910) that memory attitudes are remembered more easily and accurately than memory content has apparently never been properly tested. Both Bartlett (1932) and Spiro (1980) furnished suggestive examples. With a refined concept of attitude, more satisfactory evidence may perhaps be envisaged.

ACKNOWLEDGEMENTS

We are grateful to Bill Brewer who gave us a head start in this research by sharing insights and references from his broad reading in the psychology of Bartlett's time. Furthermore, numerous suggestions by the editor have helped substantially to improve on earlier drafts.

NOTES

1   We have not had access to this unpublished dissertation, in which Bartlett also gave the first report of the memory experiments.
2   A similar meaning is apparent in the *Dictionary of Psychology* by Bartlett's contemporary Drever (1952) who defines *attitude* as 'a more or less stable set or disposition of opinion, interest or purpose; . . . attitude tests and attitude scales are scales and tests devised to throw light on temperament or personality traits' (p. 22).
3   To the reader who has sensed a certain influence of behaviourism in Bartlett's (1936) identification of attitude with 'reaction tendencies', it may be of interest that Betz (1928) had already been fully converted to interpreting *Einstellung* as a conditioned reflex.

4   Though Russell here rejects Brentano's theory of mental acts, his notion of attitude actually retains an essential part of the meaning of intentionality.
5   This was probably not due to lack of interest. Russell was busy with pacifist politics, for which activity he was fired from Cambridge four months later (July 1916) and imprisoned in 1918; he actually finished *The Analysis of Mind* in Peking in 1920–21.
6   The second discussion paper in the symposium was an exceedingly arrogant defence of Russell by his close colleague G.E. Moore. However, both discussion papers were strongly rebuked by Wildon Carr, the president of the society. Moore's was described as being mostly 'very unimportant' (which seems true to us), while Bartlett 'in treating the problem as one of descriptive psychology has failed to see its importance for philosophy' (Carr, 1916, p. 231). In addition, Bartlett was accused of making a fatal error in his main argument by assuming that sense-data can be exactly repeated; therefore, his views did not merit further consideration.
7   Sensory Experience and Other Content were not included as categories because they were seldom used by subjects. Extended Event was added because researchers since Barsalou (1988) have found this to be a common structure in autobiographical memory. Extended Event was defined as a course of episodes that are temporally and causally related, such as a holiday trip, and that last at least one day and could last up to a few months.
8   A lifetime period was defined as a period in the person's life characterised by a specific social context, e.g. The time I lived with X, The time I worked at Y. Thus, more than one lifetime period could be present across the same chronological period (cf. Conway, 1996).

CHAPTER EIGHT

Repeated reproduction from memory

Henry L. Roediger III, Erik T. Bergman and Michelle L. Meade

The most famous psychological studies conducted by Frederic Bartlett (1886–1969) were those of repeated reproduction of 'The War of the Ghosts', which he reported in *Remembering: A study in experimental and social psychology* (1932; hereafter cited as *Remembering*). He used other materials in repeated reproduction studies, too, but 'The War of the Ghosts' experiments are the ones that are recounted in virtually all textbooks on introductory psychology, cognitive psychology and human memory. Discussion of these studies is the primary focus of our chapter. Other writers in this volume describe Bartlett's many other accomplishments, so we permit ourselves to consider a relatively circumscribed topic, albeit the one for which he is best known within contemporary psychology.

To provide an overview of the chapter, we first briefly summarise 'The War of the Ghost' studies. Although they are so well known that one might think this step unnecessary, we provide a few points that we find missing in standard treatments of this work. In the second section of the chapter we compare and contrast the repeated testing tradition of Bartlett (1932) with an older tradition dating to Ballard (1913), who obtained different results from those of Bartlett. In a third section of the chapter we consider various follow-up studies to the famous repeated reproduction experiments, ones that generally cast doubt on the reliability of Bartlett's (1932) findings. In a fourth section we describe work that attempted a close replication of Bartlett's repeated reproduction experiments. Fifth, broadening our focus a little, we consider the latter chapters in Bartlett's (1932) book on *Remembering*, on social influences. We review the little experimental work that has been concerned with direct social influence on individual memory and report a preliminary experimental study of this topic we have conducted. We conclude with some thoughts about Bartlett's enduring influence on the study of remembering.

BARTLETT'S STUDIES OF REPEATED
REPRODUCTION

In the Preface to *Remembering*, Bartlett (1932) wrote that the beginning of the book dated to 1913, so the volume was 19 years in the making. Along the way, Bartlett published some of the studies in various journals. For example, the interesting experiments on perceiving reported in chap. II had been previously published in the *British Journal of Psychology* (1916a), the premier British journal of its day. Although almost never cited, the repeated reproduction studies using 'The War of the Ghosts' as material were also reported in the *Journal of General Psychology* (1928a), although *Remembering* provides a fuller account.

Bartlett used two primary techniques for studying how recollections change over repeated tellings: repeated reproduction and serial reproduction. In repeated reproduction one subject learns material and then recalls it repeatedly over various testing occasions, with no further study of the material. In serial reproduction a subject is exposed to material and recalls it; then a second person is exposed to the first person's recall protocol and later attempts to recall it; a third person then examines the second person's recollections and provides recall of that protocol, and so on for as many people as desired. Bartlett's studies seemed to show that serial reproduction leads to much greater cumulative error than does repeated reproduction. In repeated reproduction, the same person provides the narrative each time and each recall serves to consolidate and enhance future recalls. So, although forgetting occurs and errors creep in during repeated reproduction, the narrative is relatively stable, at least in comparison to errors obtained in serial reproduction. In the latter technique, essentially the same as the children's game of telephone or rumour ('Chinese Whispers' in the UK), it takes only one weak link in the communication chain to effect great changes in the narrative. Some of Bartlett's transcripts in *Remembering* show exactly these dramatic changes in serial reproduction (see pp. 129–138, for example, in serial recollections of the tale of 'The son who tried to outwit his father'). The serial reproduction technique has been replicated in many studies (e.g. Paul, 1959) and was used by psychologists as a model for how rumours might spread and change in their spreading (e.g. Allport & Postman, 1947). In cognitive psychology, the repeated reproduction studies are better known. However, despite being so well known, the repeated reproduction technique has been used only rarely in later work.

Bartlett's (1932) work on memory was, in part, a rebellion against traditional studies of the topic. He wrote that he wanted to avoid the approach Ebbinghaus had used—research involving the learning and re-learning of nonsense syllables under strict and artificial conditions—in favour of a more naturalistic studies. However, in spite of use of the term *experimental* in the sub-title of *Remembering* (1932), Bartlett did not report one true experiment in the entire book. There is no case in which an independent variable was manipulated with other factors held constant to observe its systematic effect on some dependent variable. Rather,

Bartlett reported demonstrations, ones which sometimes amounted to little more than partially controlled anecdotes. His methods were casual in the extreme. He did not hesitate to adjust his procedures from subject to subject as he felt necessary (p. 49) and in the repeated reproduction studies he seemed to test people after varying intervals as he came upon them on campus. He presented no aggregate data even from these descriptive studies, noting in chap. I that 'In this book there will be no statistics whatever' (p. 9), as though that were somehow a desirable quality. In the Introduction to the new edition of *Remembering*, Kintsch (1995) noted that the informal conduct and reporting of the experiments 'is the weakest aspect of the book and has somewhat limited its historical influence' (p. xiv). Indeed, the Bartlett studies also seem questionable on grounds of external validity. 'The War of the Ghosts' is about as similar to normal prose as Ebbinghaus's (1885/1913) nonsense syllables are to words.

Despite these possible drawbacks, the repeated reproduction experiments became highly cited. In 'The War of the Ghost' experiments, Bartlett had students read the story twice at their own pace. Then, after a 15-minute delay, he required them to recall the story. He would then test people later in an apparently rather unsystematic manner, after periods of weeks, months or (in a few cases) years. People were often tested repeatedly. The exact testing conditions are not stated with precision; we do not know what instructions Bartlett gave to his student subjects before they recalled the target materials, a point to which we shall return below. Bartlett's results were given in the form of protocols reprinted in the book, which he analysed for various types of errors. However, he never developed a systematic coding scheme for errors of the different types.

Bartlett noted several types of systematic errors that his subjects seemed to make: rationalisation, levelling and sharpening. He provided examples of these errors from protocols in both the repeated reproduction and the serial reproduction experiments. As is well known, he interpreted these errors as support for his schema theory. Briefly, he thought his subjects retained only the general framework or theme of the story, with bits and pieces of detail, and filled in during recall by using their general knowledge. To use Hebb's (1949) metaphor, perhaps made even more famous by Neisser's (1967) favourable citation of it in his great book, *Cognitive Psychology*, remembering an episode from one's distant past is rather like a palaeontologist's reconstruction of a dinosaur from partial remains found in a dig. The assorted bones and teeth would be like memories for specific events. They are placed into a coherent model of the dinosaur based on prior knowledge shaping the palaeontologists' mental model (or schema) of what the dinosaur must have looked like. In reconstructing from memory, the bits and pieces recollected about specific events are woven into a coherent story through activation of past knowledge (schema) of what the event was probably like. The resulting story of the event may often capture a true sense of its general character, but many details may be quite erroneous. Indeed, under the right conditions, the entire reconstruction may be filled with error.

Bartlett provided many examples of protocols in his book that he thought supported this view, but as noted previously, he never developed a systematic set of scoring criteria. How would rationalisation be operationalised? How could protocols be scored reliably for this and other errors that he noted? Providing examples is a first step, but only a first step, in a very long journey. Before dealing with these issues, in the next section we turn to other research from Bartlett's era that led to different conclusions.

REPEATED TESTING: REMINISCENCE AND HYPERMNESIA

Bartlett gave students passages and tested their memories repeatedly. He notes a debt to a French researcher, Philippe, who published similar work in *Philosophical Review* in 1897. Bartlett noted (1932, p. 63) that the method of repeated reproduction 'follows almost exactly the plan of investigation adopted by Philippe in his experiments . . . except that the material used was different and the experiments themselves were continued for a much longer period.' (Davis, 1996 argues that Bartlett's work and conclusions were also anticipated in research by Henderson, 1903, published as a monograph supplement in an American journal, but there is no evidence Bartlett came across this work.) Bartlett's citing of Philippe (1897) is admirable, especially in a book practically devoid of references. However, this citation makes it all the more curious that Bartlett seemed to ignore other work being published at about the same time in leading British journals.

Ballard (1913) reported an influential series of studies using (essentially) the repeated reproduction method in the *British Journal of Psychology*. In his best-known experiments, Ballard asked schoolchildren to remember passages of poetry and tested them both soon after learning and on later tests for a period of up to one week. Although his findings were rich, Ballard was primarily interested in the fact that the children would often remember lines of poetry on later tests that they had failed to recall on earlier tests. He termed this phenomenon *reminiscence*, which he defined as 'remembering one or more [items] that were not remembered in a [prior] test' (Ballard, 1913, pp. 17–18). Ballard noted that sometimes the overall recall score would improve on the later test; that is, the passage of poetry would be better recalled overall on later tests than on earlier tests, because recovery of lines of poetry from a first to a second test was greater than forgetting of lines between tests. The basic phenomena were replicated by Williams (1926), albeit under quite circumscribed conditions, causing later textbook writers to refer to the effect as the Ballard–Williams reminiscence phenomenon (Osgood, 1953, pp. 564–566). The idea that retention could improve over repeated tests is, of course, directly opposite what Bartlett (1932) claimed to find in chap. V of *Remembering*.

Other research of the time also showed that repeated recall could lead to gains rather than losses of information and that people could be more accurate

TABLE 8.1
Data from Brown's (1923) experiments on repeated testing

	States	*Word list*	
Test 1	36.31	25.48	
Test 2	39.66	26.77	
Difference (T1–T2)	3.35	1.29	Hypermnesia
CN (Forgetting)	1.94	3.04	
NC (Recovery)	5.29	4.33	Reminiscence

on later tests than on earlier tests. In Warner Brown's (1923) famous paper, he posed the question forming the paper's title: 'To what extent is memory measured by a single recall?' He gave various groups of US college students one of two tasks during a class period. In one case they were asked to free recall the (then) 48 states at the beginning of class for 5 minutes and then to perform the task again, about a half hour later, towards the end of class. For another group of students two tests were given, but in this case they were tested on a 48-word list that had been presented to them twice.

Brown's basic findings are shown in Table 8.1 and reveal both recall of items on a later test that could not be recalled earlier (the NC component of recall, for items *N*ot recalled on the first test but *C*orrectly recalled on the second test). Therefore, Brown (1923) replicated Ballard's (1913) reminiscence phenomenon with different materials. Reminiscence is the NC component of recall across two successive tests. In addition, this NC (or recovery) component of recall outweighed the CN (forgetting) component (items *C*orrectly recalled on the first test and *N*ot recalled on the second test). Therefore, overall performance improved numerically across the two tests. No statistics were applied to bolster these conclusions, but these phenomena have been replicated quite consistently in later work. Erdelyi and Becker (1974) termed the overall improvement in recall across repeated tests hypermnesia. Today a massive literature attests to the reality of improved recall on repeated tests (see Erdelyi, 1996; Payne, 1987; and Roediger & Challis, 1989 for reviews).

It seems remarkable that, writing in the early 1930s, Bartlett should not cite research directly related to his own in terms of the repeated testing technique. Ballard (1913), Brown (1923) and Williams (1926) all published in prominent journals. In the last chapters in *Remembering*, Bartlett discussed social factors that cause forgetting and distortion of the historical record. To these we might add the tendency to disregard or ignore evidence contrary to one's own conception as being a root cause of the historical forgetting of research.

Wheeler and Roediger (1992) noted and discussed the disparate results obtained in the traditions of Ballard (1913) and Bartlett (1928a, 1932) and set out to determine their causes by experiment. The two most prominent differences between the sets of studies were the types of materials used and the intervals between tests. Bartlett's repeated reproduction studies had used 'The War of the Ghosts', although he mentions in passing on p. 64 that he had carried out corresponding demonstrations with 'graphic material' and these studies led to similar conclusions. Work in the tradition of Ballard began with poetry as the target material, but in later years researchers used lists of pictures or words, as well as repeated testing of general knowledge (American states or Presidents, for example).

Wheeler and Roediger (1992) used 60 pictures as their materials, but for different groups of subjects these were either embedded in a story or were given along with their names. In the story condition, students listened to the story and pictures appeared on the screen for 5 seconds each when the relevant objects were named in the story. This technique permitted subjects to be tested on a set of relatively unambiguous items, the 60 pictures, while retaining the story as an aid to recall of the pictures. The story could provide schematic processing, but having subjects recall the pictures would obviate the challenging difficulties of having to score complex prose recall. In a separate set of conditions, another group of subjects was presented and tested with the list of 60 pictures, with no story. In this condition each picture was shown and at the same time the word naming the picture was read aloud. This condition is like that used in experiments showing hypermnesia over tests. If improvements across repeated tests occurred in this latter condition, whereas distortions over tests occurred in the story condition, then the type of materials would have been shown to be a critical determinant of when repeated reproductions lead to improvement or to distortion over time. A critical feature of the design is that the target material that subjects were to recall was held constant; both groups recalled the 60 pictures. The independent variable was whether the pictures were embedded in a story context or simply given as a list.

The other variable investigated by Wheeler and Roediger (1992) was the number of tests given and the retention interval between tests. Immediately after subjects saw the pictures (either in the context of the story or not), different groups received either zero, one or three tests under conditions of free recall. Those taking three tests received short breaks between tests. We expected to obtain the typical finding of hypermnesia in the three-test condition, especially for subjects who had studied the list of pictures with no story context. A week later all students returned for more testing and were given three free recall tests in succession. We expected that recall would decline over the week delay and we expected to observe distortion and misremembering, confirming Bartlett's conclusions, at least in the conditions in which the pictures had been given in the context of the story (and thereby had engendered schematic processing).

The results are shown in Table 8.2 and they partially supported and partially confounded expectations. The experiment can be considered as having six conditions defined by the orthogonal manipulation of study condition (subjects studying the 60 pictures with either their names provided or with the story provided) and then having three testing schedules. The three schedules of testing

TABLE 8.2
Results from Wheeler and Roediger (1992): Mean number of
pictures recalled as a function of presentation context and testing schedule

Group	Initial tests				Delayed tests			
	T1	T2	T3	T3–T1	T1	T2	T3	T3–T1
Pictures + Names								
3–3	26.6	27.2	28.4	1.8	25.2	26.3	26.0	0.8
1–3	25.7				20.2	21.7	23.0	2.8
0–3					16.7	17.5	17.5	0.8
Pictures + Story								
3–3	32.7	35.0	36.4	3.8	31.8	33.0	33.4	1.6
1–3	31.8				23.3	25.0	25.6	2.3
0–3					17.4	17.2	18.4	1.0

are indicated in Table 8.2 for each of the three groups receiving the three types of material. The first number indicates the number of tests taken soon after presentation (0, 1 or 3) and the second number indicates the number of tests taken after the week delay (always 3).

Several results are of interest. First, notice that subjects who heard the story surrounding the pictures generally recalled more pictures than did subjects in the condition in which pictures were given with their names. Therefore, the story seemed to have instantiated schematic processing, which enhanced overall recall. Second, notice that, on the first day, hypermnesia occurred for groups receiving three tests. In fact, improvement was greater for the group having heard the story than for the other group that heard only names, an outcome that fits with other findings about level of recall and hypermnesia (Roediger, Payne, Gillespie & Lean, 1982). Third, when a week intervened between tests, forgetting occurred (as Bartlett found in his repeated reproduction experiments), and for both types of material. Therefore, the interval between tests seems to be a critical factor in whether increases or decreases in recall occur across repeated reproductions. Fourth, although not of primary interest here, Wheeler and Roediger (1992) also showed the power of testing. When recall on delayed tests is examined, we see that the number of tests taken the week before powerfully affected performance. For example, for the subjects who heard the story while watching the pictures, retention a week later was 83% better on the first test for subjects who had previously taken three tests (31.8 pictures recalled) relative to those who had not been tested (17.4 pictures recalled). Even a single test improved recall 34% a week later, from 17.4 to 23.3. Testing not only assesses retention, but can alter performance and also 'fix' it in a common pattern. Bartlett noted the same fixing tendencies in his recall protocols, for both accurate and inaccurate recollections, although he did not have appropriate control groups for comparison.

Another finding from Wheeler and Roediger's (1992) experiment is not apparent in Table 8.2, but was perhaps most important. They did not observe much distortion of subjects' recall protocols in their experiment, even on the tests delayed for a week. Subjects generally recalled the pictures accurately. Of course, this might simply mean that the particular set of materials used may not have induced enough schematic processing, even in the story condition, to lead to errors. Therefore, they conducted two further experiments using 'The War of the Ghosts' (and, later, another story) as materials. Mandler and Johnson's (1977) analysis of 'The Ghosts' parsed it into 42 idea units, which were used in scoring recall. In a classroom experiment, Wheeler and Roediger (1992) had students read the story twice at a comfortable rate, then recall US Presidents for 5 minutes as a distracter task. They then recalled the story for 8.5 minutes, recalled the states of the US for 5 minutes, and then recalled the story again for the same length of time as on the first occasion. They found that subjects actually showed improvement in the number of idea units recalled over the two tests, from 21.4 units recalled to 22.9, contrary to what Bartlett (1932) found. Although the effect seems small, idea units in the story are composed of about eight words, so the effect would seem larger if measured in words recalled. More importantly, 37 out of 47 subjects showed the improvement, highly significant by a sign test.

The final experiment used two passages and a longer delay, as well as a manipulation of recall instructions. Subjects either received 'The War of the Ghosts' or a John Updike short story ('The Kid's Whistling') of about the same length (41 idea units). Subjects then took two immediate tests under either strict instructions for accurate recall or under more relaxed instructions that emphasised less verbatim responding to the wording of the story. Subjects returned a week later for a final test. On the two immediate tests, subjects recalling both stories showed improvements between tests, and for both instructional sets. On the test given a week later, subjects did show forgetting, but error analyses failed to show much distortion, even in recall of 'The War of the Ghosts'.

These experiments with prose confirmed the earlier experiment with pictures as the study material: With short delays between repeated reproductions, improvements in recall occur; with a week delay, forgetting occurred. However, the dramatic distortions touted by Bartlett (1932) failed to materialise. We inquire as to why this might be the case, and as to whether Bartlett's repeated reproduction results can be replicated, in the next two sections of the chapter.

HAVE BARTLETT'S REPEATED REPRODUCTION EXPERIMENTS BEEN REPLICATED?

After conducting the Wheeler and Roediger (1992) experiments, the first author of this chapter became curious about whether Bartlett's repeated reproduction observations had ever been replicated. After all, the studies are among the most famous in the entire experimental psychology of learning and memory. Every textbook reports them as fact. Surely, somewhere, sometime, since 1932 someone had collected similar observations under better controlled conditions than Bartlett had used, and had done the experiment 'right' by using many subjects, a rigorous scoring procedure, well-specified study and testing conditions, with the retention interval varied systematically, and so on. A check of dozens of textbooks left the search unfulfilled; the Bartlett repeated reproduction experiments were usually followed by studies of reconstructive processes in memory that used entirely different techniques from repeated reproduction.

A next step was to ask many knowledgeable luminaries in the field. Doing so produced an interesting result: Most people thought Bartlett's studies had been replicated, but they were unclear on who might have done it and where the report might have been published. Several pointed to Paul's (1959) experiments, but he used the serial reproduction technique exclusively. Results from the serial reproduction technique have been well replicated, although it is also rarely used today.

At the meetings of the Attention and Performance group in Ann Arbor, Michigan in 1991, Roediger approached Donald Broadbent, who had been Bartlett's student, and asked the question about whether anyone had ever successfully replicated the repeated reproduction experiments. Broadbent thought for a moment and replied yes, he felt certain they had been replicated. However, he was unclear on the details. He promised to supply them when he returned to his office in England and could consult his journals and files. After the conference, Roediger waited a few weeks and wrote to Broadbent, reminding him of the conversation. Broadbent wrote back after a time and said yes, he remembered the conversation quite well, had searched his sources when he returned, but could find nothing indicating that the repeated reproduction experiments had ever been replicated.

A check with Ulric Neisser on the same question turned up a promising lead: Neisser wrote that he thought a paper by Gauld and Stephenson published in the *British Journal of Psychology* (1967) might be relevant. Indeed it was. These authors did investigate reconstructive recall in 'The War of the Ghosts' but their findings undercut, rather than replicated, Bartlett's observations. Gauld and Stephenson investigated whether Bartlett's instructions to his subjects might have caused the appearance of great construction in their recollections. Bartlett (1932) was vague about his instructions to subjects, saying that 'I thought it best, for purposes of these experiments, to try to influence the subjects' procedure as little as possible' (p. 78). Gauld and Stephenson noted that if subjects took their task as being one of retelling the story, rather than remembering it, Bartlett's results showing much invention and construction would be expected. As they put it:

> Most people who retell a story are unlikely to care very much whether the story they retell is the same, detail by detail, as the story they originally heard. In other

words they are most unlikely to take pains so that what they come out with is always what they remember rather than what they guess at or even consciously invent. Now if the changes and inventions in reproductions of stories . . . are to serve as the foundation for a theory of remembering, [then it should be established that the subjects] were indeed seriously trying to remember, and were not more or less consciously romancing or guessing in order to fill in gaps in their memories.

(Gauld & Stephenson, 1967, p. 40)

Gauld and Stephenson (1967) performed three experiments varying recall instructions and reached the conclusion that Bartlett must have used very loose instructions, ones that encouraged subjects to tell a good story rather than to try to remember carefully the facts of the story. When subjects in Gauld and Stephenson's experiments recalled 'The War of the Ghosts' when instructed to remember the story as well as possible, they made few errors (just as Wheeler & Roediger, 1992 found 25 years later). In addition, when subjects were asked to pick out their own possible errors, they were quite accurate in doing so. Gauld and Stephenson concluded that their results cast doubt on Bartlett's whole approach to remembering: 'It will be clear from the discussion of results that we feel our experiments to some extent undermine Bartlett's theory of the reconstructive nature of recall' (p. 67). Further, 'to draw, as Bartlett has, conclusions about the nature of remembering from those parts of reproductions of prose passages which are most likely to be conscious guesses or inventions seems somewhat incautious' (p. 66).

Of course, with the 20/20 wisdom of hindsight, Gauld and Stephenson's (1967) sweeping generalisations about the accuracy of Bartlett's theorising from one set of experiments seems itself 'rather incautious'. After all, a huge amount of experimental work beginning just after 1967 on memory errors and illusions has supported Bartlett's (1932) general approach, championed so strongly by Neisser (1967/1979) in his famous book that appeared the same year as Gauld and Stephenson's paper (see Roediger, 1996; Roediger & McDermott, in press; and Schacter, 1995 for general reviews of the evidence on memory illusions and false memories). Further, recollections in which subjects are induced to make errors show them remarkably prone to continue those errors on later tests (e.g. Ackil & Zaragoza, 1998; Roediger, Jacoby & McDermott, 1996; Roediger, Wheeler & Rajaram, 1993). However, as argued later, Gauld and Stephenson (1967), like Wheeler and Roediger (1992), did not attempt direct replications of Bartlett's experiments, using the same conditions that he did.

Wynn and Logie (1998) also asked 'if Bartlett got it right' in the title of their paper and they concluded, like Gauld and Stephenson, that he did not. However, their study by no means represented a replication of Bartlett's repeated reproduction experiments, nor was it intended as such. Instead, these authors tested students about their recollections of an event occurring near the beginning of their first year at the university. The students performed an initial recall just after the session and then were asked to recall the events up to several more times over the next few months. Wynn and Logie interpreted their results as showing relatively good retention of the event, which did not change much over repeated tests. They concluded that the results suggested 'very limited use of reconstructive processes' in repeated recollections. However, to draw this sweeping conclusion from recollections of one fairly salient event, the early days of university life, also seems rather dramatic, especially in the face of powerful evidence showing inaccuracy of recollections in many other circumstances.

In short, after searching the literature and asking various scholars about this issue for a half dozen years, we could turn up no direct replication under better controlled conditions of Bartlett's (1932) repeated reproduction experiments. In fact, the studies by Gauld and Stephenson (1967) and by Wheeler and Roediger (1992), both of whom used repeated testing of 'The War of the Ghosts', actually failed to replicate Bartlett. Gauld and Stephenson concluded that Bartlett's instructions were probably faulty by being too lenient ('tell me a story like the one you read' rather than 'remember as accurately as possible the story you read'). Wheeler and Roediger actually found improved recall across repeated tests, at least with short delays between tests, exactly the opposite of what Bartlett found. With a week's delay between tests, they found forgetting, but still did not report much distortion. However, neither set of authors actually tried to replicate Bartlett's (1928a, 1932) experiments under conditions that were close to the ones he used. The research by Bergman and Roediger (in press), reported in the next section attempted a direct replication of Bartlett's research. In the course of conducting it, while looking for a systematic scoring scheme to analyse our results, we stumbled across a paper that can be construed as a replication of Bartlett's repeated reproduction experiments, by Johnson (1962), even though it is obviously less than well known. We review our work and that of Johnson in the next section.

REPLICATING BARTLETT'S REPEATED REPRODUCTION EXPERIMENTS

Exactly what it means to replicate Bartlett's research is not an easy matter to determine. He never provided a clear description of his methods and he never developed a rigorous scoring scheme to analyse subjects' protocols. The instructions he gave subjects are also in debate, as noted in the previous section. Therefore, replicating his work means attempting to make reasonable inferences about what his methods were, but in some cases we may have substituted what, in our opinion, he should have done rather than what he actually did. Still, we read chap. V of *Remembering* (1932) as carefully as possible to devise our methods. Our full report appears in the Bergman and Roediger (in press) paper, but we provide a summary here.

Thirty Washington University undergraduates participated in the experiment for course credit. Everyone received instructions to read a story twice and were warned that their memories would be tested later. They then read 'The War of the Ghosts' twice, at their own pace. After a 15-minute distracter task that involved performing maths problems, 10 subjects recalled the story under strict instructions to remember it correctly, 10 recalled it under lenient instructions, and 10 did not take a test. The lenient instructions told subjects to write down the story they had read earlier without worrying about being exact. 'Just tell the story as you remember it. Imagine you are relating it to a friend who has never heard the story before.' All subjects returned a week later and were asked to recall the story again, with half the subjects receiving strict and half receiving lenient instructions. (Instructions on the second test turned out not to matter, so results were collapsed across this variable.) Finally, as many subjects as possible were contacted six months later, brought back to the lab, and tested one more time under general instructions to recall the story as well as possible. Therefore, unlike the earlier research of Gauld and Stephenson (1967) and Wheeler and Roediger (1992), a long delay was built into the design, albeit without all subjects participating at this delay.

Scoring prose recall protocols is challenging. Bergman and Roediger (in press) adopted Mandler and Johnson's (1977) analysis of the story into 42 idea units and used these as a basis for scoring. Further, following the lead of Johnson (1962), they scored for various kinds of errors. The errors were placed into the two general classes of major distortions and minor distortions. Minor distortions were changes in wording that retained the sense of the original; they reflected changes in the surface structure of the proposition. Major distortions were changes in meaning and were of three possible types: normalisation, inference or importation. For example, normalisation would consist in remembering the story as occurring during the day rather than at night, because hunting trips would normally occur during the day. A proposition was judged to show inference-based distortion if information that was merely implied by the story was added to the proposition. For example, if subjects recalled that the Indian was hit by an arrow, this inference type of error was scored, because the story never specifies what hit him. Finally, importations were scored if entirely new elements were added to the proposition during its recall, either from another part of the story or from outside the story altogether. A rigorous scoring scheme was developed and the subjects' recalls were assessed by two scorers, whose judgements correlated at +.87 for the accuracy measure and +.92 for the distortion measure.

The results are fairly complex, but here we present one figure that summarises them and gets our main point across: We did replicate Bartlett's results. In Fig. 8.1 are the recall data from those subjects who were tested on the six-month delayed test, as well as the earlier tests. The left side of the figure shows data from subjects who received the first test shortly after reading the story twice. The data on the right are from control subjects who did not take this first test, but who were only tested after one week and again six months later. Note first the general positive effect of taking the first test: More was recalled (both accurately and inaccurately) on later tests if subjects had taken an initial test,

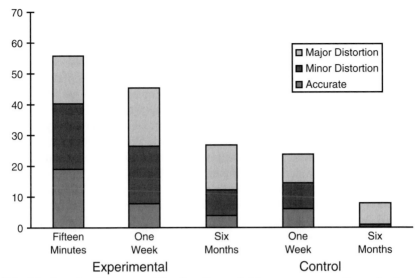

FIG. 8.1   Data from Bergman and Roediger (in press): Mean percentage recall as a function of type of information and time delay. The results show forgetting of information, but more importantly, show an increasing tendency over tests for the content of what is remembered to be distorted.

replicating work using other paradigms (e.g. McDermott, 1996; Roediger & McDermott, 1995). However, the most interesting features of the results are that, as would be predicted from Bartlett's theory and anecdotal results: (1) subjects recalled less material accurately over time, exhibiting forgetting; (2) the amount of distortion in recall grew over time; and (3) the amount of major distortion greatly increased over time. After six months, most of what subjects recalled from the story fell into the category of major distortions. The most impressive measure documenting this fact is to consider, for all propositions that were recalled from the story, the proportion of propositions that were deemed to have been distorted in a major fashion. For subjects receiving all three tests, the proportion of major distortions was 0.29, 0.39 and 0.58 across the three tests. For subjects taking only the one-week and the six-month tests, the corresponding proportions were 0.41 and 0.93.

Bergman and Roediger (in press) concluded that, yes, contrary to the claims of Gauld and Stephenson (1967), Wheeler and Roediger (1992) and Roediger et al. (1993), Bartlett's (1928a, 1932) repeated reproduction experiments can be replicated and that his conclusions are upheld. Indeed, while the authors were searching the literature for ways to score the data, they came across Johnson's (1962) research, which provided the basis for our scoring of errors. In reading Johnson's experimental work, which reported the research for his doctoral dissertation at Ohio State University, we discovered that it contained a replication of Bartlett's repeated reproduction experiments. Johnson did not make the point that he had replicated Bartlett (he seems to have assumed that there was no reason to expect otherwise), so his report dealt with other issues, such as the types of errors subjects made in recalling the story. Yet, in fairness, it should now be said that both Johnson (1962) and Bergman and Roediger (in press) have replicated Bartlett's (1928a, 1932) repeated reproduction experiments. The Johnson paper has existed in the literature for the 37 years, of course, but has never been cited as a replication of Bartlett's research so far as we can tell.

Why were Bergman and Roediger (in press) and Johnson (1962) able to replicate Bartlett's results, whereas others have not? We suspect the answer lies in the delay between study and test and between the tests themselves. All studies finding forgetting and distortion have employed a brief delay (15 minutes) between study of the passages and the first test. This delay might be important in that some forgetting of the story occurs even during this delay. If the first test occurred immediately and people were quite accurate, this consolidation or freezing due to the test might prevent further changes. However, probably more important is the fact that the successful demonstrations of Bartlett's results have employed long delays between tests. As we have seen, with very short delays between tests, people actually show improvements in recall over repeated testing, even for 'The War of the Ghosts'. However, when weeks or months occur between repeated tests, then Bartlett's predicted forgetting and distortion occur.

A larger issue is whether the replication matters. Bergman and Roediger (in press) argued yes. Replicating Bartlett is not some dry exercise in historical scholarship; rather, because we repeatedly remember the important events from our lives, knowing how retention changes over repeated reproductions is critical to a proper understanding of remembering.

SOCIAL INFLUENCES ON MEMORY

The latter part of *Remembering* (1932), to which cognitive psychologists have not much attended, is about social influences on memory. Part II of the book, comprising seven chapters, is entitled 'Remembering as a study in social psychology'. Although social psychologists have taken up the study of memory in the past few decades, many nuggets in Part II of Bartlett's book still seem not to have been mined empirically. Bartlett was primarily concerned with several issues, which included transmission of culture from one person to the next and from one generation to the next. He thought insights gleaned from studies of serial reproduction could aid in understanding these complex processes, although social psychologists have not much followed his lead in this direction.

We direct our attention here to one aspect of social influence that Bartlett (1932) did not much consider, and which has largely been neglected by modern social psychologists, too: the influence of other peoples' accounts on the recollections of an individual. Remembering is usually considered a private matter. The standard laboratory study of the topic, as in the repeated reproduction experiments, has subjects presented with some material and tested on it later. A hallmark of the typical experimental approach is that subjects are essentially tested alone, attempting to recollect the prior events by themselves. (Even if tested in a group, subjects usually work alone.) However, in many circumstances in society, remembering is a social event. A family group may reminisce about a vacation years ago; two people who witnessed a great sporting event, or a crime, or an accident, may discuss it and compare their recollections. A committee may meet and try to remember their conversations on some topic which occurred at a previous meeting. In all these cases and many more, remembering is a fundamentally social activity and we may expect all manner of social influence to be at work, operating to improve and to harm the individual's recollections. If a friend suggests an accurate rendition of events to you, your later recollection may be improved. However, if your friend suggests wrong information—she portrays events differently from the way they happened—your recollections may become distorted. Surprisingly, the magnitude of these types of social influence has been relatively little studied.

The largest systematic body of relevant research comes from the so-called misinformation paradigm developed by Elizabeth F. Loftus and her colleagues and studied by many others researchers, too (e.g. Loftus & Palmer, 1974; Loftus, Miller & Burns, 1978; see Loftus, 1991 and Ayers & Reder, 1998 for reviews). In the typical experiment, subjects witness slides or a videotape depicting an accident or a crime. Later, subjects either read a narrative or receive a question-naire about the events and, for some items, misinformation is inserted into the material. For example, if subjects had witnessed a traffic accident in which a car failed to stop at the stop sign, the information in the narrative describing the scene might refer to the sign in a neutral manner (a traffic sign), a consistent manner (a stop sign) or in a way inconsistent with respect to the originally viewed sign (a yield sign). This last condition is the misinformation condition and is of most interest: Will people come to remember the traffic sign as a yield sign rather than stop sign when they are exposed to the misleading information? The answer, in general, is *yes*, although the magnitude of the effect depends on the exact method of testing (e.g. Payne, Toglia & Anastasi, 1994). The Loftus misinformation effect then represents a form of social influence: People pick up information about an event in the past from another source and seemingly update their own memories with this bit of information. If the information provided in the narrative is correct, they remember the events better, but if it is wrong, their recollections become distorted. A typical result of both patterns is shown in Fig. 8.2.

Although the Loftus paradigm represents a kind of social influence, it is a rather curious kind. The narrative describing the event is often not portrayed as coming from one person in particular, but from some observer who might have been right or wrong. Still, because most of the facts asserted in the narrative do correspond to actual events from the scene, subjects might be led to think that the

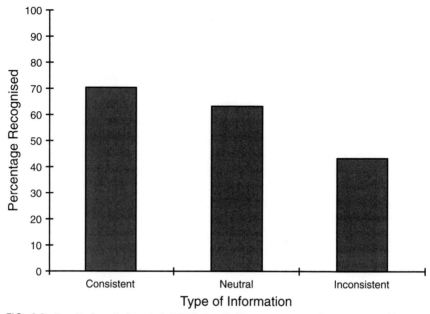

FIG. 8.2 Results from Loftus et al. (1978) Exp. 2: Mean percentage of correct recognition as a function of whether the information provided in a narrative was consistent, neutral or inconsistent (i.e. misleading) with respect to the information originally viewed. Consistent information improved later recognition, whereas inconsistent (misleading) information harmed recognition.

narrator was a good observer. Betz, Skowronski and Ostrom (1996) performed a memory experiment in which subjects were given a story and then tested on recollections of the story. They were shown a tally sheet that purported to provide responses of other subjects to see if this information would influence subjects' own judgements. It did. On a later cued recall test, subjects tended to provide responses in line with the dominant responses on the sheet they had been given. However, in this case, like that of the typical misinformation paradigm, the other people were virtual (represented by the tally sheet) rather than a real person or group giving their opinions verbally, face to face.

Relatively few experiments have used the tactic of having an actual person provide responses to see if subjects will be swayed by hearing incorrect answers from another person. A reasonable expectation is that face-to-face contact would lead to more powerful effects than reading anonymous narratives, although this outcome might depend on the credibility of the communicator in the situation (Underwood & Pezdek, 1998). The only published account of which we are aware showing social influence exerted by another person on recollections is by Schneider and Watkins (1996). They conducted a recognition memory experiment in which pairs of subjects were presented with a list of words. In their Exp. 2, one subject in each pair was a confederate. After studying a long list of words,

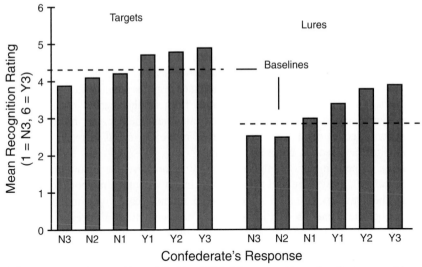

FIG. 8.3   Data from Schneider and Watkins (1996): Mean recognition ratings for targets and lures to which confederates had previously responded yes or no. The judgement of the confederate had systematic effects on subjects' recognition responses, changing them to be consistent with the confederate's response.

participants took a recognition test in which the subjects took turns calling out their answers to items. They responded on a six-point scale, ranging from 'sure that they item was in the list' to 'sure the item was not in the list'. The question of interest is whether the true subject's recognition responses would be affected by the prior response of the confederate. The results are shown in Fig. 8.3 and the answer is clearly yes. The figure shows the mean recognition rating of subjects, on the six-point scale, as a function of the confederate's previous response to the same item. On the left are responses to targets, where it can be seen that social influence was greater to correctly say yes (a target was old) than to say no (the target was new). In this case the confederate's response aided accurate respond-ing without affecting inaccurate responding very much (although the negative effect was significant). However, data for the lure items on the right show that subjects' responses were affected in both directions here. That is, if the confeder-ate had provided an erroneous positive response, subjects tended to follow suit. Thus social influence serves to push responses towards reporting of false mem-ories. However, negative responses by the confederate also led subjects to make more accurate negative responses. Schneider and Watkins (1996, p. 481) con-cluded that their 'experiments illustrate a powerful effect of social pressure on recognition responses'.

In recent research at Washington University, we are also studying the influ-ence of one person's memory reports on another person's later recollections. The experiment, like those of Schneider and Watkins (1996), was modelled rather loosely after Asch's (1956) famous experiments on conformity in perceptual judgements. The question we raised is whether a subject's wrong response during a first test will contaminate another person's memory for the event. Essentially, subjects receive misinformation from another participant in the experiment rather than from an anonymous narrative. Unlike Schneider and Watkins (1996), we were interested not in social pressure on immediate responses, but rather on whether subjects who received wrong recollections from another person in the experiment would incorporate these responses into their memory of the event. We consider selected conditions from one of our experiments here, to give the flavour of the research, but it is ongoing.

Pairs of people came to the psychology laboratory, one a confederate and one a subject. They were told that the experiment was about memory for scenes. They then saw six common scenes for 15 seconds each, with instructions to remember the scenes as well as possible. The scenes were pictures of rooms (a kitchen, a bedroom, etc.) in which many objects appeared. After viewing the scenes, subjects were next asked to recall items from the scenes, with each scene tested in turn. So, for example, the experimenter asked for the two people to recall as many items from the kitchen scene as they could. The confederate and the subject took turns recalling items from the scene until they reached 12 items. Then the experimenter stopped them and moved on to the next scene, until 12 items from all six scenes had been recalled.

For three scenes the confederate provided six responses that were all accurate (no misinformation was given), but for the other three scenes the confederate provided two items that were not actually in the scene. One of the fictional items provided was very likely to have been in the scene a priori and one was not so likely. So, for example, for the kitchen scene the confederate recalled toaster or oven mitts, neither of which was in the scene. Although oven mitts could appear on a kitchen table, pre-testing made it clear that subjects found this item less likely to appear in a kitchen scene than a toaster.

After the subject and confederate finished recalling all six scenes, they were separated and taken to different cubicles. Now the subject was told that he or she would receive a final test of items that had appeared in each scene. They were told to write down only items they were sure had appeared in the scenes and not to be influenced by the other person's prior reports, because some of the items recalled by the other person might have been wrong. The question at issue is whether subjects would still be more likely to recall items suggested by the other person as actually having been in the scenes. The results are in Fig. 8.4 and show that subjects were influenced by the confederates' responses. They did indeed recall items as being in the scene that had only been suggested by the confederate; however, this tendency occurred at much higher rates when the item was more plausible. To follow through with the earlier example, it was much easier to insert a non-existent toaster into subject's memory for the kitchen scene than non-existent oven mitts.

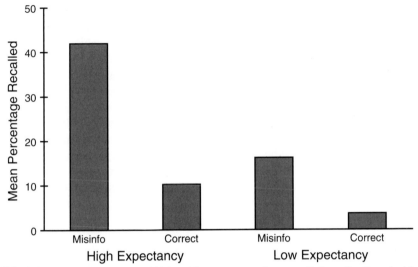

FIG. 8.4   The mean percentage of high and low expectancy items recalled as a function of misinformation or correct information. Subjects incorporated items suggested by a confederate into their own recollections, but this tendency was greater when the inserted item was one likely to occur in the situation (high expectancy items).

We are conducting further experiments using this general technique. One critical issue is the degree of confidence subjects have in these implanted memories. In the Asch (1956) conformity experiments using perceptual judgements, the general finding is that subjects' conformity responses are intentional. They know the correct answer to the question put to them, but are responding erroneously to accede to group pressure. However, the case is not so clear in remembering. False memories developed through social influence may come to be accepted and believed to be real. This seems to be true in the Loftus misinformation paradigm (e.g. Weingardt, Toland & Loftus, 1994) and we suspect the same is true in our paradigm, too, but we do not yet have the data at hand to demonstrate this conclusion.

To return to our theme at the beginning of this section, Bartlett's (1932) writings on the social aspects of remembering are still worth reading today. Most of the research programme that he outlined still has not been carried out. In fact, most chapters in *Remembering* contain interesting research ideas that have not yet been seen fruition in empirical research (Roediger, 1997).

CONCLUSIONS

This chapter focused primarily on the repeated reproduction studies that Bartlett (1932) carried out and that became a staple of cognitive psychology. We criticised Bartlett's casual methods and anecdotal presentation of his results, but the most surprising feature of our story is that almost no one, until recently, worried about the reliability and validity of the claims he made. The studies became a staple of standard treatments of memory in textbooks and achieved legendary status in the field. Exactly how this could have occurred we leave to sociologists and psychologists of science. We suspect that the processes are the same as those that establish belief in other realms: The repeated anecdote comes to be accepted as a truth in science as in society at large. However, at least in this one case, the common wisdom turns out to be vindicated, we believe. Bergman and Roediger (in press) showed that Bartlett's conclusions from the repeated reproduction experiments could be replicated and dozens, perhaps hundreds, of studies support his contention that remembering is largely a matter of construction, or reconstruction. In fact, we might say that the research on memory errors and illusions from many different paradigms over the past 30 years supports Bartlett's conclusion from his own research:

the one overwhelming impression produced by this more 'realistic' type of memory experiment is that human remembering is normally exceedingly subject to error. It looks as if what is said to be reproduced is, far more generally than is commonly admitted, really a construction, serving to justify whatever impression may have been left by the original. It is this 'impression', rarely defined with much exactitude, which most readily persists. So long as the details which can be built up around it are such that they would give it a 'reasonable' setting, most of us are fairly content, and we are apt to think that what we build we have literally retained.

(Bartlett, 1932, p. 176)

CHAPTER NINE

Re-fusing anthropology *and* psychology

Jennifer Cole and Michael Cole

For as long as psychology and anthropology have existed as distinctive disciplines, there have been those who contested the institutionalised division of labour initiated by their founding (Jahoda, 1992). We understand the current interest in the work of F.C. Bartlett to reflect, in part, the fact that disciplinary boundaries separating the social-behavioural sciences are again being actively questioned, and Bartlett's ideas provide sources of inspiration for those who would like to re-establish the unity between the individual, culture, and the social group that was torn asunder immediately preceding and following the turn of the 20th century.

Bartlett began his career at a time when disciplinary boundaries between psychology, anthropology, and sociology were still fragile and border-crossing was routine. Many of his teachers made important contributions to the establishment of the emerging social science disciplines in the course of their careers, but they were acutely aware of the problems that disciplinary isolation engendered, even as they, like Bartlett himself, were swept into disciplinary isolation by the intellectual forces that have dominated 20th-century social sciences. We hope that by retracing the development of Bartlett's ideas and applying them to current theory and research we can advance one of the projects for which he is well known: the effort to understand the relations between cultural and mental processes.

EARLY WRITING

By his own account, Bartlett participated in the founding of the Psychological Laboratory at Cambridge in 1913 (Bartlett, 1958, chap. 8). However, he showed an interest in ethnographic materials from the outset: one of the major influences on his early work was W.H.R. Rivers, whom he identifies as an anthropologist, and some of his earliest experiments were motivated by A.C. Haddon's ethnographic studies of decorative art forms in New Guinea. Rivers and Haddon, were, of course, central figures in the Torres Straits expedition, the first attempt to combine anthropological/ethnographic and psychological/experimental methods in the study of a social group.

An indication of how indistinct the disciplinary lines among anthropology and psychology were at the time is the fact that Rivers, trained initially in medicine, was included in the Torres Straits expedition as an expert on experimental methods because Haddon believed that 'no investigation of a people was complete that did not embrace a study of their psychology' (Haddon, 1901, p. v).

Over the next few decades, as Bartlett was growing to intellectual maturity, the divisions between anthropology, psychology and sociology became more sharply drawn. Rivers, upon returning from the Torres Straits, carried out a variety of experimental psychological studies, before turning to ethnology and sociology.[1] Like Durkheim in France, Rivers favoured keeping these scientific enterprises separate, arguing that the study of the customs and institutions that make up social behaviour should be pursued independently of the instincts, feelings and thought processes of individuals. Although he anticipated that the two approaches would converge at some future time, he was particularly concerned to avoid the reduction of social facts to psychological processes (Rivers, 1914a).[2]

Although he is known to the current generation of psychologists primarily for his elaboration of the concept of schema and his work on remembering, Bartlett's first monograph (1923) was on the topic of psychology and culture. In it he explicitly cites and agrees with Rivers that the sociologist should 'rigorously confine his attention to purely social determination' (p. 25). However, he simultaneously argues that the reverse is *not* true.

> it is frequently necessary to take established social conventions and institutions as facts determining the character and relations of individual response. Such institutions and conventions are legitimately regarded as group responses. They are social facts, but they exercise a direct and important determining influence upon varied series of individual reactions.
>
> (Bartlett, 1923, p. 25)

Despite his explicit acknowledgement of the importance of social processes in mental life, a contemporary reader looking for a connection between Bartlett's treatment of mind and culture in *Psychology and Primitive Culture* (1923) and contemporary cultural psychology may come away disappointed. There are several sources of difficulty. First, Bartlett develops his arguments entirely from secondary sources, which were still relatively scant at the time (he did not conduct research in a society of the kind he wrote about until several years later). Although he cites the work of Boas, Kroeber, Lowie and others who were elaborating the concept of culture, he depends largely upon catalogues of cultural elements (arts, weapons, writing systems) handed down from the 19th century. Second, he lacked a currently acceptable psychological theory, relying heavily on McDougall's (1920) theory of the instinctual basis of 'tendencies for action', which, despite some reservations, he accepted as a starting point for what he termed a psychological study of social life (Bartlett, 1923, p. 31).

None the less, one can find in this early effort several ideas that resonate with contemporary work on culture and mind (see Rosa, 1996 and Chapter 5 for a more extended discussion of these affinities; here we concentrate on those which will be most pertinent to the empirical examples to be presented later). First, like contemporary cultural psychologists, Bartlett (1923, p. 1) explicitly argued that 'we must guard against the temptation to separate the individual entirely from his group, and to seek a pre-social origin for social behaviour'. Rather,

> The individual who is considered in psychological theory, in fact, is never an individual pure and simple. The statements made about him always have reference to a particular set of conditions. The individual with whom we deal may be the-individual-in-the-laboratory, or the-individual-in-his-everyday-working-environment, or . . . the-individual-in-a-given-social-group.
>
> (Bartlett, 1923, p. 11)

Second, he offers a rudimentary version of the idea that the elements of culture, whatever they might be, operate in patterned ways that respond to the historical experience of the group and that selectively conserve and modify the cultural resources upon which people can draw in organising their actions with each other in the present. Third, he saw the relationship between culture and mind as reciprocal:

> When we set out to explain human behaviour of any kind we must be prepared to take into account facts of the external world, and facts of social structure. At the same time all such facts must be considered in their relation to tendencies towards thought, feeling, and action expressed in the individuals who are being studied.
>
> (Bartlett, 1923, p. 6)

Finally, although the focus in his first monograph was on the explanation of cultural difference, he repeatedly reminds the reader that the principles relating mind to what he refers to as 'social structure and cultural possessions' apply universally. In words that presage the title of a recent, authoritative, summary of cultural psychology ('The cultural psychology of development: One mind, many mentalities' by Shweder, Goodnow, Hatano, LeVine, Markus and Miller, 1998, pp. 865–937), Bartlett writes that 'It is in their conditions and inter-relations, rather than in their character, that primitive mental processes differ from our own.' In short, cross-cultural psychology is a specific application of a more general enterprise, which Bartlett called social psychology, but which we currently refer to as cultural psychology.

REMEMBERING AND THINKING

As others have noted, the overall trajectory of Bartlett's career appeared to represent a steady movement away from the principles enunciated in *Psychology and Primitive Culture* (1923) (Middleton & Crook, 1996; Rosa, 1996, and Chapter 5). Although his most influential book, *Remembering* (1932), contains the results of the only empirical research that he carried out in a primitive society, that section of the book is not the major source of its subsequent influence; it is not remarked upon either by those who assimilated his work into cognitive psychology (see Brewer, Chapter 6) or by those such as Middleton and his colleagues (Edwards & Middleton, 1986; Middleton & Crook, 1996) who have appropriated Bartlett's work into discursive psychology, or by Rosa (1996, and Chapter 5) who argues for strong affinities between Bartlett's early theorising and the form of cultural psychology being developed in the Soviet Union at the same time (see M. Cole, 1996 for an account of these developments). There is probably good justification for this neglect, since neither of the two key concepts that have become entry points into the use of Bartlett's ideas among psychologists, schema and conventionalisation, play a central role in his account of remembering among the Swazi.

When we arrive at Bartlett's last book, *Thinking* (1958), not only the Bartlett of 1923 but the Bartlett of 1932 appears to have been left behind. Rivers and Haddon now figure only in a brief autobiographical section devoted to an analysis of Bartlett's own experimental thinking. The words 'culture', 'schema' and 'conventionalisation' are to not to be found in the index. *Remembering* does appear in several footnotes, but in its only appearance in the body of the text it has been assimilated to information-processing theory where it finds its niche in 'long term information store'. The only hint that Bartlett may have retained his interest in culture appears in a footnote early in his chapter on everyday thinking (p. 166) where he refers to a series of studies, few of which were published, that sought comparative studies of everyday thinking in Greenland, India, Africa and central Europe.

Although there appears to be ample justification for reading the trajectory of Bartlett's ideas as a gradual rejection of his early interdisciplinary interests, and hence a movement away from our interest in his ideas as tools for understanding the relation of culture and thought, we think it is more useful to interpret his later work, despite differences in emphasis and vocabulary, as bearing important continuities with his earlier work. Next we point to three ideas for which we think the argument of continuity is theoretically fruitful, and then turn to two contemporary examples to show how these theoretical ideas can help to make sense of empirical research. Of particular concern to us are three notions, schema, conventionalisation and the social context of cognition.

Schemata, conventionalisation and the social context of cognition

One of the central ideas of cultural psychology is that many structures viewed as internal to the individual by classical cognitive psychology need to be reconceptualised as distributed, e.g. as existing simultaneously (albeit in different media) within, between and among individuals. Jean Lave (1988, p. 1), for example, refers to the need to shift the boundaries of cognition and the environment such that, in her terms, cognition 'is stretched across mind, body, activity and setting' (a perspective sometimes referred to as 'distributed cognition' (Hutchins, 1995; Norman, 1991; Salomon, 1993).

As noted by Edwards and Middleton (1986) and Middleton and Crook (1996), this is precisely the way in which Bartlett conceived of schema in *Remembering* (1932). Although he adopted the term from Head, for whom it definitely had an 'in-the-brain' sort of existence, Bartlett quite explicitly indicates that Head's use of the term fails to indicate that the results of past experience are actively influencing us all the time, and that these influences are best thought of as 'organised settings'. As Middleton and Crook remark:

> Schemata in such a view are not knowledge structures stored in the brains or minds of individuals for the interpretation of experience, but functional properties of adaptations between persons and their physical and social environments.
> (Middleton & Crook, 1996, p. 382)

Both they and Rosa (1996, and Chapter 5) note the close affinity between this interpretation of schema and the notion of mediation in cultural-historical approaches to cultural psychology (M. Cole, 1996). Bartlett's (1932, p. 208) statement that schemata are 'not merely something that works the organism, but something with which the organism can work' echoes many contemporary cultural psychologists (compare it, for example, to Jerome Bruner's (1996, p. 4) assertion that culture, 'though man-made, both forms and makes possible the workings of a distinctively human mind').

A second central concept in Bartlett's work is conventionalisation, 'a process by which cultural materials coming into a group from outside are gradually worked into a pattern of a relatively stable kind distinctive of that group' (1932, p. 280). He adapted the notion from Rivers, who used it to refer to the process by which forms of artistic expression become modified 'through the influence of the conventions and long-established technique of the people among whom the new notions are introduced' (quoted in Bartlett, 1932, p. 244).

Although Bartlett seems to have developed the term 'conventionalisation' specifically to refer to the processes of transformation that took place in cases of intercultural contact, the concept is clearly related to both remembering and schema formation because, as he put it, 'conventionalisation always illustrates the influence of the past upon the present' (1932, p. 244). The way in which a new conventionalised pattern is created exhibits many of the same constructive processes that Bartlett also found to characterise remembering. This linkage, in turn, points to the intimate relationship between conventionalisation and schema, since conventionalisation itself involves the formation and modification of schemata.

When we interpret the process of schema formation and use with the process of conventionalisation as basically two manifestations of the same process, we approach contemporary views in cultural psychology that see mind as constructed in culture, conceived of as the precipitate of past experience, deployed in the present through artefacts, aspects of the material world that have been modified over the history of their incorporation in goal-directed human action:

> By virtue of the changes wrought in the process of their creation and use, artefacts are *simultaneously ideal (conceptual) and material.* They are manufactured in the process of goal directed human actions. They are ideal in that their material form has been shaped by their participation in the interactions of which they were previously a part and which they mediate in the present.
>
> (M. Cole, 1996, p. 117)

The final concept we need to examine is that of the socio-cultural context of action. As Middleton and his colleagues emphasised, Bartlett thought of schemas in terms of 'organised settings'. Although he created special, experimental, settings in his research on serial reproduction, he recognised that his experimental methods represented especially constrained circumstances, and were not representative of the conditions of remembering in everyday life, despite his attempts to make the materials meaningful and familiar. These methodological restrictions concerned him because he believed that central to human thought is the ability of human beings to transcend prior experience (embodied in schemata) by 'turning round' on their own schemata. To explain how this ability arises, he argues, we 'must turn away from the fact of "schematic" organisation to the conditions which direct the formation of these active settings' (1932, pp. 301–302), for example, to the social context of action.

Broadly speaking, the process of 'turning round on one's schema' is what we ordinarily consider 'thinking'. As Bartlett comments in his 1958 book by this title, he had wanted to take on this topic at the time he completed *Remembering* (1932), but his work in this direction was interrupted by World War II, which channelled his energies into the study of bodily skills and other matters of urgent national interest.

Bartlett defines thinking as a process of 'gap filling'. His introduction to the topic provides a variety of examples: We meet somebody after a long absence and something about him seems different, so we try to think about what might have occurred in the interim to account for the change; or a man is tracking an aeroplane that disappears and then appears again, so he must figure out what happened while it was lost. He characterises the general process as follows:

The process begins when evidence or information is available which is treated as possessing gaps, or as being incomplete. The gaps are then filled up, or that part of the information which is incomplete is completed.

(Bartlett, 1958, p. 75)

Bartlett distinguishes several varieties of thinking in connection with the constraints thinkers must deal with and the purposes they are trying to achieve. *Closed systems* are cases where all the elements in the problem are known at the outset, the goal is well defined, and the possibility of solution is assumed: Logical and mathematical problems are Bartlett's prototype. He contrasts closed systems thinking with a variety of thinking activities that are, to a greater or lesser degree, open. *Experimental thinking*, for example, often confronts the thinker with a puzzle for which the tools for solution may need to be created; and the ordering of steps in the gap-filling process is relatively unconstrained. Even less constrained is *everyday thinking*, when people are at least as concerned with accomplishing some social goal as in arriving at a logical solution to a problem. Bartlett uses the term 'immediate communication thinking' to characterise this genre. Thinking about how to end the conflict in Northern Ireland, or whether the home team won its most recent game because of its good defence or the other team's poor offence would be typical examples.

In contrast with either closed system or experimental thinking, Bartlett reports that everyday thinking is often accomplished by people recalling an example they think appropriate from their own experience, and offering this example to 'fill the gap' posed by the problem. The thinker, he writes 'appears to adopt as his own, without any further examination, the first conventional generalisation which "comes to mind," as we say' (1958, p. 182).

It should be apparent that the three concepts that we have chosen to examine from Bartlett's work are all closely inter-related. Schemata arise as 'organised settings' and undergo a process of conventionalisation over time. Thinking is intimately bound up with remembering. This is especially prominent in the case of everyday thinking, where instances of past experience are selected to fill the existing gaps in. As Bartlett notes,

Whatever goes into long-term storage, thereafter can undergo all those kinds of change which were the main topic in my *Remembering* book. So when it is drawn upon, it can be reconstructed in all sorts of ways to meet the demands of the current situation.

(Bartlett, 1958, p. 91)

APPLYING THE CONCEPTS

Although conventionalisation, schema formation and social context are all mutually implicated in the processes of thinking and remembering, which are themselves thoroughly intertwined, the particular way in which these different elements combine on any given occasion can be expected to differ dramatically.

We have chosen the examples we present here with two major goals in mind. First, we want to illustrate that ordinary behaviours involving remembering and thinking highlight different mixes of their elements. Second, we have chosen examples based on ethnographic methods. Whereas Bartlett appears to have moved more and more toward the creation of artificial experiments to test his ideas, we believe that ethnographic methods, no less than experimental ones, offer methodologically sound evidence for the workings of psychological principles.

Conventionalisation and remembering as a socially distributed cognition

In the 1980s, Edwin Hutchins undertook the analysis of learning and problem solving that occurred in the navigation room of the USS *Palau*, an amphibious helicopter transport ship. Hutchins had come to adopt a perspective that he then termed 'naturally situated cognition', the analysis of human thinking in real-life settings. The proper unit of analysis for the study of cognition in such settings, he believed, had to include the 'socio-material' environment, including the artefacts that mediated and co-ordinated the actions of participants. He conceived of learning as 'adaptive re-organisation in a complex system' (Hutchins, 1995, p. 289).

One day, when the ship was entering San Diego harbour, it suddenly lost power. After several anxious minutes, the crew was able to slow the ship sufficiently to allow it to drop anchor. A short time later, power was restored and the ship docked at its pier.

The loss of power not only affected the ability to manoeuvre the ship, it also disabled the gyroscope, a device critical to navigation. And continued successful navigation was essential because the ship could not stop just anywhere. It had to find a way to anchor out of the main shipping channel at a spot close to dangerous shoals. Ordinarily, a backup gyrocompass would begin to function, but unluckily, it, too, failed to work. The navigators had partial information which they could use to calculate the bearing of a landmark with respect to the ship that would locate them correctly in the channel. One bit of information they could obtain was the bearing of a conventional landmark such as a lighthouse with respect to the head of the ship. This is called the *relative bearing* (RB). Full information about the true bearing, which a working gyroscope would provide directly, required more. First, it required determination of the compass point known as true north (T). Unfortunately, a ship's compass does not automatically indicate true north. Rather, it indicates the direction of the ship's head with respect to magnetic north (C), which deviates from true north depending on the specific compass, and the direction in which the ship is heading (D). It also requires knowing the difference between true north (T) and magnetic north (M) which depends upon the ship's exact geographical location. The navigators could obtain this information, called variation (V), because it is recorded on nautical maps for all regions of the world. Full navigation required putting together all of this information, quickly, in order to know the ship's heading.

Although they were lacking a gyroscope, the navigators had at their disposal a mnemonic device that summarises how to calculate the ship's true heading: 'Can Dead Men Vote Twice', which stands for the algebraic expressions, $C+D=M$ and $M+V=T$ (compass heading plus deviation = magnetic heading, magnetic heading plus variation = true heading). This information is essential to calculating the ship's exact location; but note that the mnemonic says nothing about relative bearing. Yet relative bearing was a crucial piece of information that was available to the navigators in this emergency situation.

The information they do have (V, C, D and RB) is sufficient to calculate the line of position of the ship. For each calculation of the line of position, it was necessary to calculate three numbers: $C+D=M$, $M+V=T$, $T+RB=TB$. Three such calculations provide the triangulation to fix the exact position of the ship.

Hutchins notes that if the individual addition operations are made in any arbitrary order, it requires nine additional operations in all to reach a position fix. However, for any set of three line-of-position calculations, the position of true north (T) is likely to be the same, since the calculations are taken as nearly simultaneously as possible. So there would be a real savings of calculational steps if the team first calculated $C+D+V$ and then added the result to RB.

Hutchins recorded every calculational step the team of plotters made, as well as the way they divided the labour. He found that at first they had no set division of labour, that they added elements of the needed formula in different orders, and that for a long time they failed to include the Deviation term needed for correct calculation of the ship's line of position. Fortunately, the ship's heading was such that the deviation was effectively zero. After several attempts at carrying out the operations in their heads, following different orders each time, the team start to use an electronic calculator.

After a little over 20 calculations of the line of position, the ship swung on its anchor sufficiently to make the Deviation term significant, which the plotter quickly picks up on. But the two-man team has still not settled into a fixed order of calculation in which they simplify the problem by first calculating $C+D+V$ and then RB, and the division of labour is still variable. After 38 calculations of line of position, the pair finally arrived at a stable, efficient procedure. At this point, they not only calculated $C+D+V$ as a module, to be used with three calculations of RB, they gave this module a spontaneously arrived-at name, 'total', which functioned as a new, fused, cultural artefact, simplifying and increasing the reliability of their work.

Here we see in microcosm the process of conventionalisation/schema formation being accomplished in a real-world setting that definitely would fall under Bartlett's definition of thinking as gap-filling. Remembering enters the activity at many points, far more than we have time to explicate here (Hutchins provides a detailed analysis of the changes we have summarised over 20 pages of text interspersed with verbatim dialogue and detailed description of the dynamically shifting division of labour). But remembering (such as recalling the conventionalised mnemonic device 'Can Dead Men Vote Twice') is clearly subordinated to a process of conventionalisation that serves to reduce the mental labour involved in each set of calculations, terminating in a modularised treatment of part of the problem and the lexicalisation of the spontaneously created cultural artefact called 'the total' (which would not be considered 'the total' outside of the micro-cultural situation instigated by the broken gyroscope).

It is not entirely clear how to characterise this example with respect to the continuum from closed to open forms of thinking, nor does it seem necessary to pigeonhole the example with respect to Bartlett's typology. It clearly was thinking under severe constraints, but the order of operations to fill in the needed gaps was not standard. This order shifted with the division of labour and the level of expertise needed to deal with the unusual problem conditions that developed over repeated attempts to calculate lines of position. Yet this process just as clearly illustrates aspects of the kind of thinking Bartlett characterised as everyday. People worked together fluidly as one person or the other contributed information that could help to fill in the gaps in the solution process, and one or another of the participants made comments that were entirely beside the point of the task logically speaking (as when the Recorder says, 'Chief, the computer just beat you' and the Plotter glares at the Recorder, who says 'Just kidding', at which the two of them laugh).

There seems to be little doubt, however, that Bartlett would be pleased to see this kind of analysis. It richly illustrates his emphasis on thinking as situated action in which the thinking that occurs is distributed across people and the artefacts that mediate their actions in a flexible manner. It also illustrates nicely that an analysis of thinking/remembering in context applies as much to modern as to 'primitive' people.

Bartlett and remembering among primitive peoples

Our second contemporary empirical case focuses on the prominence of conventionalisation and schema utilisation in the process of remembering. It also applies these ideas to the lives of people living in the kind of society that Bartlett had in mind when he used the term, 'primitive'. As we noted earlier, Bartlett's own research in such societies is overlooked in the current renaissance of interest in his work. There are good reasons for this oversight, but there are also good reasons for trying to retrieve the virtues to be gained from applying his ideas in such settings.

In *Remembering* (1932), Bartlett suggests that many of the processes such as schema formation that he describes as central to remembering are also relevant to understanding the processes of cultural transformation that accompany intercultural contact. In particular, he argues that whenever two groups come into contact, particular practices or material items may undergo a process of conventionalisation, which includes processes of assimilation, simplification or elaboration as the new item is absorbed into the new group. Further, any new element 'will be conventionalised either as a mere additional instance of an old convention or as the starting point of a new one' (1932, p. 245). The particular direction or form that the new practice takes is shaped by the 'preferred persistent group tendencies' (akin to schema?) characteristic of a group. Bartlett (1932, p. 258) identifies these tendencies as characteristics which can be identified in: (1) multiple historical periods, (2) from different zones in a group's culture and (3) from comparison of the group under normal conditions with the same group in a time of crisis.

In the only foray into research among a primitive group included in *Remembering* (1932), Bartlett reports on what must be considered pilot studies among the Swazi of East Africa. As an example of how 'persistent group tendencies' are reflected in remembering, he reports on an informal experiment he conducted among the Swazi. A farmer with whom he was visiting proposed that Bartlett query his herdsman, who had been present a year before when the man had bought some cattle and who had driven them home after the sale. The farmer had recorded each sale with a description of the cow in a book, which was used as evidence against which to test the herdsman's memory. The herdsman was sent for, and asked to list the cattle his employer had bought the year before and any details he cared to give. The man recalled all the purchases—their prices, their markings and their previous owners—with only two errors on details. Typical descriptions included:

> From Gampoka Likindsa, one young white bull with small red spots for 1 pound;
> From Lolalela, one spotted five year old cow, white and black, for 3 pounds, which was made up of two bags of grain and 1 pound.
>
> (Bartlett, 1932, p. 250)

Although this performance was quite impressive (the man provided information on about a dozen cows although he had not been responsible for the transactions), Bartlett treats it as in no way extraordinary because it presumably reflects the operation of dominant interests of this person and his group.

Bartlett also hypothesised the existence of a second kind of recall in which temporal order serves as the organising principle. 'There is,' he wrote, 'a low-level type of recall which comes as nearly as possible to what is often called rote recapitulation. It is characteristic of a mental life having relatively few interests, all somewhat concrete in character, and no one of which is dominant' (1932, p. 266).

His evidence for rote recapitulation came from the transcripts of a local law court where a man was being tried for the murder of a woman and another woman was called as a witness. The outstanding characteristic of this woman's recall was that she began her account with arising in the morning and proceeded to provide an account of her day in what the magistrate (and we) consider excruciating detail. Each time the magistrate asks her to jump ahead in her narrative to the crucial events, she begins again at the beginning. In defence of his claim that Swazi culture might lend itself to rote recapitulation Bartlett speculated that it was a culture 'with plenty of time, in a sphere of relatively uncoordinated interest, which combined to create this form of recall' (1932, pp. 265–266).

This kind of speculative interpretation of 'the native system' illustrates the very dangers against which Bartlett warned in his earlier work. But even as he erred in his amateur excursion into the ethnography of remembering, he offered an alternative explanation for the woman's behaviour that resonates quite clearly with the contemporary insistence of discursive psychologists on the strategic and situated nature of remembering. In particular, he insisted that when the audience changes so too does the manner of recall and that the most important element in determining the style of remembering was the particular social context in which it occurred.

In the following example, we want to suggest that it is productive to follow Bartlett's principles, but to do so in an ethnographically sophisticated manner that avoids the Eurocentricism of referring to strategically deployed narrative recall as 'rote recapitulation'. We will also highlight the feature of his theory of remembering that is most conspicuous by its absence in his discussion of the Swazi, conventionalisation.

CONVENTIONALISATION AND REMEMBERING THE COLONIAL PAST IN EAST MADAGASCAR

In the last 10 years, anthropologists have addressed the various techniques of colonial transformation and rule, as well as the ways in which the lingering impact of colonialism has transformed the consciousness of people once colonised by a major European power (Comaroff & Comaroff, 1991; Cooper & Stoler, 1997; Dirks, 1992; Mitchell, 1988). In so far as consciousness is constructed through the webs of significance and social practice that constitute culture, the question of remembering cannot help but be relevant to the issue. It is our view that the concept of conventionalisation is especially helpful in understanding how formally colonised peoples reconstitute—and hence re-member—the symbols and material residue of the colonial past in their daily lives.

The Betsimisaraka: A thumbnail sketch

The work we describe here was carried out by the first author among the Betsimisaraka, a group of peasant farmers who inhabit the rainy, and in parts densely forested, east coast of Madagascar. The term Betsimisaraka literally means, 'they who will not be rendered asunder'. Yet ecological circumstances and history have seemingly conspired to 'split apart' the Betsimisaraka many times.

To begin with, communication throughout the area is difficult, hindered by the poor condition of the roads and multiple rivers that cut across the coast. Dating from the colonial period, slow ferries designed to transport cars or cargo can still be found at most river crossings. Today, however, owing to the disintegration of state infrastructure that has characterised Madagascar since 1975, these ferries are in a state of disrepair. As a result, most movement through the area takes place by foot and dugout canoe, as has been true for at least 200 years.

Unlike some Malagasy peoples, the Betsimisaraka never had a centralised kingdom or any institutionalised form of ranking. Instead, Betsimisaraka society is composed of many different exogamous clans or 'kinds'. Although these clans were originally associated with a particular territory, today they are non-localised groupings of people who share a common family origin and taboos. Each ancestry is further composed of several 'great houses' inhabited by the *tangalamena*, the ritual specialist in charge of mediating between the living and the dead. Localised groupings are built around the central plaza where sacrifices take place. Each great house is also linked to a particular tomb. Although certain clans extend over several different villages, the actual ritual/political/communal environment people participate in on a regular basis is the much smaller grouping of the *tangalamena* and his immediate descendants.

The dispersed nature of Betsimisaraka social organisation has made them easy prey for powerful outsiders seeking to use them to their own ends, even while their decentralised way of life also served to shield them from colonial power. In the 19th century, the Merina, the people who inhabit central Madagascar, conquered the Betsimisaraka area in a series of military expeditions. Although early Merina rule affected Betsimisaraka life relatively little, by the late 19th century Betsimisaraka were subject to increased taxation and forced labour in the service of Merina queens. During certain seasons, those who served the Queen had barely enough time to return home before they were called back to work yet again. In addition, Merina officers explicitly sought to deconstruct and reorganise local societies. Their battle was carried out on three fronts: against the cutting of trees in the forest for constructing canoes, against the practice of burning the forest to plant dry rice, and against the construction and inhabitation of temporary shelters in the fields.

In 1895 when the French colonised Madagascar, Betsimisaraka were forced to submit to a new, invasive, predatory, regime. Like the Merina who preceded them, French administrators were also interested in extracting resources and labour from the Betsimisaraka. In addition, however, the French administrators waged an extensive campaign to transform the local culture, or what Bourdieu (1977) refers to as 'habitus'—the local ways of seeing and being.

French efforts at 'civilising' the Betsimisaraka involved a three-pronged strategy of the resettlement of single families into large, multifamily villages, the creation of a cash economy, and the restructuring of local authority structures. By gathering many families together in a single town, French administrators hoped to increase what they called social solidarity, which they believed would lead naturally to the creation of new forms of needs and desires. In turn, these new desires were supposed to motivate Betsimisaraka to work for settlers to obtain cash, which they would then use to pay their taxes. Attacking the problem from several directions, French administrators also imposed a series of taxes that were supposed to make Betsimisaraka need money, which in turn required them to work.

For our purposes here, two new practices that the French introduced need to be singled out for attention, because the ways in which the Betsimisaraka responded to them demonstrate with special clarity the Barlettian notion of conventionalisation at work 'in real life'. One practice was the growing of coffee, and the other was building houses with tin roofs.

The French introduced the practice of growing coffee in two, interrelated ways: On the one hand, the Betsimisaraka were supposed to work for the settlers harvesting their coffee, which was a primary source of wealth in the colonial economy. On the other hand, they were supposed to plant coffee for themselves in order to have a cash crop from which to pay taxes. As one old man explained, an order had come 'from above' telling everybody to plant a certain number of coffee trees, among other things. 'You'd hear, the chief is coming, the chief is coming! And you'd run clean everything. Coffee! Sweet potatoes! Manioc! And they'd come looking for it and if you didn't have the allotted number—15 days in prison in Mahanoro. Fifty coffee plants!' (J. Cole, Fieldnotes, 12 June 1993, p. 163). Yet coffee was not only planted because of administrative constraint. As Fremigacci (1977) points out, planting coffee also liberated Betsimisaraka, because it allowed people to pay off their taxes and so freed them from having to work for the settlers.

Houses with tin roofs enter the picture because, as a way to lessen the costs of local administration, French colonial administrators sought to identify and shape a subaltern élite who were then supposed to help with local administration. French administrators complained constantly that it was impossible to find a local élite because the local groupings were so dispersed. The Betsimisaraka, however, perceived the situation differently. In particular, the possibility of participating in the creation and maintenance of the colonial order provided them with new forms of power on which they might draw. Betsimisaraka society had always been somewhat differentiated, with some families owning slaves whereas others did not. French attempts to incorporate Betsimisaraka into the subaltern ranks of the administration exacerbated these differences in power by providing institutionalised mechanisms for channelling colonial power to particular families. Those Betsimisaraka who participated in the colonial regime took up the practice of building tin-roofed houses like the French administrators and Creole settlers they saw around them. Because they participated in colonial power and to some extent accepted the practices and values of the colonial regime, local administrators, although ethnically Betsimisaraka, might also be called *vazaha*, the word typically used to refer to Europeans. Along with coffee, then, the tin-roofed house became emblematic of the power of the colonial regime, and the different form of social relations for which it stood.

Coffee, tin-roofed houses and ancestors

As a result of the colonial encounter, Betsimisaraka came to perceive the kinds of social relations that coffee and tin-roofed houses symbolised as fundamentally opposed to local forms of social life. For Southern Betsimisaraka, the traditional political, ritual and moral order is predicated on the fundamental connection between the living and the dead, people and their ancestors. Unlike the French, they believe that their village and rice fields are all peopled with the dead among whom the living move. In many ways, the dead are just like the living and share many of the same predicaments and concerns. The most important difference, however, is that the dead can only exist in the memories of the living; if the living forget the dead, the dead are consigned to oblivion. So the dead need the living to remember them, in order to exist. At the same time, the living require the dead, for ancestors are simultaneously the root of prosperity and the sign of any form of social standing one might hope to achieve. Ancestors define one's position among the living; to have powerful ancestors is the mark of a powerful person. Conversely, a powerful and prosperous family is evidence of the potent and efficacious ancestors from which it springs.

Ideally, all ancestors are equally efficacious. As Betsimisaraka often observe, 'God makes equivalent that which he takes', which means that once they die and reach God people are made equal. Whatever a person's status or character in life, no matter how poor, once dead he or she becomes a fat prince or princess who rules over his or her descendants. One indication of this princely status is that all ancestors are believed to have cattle, a primary form of wealth in Madagascar. Precisely because all ancestors are supposed to be equal, however, they are also said to compete incessantly with one another as each seeks to assert his or her power and influence in the world of the living.

When the French introduced coffee and tin houses to the Betsimisaraka, Betsimisaraka found themselves faced with a conflict. On the one hand, they wanted to participate in the new practices brought by the colonial power. On the other hand, however, these new practices were emblematic of the colonial regime, which Betsimisaraka regarded as antithetical to the power of ancestors. At least initially, participation in the colonial regime was perceived as the rejection of the ancestral. This tension is revealed in the fact that although Betsimisaraka made a good deal of money planting coffee, coffee came to represent the acquisition of unseemly quantities of money:

It used to be that few people drank coffee—people who had money drank coffee, princes drank coffee. Coffee used to kill those who planted it (manofa). You'd plant coffee and get huge sacks, and all of a sudden you'd go from not having to having. It was too much for their heads! Their heads would turn with the money! They would go to the Chinese merchant to sell their coffee and get cash and some would be too embarrassed to take the money. Stop, stop they would say! It's too much money. And the merchant would write your name down and give the remaining money to your wife. And some would throw off their ugly raffia clothes and buy fabric. Too much money and their heads would turn! So they started to do the *fafy kafe*—like something transgressed.

(J. Cole, Fieldnotes, 4 September 1993, pp. 221–228)

Further, many people came to believe that coffee, because it was associated with forms of prosperity derived from colonial power, had the power to kill whoever planted it. A similar fate was expected of those who tried to copy the lifestyle of the District Officer by living in a tin-roofed house.

Betsimisaraka responded to the tension they perceived between ancestral and colonial practice by actively trying to transform the meanings associated with coffee and houses through ritual. As the woman quoted earlier mentioned, people started to do *fafy kafe*. A *fafy kafe* is the name for the sacrifice of a bull performed specifically when someone's coffee has been particularly fruitful and brought the owner great wealth. It follows the typical pattern for sacrifice (J. Cole, 1997), except that during the speech performed for the assembled village the amount of coffee is publicly announced and, once the cow is sacrificed, the blood of the bull is poured directly onto one of the coffee plants.

A similar ritual is required of those who complete a house with a corrugated tin roof. The invocation of the ancestors on this particular occasion explicitly notes how the house is made differently than in Malagasy custom. Boards that are used on the floor of a traditional Betsimisaraka palm-thatch house are taken and placed on the walls, trees frequently bought in other parts of the country are used to build the frame, and finally the corrugated iron for the roof and the nails are imported from abroad. As one man explained:

> Let's say I covet the house with the corrugated iron roof over there, I covet the functionary's house over there. I decide to make one too. So I take the corrugated tin from overseas, I take the nails that come from overseas, I take palm thatch, and floor boards. But those things—they're not the same. You take the European and you take the Malagasy and you mix them. You make the European and the Malagasy like kin so that they won't harm the people that live in the house.
>
> (J. Cole, Fieldnotes, 31 July 1993, p. 189)

In short, to prevent the inhabitants of the house from suffering, possibly dying, the house is 'entered' by the ancestors, so that what was originally quite the opposite of ancestral—the functionary's, perhaps the District Officer's house—is made ancestral and thus acceptable for ordinary Malagasy to live in.

The way Betsimisaraka responded to the introduction of coffee and tin houses, which symbolised a cash economy and the power of the state, respectively, reveals many of the characteristics of conventionalisation of which Bartlett wrote. As Bartlett pointed out, new practices may be conventionalised as 'either a mere additional instance of an old convention or the starting point of a new one' (1932, p. 245). Given the ideas about ideal forms of social relations embodied in Malagasy houses and the practices associated with them, it seems clear that the 'house cleansing' is an example of how ritual practice may enable the assimilation of a new instance into an existing framework.

For example, the need to appease houses has a long and developed precedent in Betsimisaraka practice. In traditional Betsimisaraka practice, houses are a constant source of worry, and must be mollified, inhabited and cared for or else they make their inhabitants sicken and die. An inauguration for a plain Malagasy palm-thatch house is required as well, but it differs from the more elaborate ritual performed for a European-style house in that it can be finished with mere rum and doesn't require a sacrifice. The reason given for the 'traditional' house inauguration is that many kinds of trees, each associated with certain qualities and each coming from a different patch of land with a different spirit must be combined and bound 'as one'. Should the spirits of the different trees fight, or should a kind of tree that should be placed high be placed low, then the inhabitants will suffer the consequences.

Another way in which the Betsimisaraka case enriches our understanding of Bartlett's ideas about conventionalisation is that—contrary to the examples where conventionalisation appears to occur without any identifiable human agency —we can identify the social struggles through which the transformation of growing coffee and building tin-roofed houses took place. In particular, several Betsimisaraka actually identified the creation of the cleansing rituals with the social competition between different families, mediated through their remembered ancestors. As one old man put it, when queried about the origins of the ritual: 'Coffee came recently but didn't rule in the days before. It was only when Europeans got the land that coffee came but there wasn't any before. Fafy Kafe is mimicry. Someone's coffee prospered and so they killed a cow and someone copied him and the disease was catching. You show off that you have something good and the disease was catching!' (J. Cole, Fieldnotes, 23 October 1993, p. 256).

Although oral histories suggest that villagers initially perceived ancestral and colonial forms of power as opposed, contemporary practice implies that villagers use the signs and symbols of colonialism in order to constitute ancestral power (see also J. Cole & Middleton, unpublished). New practices such as cash cropping, or styles of building and the ways of life they implied, were symbolically appropriated by local people to their own ends, in part because of local social struggles and the variable ways that Betsimisaraka experienced colonial power. Since coffee and tin houses were emblematic of new forms of power, they became the occasions for social competition, which in local terms plays out in struggles around ancestors. In turn, the demands of the ancestors for sacrifice provided the idiom through which meanings associated with alien practices were configured. Villagers incorporated these alien elements through rituals that simultaneously begged permission from, and offered wealth to, ancestors, thereby symbolically reaffirming their belief that prosperity springs from the ancestors. But the practice of 'cleansing' alien elements also gives additional proof of what the Betsimisaraka already assume: Some ancestors are more powerful than others, and thus have more wealth to command. In both the case of cleansing a tin roof and cleansing coffee, the connection between ancestors and the production of wealth is visually marked by the skull of a bull, which the owner of the house would proudly nail either to the northern edge of the roof or the most abundantly productive tree in his grove. No longer the symbol of alien rule, the tin roof or the coffee have come to symbolise the owner's powerful *ancestral* connections. But as we have shown, that power is partially constituted by those ancestors' ability to command wealth like *vazaha*.

Remembering the rebellion

Before concluding, we want to turn briefly to a different manifestation of the relationship between conventionalisation and remembering among the Betsimisaraka, and particularly to the way in which the content of what is remembered is intimately connected with the social discourse of which it is a part. As we mentioned earlier, Middleton and Crook (1996, p. 382) argue that schemata arising from a process of conventionalisation 'are not knowledge structures stored in the brains or minds of individuals for the interpretation of experience, but functional properties of adaptations between persons and their physical and social environments'. Consequently, they make a convincing case for the claim that 'In a sense germane to the psychology of participants, the truth of original events is the outcome of, not the input to, the reasoning displayed in talk' (p. 391). The power of social discourse to shape memories for events is sharply revealed in the way Betsimisaraka remembered the anti-colonial rebellion of 1947 in state elections that took place in 1993.

The anti-colonial rebellion of 1947 occurred following the electoral victory of the Democratic Movement for Malagasy Renewal (MDRM), a moderate political party that advocated independence for Madagascar but within the context of a French Union. Immediately following the elections, rebel bands began to attack French military bases. In response, colonial officials throughout Madagascar, including the Betsimisaraka area, arrested anyone thought to be an MDRM supporter and held them responsible for the attacks. In the town where J. Cole did her fieldwork, the rebels arrived from the south, whereupon the local residents joined the rebel forces and set out in bands to attack colonial concessions. Ultimately, the French crushed the rebellion with considerable loss of life.

The Betsimisaraka do not normally refer to these events in the contexts of their everyday lives. However, during elections held in 1993, elders constantly evoked the rebellion in conversation as a way to warn younger members of the consequences of certain kinds of political choices that would involve them with the state. In this context, the aspect of the rebellion that elders selectively highlighted was the terrible consequences that resulted from their attempts actively to involve themselves with the colonial state through a modern form of political engagement (voting). Older villagers hoped that by using the rebellion as a moral example, they might influence the outcome of the elections in favour of a candidate they hoped would create a less active state political presence in the village (J. Cole, 1998). Even though the actual events around the rebellion were considerably more complex and might have been mined for other purposes, it was the connection between engaging in state politics and subsequent violence that they chose to deploy. Although it is impossible to predict exactly how the rebellion will be remembered in the future, we can nevertheless hazard a guess that the state–local angle of the events may play a role.

Although one of our examples from the Betsimisaraka focused on practices while the other features discourse, they are united in suggesting that conventionalisation is relevant to understanding several planes of social practice. Conventionalisation implies that processes of reconstruction are relevant to how dominated groups may assert their cultural and political autonomy. Moreover, it should also be clear that Betsimisaraka culture is not a closed system. People's local understandings in the present operate in open systems which are constantly informing and being formed by the ways that alien elements play into local social struggles. Although Bartlett's own work among the Swazi never elaborated the concept of conventionalisation and its relationship to remembering that are so central to his broader work, these examples suggest that, had he applied them, they would have been equal to the task.

CONCLUDING REMARKS

As we noted earlier, we selected our examples to highlight both the relative prominence of conventionalisation and schema formation in different forms of activity where psychological processes such as remembering and thinking are evoked. Our examples were chosen to highlight the usefulness of close ethnographic description as a source of evidence for such psychological processes occurring in context.

We hope that the examples convince the reader of our major point. It is possible to see connections between Bartlett's early and late work and to assess the relative usefulness of different ideas from his entire career. We find it useful to imagine integrating the early and late parts of Bartlett's work, reading the overall corpus as the working out of a common set of ideas on vastly different substantive contents and social conditions. At the present time, the ideas we have discussed here are being actively used across the social sciences. They may, in fact, help us to achieve Bartlett's youthful ambitious goals of a more social psychology of the individual. If so, we might arrive at a set of ideas that would be as productive in the 21st century as they have been in the 20th.

NOTES

1   During the war he also served as a psychiatrist, but this aspect of his work does not appear to have been a major influence on Bartlett.
2   For an informative discussion of the ongoing debates on this issue at the time, see Slobodin, 1978, pp. 160ff.

CHAPTER TEN

Multilevel analyses of social bases of cognition

Akiko Saito

BARTLETT'S WORK ON SOCIAL BASES OF COGNITION

In the general history of psychology, Bartlett's work has suffered a similar fate to that of Wundt in that it has mainly been his experimental cognitive psychology that has been widely acknowledged; the fact that with his social psychology he attempted to develop a systematic study of social bases of cognition has attracted far less attention. After a long period of neglect, occasioned at least in part by the widely established view of Bartlett as a founder of cognitive psychology (which is generally taken as asocial), it is only very recently that his social psychological studies have begun to be scrutinised (e.g. Costall, 1991, 1992; Edwards & Middleton, 1987; Middleton & Edwards, 1990b; Rosa, 1996; Saito, 1994, 1996a; Shotter, 1990). Although these recent studies have done much to highlight Bartlett's extensive concern with social bases of cognition, few attend to what I find to be one of its most distinguishing features, namely that taken in its entirety his approach countenances multilevel analyses of social bases of cognition.

Bartlett does not himself explicitly propound an approach to cognition based on multilevel analyses. Therefore, the first section of this chapter aims to distinguish the various levels of analysis Bartlett adopts in his work; these I term the individual, social–individual interactive, microgenetic, sociogenetic and phylogenetic levels of analysis. The second section of the chapter focuses on one particular level, namely sociogenetic analysis, examining this in some detail both theoretically and empirically. I then go on to discuss Bartlett's sociogenetic analysis in relation to social representation theory, a current research paradigm in social and cultural psychology, illustrating the contemporary relevance of some of Bartlett's ideas. The chapter concludes by suggesting how his multilevel analyses might be extended and incorporated in current efforts to develop a unified framework to encompass biological/cognitive and social studies of human cognition and action, which, I argue, is important for the development of contemporary cultural psychology.

BARTLETT'S MULTILEVEL ANALYSES

Bartlett's work (e.g. 1923, 1932, 1958) taken in its entirety can be seen as comprising multilevel analyses of human cognition. Provisionally, I term these levels of analysis the 'individual', 'social–individual interactive', 'microgenetic', 'sociogenetic' and 'phylogenetic' (Saito, 1996b). Although these are not necessarily fully developed, definitive, or even explicit analyses, none the less in my view they do indicate the distinct nature and scope of Bartlett's work.

The individual analysis

At the level of the individual, Bartlett is concerned with the conditions and functions of cognition, as opposed to its nature. Specifically, he focuses on elucidating a generative process of cognition. There are several notable features of this individual level analysis by Bartlett, which I have expounded upon elsewhere as 'embodied mind' approach (Saito, 1996b), including: recognition of social, individual psychological and biological bases of cognition; placing affect and conation (e.g. values, interests) at the root of cognition; and emphasising the inter-relatedness of various cognitive processes (e.g. perceiving, recognising, remembering, imaging and thinking).

From his experimental studies of individual cognitive processes, Bartlett finds cognition to be an active, selective and constructive process, continuously developing from moment to moment (and hence his consistent use of expressions such as remembering, perceiving and thinking, instead of memory, perception and thought). He describes this generative process of cognition as 'effort after meaning' (e.g. Bartlett, 1932, pp. 20, 44, 188, 227), and proposes that it is constituted to a considerable extent by sociocultural factors such as the individual's social group membership (i.e. social identity) and the group's conventions and values. Bartlett's social psychology (e.g. 1923, 1928b, 1932, 1939b, 1940) was developed specifically to investigate these sociocultural factors.

To address the developmental systems nature of cognition, Bartlett introduces the notion of 'schema', borrowing from Henry Head's (1920) neurophysiological notion (e.g. Bartlett, 1932, p. 200). Criticising Head's notion as being too static, Bartlett redefines schema as 'active organisation of past reactions, or of past experiences' which are 'developing, from moment to moment' and which are 'actively *doing* something all the time' (p. 201, italics in original). To stress this ongoing, open-ended developing constitution, Bartlett uses interchangeably with 'schema' other terms such as 'active, developing patterns', 'active organised setting' (e.g. p. 201) or 'living, momentary settings' (p. 202), which he feels more adequately capture their momentary unfolding formation. He warns against the use of the notion as a 'store-house notion' (p. 200) or 'some persistent, but fragmentary, "form of arrangement"' (p. 201).[1]

Bartlett (1932) finds that when presented with a cognitive object, a responding individual does not take such material detail by detail, meticulously building up the whole, but instead forms a general impression and then constructs the whole in such a way as to justify the general impression. In Bartlett's term, whatever material is presented, there first occurs an arousal of 'attitude' or 'psychological orientation' towards the object, which is largely a matter of 'affect'. The arousal of attitude usually involves immediately beforehand the 'naming' of the object, which sets the object or an aspect of it in relation to some existing already familiar object thus labelled in the social group. The naming renders certain details of the whole dominant, around which other details cluster by way of inference and rationalisation in such a way as to justify or provide a rationale for the initial attitude. In determining the dominant feature, 'physical factors of the material have comparatively little weight in the life of the higher animals and man' and it is 'appetite, instinct, interests and ideals, the first two being much the more important in early stages of organic development, and the last two advancing to positions of great, and very likely of chief, importance at the human level' (p. 210). Such interests and ideals are found to be an interplay of individual (e.g. temperament, character) and social factors.

Further to the psychological and social, Bartlett also recognises physiological bases of individual cognition. For example, he explains auditory perception as involving a combination of two factors, namely hearing and listening. Hearing is immediately physiological, contingent upon the reactivity of the auditory mechanisms whose selectivity is based on stimulus differences of intensity, duration, frequency and so on. Listening is also selective, but here the physiological characteristics of the stimulus play a secondary, though prerequisite, part, determined mainly by the qualitative differences of stimuli in relation to 'predispositions', which are 'cognitive, affective and motor' (Bartlett, 1932, p. 190), and the psychological orientation or attitude (e.g. interests, goals, values) of the listener. In short, in Bartlett's writings, physiological bases are assumed to be prerequisite for human cognition, though they are seen as insufficient by themselves, requiring processing and meaningful organisation by psychological (including social) factors. Bartlett cites the case of a child with speech and hearing difficulties arising from psychological factors, without any particular physical or physiological impairment (pp. 188–191) in his discussion of this.

Although he does not fully develop the idea, Bartlett identifies imaging, which he sees as being closely linked with affect and conation, as playing a pivotal role in bridging the bodily and the psychological and social bases of cognition by constructing a sensory pattern into something having a significance that goes beyond its immediate physiological feature or sensory character. Imaging is also conceived to underlie and thereby interrelate all other 'higher mental processes' such as perceiving, recognising, remembering and thinking (Bartlett, 1932, pp. 215–226).

Similar ideas, albeit in more up-to-date and sophisticated forms, underpin some recent works in the fields of neuroscience and cognitive science (for a review, see Saito, 1996b), which have been proposed as an alternative to the classical cognitivist approach to human cognition, which is largely Cartesian, disembodied, aconative and asocial (e.g. Gardner, 1985). Various terms have been used to describe these new works, including for example 'embodied mind', 'dynamic systems' or 'developmental systems' approaches to human cognition (e.g. Damasio, 1994; Edelman, 1992, 1998; Johnson, 1987; Lakoff, 1987; Varela, 1992).

The social–individual interactive analysis

In his social psychology, Bartlett investigates three main social processes. The first is the way in which 'persistent tendencies' (Bartlett, 1923, 1932) of a social group direct and inform the individual members' cognition. By 'persistent tendencies' of a social group, Bartlett means such 'social facts' as conventions, institutions, norms, values and beliefs that are characteristic of the social group to which the responding individual belongs. From his experimental studies, Bartlett observes that such persistent tendencies of a social group provide the setting of affect, interest and ideal, and thereby direct what individuals observe, notice, perceive, image and remember in their environment:

> In perceiving, in imaging, in remembering proper, and in constructive work [i.e. thinking], the passing fashion of the group, the social catch-word, the prevailing approved general interest, the persistent social custom and institution set the stage and direct the action.
>
> (Bartlett, 1932, p. 244)

Accordingly, Bartlett's study of 'group tendencies' that influence individual members' cognition involves researching the particular 'persistent tendencies' of a social group *per se*, which he postulates to be crystallised in the group's culture, such as its traditions, institutions, moral and religious practices, and material artefacts. Further to such pre-existing features of culture, 'group tendencies' more significantly include 'trends of development' of the group. As far as Bartlett is concerned, every significant social group has not only 'history' but also 'prospect', that is, certain tendencies and lines of development, which 'need not be, and in the majority of cases it certainly is not, present in the mind, or fully represented in the behaviour, of any individual member of the group' (Bartlett, 1932, p. 275).

Taken together, group tendencies as such emerge only out of the collective, interactive (including both co-operative and conflictual) activities of the group members. In this sense, Bartlett's notion of 'persistent tendencies of a social group' or alternatively 'group tendencies' is inherently developmental and open-ended. It is furthermore dialectical in the sense of assuming a dialectical relationship between a social group and individuals.

Rather than assuming a one-way influence from the group to individuals, Bartlett assumes a mutually constituting and two-way influencing relationship between a social group and individuals. In Bartlett's view, a social group is more than a collection of individuals; it is held together and organised with some active tendencies which on the one hand inform the individual members' cognition, and on the other come to manifest themselves only with and through the actions of the individuals (e.g. Bartlett, 1932, pp. 253–255, 275, 311). It is to make explicit this dialectical assumption of the relationship between the social group and individuals, that I term Bartlett's study of group tendencies influencing the individual members' cognition 'social–individual interactive' analysis.

The microgenetic analysis

The second social process Bartlett investigates is the 'actual social presence' (Bartlett, 1932, p. 245) of other individuals influencing an individual's cognition. This includes the interlocutor's effect (i.e. the phenomenon that the mere presence of others influences action and cognition of an individual), as well as other various social situational and interactive factors involved in the particular generative context of cognition at that moment in that place. For example, Bartlett reports that recall in the presence of and for the hearing of other members of the recaller's social group, differs from recall in the presence of and for a foreign audience. The former displays characteristic features of the group; by contrast in the latter the manner and the matter of recall are affected by such factors as the recaller-narrator's social position in her own group and her relation to the audience group (Bartlett, 1932, p. 266). For its analytical focus on intercommunication and social interaction out of which particular cognitive processes are generated, elaborated and/or negotiated, I term this second social process investigated by Bartlett 'microgenetic analysis'. In the aspect of addressing the strategic and socially situated nature of cognition as well as the socially distributed nature of cognition, it is relevant to works of some contemporary cultural psychologists (e.g. Hutchins, 1995; Lave, 1993; Rogoff & Lave, 1984; see also Cole & Cole, Chapter 9).

The sociogenetic analysis

The third social process Bartlett investigates in his social psychology is what he terms 'processes of conventionalisation' (1932, p. 243), that is the processes involved in the development and transmission of shared practice and cognition (e.g. memory, knowledge) that take place *in* and *between* social groups. I term this 'sociogenesis of cognition', and it is examined in some detail later in this chapter.

The phylogenetic analysis

An evolutionary perspective informs the work of a number of seminal early
modern psychologists, including Wundt (1832–1920), Mead (1863–1931), Freud
(1856–1939), Baldwin (1861–1934), Piaget (1896–1980) and Vygotsky (1896–
1934) as well as Bartlett (for detailed analyses of their evolutionary views, see
e.g. Farr, 1996 for the first three; Kahlbaugh, 1993 for Baldwin; Chapman, 1988
for Piaget; van der Veer and Valsiner, 1991 for Vygotsky). For our purposes it
is useful to clarify that Bartlett's evolutionary perspective is distinct from some
others' (e.g. Wundt, Piaget), whose works, however unwittingly or indirectly, led
to the proposition of different stages of cognitive development amongst different
racial or cultural groups (i.e. social evolutionism). Bartlett is evidently opposed
to such a position, regarding it as misconstruing cultural diversity and dis-
tinctiveness (Bartlett, 1923, 1932).[2] Instead, Bartlett's evolutionary approach is
to treat humankind as one and the same species and to place its mind in an evolutionary continuum in relation to other biological organisms. Adopting an evolutionary approach in this way, Bartlett views the human mind or 'higher mental
processes' (e.g. Bartlett, 1932, pp. 2, 248) as the most advanced form of biological adaptation, capable of meeting the variable demands of the external environment, evolved over a long duration of time (e.g. Bartlett, 1932, pp. 217–220,
225, 314). This is of course an outmoded view of phylogeny of human cognition
which assumes a hierarchical relationship between human cognition and those
of the other species. It has to be noted also that Bartlett does not carry out
phylogenetic analysis in any systematic way; rather it is discernible throughout
his writings, as assumptions informing his other analyses of various cognitive
processes (e.g. remembering, imaging, thinking). None the less I provide an
outline of it here, as it is pertinent to the elucidation of the overall scope of
Bartlett's work, especially the multilevel analyses of cognition, and because of
the relevance of phylogenetic analysis to contemporary cultural psychology.

Bartlett (1932) conceives the emergence of higher cognitive processes to
entail, very broadly speaking, three evolutionary stages. He postulates that at the
least developed stage of mental life, an organism's responses are predominantly
determined by physical or 'external static' characters of stimuli, being most
immediately and directly constrained by the organism's own biological constitution. At a more advanced stage, 'psychological orientations' or 'active tendencies'
of the responding organism come into play. Within this stage Bartlett distinguishes subtler levels of development. At the lower level, more elemental and
immediately biologically significant psychological orientations (e.g. 'appetites,
instincts') predominate. At the higher level, more 'advanced' orientations (e.g.
'interests, ideals') predominate, which yield an increase in the diversity and
sensitivity of responses. Furthermore, these advanced psychological orientations
tend to be individually directed at early stages, and at later stages they become
more and more socially directed, being controlled by, say, social conventions,

norms and cultural values. This constitutes the third and organically most advanced stage of mental life, where higher cognitive processes arise. The prerequisite of this stage is the development of a highly complex social life and greatly enhanced ability for communication, which needs precedently the achievement of necessary biological evolution (p. 206).

According to Bartlett's postulates (e.g. Bartlett, 1932, pp. 217–220), 'all important biological advances are marked by two outstanding characteristics'. One is an 'increase in the diversity of reactions to match more nearly the variety of external existing conditions'. The other is 'growth in the capacity to deal with situations at a distance' in terms of time and space ('distance senses' or 'distance reactions') whose biologically earlier examples include sight, hearing and smell. The two together 'mark the superiority of the higher forms of organic life' (p. 217). 'The less developed organisms' (e.g. amoeba) have but a few ways of coming into contact with the external world, and these all result in a few stereotyped responses (p. 218). With a more developed organism, there gradually grows up a greater range of sensory organs and special sense avenues, and correlated movements and reactions. This increase in number and range of reactions is biologically advantageous, making possible greatly increased speed, sensitivity and diversity of reactions, each more or less specialised to its appropriate stimuli. Parallel to this, Bartlett postulates, another process is continually developing, namely 'the ability to be influenced by past reactions' (p. 217), which falls into line with the development of distance senses. Higher cognitive processes are, according to Bartlett, instances of this ability.

In order to explain the evolution of the ability to be influenced by the past, Bartlett elaborates upon his notion of 'schema/ta'. The earliest schemata follow the lines of demarcation of the special senses, giving rise to schemata of, for example, visual, auditory and various types of cutaneous impulses. In a less developed organism, reactions and experiences of immediate biological significance predominate in the generation of schemata, and only in a more developed organism do those connected by its 'active psychological tendencies' (e.g. interests, values) come into play. Epigenesis of schemata concerns not only their range but also their functioning (e.g. Bartlett, 1932, pp. 202–204). At 'the low-level mental life', schemata operate in one direction only; past reactions and experiences which constitute a schema operate in the sequence in which they occurred originally. The general effect is to produce fixed serial reactions and habit behaviours where repetition and circularity of reactions are prominent; if the series fails at any point there is a tendency for complete collapse to set in, or else for the whole series to begin all over again. This has certain biological drawbacks. First, it is uneconomical, because to resume a whole series of behaviours and reactions is often a waste of time. Second, it is unsound, as fixed serial reactions conflict with the demands of a diverse and constantly changing environment. If any marked further advance is to be achieved, an organism must develop an ability to break up this fixed sequence and go directly to that portion which is most relevant to the needs of the moment. Bartlett calls this ability the capacity to 'turn round upon its own schemata' (i.e. reflexivity) and construct them afresh (e.g. pp. 206, 301). This emergence of reflexivity is, according to Bartlett, when and why consciousness arises and is contingent upon a great growth of organised, complex social life where an organism's responses are constantly checked and facilitated by those of others living in the same community (e.g. p. 206). With the evolution of reflexivity and consciousness, which together mark 'a crucial step in organic development' (p. 206), schemata become able to utilise the past in relation to the somewhat changed conditions of the present. Since conditions are always changing (at least in a temporal sense), this is biologically more advantageous. They become 'not merely something that works the organism, but something with which the organism can work' (p. 208). It is the difference between schematic determination and active formation of 'organised settings', the difference between reproduction or recapitulation and construction. At this level, instead of the original sequence of a set of responses, schema construction is controlled by certain elements of the whole, which become dominant in relation to the present (p. 209), and are in turn directed by the interplay of 'appetites, instincts, interests and values' (e.g. pp. 210, 309) of an organism, the latter two being of chief importance at the human level. These cross-streams of organising influence mean that many objects, reactions, stimuli and experiences get organised simultaneously into different active settings or schemata (p. 212).

Through the direct influence of Henry Head and W.H.R. Rivers, Bartlett's ideas on phylogeny of 'higher mental processes' are broadly Jacksonian, a view that was current at the time.[3] Although many of the specific details would not be of much help to contemporary research, Bartlett's analysis is significant in pointing to the right direction, by explicitly taking into account social bases in the evolution of human cognitive processes. This presages contemporary research on social bases in the phylogeny of *Homo sapiens* and its mind (for a review, see e.g. Saito, 1996b).

Analysis of social bases in the evolution of the human mind and cognition, including phylogenetic continuities and discontinuities between *Homo sapiens* and other species, is a requisite for contemporary cultural psychology (Cole, 1990, 1996; Saito, 1996b). It is, however, one of the least developed areas in the field, and merits urgent attention. There are two areas of research that are particularly pertinent to the field. One is sociocultural evolution, a closely related though distinct process from biological evolution, with a significant effect on the evolution of mind and cognition (e.g. Boyd & Richerson, 1985; Plotkin, 1998). The other is the relation between the evolution of sociality and parallel changes in life history and behaviour (e.g. Foley, 1995; Foley & Lee, 1989; Keller & Genoud, 1997). To carry further these areas of research in cultural psychology, one useful line of investigation is to extend one school of social intelligence research which views social intellect, whose defining features include sympathy and morality, as being morphologically more complex than Machiavellian intellect (e.g. Humphrey, 1976; Ridley, 1996; Sober & Wilson, 1998; see also Dugatkin, 1998; Frank, 1998). Other relevant lines of investigation include the study of life course as a social institution (e.g. Buchmann, 1989; Kohli, 1986) and the research on life-span development of *Homo sapiens* from an integrated behavioural, neurobiological and psychosocial perspective (e.g. Cairns et al., 1996; Magnusson, 1996).

SOCIOGENESIS OF COGNITION: CONVENTIONALISATION

As seen in the preceding section, Bartlett's concern with social bases of cognition was more substantial or 'radical' (Costall, 1992) than being simply concerned with social influences on individual cognition: Analysis of cognition at the individual level comprises only one part of his multilevel analyses. Bartlett's research encompasses the socially situated nature and socially distributed and interactive origins of cognition (i.e. microgenesis), and the collective generation of shared cognition (e.g. memory, knowledge, thinking) in and across social groups (i.e. sociogenesis). This section focuses on Bartlett's sociogenetic analysis to examine it in some detail both theoretically and empirically.

Social constructiveness

Bartlett's sociogenetic analysis of cognition is composed mainly of his work on '(social) conventionalisation'. It concerns the social collective generative process of conventions and conventionalised forms of understanding, which typically take the form of the development of shared knowledge, memory and practices in a social group.

As he explicitly acknowledges (e.g. 1932, p. 244; 1958, p. 143), in developing his analysis of 'conventionalisation' Bartlett borrowed the term from Haddon (1894b, 1895) and Rivers (1914d). Bartlett developed the analysis through his series of studies on various cognitive processes including perceiving, imaging, remembering and thinking (e.g. 1916a, 1916c, 1920a, 1920b, 1921, 1923, 1928b, 1932), to expound specifically upon their constructive (as opposed to passive or purely recapitulatory) nature and generative processes.

For example, in *Remembering* (1932), where his analysis of conventionalisation more or less culminates, Bartlett progressively develops the analysis in his experimental studies of memory, including his studies of repeated reproduction (Bartlett, 1932, pp. 63–94) and serial reproduction (pp. 118–185) to account for the systematic changes he was observing. I do not repeat here the details of these experiments and results, which are included elsewhere in this book. He also applies the analysis to his social psychological studies (e.g. pp. 243–244, 268–280). The central question posed in Bartlett's social psychological research on conventionalisation is: 'Here is an element of culture coming into this group from another. What are the main principles of the changes it must undergo before it finally settles down to an accepted form in its new social setting?' (p. 268). In other words, it concerns cultural transmission and transformation.

The specific processes and main principles of conventionalisation which Bartlett expounds in the social psychological studies (i.e. the social group level analysis; for details, see later) are extensions of those he delineates in his experimental studies (i.e. the individual-level analysis). Although Bartlett uses 'conventionalisation' to refer to the processes he observes at both levels, I use the term 'social conventionalisation' in this chapter to make explicit the reference to 'conventionalisation' taking place at the social group level. This follows Bartlett's own convention, as he occasionally prefixes 'social' to some of the main notions he introduces to expound conventionalisation (e.g. 'assimilation', 'schema') when he is referring to the said operation at work at the social group level, as opposed to the individual.

Through his studies of social conventionalisation, as well as his experimental studies on conventionalisation, Bartlett became convinced that mere assimilation and simplification in accord with the pre-existing cultural schemata were insufficient to account for the constructive changes he was observing in his studies. In order to articulate this constructive nature of the transformation process, he introduced the notion of 'social constructiveness'. The idea of social constructiveness marks the clear divergence of Bartlett's notion of conventionalisation from that of Haddon, which stresses the conservative nature of culture only.[4]

'Social constructiveness' refers to the process of transformation being directed not only by existing culture (e.g. social conventions and institutions), but also by the trend of development of the receptive group in relation to the sphere of life involved:

> when any cultural features come from outside, they may be transformed, not only by assimilation, by simplification and elaboration, and by the retention of apparently unimportant elements, but positively *in the direction along which the group happens to be developing* at the time.
>
> (Bartlett, 1932, p. 275, italics in original)

To rephrase Bloor (Chapter 12), Bartlett's work on social conventionalisation elucidates the nature and genesis of group tendencies and cultural schemata (which are in turn embodied in material artefacts, social norms, values, institutions and so on) that influence individual cognition, as being social collective entities themselves.[5] It does this with an explicit emphasis on the constructive nature of culture or the social group; a social group is maintained by its *activity* as well as its more or less stable structure, possessing not only a 'history' but also current needs and a 'prospect', that is, certain directions rather than others in which it tends to develop (e.g. Bartlett, 1932, p. 275).

Bartlett finds that the study of cultural transmission and transformation provides a particularly useful means to research the social collective nature and generative process of conventionalised forms of understanding (e.g. shared knowledge, memory, thinking and practices). I surmise that this came about for several reasons, including the following. First, the study, by being intrinsically cross-cultural, provides an initial reference point from which to analyse the generative, transformation process. Second, 'social constructiveness', that is, the genuinely creative and constructive nature of culture or a social group, was one of the main focuses in Bartlett's study of the generative process of conventionalised forms of understanding, which can be demonstrated in a striking manner in cross-cultural comparative studies.

Four principles

Bartlett expounds upon the processes of social conventionalisation as entailing four main principles or operations. They are 'assimilation', 'simplification and elaboration', 'the retention of novel though trivial details' and 'social constructiveness'. For the following expositions, I draw on Bartlett's chapter on conventionalisation (1932, pp. 268–280), supplemented by his accounts of these processes given in his experimental studies (1932, chaps. I–VIII), which are very informative in providing illustrations of the finer details.

Assimilation refers to a process in which only those aspects or details of a cultural element or material transmitted to a social group for which there already exists a suitable background in the culture of the receptive group, become adopted (Bartlett, 1932, pp. 270–271); conversely, those elements or certain details for which there is no suitable background will fail to be adopted. Assimilation involves the assignment of a 'name', i.e. 'naming' (e.g. pp. 32, 107, 116, 128, 179, especially 183–185). Through 'naming', the material is accorded a distinctive 'name', through which in turn it becomes classified into a '(social) schema' and then situated into a specific sphere of life of the receptive group. Through 'naming', the material is given a specific identity and starts to acquire representational significance and concrete features associated with the label (i.e. the 'name') in the group. Through classifying, i.e. being mapped onto the concrete life of the group, it acquires further embodied features and significance which are conventional and meaningful in the new group. Providing this specific 'name' and 'social schema' often involves 'affective attitude'. The experience of a certain feeling is attached, not to the material as such, but to the mental process of assigning to it a more or less definite significance. This assigned 'name' and 'social schema', along with the 'persistent tendencies' (e.g. existing social conventions, institutions, values, trends of development) of the group, make certain details of the element dominant. These details then serve to act as the central feature, a nucleus around which other details will cluster. In this way, the element becomes gradually transformed into a new whole, which appears 'familiar' and 'conventional' to the group (i.e. 'conventionalised').

This gradual transformation involves 'simplification and elaboration', whose primary function is defined as 'the changing of the unfamiliar into some more familiar counterpart' (Bartlett, 1932, p. 138). Details which appear to the new group detached from the central feature of the conventional representation of the element, and details which appear irrelevant to the construction of a more coherent whole as far as the recipient group is concerned, are likely to be omitted or simplified. In turn, the element is elaborated along the direction of the 'persistent tendencies' of the new group. Elaboration takes various forms. One is the interpolation of details which are not in the original. Some such elaborations are described by Bartlett as 'inferences' and 'rationalisation' (e.g. pp. 174–175), for their effect of making the whole appear more logically coherent for the new group. Another common form of elaboration is 'bias towards concrete' or 'concretisation', which refers to 'a strong tendency to develop a concrete form whenever possible', achieved through, for example, a tendency 'to take on a personal form' and the use of 'popular phraseology' and 'conventional social phrases' current in the group (e.g. pp. 172–173).

Further to the transformations brought about by simplification and elaboration, the third principle, the retention and sometimes even exaggeration of peculiar though minor details may give an entirely new bias to the element concerned (Bartlett, 1932, pp. 273–274). Bartlett suggests that this persistence of the apparently unimportant, detached, though novel details of a complex whole must somehow have a significance for the group which retains them. He surmises that this significance may in some cases be no more than that by standing apart from those features of the whole that have an immediate social background and representative significance, they are most of all free from the transforming influence of assimilation. He also suggests that, in other cases, the significance may be more positive, in that their retention forms the readiest means of identifying the home from which the material came, so that a clear mark of its 'exotic origin' is maintained while at the same time the form of the whole is progressively conventionalised.

Finally, the series of transformations is directed not only by the pre-existing culture, but also by the trend of development of the group, i.e. 'social constructiveness'. This has a parallel effect, that the development of a new whole entails not only changes in the newly assimilated cultural element, but also changes in the social schema to which the element is classified and in the sphere of life of the group into which the element is set and incarnated. For Bartlett, the schema is initiated by the naming of the element, which takes place at the initial stage of the processes of conventionalisation. The schema sets the element into relation with other extant ones which are already in the culture and social possessions of the group, and subsequently determines the direction of its transformations. However, here the group's social constructive forces are also operating at the same time in determining the direction. As a consequence, in the course of the series of transformations, the schema itself is constructed afresh integrating certain new features of the element in the direction along which the group is developing, while the element becomes thoroughly enfolded into it. In this way, the new element comes to constitute an integral part in its own right of the given schema and the culture of the group, and contributes thereafter in assimilating other cultural elements.

Each single transformation may be small and is often hardly noticeable when viewed in isolation. Yet its cumulative effect, accrued in the course of the cultural element being passed on from one group to another and from person to person within the group, can be radical. The new whole constructed out of the cumulative changes invariably gains features characteristic to the recipient group while losing features characteristic to the group of its origin.

It has to be noted that the four principles or operations recounted earlier carry no implication of chronological order in relation to the transformation process, and may very well operate concurrently, except for 'assimilation', which is involved at the very first stage.

A major function of conventionalisation, especially social constructiveness, is, according to Bartlett (1932, p. 275), 'to weld together elements of culture coming from diverse sources and having historically, perhaps, very diverse significance'. This creative nature of the process is attributed to the dynamics and constructive nature of a social group; as far as Bartlett is concerned, 'while probably the most effective *stimulus* to change comes in the main from social contacts, important social *forms* of culture may genuinely grow up within the group' (pp. 275–276, italics in original).

At the same time, however, Bartlett assumes a dialectical relationship between culture or a social group and individuals, which he sees as two-way influencing and mutually constituting, as noted earlier. Accordingly, he attempts to investigate social group–individual interaction and dynamics involved in the process of social conventionalisation (e.g. Bartlett, 1923). They include the social status of the pivotal individual(s) who introduces the new element (hereafter 'innovator') and their particular individual styles, the development of a new social group which pro-actively accepts the new element (hereafter 'special interest group'), the relation between the innovator(s) and the special interest group, and that between the special interest group and the rest of the society. None the less, this work is not elaborated, and is even expunged in the subsequent writings of Bartlett on social conventionalisation (1932). In order to elucidate social group dynamics and social group–individual interaction involved in the process of social conventionalisation, it would appear to merit further attention from researchers today.

Finally, on a methodological note, Bartlett's study of social conventionalisation involves a social collective analytical perspective, which has been a distinctive element of European social psychology since its foundation (Farr, 1996; Saito, 1998). Bartlett maintains that many of his social psychological studies, including the study of social conventionalisation, are not amenable to experimental studies: 'Most of these are beyond the reach of experimental investigation', as he puts it (Bartlett, 1932, p. 12). Concomitantly he claims social psychology 'is not to be treated as if it were independent of sociology' (p. 2), himself drawing on anthropological and sociological methods, including field research and ethnological studies.

A case study: Conventionalisation of Zen in Britain

Concerning the operationalisation of his notion of conventionalisation, in particular social constructiveness, Bartlett makes several suggestions. First, he suggests the development of a religious or political group such as the Society of Friends (i.e. the Quakers) and the English Labour Party as (potentially) providing good empirical illustrations (e.g. Bartlett, 1932, p. 279). Second, he recommends selecting social groups that possess sufficiently distinct cultures and social conventions as subjects of study; the more divergent their social conventions, the greater chance there is for observing marked transformation, providing an opportunity for probing analyses. Taking into account these suggestions by Bartlett, I conducted a case study to examine empirically his notion of conventionalisation by investigating the transmission of Zen to Britain from Japan.

The case study comprised two parts. The first was a historical and sociological investigation of Zen's transmission to Britain from Japan. It investigated the history and social organisation of Zen in the two societies, using archival research, mass-media analyses and ethnological studies involving participant observation as well as interviews among Zen professionals (e.g. monks, scholars, Zen group or institution leaders). This was aimed at providing a macro-level analysis of the transformation, examining large-scale phenomena such as the establishment and nature of social organisations relating to Zen and the relation of Zen to general culture. The second part of the study consisted of an examination of current, everyday conceptions of Zen held by members of the general populace in the two societies. In-depth, semi-structured interviews were conducted among 40 respondents, 10 (5 men and women, one each in their 20s, 30s, 40s, 50s and 60s) from each of the following groups: Japanese Zen practitioners, Japanese Zen non-practitioners, British Zen practitioners and British Zen non-practitioners. The definition of a 'practitioner' is a lay person who takes an active interest in Zen, and excludes professionals (e.g. Zen monks or scholars) whose views were covered in the first part of the study.

For detailed results of the study, please see Saito (1996a). Here I provide only an abstract of the findings to illustrate that such an operationalisation or empirical application of Bartlett's notion of social conventionalisation is indeed possible, and that his notion contains interesting research ideas that are worth further empirical research. It has to be stressed that in isolation this case study is inadequate to justify fully the relevance of Bartlett's work on social conventionalisation, and further studies would be required to test his propositions thoroughly.

Both parts of the study revealed a notable transformation of Zen in its assimilation in Britain. In Japan Zen was identified as *zazen* (sitting practice), which is in turn a means of *shugyo* (disciplining and training the physical through which the mind is also disciplined; e.g. cultivation of perseverance and self-discipline), a conventional social value in Japan. In Britain, Zen is a form of Eastern religion that is esoteric and mystical, unlike traditional religions such as Christianity, and which is closely associated with the counter-culture of the 1960s and its adjunct features (e.g. experimentation with drugs, transcendental experience and psychotherapies).

Results obtained from both parts of the study broadly supported the four main principles of social conventionalisation, namely assimilation, simplification and elaboration, the retention of novel though not central details and social constructiveness. Some finer details of each principle were also discerned. For example, 'concretisation' as a form of 'elaboration' was illustrated in this study in a number of ways. These included 'the use of conventional social phrases' (e.g. 'to enter from a [physical] form', 'state of nothingness' amongst the Japanese; 'paradox' amongst the British), 'the use of popular phraseology' (e.g. 'Zen and the Art of . . .', 'Zen and Motorcycle . . .' amongst the British), as well as 'taking on personal forms' (e.g. features of Zen comprising a part of social identity for individual British Zen practitioners; attributes of Zen discussed by the Japanese with illustrations from their own everyday, mundane activities in general spheres of life). However, the results also suggested that some details require elaboration and refinement, in particular the concept of 'rationalisation' and some aspects of 'retention of novel though not central details'.

The main effect of conventionalisation, especially social constructiveness, i.e. that the element becomes constructed into a new whole which acquires features characteristic to the recipient group, replacing those features characteristic to the communicating group, was also observed. British Zen was found to omit physical details (which constitute the central feature of Japanese Zen) and instead acquired features distinctive to the British.[6] Foremost amongst these were an association with 'the East', which is in turn closely linked with mysticism and esotericism, as well as the interpolation of philosophical, theistic and mental details that are delineated in comparison with Christianity.

One issue suggested from this case study was the need to develop Bartlett's insight that social–individual interaction and social (sub-)group dynamics underpin in an important way the process of social conventionalisation. In the first part of my study, I distinguished three broad epochs in the transmission and assimilation of Zen in Britain. The first epoch is pre-1930, which is characterised by the very limited transmission of Zen in the UK. The second epoch is 1930–70, which witnessed the appearance of three key exponents of Zen (i.e. D.T. Suzuki, Christmas Humphreys, Alan Watts), the beginning of a wider diffusion of Zen and the establishment of the first Zen groups amongst an interested British public. The third epoch is post-1970, when Zen has become more widely diffused throughout society; there were approximately 50 Zen groups and organisations in Britain at the time of the study, circa 1990–92, which were scattered across the country from Aberdeen (in the most north-eastern part of Britain) to Penzance (in the most south-western part of Britain). The first part of the study demonstrated that certain aspects raised by Bartlett, such as the social status and personal styles of the innovators, their relation to the special interest groups and the status of the special interest groups in the society, strongly inform the conventionalisation process. The study also suggested that the relationships amongst the innovators, amongst members of special interest groups and amongst different special interest groups, were also pertinent to the conventionalisation process, and that the nature of these relationships included the distribution of power and resources.

IN RELATION TO SOCIAL REPRESENTATION THEORY

The theory of social representations was proposed by Serge Moscovici (1961/ 1976) in his study of assimilation of psychoanalysis into 1950s French society. It is generally understood as a social-psychological revising of Emile Durkheim's (1898) concept of collective representation to research socially shared cognition, in particular common sense or everyday knowledge (Graumann, 1988; Leyens & Codol, 1988; Leyens & Dardenne, 1996). Research associated with the new theory was initially carried out primarily in France (e.g. Abric & Kahan, 1972; Chombart de Lauwe, 1971/1978; Codol, 1974; Doise, 1985; Herzlich, 1973; Moscovici, 1972). During the 1980s it began to attract the attention of other European social psychologists, especially following the publication of the first compendium of social representation research to appear in English, *Social Representations*, edited by Farr and Moscovici (1984). Since then, social representation theory has fast ascended in popularity to become one of the major research paradigms in European social psychology, and today secures for itself a routine entry in European social psychology textbooks (e.g. Hewstone, Stroebe, Codol & Stephenson, 1988; Hewstone, Stroebe & Stephenson, 1996; Hogg & Vaughan, 1995). In particular, it is generally credited as revitalising a distinct tradition of European social psychology that takes into account the social collective perspective in the analysis of human cognition and behaviour, complementing the dominant trend of North American social psychology whose primary analytical unit remains restricted to the individual (Farr, 1996). Besides Europe, there is a rapidly growing community of social representation researchers in Asia and South America (e.g. Campos, 1998; Ho & Chiu, 1998; Kim, 1997), and the theory also appears to be catching on in North America and in the South Pacific (e.g. Augoustinos, 1990; Goodnow, 1996; Oyserman & Markus, 1998).

In the early stage of introduction of social representation theory to the English social psychological literature, Jahoda (1988, p. 205) noted its Bartlettian heritage: 'A much more direct intellectual ancestor is Bartlett (1958) whose idea of what he called "everyday thinking" seems to have been utilised by Moscovici in his theory, though Bartlett is not given any credit.' More recently, the Bartlettian lineage has begun to be acknowledged explicitly in social representation research literature. For example, Farr (1998, p. 279) states 'An important source of inspiration for Moscovici in developing his theory were the studies by Bartlett.' Moscovici himself refers to his analysis of 'objectification' in his theory as being influenced by Bartlett's work (Moscovici & Marková, 1998, pp. 389–389). Taking these comments further, in this final section, I will examine affinities between Bartlett's work, especially on social conventionalisation, and social representation theory with a view to providing an example of contemporary application of Bartlett's work.

According to Moscovici, one of the strengths of his theory is that the lack of precise definition avoids the premature restriction of intellectual advance by tying the concept to a single empirical procedure (e.g. Moscovici, 1985). None the less, in order to provide some orientation as to the nature and contour of the theory for those who are unfamiliar with it, one of the most cited delineations of the theory is offered here:

> By social representations we mean a set of concepts, statements and explanations originating in daily life in the course of inter-individual communications. They are the equivalent, in our society, of the myths and belief systems in traditional societies; they might even be said to be the contemporary version of common sense.
>
> (Moscovici, 1981, p. 181)

In Moscovici's theory (e.g. 1981, 1984), social representation[7] is composed of two processes. The first one is 'anchoring', which is in turn constituted by 'classifying' and 'naming', through which the unfamiliar is assimilated into the familiar categories of everyday cognition. The second is 'objectification', through which still abstract representations are gradually transformed into something concrete by being projected into the world. 'Objectification' entails two stages. In the first stage, a new, still abstract representation becomes more concretised (e.g. psychoanalysis is understood as being similar to religious confession and becomes associated with some of its attributes). In the second stage, the elaborated representation achieves independence from the original milieu and becomes accepted as a 'conventional' reality (Moscovici, 1984, p. 39).

These major constructs, namely 'anchoring', 'classifying', 'naming' and 'objectification', all seem to have equivalents in Bartlett's notion of social conventionalisation recounted in the prior section. The first three constructs are explained in Bartlett's work under 'assimilation' and 'naming'. As for 'objectification', Moscovici himself acknowledges Bartlett's influence as noted earlier. The first stage of objectification is effectively explained in Bartlett's notion under the operations of 'naming', 'social schema' and most pertinently 'elaboration', which includes 'concretisation'. Incidentally, Bartlett's examples of 'concretisation' include 'the use of popular phraseology and social phrases' and 'taking on personal forms'; Moscovici also notes the use of popular phraseology in his exposition of objectification (e.g. Moscovici, 1984) as well as 'personification' (Moscovici & Hewstone, 1983). The second stage of objectification corresponds to Bartlett's accounts of the final stage of conventionalisation: the new element becomes an integral part of the life and culture of the group in its own right, while becoming thoroughly conventionalised.

Besides these major constructs, other important affinities include 'making the unfamiliar familiar' as a primary function of conventionalisation and social representation respectively (e.g. Bartlett, 1932, pp. 128, 138, 174, 178, 181, 182; Moscovici, 1981, p. 188, 1984, pp. 23–28, especially p. 24), and the most fundamental role of social representation, namely to 'conventionalise' (Moscovici, 1984, p. 7, italics in original.) Similarly Bartlett expounds the 'affective'[8] attitude involved in 'naming', while Moscovici stresses the 'affective' nature of social representations. Furthermore, Bartlett's notions of 'concepts', 'percepts', 'image' and 'meaning'[9] could be seen as presaging Moscovici's idea of a social representation occupying a curious position situated between 'concepts' and 'percepts', entailing two interdependent facets of 'image' and 'meaning' (e.g. Moscovici, 1984, p. 17).

Perhaps the most significant affinity between Bartlett's work on social conventionalisation and Moscovici's social representation is the object of study, that is the development and transmission of a conventionalised form of understanding, or alternatively put, everyday knowledge/thinking and practice, which is continuously developing in a social group. Yet there are subtle but none the less important differences in the ways in which the two approach this object of study. The first difference is the intended scope. Bartlett's work on social conventionalisation concerns sociogenetic analysis per se, which constitutes one element in his overall multilevel analyses of cognition. Social representation theory, on the other hand, although commencing with sociogenetic analysis (i.e. Moscovici's La Psychanalyse: Son image et son public, 1961/1976), is now being expanded to include explicitly other levels of analysis such as the ontogenetic (for further details, see Duveen & Lloyd, 1990). Moscovici's vision of his theory is indeed ambitious. He sees it 'to be theory unifying the field of social psychology' (Moscovici & Marková, 1998, p. 409) and also as providing 'the modern theory of cognition', the embryo of which, in his view, lies in the works of Durkheim and Lévy-Bruhl, which was developed by Piaget's and Vygotsky's 'developmental psychology and . . . elaborated in social psychology in the theory of social representations' (Moscovici, 1998a, pp. 427–428). Taken together, the intended scope of social representation theory is much broader than that of Bartlett's work on social conventionalisation.

The breadth of social representation theory has been seen as a strength and a weakness at the same time. It is taken as a strength by social representation researchers demonstrating the 'versatility' of the theory (e.g. Allansdottir, Jovchelovitch & Stathopoulou, 1993); but a weakness by critics who see it as a cause of both the theory's 'fuzziness' (e.g. Leyens & Dardenne, 1996), and its numerous logical contradictions and theoretical inconsistencies (e.g. Gergen, 1989; Harré, 1984, 1985; Jahoda, 1988; McKinlay & Potter, 1987; Parker, 1987). In my view, one way in which to answer the criticisms is to distinguish explicitly and expound in detail the various levels of analysis that are envisioned as constituting social representation research; in other words, to adopt a multilevel analysis (although this may take a different form from Bartlett's). This may have already been implicitly recognised by some social representation researchers. For example, in introducing their edited volume, which compiles developmental psychological studies that apply a social representation framework, Duveen and Lloyd (1990) attempt to distinguish three levels of social representations, namely ontogenesis, microgenesis and sociogenesis.

The second difference lies with the cultural dimension. As discussed earlier, the focus on the creative and dynamic nature of a social group and culture *per se* is a primary feature of Bartlett's work on conventionalisation. This focus does not appear to figure centrally in Moscovici's theory. A similar point is raised by Farr who calls for a modernisation of the theory 'to restore the cultural dimension' (1998, pp. 288–293, 279–281). Moscovici, though, claims that 'the idea of social representations is fundamental not only in the past but also in the future for a vigorous cultural psychology . . . [being] at the core of its genetic code' (1998a, p. 428). It is true that social representation theory emphasises the dynamics of social representation by distinguishing itself from Durkheim's 'collective representation', on which ground it is widely taken, amongst social representation researchers, as addressing cultural dynamics. However, when contrasted with Bartlett's work, one aspect missing in Moscovici's theory is the notion of 'social constructiveness', that is the idea that the genetic process of a conventionalised form of understanding or shared knowledge/thinking is directed by existing culture and social conventions as well as by the current needs and trends of development of the social group.

Other examples of Bartlett's insights on social-group and cultural dynamics that do not appear to feature strongly in social representation theory include the mutually constituting dialectical relationship between a social group and individuals, and the social (sub-)group interactions and the social group–individual interactions. Moscovici (e.g. 1988) does refer to, for example, conflicts between different social representations held by the different social sub-groups that make up society; none the less, his focus is on the conflicts in terms of the content of social representations, and not the social relationships or interactions between the social sub-groups *per se*. However, Moscovici is also acknowledged as a researcher on minority influence, and this work may merit being explicitly brought in line with his social representation theory. This might contribute to the contemporary extension of Bartlett's unfinished work on social group dynamics and social–individual interaction underpinning the sociogenesis of everyday thinking and practice.

Social psychology of knowledge

Moscovici's theory has been claimed to constitute a 'social psychology of knowledge' or occasionally a 'social constructionist' approach to knowledge (e.g. Moscovici, 1988; Moscovici & Marková, 1998). This raises two issues that provide further points of affinity between Moscovici's theory and Bartlett's.

The first issue concerns the two works' similar relation to particular forms of 'social constructionism',[10] which Marková calls 'radical forms of discourse analysis' (Moscovici & Marková, 1998, p. 404) or borrowing Danziger's (1997) term 'the dark forms of constructionism' (Moscovici & Marková, 1998, p. 394). In relation to the view that discourse analysis and social representation theory are essentially similar, Moscovici and Marková (pp. 404–407) expound important differences between the two approaches; however, Moscovici also points out that the majority of discourse research (e.g. Billig, 1987; Harré, 1998; Potter & Litton, 1985; Potter & Wetherell, 1998) does not contradict but complements aspects of social representation research concerned with language (Moscovici, 1998b, p. 246; Moscovici & Marková, 1998, p. 405). Similarly some discourse analysts (e.g. Edwards & Middleton, 1987; Middleton & Edwards, 1990b) have argued that Bartlett's work is compatible with and provides support for their position, namely 'discourse provides the most natural basis for studying social cognition in general' (Edwards & Middleton, 1987, p. 89). To this view, others have noted (e.g. Rosa, Chapter 5; Saito, 1996b) that discourse analysis may well be an important element to further Bartlett's (and others') work concerned with social bases of cognition; none the less, there are some issues to be resolved, including the modification of a strong claim amongst some discourse analysts for the hegemony of discourse at the expense of other integral bases of cognition such as the biological and the other social. Cole and Cole's study (Chapter 9) suggests a fruitful convergence of discursive psychology (e.g. Middleton & Crook, 1996) and Bartlett's work. Such mutual fertilisation amongst discourse analysis, social representation research and Bartlett's psychology is to be encouraged, whilst paying due attention to current differences. In this undertaking, it would also be beneficial to take into account other contemporary approaches in cultural psychology that are concerned with language, communication and cognition, such as for example narrative approach (e.g. Bruner, 1990; Nelson, 1989, 1993b).

Second, one of the main topics in social representation research has been the transformation of scientific knowledge. Bloor (Chapter 12) shows that Bartlett's work on 'social constructiveness' is a precursor to today's social constructivism in the sociology of scientific knowledge. He suggests that, in Bartlett's work, the main ingredients of today's sociology of scientific knowledge can all be found, including underdetermination, conventionalisation, the study of reception, the importance of conflict, concern with practice, the role of metaphor, anti-individualism, methodological symmetry and reflexivity. This dimension of Bartlett's work might be used to extend the aspect of social representation theory that is concerned with research on scientific knowledge. This might entail, however, a careful examination of Moscovici's distinct concern with 'the problem of modernity' (e.g. 1998a), which includes his view that in 'the modern society' we should study the transformation of scientific knowledge to common sense, as opposed to 'the traditional society' or 'the pre-modern world', where the reverse, that is, the transformation of common sense to scientific knowledge, constitutes a more pertinent question to research.

It should also be noted that, within social representation research, attempts to apply aspects of Bartlett's work to the investigation of the diffusion and transformation of scientific knowledge into common-sense knowledge have just begun to emerge (e.g. Bangerter & Lehmann, 1997) and whose development is keenly awaited.

Dialectical paradigm

Marková discusses 'the dialectic paradigm' as characterising social representation theory, as opposed to 'the Platonic/Cartesian paradigm' (Moscovici & Marková, 1998, p. 394). According to Marková, the dialectic paradigm is distinguished from the Platonic/Cartesian paradigm in terms of its ontological assumptions about reality: The former views culture and mind as interdependent and hence studies, for example, their co-development and the interdependence between thought/thinking and language/speaking; whereas the latter treats various cognitive processes as discrete information-processing entities or cause–effect relations, and studies them as isolated processes. This dialectic paradigm is shared, in her view, by some other social scientific approaches to mind including Bakhtinian dialogism, the Vygotskian sociocultural approach, Valsiner's co-constructivism, Nelson's theory of cognitive development and the Prague School of structuralism. I would add to this list Bartlett's approach; I have suggested elsewhere (Saito, 1996b, p. 415) that an epistemological feature of Bartlett's work, which I have termed 'embodied mind approach', is compatible with what Marková (1982) describes as 'the dialectic paradigm' as an alternative to the Cartesian. Marková (Moscovici & Marková, 1998, pp. 394–395) notes that in the approaches in the dialectical paradigm inhere epistemological differences, resulting in subtle differences in terms of operationalisation of the respective approaches. She leaves detailed analysis as a future task that merits swift follow-up. This would contribute to the development of the dialectical approaches and thereby contemporary cultural psychology (all the examples Marková mentions are approaches in cultural psychology).

CONCLUSION

In this chapter I have distinguished several levels of analysis of cognition that Bartlett uses in his work, which I term the individual, social–individual interactive, microgenetic, sociogenetic and phylogenetic. Although Bartlett does not explicitly promulgate the notion of multilevel analyses of human cognition, and moreover many of his notions require further elaboration, I have suggested that his overall approach, as well as some specific elements of his analyses, appears to merit further consideration in contemporary cultural psychology.

In particular, his various levels of analysis explicitly acknowledge biological and individual psychological as well as multiplex social bases of cognition. Some contemporary approaches in social and cultural psychology simply tend to assume the hegemony of the social or a particular social basis at the expense of the other bases; but Bartlett's work suggests ways in which the interaction of the three integral bases (i.e. social, individual psychological and biological) of cognition, as well as the relations amongst the various social bases, might be constructively explored. This is similar to recently proposed 'embodied mind' approaches to cognition and the 'framework of developmental science' (Cairns et al., 1996; Magnusson, 1996), which attempt to bring together findings from biological sciences, neuroscience and various sub-disciplines of psychology (e.g. developmental, social and cognitive). One commonality of these approaches is a developmental systems perspective, which unifies various levels of interrelated activities, for example neuronal group selection, individual behaviour and cognition, human life-span development, and phylogenetic development of *Homo sapiens* in a particular physical and social environment. Empirical research examining the interplays between individual and social bases of cognition has recently begun (e.g. Azmitia, 1996; Damon, 1996; Staudinger, 1996); further research on each particular level and on their interface is eagerly awaited.

Second, I have focused theoretically and empirically upon Bartlett's socio-genetic analysis, or what he terms (social) 'conventionalisation'. I have suggested that it would be valuable to develop some of his seminal ideas, including the notion of 'social constructiveness', and the dialectical relationship between culture or a social group and individuals. This would be consistent with Douglas's (Chapter 11) call for a new social psychological approach to take social institutions fully into account in the study of social bases of cognition.

Third, I have examined affinities between Bartlett's work, especially his sociogenetic analysis, and the contemporary theory of social representation, with a view to providing an example of contemporary research which could be seen as applying aspects of Bartlett's work in social and cultural psychology. My analysis has shown certain parallels between Bartlett's work and social representation theory; however, there are also equally important differences between the two works, including some of the focuses in terms of empirical analysis. I have suggested that in the development of social representation theory as a form of cultural psychology there may be value in restoring and developing some of the ideas stressed in Bartlett's work, in particular social constructiveness and the dialectical relationship between culture or a social group and individuals.

My analysis in this chapter has focused mainly on Bartlett's sociogenetic analysis, and it should be stressed that his other levels of analysis also merit critical scrutiny both empirically and theoretically. But if this chapter has succeeded in making a first step towards elucidating the pertinence of some aspects of Bartlett's work to contemporary cultural psychology and stimulating further debate, its goal has been fulfilled.

NOTES

1   It should be noted that Bartlett's notion of schema assumes that schemata underpin not only cognitive processes (e.g. remembering, thinking) but also physical and physiological processes. In this respect, Bartlett's notion maintains, albeit implicitly, Head's conceptualisation of schemata of neurophysiological processes underpinning behaviour: 'The active settings [i.e. schemata] . . . are living and developing, are a complex expression of the life of the moment and help to determine our daily modes of *conduct*' (Bartlett, 1932, p. 214, my italics). And also: 'When I make the stroke [in a game such as tennis or cricket] I do not, as a matter of fact, produce something absolutely new, and I never merely repeat something old. The stroke is literally manufactured out of the living, *visual and postural "schemata"* of the moment and their interrelations' (Bartlett, 1932, p. 202, my italics).

2   It is true that there are elements in Bartlett's work that might be taken as ethnocentric. For example, Cole and Cole (Chapter 9) and Douglas (Chapter 11) point to Bartlett's assumption of rote recapitulation as a typical mode of remembering amongst the Swazis; none the less, a closer scrutiny of the text (Bartlett, 1932, pp. 264–266) reveals that Bartlett also offers an alternative explanation for this, which is noted by Cole and Cole. As shown by some (e.g. Kashima, 1997; Rosa, 1996, and Chapter 5), read in the context of the time when social evolutionism was widely held amongst scientists as well as the general populace, Bartlett's cultural and cross-cultural studies are remarkably free of this view. It is possible to trace this basic approach of Bartlett at least in part to that adopted by one of his most influential teachers at Cambridge, W.H.R. Rivers. Rivers was originally influenced by the Spencerian social evolutionist view, yet after carrying out fieldwork in the Torres Straits in 1898, he no longer subscribed to this view (see for details, Herle & Rouse, 1998; Jahoda, 1982).

3   See also Rosa (Chapter 5) for Jacksonian influence on Bartlett's work.

4   See also Bloor (Chapter 12).

5   In this respect, Bartlett's sociogenetic analysis in effect subsumes his social–individual interactive and microgenetic analyses of cognition.

6   They are distinctive to the British, featured neither in Japanese Zen nor Zen in any other Western countries, such as the USA, Germany or France, where Zen has been transmitted.

7   Following Duveen and Lloyd (1990) and Wagner (1996), I use 'representation' in the singular to refer to the process and 'representations' in the plural to refer to the product or structure of social representation.

8   The notion of 'affect' constitutes a central construct in Bartlett's work on cognition and memory at large. For details, see Larsen and Berntsen (Chapter 7), Rosa (Chapter 5) and Saito (1996b).

9   Bartlett (1932) provides detailed accounts of the interlinkedness as well as the distinction in terms of the functions and conditions, amongst 'concepts', 'percepts', 'image'

and 'meaning' (chap. IX, 'Perceiving, Recognising, Remembering', chap. XI, 'Images and their Functions', especially pp. 216–217, 224–226, and chap. XII, 'Meaning').

10   Please note that what is generically referred to as 'social constructionism' in psychology is somewhat different from 'social constructivism' in the sociology of scientific knowledge. The former is an umbrella term to encompass a broad range of approaches concerned with social bases of human cognition and behaviour in psychology and sociology. The latter is a specific approach known as 'social constructivism' in the fields of the history, philosophy and sociology of science and technology (for details, see e.g. Bloor, 1997).

CHAPTER ELEVEN

Memory and selective attention: Bartlett and Evans-Pritchard[1]

Mary Douglas

'There is no theory of culture.' Thus spoke a distinguished sociologist recently. In fact a powerful theory of culture is being developed and tested internationally in interesting research projects, with a growing bibliography in several European languages (see for example Benjamin, 1996; Douglas, 1992, 1996; Douglas & Ney, 1998; Ellis & Thompson, 1997; Ellis, Thompson & Wildavsky, 1990; Grendstad & Selle, 1996; Gross & Rayner, 1985; Karmasin & Karmasin, 1997; Rayner & Malone, 1998). But looking round for a general theory of cultural behaviour, our nameless speaker only saw an empty desert. The career of Bartlett confirms to some extent that such a theory should be difficult to develop, and explains why it should be elusive and hard to call to mind, almost invisible. The reason why there seems to be no theory of culture is because no one wants one. If they really wanted it, they could have it. They don't want it for good reasons which can be explained within the theory itself.

SELECTIVE ATTENTION

To read F.C. Bartlett on the subject one would expect that the cognitive theories which his work helped to establish would give recognition to an important cultural element. Bartlett and Rivers both emphasised that individual memory is supported by social institutions. In the 1920s anthropology was expected to contribute to psychology and close exchanges were made between these disciplines. Bartlett's concept of conventionalisation (e.g. 1923, 1932) was inspired by the works of A.C. Haddon, the anthropologist who led the famous Cambridge expedition to the Torres Straits in 1898–99. Haddon's work interested Bartlett. He wrote that when studying:

179

perception sequences, it seemed there came a stage when something like a stored pattern or standard representation took charge of the observer's response and principally settled what he was alleged to have perceived. Moreover, observers of much the same social group were very likely to use the same stored standard representation.

Just about this time I had become interested in the ethnographical studies of the development of decorative art forms such, for example, as those undertaken by Dr. A.C. Haddon in *The Decorative Art of New Guinea* [1894]. It was from such writings that I borrowed the plan of attempting to derive and use sequences for perceiving and remembering so as to help towards an understanding of those processes of conventionalization which not only produce standards and patterns peculiar to the decorative art of a social group, but could also, it seemed to me, play an important part in the individual's interpretation of his own environment.

The programme was now moving away from straightforward studies of the determining activities and conditions of perceiving and remembering, towards an all out experimental attack on conventionalizing in both its individual and social forms.

(Bartlett, 1958, p. 143)

Psychology and Primitive Culture (Bartlett, 1923) quoted many American and British anthropologists. It started out with the assumption, established in philosophy and psychology, that the process of cognition is a selective screening and organising of sensory inputs. And with Rivers he insisted that selective screening must be influenced by social experiences. Institutions constituted screens and selective principles. He worked this out with many ethnographic examples. His analysis of the folk tale is particularly convincing. He declared that the search for the origins of a folk tale is futile; likewise the discovery of those grand archetypal themes dear to many psychologists, or the attempts to use folk tales to establish the history of past institutions. He said firmly:

It is not the institution that is derived from the story, but the story from the institution. . . . That the folk story is a social product implies, among other things, that in its matter the popular tale must make a common-sense appeal and in its form it must be shaped as to call forth a widely readily shared response. *For both of these characters spring from the fact that the folk story is largely a mode of social intercourse.*

(Bartlett, 1923, p. 63, my italics)

Following Rivers he insisted that taboo was not to be explained by fear. Many writers of the time named fear as the primary emotion explaining taboos. 'But when we turn to popular stories . . . descriptions of fear seem to occupy no very important position' (Bartlett, 1923, p. 110). Bartlett himself explained taboo by a sociological requirement to control conflict by separating spheres of action and even creating separate cognitive spheres. For the 'general determination of boundaries' and for the social control of curiosity, Bartlett's words were remarkably explicit: 'The history of any primitive group, in fact, reveals certain spheres of activity within which curiosity is not readily to be allowed full sway. The limitation does not necessarily produce disorder. Curiosity is allowed its own realm' (Bartlett, 1923, pp. 117–118).

Psychology and Primitive Culture was a good book to put into the hands of anthropologists, full of promise for a sociological approach to perception. In it, Bartlett had been committed to the problem of how social factors influence cognition. He knew and accepted that the problem of conventionalisation could be solved only by knowing the institutions in which conventional responses were embedded. He said so over and over again. However, when he went on later to write his justly famous book *Remembering* (1932), he had made very little progress towards a sociological theory of cognition.

Working on the psychology of memory, he planned to expand and test the idea of the neurologist Henry Head that each individual attends selectively to sensations whose stored results create a cumulatively developed schema. Head supposed the schema or armature of attention to be individual, but Bartlett expected memory to be institutionally anchored. Unfortunately, the attempted draft of a book about conventionalising did not advance well:

> There came a time when I began to write this book, and I laboured heavily through two or three chapters, but it did not go well. I tore up what I had written and for some time there followed a most unpleasant period when it seemed that I had taken a lot of steps to get nowhere at all.
>
> (Bartlett, 1958, p. 144)

The young genius Norbert Wiener, who 'was at that time in Cambridge studying mathematical logic', brought the barren period to an end by helpfully suggesting that 'the Russian Scandal' game be turned into an experimental method. An experimental subject was isolated and shown a picture; the picture then being taken away, the subject was asked to reproduce it. His drawing was then presented to the next subject, who saw it equally briefly, lost it, and was asked to reproduce what he recalled, and so on until as many subjects as were required had worked on successive transformations of the original design. By this means he could show some of the perceptual processes that lead to a steady reproduction or to conventionalisation.

By two ideas, serial reproduction and subjective organisation of experience, Bartlett had found a way of exploring memory and, through memory, recognition and other faculties of the mind. The work he then embarked on was immense. Each experiment that he counted successful led him to consider new ones. An inventor of methodologies and a supreme instrument-maker, he succeeded in showing how the individual subject organises, constructs, maintains and defends the stability of its cognitive scheme. There was so much work to do in developing this approach that he relegated the programme of establishing the social foundation of stable perception.

He had certainly wished to introduce social factors to experimental psychology. He wrote that social conditions control individual recall 'by providing that setting of interest, excitement and emotion which follows the development of specific images and socially by providing a persistent framework of restrictions and customs which acts as a schematic basis for constructive memory' (Bartlett, 1932, p. 222).

But the English were working very much on their own. Alas for Bartlett's project that he did not understand better what Alfred Schutz had done and what Maurice Halbwachs was trying to do on collective memory. A pupil of Henri Bergson, of Durkheim and of Mauss, Halbwachs undertook for his main research project to demonstrate that perception and recall depend primarily upon social institutions and secondly upon physical, visible symbols.

In Durkheim's theory of religions the totem is an emblem which serves by its physical existence to fix an otherwise fleeting, abstract idea. If it were not for this physical existence as a point of reference, ideas about religion would have no stability. Second, for Durkheim's theory religious ideas are particularly vulnerable to destabilising forces because they are second-remove ideas about another abstraction, society itself. They depend on social commitment. Insofar as the individual has a commitment to society, that commitment has to be hedged around with physical markings, rules of taboo. The concept of society as having overriding authority was transformed into a concept of Godhead.

Halbwachs's contribution was to work out in detail the social and physical supports of memory. The temporal stages of an event are more easily recalled if they can be given a spatial ordering that corresponds to the temporal sequence. Concern to establish the social framework of memory leads him to discuss the different memory of different social classes, pegged out by different physical memorials. Instead of considering he spatial layout of Australian camps or the seasonal movements of the Eskimos, as Durkheim and Mauss had done, he applied himself to European history and contemporary life. He was particularly interested in the negative case of how memory could be sustained without that physical structure that seemed to be its prerequisite, in the same way as Durkheim had taught that religious organisation has an inherent problem of cognitive stability unless it takes over a physical anchorage.

The work of the anthropologist, Evans-Pritchard, spanned the gap between the English psychologists' interest in the institutional frameworks that sustain memory, and the French sociologists' researches in the same direction. Thanks to this double heritage he was able to advance the sociological approach to reasoning and remembering.

The evidence shows that Evans-Pritchard adopted Bartlett's research interests and even used the same vocabulary about selective principles of attention for indicating what he held to be the central problems of cognition. Unfortunately he was the only anthropologist of his period whose work provides continuity with a major concern in perception psychology.

RECIPROCAL INNERVATION AND
DISTANCE PERCEPTORS

In the 1920s the most popular models for the processes of human reasoning were borrowed from the physical sciences, and the best were neurological. In addition to Henry Head, Sherrington was enormously influential for anthropology. He worked on the neural connections in the spinal column and brain stem that sustain the normal maintenance of muscle-tone and of posture and reflex movements in the limbs. Then, moving on from the spinal column and brain stem to the fore-brain of the cat and ape, he mapped the motor keyboard of the cerebral cortex.

So many of Sherrington's concepts were borrowed, extended, transformed by thinkers in other fields that it is impossible to separate threads in what became a common canopy of ideas. Take his demonstration of reciprocal innervation, the principle by which antagonistic muscles must relax to allow the contraction of the muscles that cause a limb to move. In psychology, Bartlett tried to focus on 'group difference' tendencies that clustered about various forms of institutions, and insisted that it is not enough to know what these tendencies are; one must also study the relationship they bear to one another; particularly, he was interested in the 'conflict of tendencies and their mutual reinforcement' (see Bartlett, 1923, chap. 4), and in processes of inhibiting antagonism. This sounds so like a vague version of Freud's model of the mind, as well as Sherrington's neurological model, that it is clear that the basic idea of reciprocal interplay between forces was freely available to contemporary thought.

An important disseminator of Sherrington's ideas was Eugenio Rignano (1870–1930). An Italian professor of philosophy who wrote on many topics and was quickly translated into French and English, Rignano worked out what he called a mnemonic explanation of attention. In his theory of mental functions the whole organism was always involved. For a human being the concept of the whole organism would have to include its social ambience. He took over Sherrington's distinction between non-distance perceptors (which permit immediate or almost immediate satisfaction of the affective tendencies with which they start) and distance perceptors (which can hold the state of attention in suspense). Among his examples: The sea anemone does not pay attention or react to the presence of food except when its metabolism has reached a state requiring more nutrients. In humans, the experience of hunger, a particular localised sensation in the wall of the stomach, is enough to activate food-seeking behaviour. Long before starvation is threatened, the immediate perception of hunger has reminded the human organism that it needs nourishment; long before death from thirst, a local sensation in the mouth and throat is a warning request for attention; the species will die out if not reproduced, but the sexual urge is called into action without waiting for the species's survival to be at risk. Rignano said that in these forms we find the substitution of the part for the whole: Hunger, thirst and sexual desire are examples of the mnemonic process by which the needs of the whole organism are continually met by short-lived local transfers of attention—early-warning reminders, as it were.

The array of slow and quick nerve pathways to the brain, the concept of reciprocal innervation, the power to suspend attention—these three ideas appear later in Evans-Pritchard's work. Several times he acknowledged Rignano's book, *The Psychology of Reasoning* (1920). He even placed Rignano alongside William James in his own programmatic statement about the need to understand the selective principles controlling attention (Evans-Pritchard, 1934). In England, Rivers and Evans-Pritchard (and originally Bartlett) were alone in their confidence that the selective principles were to be found in social institutions.

At this distance we can see that the French sociologists, Durkheim, Mauss, Lévy-Bruhl and Halbwachs, were potential collaborators working on the same problems of perception at the same time. The French theories were roundly rejected by psychologists on the English side of the Channel. The reciprocal failure of the British psychologists to develop a sociological dimension to their experimental thinking and the failure of the French to benefit from the British methodological advances in anthropology are themselves problems for the sociology of knowledge. Ignorance of each others' work does not explain it; they read, but they misunderstood. It is another case for the theory: Their attention was turned in other directions.

Evans-Pritchard studying the Nuer, a Nilotic people practising pastoralism in the south Sudan, presented their social institutions as the schematic framework of their memory. Whenever Nuer seek to clarify the definition of status they state it in terms of claims to cattle. Lines of relationship too complex for the outsider to unravel would be easy to recall for the person who stands to gain a cow or an ox from correctly computing them. Thus is keenness of individual perception institutionally encouraged along prescribed lines. Memory will be continually revived by occasions such as weddings and funerals when claims and counter-claims are made. The major crises of loyalty and alignment in warfare activate other aspects of memory. Everyday life selectively focuses attention. Evans-Pritchard's field reporting illustrated principles of selection which automatically send some information to oblivion, and exemplified how benchmarks are used to organise time past and to group historical series for easy retrieval.

Before describing the Nuer case study, first let me set the question of logical discrimination back into its old anthropological context. Recall that there are still extant societies that have no words for counting beyond the number three, and others in which four to seven is the limit of the numerate skills. Apparently people with no worldly possessions worth counting can manage quite comfortably with a linguistic competence for distinguishing numbers only up to three. Asked, 'How many of your children are living with you?' a mother with six around her knees will feel content to reply something like 'a lot' or 'many' or 'all these'. This does not mean she cannot name them all in order of birth or notice when one is missing. Judgement of quantities is an even more complex matter. Some shepherds are said to scan a large flock of sheep and register how many and which are absent in much less time that it would take to count them. However, a hundred years ago it was naturally tempting to consider these non-numerates as simple children of nature, and to try to work out a social developmental sequence that paralleled that of the stages in which children learned to count. The implications of ranging such societies on a series from the most infantile to more numerate were never tested because extraordinary discrepancies in the capacities for reckoning, judgement and memory rendered any single grading criterion useless. Some people whose technology might cause them to be placed at a primitive stage performed prodigious feats of memory when it came to reciting genealogies of kings or ancestors. The idea came to be accepted that primitive people were good at learning by rote and that their best remembering was the result of mechanical mnemonics.

Bartlett thought that a strong social support to memory was inclined to produce a mechanical style of recall. His idea was that when the social institutions provided the mnemonic setting, recall was of the recitative type; by contrast, when an individual, free from the guidance and constraints of his society, had to remember, he did so 'with none of that relatively effortless, recitative, copying manner which marked the recall of the native. The plan was built up bit by bit, a detail here, a filling up there, then another key and so on. The whole process had every appearance of a genuine construction' (Bartlett, 1932, p. 251). The idea that institutions are something which the primitive takes as given—a fixed, unalterable part of his environment—dies hard. It is one of the sources of a theoretical division between ourselves, modern industrial man, thought to be free of tradition's grip, free to argue the toss and exert our influence over institutions, and they, the primitives, who are supposed to accept the encrusted yoke of custom.

REMEMBERING DEGREES OF KINSHIP

Prohibitions on incest often figure in the perennial controversy about human behaviour and its psychological basis. Sometimes it is argued that humans have a natural aversion to sexual congress with close kin, in which case the rules that they observe are not intellectual constructions but instinctive responses. The counter-argument rests on the observation that humans are frequently not deterred by the alleged instinctive aversion: Humans seem to be no different from animals in their readiness to mate with kin; and on this argument, social considerations explain the prevalence and form of such regulations. Fieldwork among the Nuer shows that the Nuer themselves come down unequivocally on the side of a sociological explanation of incest regulation. Nuer say that it is unthinkable for a mother and son to have sexual relations. The whole context for this unthinkability is laid out by their justification of the regulations in less heinous cases. Basically sex and marriage are organised by the transfer of cattle. Cattle-givers cannot give cattle to themselves, so the elementary requirements of a transaction draw a boundary around kin who hold common rights as joint cattle claimants. Every prohibited relationship is forbidden explicitly 'because of the cattle'. The regulation is on a par with our law which disallows evidence given in court by a wife against or for her husband.

Nuer incest regulations are as follows. Marriage is forbidden between clansfolk—relationships traced in the male line. It is forbidden also between a man and a woman related through either father or mother (by male or female links) up to six generations. It is forbidden between close natural kinsfolk, that is, between persons related through sexual union outside of marriage; for example, a man could not marry the daughter of his maternal grandfather's natural son. Thus far the rules would seem to be concentrated on closeness of biological relationship, and might support the theory that an instinct is being codified into laws. But adoption is also a bar to intermarriage. A captured boy of the Dinka tribe, if adopted by his captors, counts as a son, and he cannot marry into their lineage. Even if he be adopted into a different lineage from that of his captors, men from his captor's lineage are forbidden to marry his daughter. The reason given is the same in all cases: when the Dinka boy marries, his captors will contribute cattle to the marriage payments for his wife, which gives them a claim to some of the cattle that will come in when his daughter eventually marries; it is impossible for them to marry a girl at whose marriage they are entitled to claim cattle: It would be an incestuous union. The rule by which they forgo sex gives them a claim to the cows due to kinship. Only if there were no recognised relationship can they have sexual intercourse or marry. When a captured Dinka girl is adopted, her adoptive kin perform a religious rite and say 'She will become our daughter and we will receive her bridewealth cattle.' The cattle of her bridewealth give her kinship, and with it she acquires the right to receive the cows due to her as paternal aunt on the marriage of her captor's sons. Marriage is forbidden between her descendants and those kinsmen in virtue of her bridewealth for several generations. Nuer state all the rules in terms of rights to cattle.

The transfers of cattle create the relationships that are incompatible with marriage. The fact that a man cannot marry his wife's sister, or any near kinswoman of his wife, as second wife unless the first wife had died without children, is also explained in terms of rights to cattle. The rules against marrying the daughter of an age-mate acknowledge the social nature of the prohibition:

> The blood age-mates have shed together into the ground at their initiation gives them a kind of kinship. In certain circumstances an age-mate may claim a cow . . . of the bridewealth of the daughter of one of his mates and a man may not be in the position of paying bridewealth and being able to claim it. Nuer also points out that were a man to marry the daughter of an age-mate her parents would become his parents-in-law, and the respect he would have to show them would be incompatible

with the familiarity with which he should treat age-mates and their wives and the liberties he may take with them. He could not, for instance, eat and drink in their home, an abstention in glaring contradiction to the behaviour expected of age-mates.
(Evans-Pritchard, 1940, pp. 34–55)

Very evidently the Nuer divides his social universe into kin and not kin. From male kin he expects support in fighting, vengeance if he is killed and cattle distribution when kinswomen are married. Kinship means claims on cattle. Every wedding is an occasion for reviving the lines of relationship in people's minds (see Evans-Pritchard, 1951, chap. 2).

To state a claim on cattle is to divide the whole universe of possible relationships into two mutually exclusive spheres of claims. Either sex claims are possible or cattle claims, but both simultaneously are contradictory and logically absurd. If this does not begin to illustrate the relentless demands of social accountability upon logic, a further glance at Nuer marriage will convince. Nothing gives more zest to drawing fine logical distinctions than the need to distinguish among competing claims. But the desire to reconcile incompatible situations is another powerful stimulus to logical exercise. A person wants to hold and yet to have the credit of giving away; to enjoy sexual adventures himself while allowing no one to disrupt his own marriages. Basically the Nuer want to have a social system in which rights are transmitted through wedlock, and at the same time not to constrain their womenfolk. Compared with Azande women, Evans-Pritchard contested that Nuer women enjoy great freedom and dignity. Although all the categories in the social system are generated through the marriage bonds, a Nuer woman is not forced to stay with a husband she dislikes. The Nuer reconcile potentially opposed patterns of behaviour by a series of legal fictions. Starting from the principle that a legal marriage is established by the transfer of cattle, they pursue this principle through all the ramifications they desire.

Legally, so long as the cattle are not returned (and this is exceedingly difficult after they have been distributed to kin), a marriage endures. The mere fact that the husband dies does not end the marriage, for he has paid over the cattle once and for all. So with no new marriage being required, the widow should normally co-habit with one of her husband's brothers. Any children begotten are still to be counted as the children of the dead man. What if she refuses to live with any of the brothers of her late husband? The brothers whom she rejects do not try to force her to stay with them against her wishes. If she wants to go away and live with a man outside their group, she can, but the children she might bear to him are still legally the children of the man who paid the cattle. If the natural father wants to legitimate the children, he only has to pay the appropriate amount of cattle. He has a material interest in doing so, for the payment entitles him to claim cows as a father at the marriage of his own daughters. If it should happen that a girl is too promiscuous to be able to settle down to marriage, her own father, not having received cattle for her, can claim the children for his own lineage.

REMEMBERING THE DEAD

The most ingenious elaboration of this legal principle is applied to the Nuer senti-ment that no man should die without leaving legitimate descendants to carry on his name. If this should happen, his kinsmen are duty-bound to collect cattle and to use them to marry a woman to the dead man. His brother or nephew would normally take on the responsibility of begetting children whose place in the lineage genealogy would be as the dead man's offspring.

Looking at a Nuer village, with the identical homesteads and cattle *kraals*, it would be impossible to disentangle the elaborate skein of relationships between living and dead. At any one time a roster of the living men would not give all the fathers of the babies being born. Dead persons are legally active, so much so that a man might inherit the widows of one brother and marry a girl to the name of another, and then, having piously begotten many children to the name of dead men, might die leaving no legitimate issue to carry on his own name. Then of course the altruistic obligation to marry a woman for his ghost falls on someone else—and so on.

The honouring of this obligation has another aspect. Individual Nuer have to be ready to defend their rights with force. They risk maiming or death when they start a fight. The confidence that kinsmen would not let your name be forgotten sets a limit on the social dangers—if one can separate the physical risks from social risks. Fear of what would happen to his family and his own good name would not stop a man from laying his life on the line: The family would be cared for, and his name avenged and perpetuated. The system of accounting has to provide the conditions for its own smooth working at any level—psychological, intellectual and institutional. The Nuer find their way through this web of legal fictions because of the simple rule that they can either marry or claim kinship and cattle. This rule working in every sexual confrontation makes it easy for Nuer to see the tribe as a single genealogical system. It also means that every possible sexual adventure is an occasion on which the relationship system has to be reviewed and its principles re-affirmed.

DISTANCE PERCEPTORS AND STRUCTURAL OPPOSITION

Thus did Evans-Pritchard show how the human faculties of reasoning develop muscle. The joint effort of accountability also produces a powerful machinery for turning social dilemmas into legalistic issues, solved by fictions. But import-ant though this was, it was not quite the big discovery that psychologists in Bartlett's day would have needed to put them on another trail of enquiry. The main interest to them should have been Evan-Pritchard's analysis of how con-sciousness itself is structured.

Two approaches to this problem may be mentioned: One was according to the idea that the individual does his own work of accountability, sifting information and organising it upon a personal evolving scheme, his social interests being his guide (this approximates to Bartlett's assumptions); the other (corresponding to Halbwachs's idea), took more deliberate account of social pressures and of physical aids to support the meanings. Neither approach invites one to think of the blanks in memory as being social constructs, nor did they suggest that the gaps over which recall is impossible are more than a mere incidental result of the restructuring of attention by social interests. Yet amnesic blanks are a crucial part of the social structuring, one of the conditions of its smooth working. However, in the 1920s no one transferred to sociology Freud's insight that some forgetfulness in the individual is a blessed help to sanity. Evans-Pritchard achieved this parallel insight for the working of the social system. By doing so he anticipated later work, such as Michael Foucault's, on socially constructed oblivion. He also cut the theory of memory free from physical props.

As he saw it, the Nuer articulate their experience of past time and anchor its several parts into the articulated society on which they focus attention. Most Nuer tribes have a history of only 10 or 11 generations. There is good reason to think that they have been in existence as tribes in that location much longer. The tribe is thought of by Nuer as a genealogical structure, but clearly the genealogy is fabricated. The anthropologist was bound to ask why the succeeding generations of the dead do not cumulatively lengthen the genealogical tree.

The answer in Evans-Pritchard's work is the concept of structural distance. Every Nuer can place himself genealogically in the tribe for two kinds of purposes: for calculating political alignment, and for calculating sex and cattle trade-offs. Political alignment is determined by considering the major territorial divisions of the tribe, and the skeletal spread through them of the dominant clan. A tribe does not contain more than five or six levels of segmentation, from the most inclusive to the smallest local community. At the edges of the tribe the force of law runs out. Within each of its major divisions redress for wrongs becomes progressively easier until the last level, the local community, which is like a close-knit kinship unit. The first four or five generations of the tribe's existence from its founder to the more recently dead are continually commemorated in all the political confrontations in which a person has to assess wrongs as redressable or not. Structural distance being an active political principle, there is no difficulty in understanding how Nuer manage to remember the major levels of segmentation.

The other context for reckoning genealogy, which was discussed earlier, is the taking of women in marriage and the claiming and paying of cattle. In this context the reckoning of descent starts from the opposite direction. Any adult can easily recall the relationships of his father's father's father; there will be people around alive who can corroborate. A descendant of the father's father's father may turn up at a marriage and claim a calf. It would be given to him as a sign that the limit of claims has been reached, at the fourth generation. Relatives who claim relationship up to six or seven generations back would not be refused a gift; but the main genealogical structure recognised cattle claims up to and not including the fifth generation. Anyone who knows that this is how he is related, also knows that sexual intercourse with the range of women thus defined as kin would count as incestuous.

By using one system for reckoning forwards from the beginning of time and another for reckoning backwards from the present day, the Nuer limit their historical experience. An amnesic space in the middle of the genealogy swallows up the new generations as the dead great-great-grandfathers are succeeded by the new great-grandfathers. Thanks to this structural fault in the method of reckoning, an empty hole was created. Its absorbent properties reduce the whole known past and allow it to be articulated. If every generation were included, the impossible task of remembering everything would strain the cognitive schema. Lapses of memory would be individual and fortuitous instead of social and regular. The public structuring of the consciousness of time allowed the Nuer to take full cognisance of a short historical depth. The tree under which mankind came into being was still standing in western Nuerland until a few years before the research began.

The most important sentence in which Evans-Pritchard summed up the Nuer consciousness of time is: 'Beyond the annual cycle, time-reckoning is a conceptualisation of the social structure, and the points for reference are a projection into the past of actual relationships between persons' (Evans-Pritchard, 1950, p. 108). He did not consider the material benchmarks of time's passing as so vitally important for sustaining memory. The hooves treading out paths over the land as cattle are driven from one homestead to another are material aids to memory, no doubt, but they would never take it very far back. There are no written constitutions, no enduring monuments, no scenes of battle or palace ruins. The maximum historical depth is achieved by the exigencies of the Nuer social structure: 'Time is not a continuum, but is a constant structural relationship between two points, the first and last persons in a line of agnatic descent' (ibid.).

These statements expand easily into a testable general hypothesis and a programme for relating historical consciousness to social structure. If the Nuer case, which Evans-Pritchard demonstrated, has wider implications, then other people too use their conceptualising of the social structure to give points of reference for the projection into the past of actual social relations. Immediately after World War II, younger anthropologists took up this challenge. Evans-Pritchard had not explained the steps by which the present is projected into the past. Nor did he himself attempt the comparative studies which would test the general applicability of the idea. The first exercise was performed by intensive fieldwork among the Tiv of south-east Nigeria. A whole process of clipping, eliding and openly adjusting genealogies so that history would accord with the current distribution of authority was described in a basic form that deserves not to be forgotten (Barnes, 1967; Bohannan, 1952; Cunnison, 1959; Murphy, 1967).

However when the re-writing of science textbooks was shown to be performing exactly the same function in Western society—of keeping memory of the past in alignment with the present state of scientific authority (Kuhn, 1962)—it seems probable that the Tiv demonstration had been forgotten.

A major point needs to be made about this vicarious fulfilment of Bartlett's programme: Contrary to his expectation, the peoples whose time experience is posited as being structured by their social experience must be credited with an active role in the analysis. The clipping, elision and merging of sections of history is not something that is happening to them; it is something they are doing. They are very conscious agents. The Tiv who engage in disputes about political seniority derive some of their bargaining power from the numbers they can muster in support, and some from ancient genealogical right: At the end of the day, when settlement is reached, sheer numerical strength always wins over genealogy; consequently the genealogical charter has to be amended to fit the political reality that has been accepted. Their negotiating is from a short-term perspective. They do not have in mind the final resultant structure of their society. What they do with one set of purposes creates the unintended empty spaces or the thick clusters of fine discriminations that characterise their consciousness.

Besides the sophistication of this work, other generalisations about the experience of time seem childish indeed. The extreme methodological positivism, the search for objective bases for comparison, the trial and testing of data are recognisably in the tradition of the empirical sciences, as austere in what they do allow themselves to conclude as in that which is rejected as evidence.

Well before the self-fulfilling prophecy became a tag-word in sociology, these self-limiting, self-validating processes of collective cognition were being analysed in the 1940s in greater intricacy than has since been achieved. Well before phenomenology's claim that sociological understanding must start from the negotiating activities of conscious, intelligent agents, Evans-Pritchard had seized the problem, developed a method and shown what progress can be made, achievements missed in Bartlett's work.

Bartlett himself in his own life work exemplified the lesson. He it was who had taught originally that social institutions provide the framework for memory and attention. He wrote the best book on remembering, and in it he showed that he had forgotten his earlier convictions. He was drawn to accept the institutional framework of Cambridge experimental psychology, and in doing so allowed his attention to be distracted from his first intentions. The experimental laboratory could only work with individual subjects. It was not (and still is not) adapted to testing ideas about larger units of experience. We are bound to conclude that if we want a social constructivist theory of cognition we would not be wise to look for it in this quarter, which is inherently set up for testing theories about individual cognition. Nor would there be interesting results from mass surveys, which are also focused essentially upon individual response. The main conclusion might be that a constructivist theory is going to be extremely difficult to develop.

This puts the social sciences into a position like that of medicine when the germ theory of disease reigned supreme, just before it was surpassed by immunology. The concept of an immune system is very parallel to the concept of a society that selectively screens foreign information by setting gates in every institution to control curiosity and discredit new ideas or methods. A theory about the collectivist construction of knowledge would have to be very like a theory of the immune system. And therein lies its trouble in getting accepted. Nobody wants it, least of all the scientists who are living in a culture that rewards individual success. To gain promotion, and even to attract the necessary grants for their research work, academics need to claim individual merit. Robert Merton has analysed in these terms the acrimonious controversies surrounding multiple discoveries and claimed singletons: the big rewards go to the first finder of a new principle or the first inventor of a technical innovation. The system of prizes presumes and upholds a culture of individual competition. The person whose life is engaged in that culture is led to cherish the idea of intellectual autonomy, to downplay those who have shared the struggle and contributed to the successes. To this culture a collectivist theory of the construction of knowledge is unintelligible and unacceptable: it raises the hackles and firmly closes the gateways of curiosity. Cultural theory would predict that individualists would reject a theory of culture.

We have proposed two reasons why Bartlett's forgetting did not attract attention. The same reasons explain why Evans-Pritchard's and his colleagues' analyses of what is called pejoratively 'constructivism' are not known outside of anthropology. One is that constructivism conflicts with deeply entrenched presumptions, and the other that none of the esteemed testing equipment can be applied to demonstrate it. There is a third reason, political, against what is made out to be social determinism. The background is the history of liberal resistance to totalitarian claims. Durkheim's adversaries consider his collectivist theories of cognition to be determinist, believing that he taught that some reified abstraction called 'society', *le gros animal*, controls the thoughts and affections of individual members. He could be read in that sense—it would be fairer to read him in the spirit of Evans-Pritchard's demonstration of the collective construction of memory. The late Thomas Kuhn told me personally that after World War II any form of cognitive constructivism was repugnant. It revived echoes of the communitarian claims of National Socialism and Fascism. This is the deep reason why no one wants a theory of culture. It would be politically dangerous.

The challenge then, for psychologists and anthropologists, is to try to think more profoundly about what they need to propose so as to be able to go on with the work. And they must think of the project in terms that will not earn the very reasonable political hostility. Personally I think that Rignano's formulation is the best, the idea that memory and cognition are carried in the social structure. The institutions are like hollow tubes or sounding boards, they make the music, but not the tunes. The people who individually combine to make the institutions are also collectively composing the melodies.

NOTE

1   This chapter is based on parts of Mary Douglas (1980) *Evans-Pritchard*, Fontana Modern Masters, London: Fontana.

CHAPTER TWELVE

Whatever happened to 'social constructiveness'?[1]

David Bloor

In his two books *Psychology and Primitive Culture* (1923) and *Remembering* (1932) Frederic Bartlett talked at some length about a process he called 'social constructiveness'. By contrast, his later books, *The Mind at Work and Play* (1951) and *Thinking* (1958) showed little or none of this earlier preoccupation. What happened to the idea? I don't want to explain its departure from Bartlett's personal publications—that would be a matter of biography. I want to pose the question of what happened to social constructiveness as a theme for discussion in the relevant academic circles. Has it simply disappeared from the analysis of cognition and knowledge of the kind that interested Bartlett? To begin with, however, I must define the terms involved. What is social constructiveness?

SOCIAL CONSTRUCTIVENESS

One root of the idea goes back to McDougall, who said we all have an instinct to construct, that is, literally, an instinct to build things (McDougall, 1908, p. 88). Another root is W.H.R. Rivers's observation that many conspicuous examples of building things, whether animal or human, involve co-operation (1920, p. 53). Bartlett took this social aspect of the idea and elaborated it experimentally, though it cannot be said that the term ever achieved much precision. On the one hand, Bartlett used it to refer to our ability to 'construct' society itself, that is, its institutions, customs and conventions (e.g. Bartlett, 1923, p. 43). On the other hand, he used it to denote the activity in which members of a group co-operate to produce some artefact (e.g. Bartlett, 1923, p. 180). This could be a traditional, decorative design, a piece of culture such as a folk story, or even some product of the material arts such as a canoe, a tool or a pot. A material artefact has some sort of existence distinct from society, but it would not exist in the form that it does, or have the identity and meaning that it does, were it not for the traditions and practices of the group who produced it.

Experimentally, Bartlett treated social constructiveness in connection with another idea, that of 'conventionalisation', taken over from A.C. Haddon. For Haddon, conventionalisation was the sheet anchor of ethnography (Bartlett, 1923, p. 6). For Bartlett, it was the key to social constructiveness. Recall the classic studies described in *Remembering* (1932). A folk story from culture A was told to subjects from culture B. Two methods were then used, the method of 'repeated reproduction' and the method of 'serial reproduction' (pp. 63, 118). In the first, the method of repeated reproduction, the subjects each had to recall the story at a number of different time intervals after the original encounter. The result was that the story underwent systematic changes in the memory. Details and themes characteristic of culture A, the culture of its origin, were gradually replaced by those characteristic of culture B, that of the person who was remembering it. The memory image, in Bartlett's terms, became conventionalised. In the experiments using serial reproduction, the first subject reproduced the story from memory and then this subject's version was given to the second subject for recall, and so on. The story was passed from person to person. The result was similar to that of repeated reproduction. Cultural stereotypes rapidly asserted themselves so that the story was reconstructed in accordance with the conventions current amongst those who were seeking to remember it.[2]

The difference between Haddon's and Bartlett's idea of conventionalisation is that Haddon emphasised its conservative aspect whereas Bartlett emphasised its creative aspect. For Haddon, to conventionalise meant little more than making something fit into a pre-existing mould; but mere assimilation and omission did not add up to genuinely constructive change. For Bartlett, each significant social group contained within itself certain tendencies or lines of development. He saw these as irreducible dispositions of the group itself which need not, and typically did not, find representation within the minds of its individual members.[3] When such tendencies found expression in the process of cultural assimilation the merely conservative aspect of assimilation was transformed. The group tendency blended together diverse elements of culture to form something qualitatively new.

> This is what I wish to call social constructiveness. It is a characteristic reaction towards imported elements of culture adopted inevitably by all strong and vigorous groups. It means that imported elements suffer change both in the direction of existing culture and along the general line of development of the receptive group.
>
> (Bartlett, 1928b, p. 390)

This positive and creative side of the process does not appear strongly in the classic experiments on memory described previously, but I shall present one of Bartlett's examples shortly which is meant to embody this aspect of the matter.

My impression is that after a flurry of interest, such as that evinced by the symposium on social constructiveness published in the *British Journal of Psychology* (1928b), and the impact of Bartlett's book itself, there was little sustained development of these themes by psychologists.[4] The disciplinary tradition during the 1940s, 1950s and 1960s was certainly not wholly individualistic, but Bartlett's socially oriented work was primarily read as a comment on an individual, psychological process. His reputation was tied up with the idea that individual memory is influenced by cultural stereotypes. The nature, construction and status of the stereotypes themselves, as social entities, was not the object of much active enquiry. Does this mean that the theme of social constructiveness should be consigned to history? Was it a mere phase through which experimental psychology passed, *en route* to different and more sharply defined problems? For the discipline that may be true; but for the theme of social constructiveness itself, that is not the end of the story. After lying more or less dormant, the idea experienced a rebirth in the early 1970s within the new sociology of scientific knowledge which was beginning to emerge at that time.[5]

My thesis is that social constructiveness is alive and well and living in departments of sociology and departments of history and philosophy of science, indeed, anywhere where the sociology of scientific knowledge is being pursued. Even the terminology is very similar. Today the preferred label is 'social constructivism' but social constructivism is just Bartlett's social constructiveness. To show that this continuity is genuine, and not just a matter of words, it will be sufficient to show that Bartlett himself was serious about the social construction of scientific knowledge. If I can show Bartlett convincingly assuming the role of a prototype sociologist of scientific knowledge, the case will be made.

BARTLETT ON SCIENCE AND TECHNOLOGY

In chap. XVI of *Remembering*, Bartlett (1932, p. 276) said he would offer a 'few instances of social constructiveness', though 'no attempt will be made to work them out in full detail'. After all the use of folk stories as experimental material, the first and most prominent of these instances comes as something of a surprise: It concerned teamwork in science and technology. Both practically and theoretically 'specialists belonging to different fields must co-operate'. How the final product of the team is achieved, he said, 'presents an interesting series of problems'. During the war of 1914–1918, he went on:

> the demands of aircraft defence stimulated every large nation group concerned to develop mechanical, or semi-mechanical, devices for the detection of attacking aircraft at night. These all, by physical and physiological necessity, followed broadly the same lines; but there were important differences which, for the time being, were not fully known as between group and opposing group.
>
> (Bartlett, 1932, p. 276)

After the war, development continued in Europe, the United States and elsewhere. The new instruments differed in many respects from the originals, with a significant transfer of features resulting from contact between the groups involved. Bartlett observed that no instrument was the work of a single person, nor were they the result of a simple aggregation of individual contributions. Individuals played a vital part in the story, but their contributions were changed in the course of interaction.

> A, perhaps, proposed this; B that; C the other thing; and E, very likely proposing no specific detail himself, worked all the details derived from the various sources into a practical form, so that the A, B and C details are not any longer exactly as A, B and C thought of them.
>
> (Bartlett, 1932, p. 277)

We see here the scope for those mental mechanisms uncovered by Bartlett's experiments. As A's idea is transmitted from A to E it will be subtly reconstructed in E's mind. As the various contributions circulate in the thinking and discourse of the group developing the technology, the conditions of the serial reproduction experiments are recreated. There will be a tendency to reconfigure thoughts and ideas in accordance with accepted elements of culture while, at the same time, constructing new conventions of design and procedure. The technical device will be unwittingly shaped by tendencies that are characteristic of the group.[6]

Bartlett laid particular emphasis on the subtle changes that detection technology underwent as it moved from the stage of initial design to its actual use, even when that use was still of a somewhat experimental character. In the course of practice, changes were made, which no individual had thought through in advance and whose resultant effects were not the achievement of any single person. When, as Bartlett put it, 'the apparatus came into experimental use, it suffered various modifications of its functional parts which nobody ever thought out very clearly, if at all' (Bartlett, 1932, p. 277). Changes produced at this stage were seen by Bartlett as particularly significant for the expression of social dispositions: 'the group trend,' he said, 'is apt to come in by way of unwitting modifications produced by practice' (Bartlett, 1932, p. 277).[7]

The social aspect of the technology does not just inform its creation, it also applies to its operation. Both involve team-work. Bartlett connected these two points together when he said:

> The commonest aircraft detection instruments have to be controlled by a group, or by a team. There are some forms which demand very much greater interdependence among the members of the team than is the case with others. Each has developed within its own special social *milieu*, so that a well-instructed onlooker, asked to furnish a *rationale* for differences in the type of instrument in common use, will often find himself speaking in social, group terms.
>
> (Bartlett, 1932, p. 277)

This is a slightly enigmatic formulation, but the message is clear. Different groups will reveal something about themselves by the artefacts they produce—even artefacts like aircraft detection systems.[8]

Writing, in 1932, about World War I, Bartlett could not have been referring to radar, so what were the detection systems he had in mind? Unfortunately he did not tell us. There is not a single reference given to accompany these passages in *Remembering*, but any standard military history of the period makes it clear that he must have been talking about the technology of sound-location (e.g. Jones, 1935, p. 73). This is borne out by a paper Bartlett contributed to *The Royal Engineer's Journal* called 'Psychology and the Fighting Services' (Bartlett, 1929, p. 236). So let us have a look at this technology.[9]

SOUND-LOCATORS

A typical sound-locator used for aircraft detection employed four listening trumpets and used what is called an 'alt-azimuth' mounting. This means that two of the trumpets were mounted horizontally and used to determine the azimuth, or compass-bearing, of the source of sound, while the other two trumpets were mounted vertically and used to establish elevation (see Fig. 12.1).

FIG. 12.1   Standard early British sound-locator (with permission, Imperial War Museum).

Bartlett was right about the teamwork involved. Each pair of trumpets fed, via a stethoscope, into the ears of a single listener, so there were two listeners, one trying to get the azimuth, the other trying to get the elevation. If there were a number of unseen aircraft in the night sky, the two listeners had to be alert to the danger that they would be locked onto different sources. Sound-locators were used in conjunction with searchlights. A third person, the 'sighting number', had to use an instrument (such as a ring-sight) mounted on the locator to keep track of the direction in which the whole system was pointing at any given time. This continuously changing information was passed to a searchlight crew who would point the light in the direction they were told. The instructions had to allow for the time-lag in receiving the sound from the aircraft, during which it would, of course, have changed position.[10] Then there had to be a 'flank spotter' who stood to one side ready to see if the light actually picked up an aircraft (this being nearly impossible for the sighting number and the light operator to see for themselves). If the moving beam flicked across an aircraft the flank spotter had to assume immediate responsibility for guiding the light. The final step was to bring a battery of anti-aircraft guns into operation against the illuminated enemy. We can certainly see here the involvement of an ever-widening team of people.[11]

Why should Bartlett choose this example? How did he know anything about sound-locators? His own work during World War I had not been in this field, though he had worked on the related problem of training hydrophone operators for the acoustic detection of submarines.[12] The question is, however, sufficiently answered for our purposes by his membership, at the time of writing *Remembering* (1932), of the Medical Research Council's Physiology of Hearing Committee. Papers in the Public Record Office indicate that this was originally set up, in 1928, at the prompting of the military to organise research into scientific problems thrown into prominence by sound-locator technology.[13] The acoustics of collecting trumpets and the nature of the sound emitted by aircraft were still under analysis, while the fundamental, psychological capacity to use our two ears to locate sources of sound was still very obscure.[14] As a member of this committee Bartlett would almost certainly have had access to otherwise restricted military documents such as the *Theory and Use of Anti-aircraft Sound-locators* issued by the Army Council (Hill et al., 1922). This document was not a drill manual or handbook but a summary of the research and development of the British sound-locator effort since its inception in response to the night raids on London, which began in September 1917.

I have no direct evidence that Bartlett read this source, but one of its authors, Major W.S. Tucker RE, was also on the Physiology of Hearing Committee.[15] Whether or not it was one of Bartlett's sources, or whether he picked up the information informally, this document supports Bartlett's claim about the team-character of the development, and not just the operation, of sound-locators. As Bartlett said, that development involved specialists from many different areas co-operating with one another. The authors, besides Tucker and a Capt. Ward and a Lieut. Col. Monkhouse, included a scientist from the National Physical

Laboratory, C. Jakeman, and the mathematician E.A. Milne (then Lieut. Milne), a recent graduate of Trinity College, Cambridge.[16] The report also mentions contributions from the psychologist Charles Spearman (p. 109) and Horace Darwin of Cambridge Instruments (p. 59).[17] The foreword was written by the eminent physiologist A.V. Hill who (with the rank of Major) supervised the development work in his role as director of the Anti-Aircraft Experimental Section of the Munitions Inventions Department.[18]

Confirming Bartlett's claim (for the British case) that sound-locators were the result of collaboration by specialists from different fields clearly doesn't take us all the way. Bartlett made specific claims about the transformation of individual ideas in the course of interaction and the unwitting modifications introduced in practice. He spoke as if he had been an observer of the day-to-day development of sound-locators, peering over the shoulders of those involved and listening to their discussions. How could he have known that the suggestions of A and B were taken up and modified so that they were no longer exactly as A and B had proposed them? Perhaps Bartlett was indeed party to such discussions and was actually in a position to make these claims as a result of direct observation. Or was he saying what must have been the case, in the light of all he knew about cognition and social interaction drawn from other sources, such as his serial reproduction experiments? So far, I have no evidence either way. It is certainly true, however, as the Hill report makes clear, that a number of modifications were introduced in the course of practice in the British model. Thick rubber tubing was replaced by thin copper tubing; greater attention was paid to the smoothness of the join between trumpet and pipe; the ring-sight was modified so the sighting number did not have to crouch at high elevations; the trumpets were covered with hessian and painted to stop them cracking; and various different sizes and mixtures of sizes of trumpets were tried out; attempts were made to put boxes round the trumpets to stop the effects of wind; and later, baffles were introduced into the mouths of the trumpets themselves; various ear-protectors were tried to protect listeners from the acoustical effect of nearby gun-fire, and so on. But again, the precise negotiation of these processes remains elusive. Perhaps, for the moment at least, it is best to say that Bartlett was here reminding us of what we ought to know or assume about the collective character of cognition, but what we so frequently forget because of the rooted individualism of the psychological perspective.

NATIONAL STYLES

Bartlett said that sound-locators developed in different countries differed from one another in significant ways. Is this true? Figure 12.1 shows a standard British model. Notice the short, wide-angled collecting trumpets. Now look at the French telesitemetre, developed by the physicist Perrin, and shown in Fig. 12.2. Notice the multitude of small trumpets within the four groups on the alt-azimuth stand.

FIG. 12.2   French telesitemetre (with permission, Mittler Verlag).

What of the German system? The apparatus developed by the psychologist E.M. von Hornbostel is shown in Fig. 12.3, and the system of E. Waetzmann in Fig. 12.4. I shall come back to the Hornbostel and Waetzmann devices in a moment. If we follow Bartlett and bring post-war developments into the story we can add others to the collection. Figure 12.5 is the American system with its large and long, exponentially shaped collectors, and Fig. 12.6 shows the Goerz system manufactured in Bratislava. The Goerz system used a mixed reflecting and collecting process. The sound was focused by reflection and then channelled down the arms of the device (see Paris, 1933).

Clearly, Bartlett was right about the facts to be explained. There was a range of devices differing from one another in interesting ways. Nevertheless, it is necessary to step with caution. Simply exhibiting diversity, as these pictures undeniably do, is not enough to substantiate the claim that the systems *commonly*

FIG. 12.3   The German Hornbostel apparatus (with permission, Mittler Verlag).

in use differed from one another. The problem is knowing whether the picture portrays equipment that was widely used or whether it is a prototype and an experimental variant. In the case of the British, French, American and German models shown in Figs. 12.1 to 12.6, the evidence is that they were in general use.[19] The point of attending to the difference between apparatus in common use and mere prototypes is that one would naturally expect more idiosyncrasy amongst prototypes. Conventionalisation, and the impress of the style of the group or nation concerned, would be more reasonably expected in the case of officially accepted and sanctioned production models.[20]

This takes us to the aspect of Bartlett's claim that is most difficult to assess. Did the development of these pieces of technology, and the emergence of the differences between them, really reflect social properties of the groups who produced them? Let us start at the beginning by looking at the development of

FIG. 12.4   The German Waetzmann apparatus (with permission, Bundesarchiv).

the standard British locator. According to the 1922 report the first phase of the British effort to produce a sound-locator for aircraft involved examining and modifying a French device called the Claude orthophone, see Fig. 12.7. This was not an aircraft detector but designed for use in trench-warfare for locating enemy guns. It was essentially a huge pipe, some 23-feet long pivoted at the centre so that it could swing round. The ends of the pipe were bent forward. The piping to the left and right of the central pivot led, respectively, into the left and right sides of a stethoscope. This allowed the operator, safe in a dugout, to turn the device until it pointed to the source of the sound made by enemy guns. Experiments at the National Physical Laboratory quickly convinced the British that a much shorter device, between five and seven feet, could be almost as accurate. As well as shortening it, the experimenters did three other things to the orthophone: (1) they added collecting trumpets to the ends of the pipe, (2) they introduced two further trumpets attached to a pipe to be used vertically to detect elevation, and (3) mounted the set-up on an alt-azimuth stand (see Fig. 12.8).

FIG. 12.5   The American exponential Horn (with permission, Mittler Verlag).

But the 1922 report by Hill et al. makes it clear that this set-up was felt to be something of a failure. The conclusion was that the trumpets were too small. Aircraft typically emit low-frequency sounds from their engine exhaust (around 80 cycles per second for a Gotha) and this required a larger trumpet to catch the sound.

Now look again at the picture of the Hornbostel system, Fig. 12.3. On the basis of these pictures the Hornbostel system looks suspiciously like the British development of the Claude orthophone. Indeed, the devices are so similar that one wonders if the orthophone might have been a common parent of the two— the model from which both sides worked. Evidence from photographs, rather than from an examination of actual artefacts, or their detailed specifications, is hazardous, but if the two systems were very similar what does this mean for Bartlett's claim? It looks, superficially, as if it spells trouble. So much, it seems, for the significance of the different groups who produced the two devices. Shouldn't they be producing different technological solutions rather than very similar ones? But then we must remember that the British rejected this model, whereas (if I am right in my assessment of similarity) the Germans accepted it. It is true that after the war, for example in Hunke's *Luftgefahr und Luftschutz*

FIG. 12.6   The Goerz apparatus (with permission, Imperial War Museum).

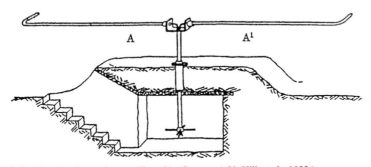

FIG. 12.7   The Claude gun-locator (French). (Source: A.V. Hill et al., 1922.)

(1935, pp. 87–88), the feeble performance of the Hornbostel apparatus was a matter for dismissive comment, but the fact remains that it came into use by the German armed forces whereas the modified Claude apparatus was not used by the British army because it was rejected at the experimental stage. The situation is therefore an interesting one and clearly supports rather than undermines Bartlett's claims. We have, roughly, the same technology rejected by one group but accepted by another. As Bartlett would perhaps have expressed it: One sensory pattern

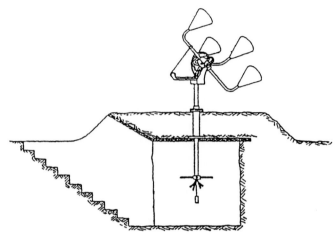

FIG. 12.8   A British experimental modification of the Claude locator. (Source: A.V. Hill et al., 1922.)

is producing a diversity of responses. Where, therefore, do we look for the explanation? Certainly not in the 'stimulus'. The answer can only be in the groups themselves. This differential response, at the group level, tells us something about the responding groups.[21]

What sort of thing might it tell us? At its boldest and simplest this type of claim suggests that we could 'read off' the alleged national or cultural character-istics of the producers from the products. It suggests there was something 'typic-ally British' about a British sound-locator, and something 'typically German' about a German apparatus and so on. Looking at the elaborate elegance of the French system, and the enormous size of the American, compared with the simplicity and modesty of the British, one can feel the temptation, as Bartlett coyly put it, to speak in social group terms.[22] In *Remembering* (1932), Bartlett did not actually refer to the typically British or typically French.[23] He said that each device developed in its own special social milieu and implied that this special milieu would find expression in the fact that some sound-locators 'demand very much greater interdependence among the members of the team' (p. 277). An undated manuscript for a course of lectures on social psychology in the Bartlett papers, however, shows him taking a step closer to the national typicality hypothesis. In a passage that otherwise looks like a draft for the discussion in *Remembering*, he said, 'A listening instrument for instance is a group affair, and in the German type the interdependence among the members of the listening unit is greater than in the British type' (Box 2, folders B1–B7, item B6).

Such a claim is difficult to assess without direct empirical observation and perhaps Bartlett based his claim on such data. Having no such data myself, and no knowledge of Bartlett's sources, I am forced to speculate.[24] I can see nothing about the Hornbostel apparatus that suggests the teamwork involved in its operation is significantly different from that of the standard British sound-locator. Photographs show the standard trio of azimuth listener, elevation listener and sighting number. The sighting system shown in Fig. 12.3 seems to be less convenient than that on all but the earliest British models, forcing the sighting number to crouch, but that would hardly provide a basis for Bartlett's claim. It is possible, however, that he had in mind the Waetzmann apparatus as shown in Fig. 12.4. The picture suggests (though it does not prove) that the azimuth and elevation listeners worked independently of one another. If there was indeed no mechanical connection between the listening devices of the two observers then the task of combining their different orientations in order to guide the search-light would be greater than using a sighting device on an alt-azimuth system. The team-work aspect of its operation might therefore be more demanding and difficult. In this sense it might involve greater interdependence among the members of the listening unit as Bartlett intimated.[25]

As I have just indicated, there are problems in assessing some of Bartlett's specific claims. There can be no doubt, however, that the general question, as to the causes of the differences in the design of sound-locators, is a real one.[26] There is also no doubt that a search for the cause of such differences is the kind of enquiry that today's sociologists of scientific knowledge would want to encourage. It would not now be readily taken for granted that national stereotypes could be read off such a piece of technology, but the assumption would still be that the explanation of the differences would, at some significant level, implicate social processes. Let me explain this. Recall the co-operation between specialists to which Bartlett alluded. We only have to imagine different degrees of co-operation and different patterns of interaction to see how the resulting techno-logy could be influenced. For example, think of the impact that might be had by a preference for laboratory work over field trials. Or suppose that laboratory-based scientists or theoretical specialists had their say first, and their conclusions fixed the terms of reference within which subsequent development was required to take place.[27] The outcome could be very different from a development pro-cess in which academics and military men rubbed shoulders from the outset. In the former, a concern for theoretical elegance might override pragmatic considera-tions, producing a device that was more advanced and sophisticated, but less handy. Different boundaries and different hierarchies, as well as different research traditions and different theoretical models, would then all leave their imprint on a piece of technology—even if they did not stamp an immediately recognisable and stereotyped physiognomy on the result.[28]

BARTLETT AND THE SOCIOLOGY OF SCIENCE

To consolidate this picture of Bartlett as a proto-sociologist of scientific know-ledge I shall briefly broaden the discussion to take in certain features of his general methodological position. This will allow me to emphasise the family resemblance between his work and certain positions in contemporary sociology of scientific knowledge.

I have already drawn attention to Bartlett's emphasis on the role of practice, his resolute anti-individualism and his realism with regard to group tendencies and dispositions. His classic studies of conventionalisation pre-figure today's studies of the differential reception and interpretation of scientific theories and results. (Elsewhere, I have compared Bartlett's results with a recent study of the reception, in Cambridge, of Einstein's 1905 work on relativity.[29]) There is also a similarity between Bartlett's account of creativity, as arising from an outside stimulus where 'realms organised by interests usually kept apart are brought together' (1932, p. 226), and recent work on what is called the interaction theory of metaphor. This inductivist account of scientific thought, particularly as it has been developed by Hesse (1974), has been influential in the sociology of knowledge. We can see Bartlett moving from the old anthropological concern with the progress of civilisation, and the contact of peoples and groups, to an attempt to spell out the cognitive mechanics of innovation. Perhaps the most characteristic, though still controversial, stance of contemporary sociology of scientific knowledge is the so-called 'symmetry postulate'. Although he did not use this label I shall now show that Bartlett's work embodied the requirement of 'methodological symmetry.' In some important respects he can be seen as one of the pioneers of this approach.[30]

In this context, 'symmetry' means giving the same, general kind of explanation for beliefs the investigator evaluates as true or rational as is given to those which are evaluated as false or irrational. (Psychologists will recognise this as a generalisation of the idea that, say, the same visual mechanisms underlie both veridical and illusory perception; see Broadbent, 1973, p. 63.) Thus, in *Remembering* (1932), we find Bartlett concerned, not with the conditions of accurate recall, but with the general process by which the past is mobilised for use in the present. He warns us against narrowing down the phenomenon of remembering to that of remembering rightly, as if the rest is not really remembering at all. This may be what philosophers want to say, but it isn't the way to get hold of biological and social reality. The 'status' of the knowledge given in recall, he said, was of no concern to him (p. 12). In extending this approach from psychology to sociology Bartlett enjoined us always to look for alternatives to a group's practices. This is how we identify what the social group contributes, as distinct from what the non-social world demands. We recognise what is conventional by identifying other actual or possible practices—like driving on different sides of the road.[31]

> Taking whatever group we are studying, we must try to find some social situation which offers alternative social solutions. If the alternative solutions definitely conflict, so much the better. If the alternative adopted can be shown, on general principles of social welfare, to be disadvantageous, best of all.
>
> (Bartlett, 1932, p. 262)

So much the better because, in the first case, conflict exposes social process which might otherwise remain hidden from view, and in the second case, the better to show the strength of traditions and conventions by exhibiting their power to overrule other forces. This was why Bartlett was interested in the different ways in which sound-locators were developed. He was not interested in judging which was the best—everybody wanted the best—but he was interested in explaining why people got the technology they did.

> In perceiving, in imagining, in remembering proper, and in constructive work, the passing fashion of the group, the social catch-word, the prevailing approved general interest, the persistent social custom and institution set the stage and direct the action.
>
> (Bartlett, 1932, p. 244)

I do not want to create the impression that I think Bartlett's sociological orientation was flawless, or even that it was particularly well-developed. It wasn't. It was programmatic and conjectural. It is impossible to read Bartlett's attempts to pin-point the essential character of social phenomena without feeling that it eluded him. In Bartlett's writings the basis of social ontology remains a mystery. Nevertheless, the main ingredients of today's sociology of scientific knowledge can all be found, in some more or less developed form in Bartlett's work: under-determination, conventionalisation and the study of reception, the importance of conflict, the concern with practice, the role of metaphor, anti-individualism, and methodological symmetry.[32]

CONCLUSION

Fortunately, for my purposes, it is not necessary to know that Bartlett was right in every respect in which he made claims or dropped hints. All that is necessary is that we can see the point and the interest of the questions he was posing, and see that, on some level, he was right about where the answers lay. It would be a fascinating exercise to try to carry through the sociological investigation at which he hinted in *Remembering* (1932). My aim has simply been to indicate Bartlett's position with regard to his antecedents and his successors. Bartlett stretched out one hand to reach for the theoretical and conceptual resources on offer from McDougall, Rivers and Haddon; with the other hand he reached forward towards the sociology of scientific knowledge. He links the pioneers of the Torres Straits to the controversial social constructivists of today.[33]

ACKNOWLEDGEMENTS

I should like to thank the helpful staff at the Public Record Office, the Imperial War Museum, the Deutsches Museum, Cambridge University Library (for the Bartlett papers), the Bodleian (for the Milne papers) and the Churchill Archives Centre (for the Hill papers). I am particularly indebted to Col. Guy Yeoman for making a copy of *Theory and*

Use of Anti-aircraft Sound-locators (Hill et al., 1922) available to me. David Edgerton, Matthias Klaes, Martin Kusch, Donald MacKenzie, Alex Roland, Steve Sturdy and Ed Westerman have given me invaluable help.

I should also like to thank the staff at the Imperial War Museum photo archive, and at the Bundesarchiv, Koblenz, for their help. The provenance of the illustrations is as follows: Figs. 12.1 and 12.6 are printed with permission from the Imperial War Museum; Figs. 12.2, 12.3 and 12.5 are reproduced with permission from M. Hunke, *Luftgefahr und Luftschutz*, Berlin, Mittler, 1935; Fig. 12.4 is reproduced by permission of the Bundesarchiv (Bild 141/2346); Figs. 12.7 and 12.8 are taken from A.V. Hill et al. (1922).

NOTES

1   This is an expanded version of a paper given at a conference on 'Anthropology and Psychology: The Legacy of the Torres Strait Expedition (1898–1998)' at St. John's College, Cambridge, 10–12 August 1998.

2   The result of repeated reproduction depends on pre-existing conventionalised forms of understanding, but where do these come from? They are the result of serial, cognitive interactions of the kind captured, at least in part, by the serial reproduction experiment. Viewed in this way, serial reproduction is the more fundamental process. Bartlett never followed through the suggestions furnished by his own experiments and so never gave an adequate account of conventions. For a treatment of the kind he needed see Barnes (1983).

3   As Bartlett said 'the social group, as such, possesses a certain trend of development. This trend need not be, and in the majority of cases it certainly is not, present in the mind, or fully represented in the behaviour, of any individual member of the group' (Bartlett, 1932, p. 275).

4   For the symposium see Bartlett (1928b) and the following papers by MacCurdy, Armstrong and Haddon. For individualistic criticisms of Rivers and Bartlett see Allport (1924a, 1924b) who thinks Bartlett's belief in the explanatory significance of social tendencies is 'gratuitous' (Allport, 1924a, p. 187). Urbach (1980) gives a methodological defence of social propensities based on Popper's propensity theory of probability.

5   For a guide to the literature see Shapin (1982).

6   Bartlett's comment that the post-war devices were significantly different from the original wartime systems can be understood as a reference to the operation of serial processes similar to those at work on his folk story.

7   Bartlett here anticipates the concern with the tacit dimension of knowledge and the emphasis on practice in current work in the sociology of science; see Collins (1985).

8   This claim is pre-figured in the folk story material by the remark that, 'there is some suggestion that material treated by way of serial reproduction may gain a kind of group stamp or character' (Bartlett, 1932, p. 173).

9   Whist it may be true that all *sound-locators* may have a certain similarity due to physical and physiological necessity it is not true that, as Bartlett said, all *aircraft detection* systems must be similar for these reasons. The limitation in question actually came from limitations of knowledge and the cultural resources that were brought to bear on the problem. Bartlett was writing before radar was known about, so it is easy to see how the mistake could have been made, but even at the time this over-

estimation of the role of physical constraints might have been avoided by reference to the possibilities of infra-red detection.

10 What about other sources of error such as wind drift and diffraction due to changes in atmospheric temperature? In the British locator, temperature corrections could be made by pivoting the ring-sight eccentrically. As for wind, it was argued that, over a considerable range, the effect of wind on the sound of an aircraft was compensated for by its effect on the aircraft itself (see Hill et al., 1922, chap. 5).

11 An alternative method involved trying to get two or three searchlights to converge on an intruder and have defending aeroplanes fly towards the point of intersection. Defending a large area such as London was a major feat of social co-ordination.

12 See Oldfield (1972, p. 134).

13 See file FD/1/7186. A document dated 20 January 1928 indicates that a request was received by the Medical Research Council from the Anti-Aircraft Sub-Committee of the Committee of Imperial Defence. Bartlett was proposed as a member of the committee from the outset, his work, with C.S. Myers, on hydrophones being explicitly mentioned.

14 For work on localisation prompted by these concerns and commissioned by the committee see Shaxby and Gage (1932), James and Massey (1932) and James (1936). Sound-locators, and their significance on the design of the study, are mentioned on pages 5 and 6 of Shaxby and Gage. For the state-of the-art by the end of the 1930s and 1940s see Woodworth (1939) and Boring, Langfeld and Weld (1948)—which has a photograph of a sound-locator on p. 339.

15 Tucker had originally worked on sound rangers, that is, devices for locating heavy guns by acoustical means. In this connection he was responsible for the development of the Tucker hot-wire microphone, which found its way into physics textbooks. Sound-rangers seemed to be a success story by comparison with sound-locators. Tucker worked hard to replace the human operator of the standard four-trumpet sound-locator by microphones. He also developed locators which consisted of large circles of microphones. For a general report by Tucker on binaural, and other, sound-locators see Tucker (1936).

16 Milne wrote to Hill (2 September 1919) that he had submitted 'that old M.I.D. report of mine' on the geometry of sound-locator sights and trumpets as part of his Fellow-ship dissertation at Trinity (see Milne papers D 63, box 429, f. 309).

17 Research was also done at the National Physical Laboratory in 1915 by A. Campbell at the behest of the Director, Sir Richard Glazebrook who had been approached by Lieut. Commander H. D. Capper of the Dover Anti-Aircraft Corp. See PRO DSIR 10/127. Flugel's (1919) paper on local fatigue in the auditory system arose out of war work with Spearman on locators (see p. 106). Flugel's interpretation was challenged by further data in Bartlett and Mark (1922).

18 For brevity I shall refer to *The Theory and Use of Anti-aircraft Sound-locators* as Hill et al. (1922). On the work of the Munitions Inventions Department see Pattison (1983) and Hartcup (1988). For a brief account of Hill's wartime role see Katz (1978) and for Milne see McCrea (1951). Hill's role was not purely nominal: see his detailed comments on Jakeman's experiments in Hill papers AVH 1/20.

19 Amongst other sources see PRO AVIA 7/3254 (Index to Sound Locators: Service and Experimental Instruments, June 1923), Tucker (1936), Paris (1933) and Hunke (1935).

20   Hunke (1935) Abbildung 16, show a photograph of a Hornbostel locator directly attached to a searchlight. Was this a general practice or an experimental prototype? Hunke provides criticisms of this method, but his language suggests that it was an experiment rather than routine practice: cf. p. 107.

21   Sociologists and philosophers call this 'under-determination'. A similar point about underdetermination could be made with respect to the short horns preferred by the British compared with the long, exponential horns preferred by the Americans, or the British rejection of multiple, small horns compared with their acceptance by the French. In another form it is a phenomenon with which Bartlett was, of course, very familiar given the perceptual experiments reported in *Remembering* (see Bartlett, 1932, p. 108).

22   There is a hint, though no more than a hint, of this thesis in *The Theory and Use of Anti-aircraft Sound-locators*. There we see the British dismissing the French system because it is too elaborate and expensive (Hill et al., 1922, pp. 121, 82), and the American system because it is too big (p. 73).

23   But he came close. He spoke with apparent agreement about the characteristic style imputed to different national rugby teams, with Irish 'turbulence', English 'persistence' and French 'individuality' (p. 278).

24   It is possible that Bartlett could have compared notes with both Hornbostel and Waetzmann after the war because, along with Tucker, they all gave papers at a conference on audition held at Imperial College on 19 June 1931. (See 'Report of a Discussion on Audition', The Physical Society, London, 1931.) Hornbostel, who had worked during the war on sound location with Max Wertheimer and Kurt Koffka, gave a paper on the time-difference theory of localisation. Waetzmann was reporting on the threshold sensitivity of the ear. Tucker talked on the intensity theory of localisation. This war work is mentioned on pp. 220–221 of Koffka (1936). On Hornbostel and Waetzmann see Boring (1942) and (1950). Bartlett's own contribution to the conference was a paper called 'On certain general conditions of auditory experiments' (1931) and explicitly mentioned problems that arise because of inner changes in the mental set of listeners engaged in binaural location experiments of the kind then being encouraged by the Physiology of Hearing Committee.

25   The only other possibility I can think of is that Bartlett was referring to the way some locators were connected mechanically to the searchlights they controlled. Such systems were developed by all the main nations after World War I. (For the French Bochet system see Hill et al., 1922, p. 166). It is unclear from this source whether this was a wartime, or a post-war, development. If this is what Bartlett had in mind it is difficult to see how it could differentiate between significant groups because it became widespread. (It is more likely that these devices were what Bartlett had in mind when he noticed that some bits of the technology, 'have been transferred bodily from one group to another'; Bartlett, 1932, p. 277.)

26   An interesting methodological question is: What is the null-hypothesis? What would be expected in terms of variation if Bartlett were quite wrong and nothing specific to the character of the group received expression in the design of the preferred type of sound locator? Presumably two, disjoint groups, which were empirically indistinguishable in terms of social structure and even, let us suppose, in terms of past culture would not necessarily generate *identical* technical solutions to the problem of aircraft detection. Though no one would be surprised if their technologies were

close, a degree of random variation would be expected. How do we know that we are not looking at such random variation? To some extent we probably are, but this cannot be the whole story. We must not forget the extent to which, especially in the inter-war years, one group knew of the other's preferences and sought actively to compare the options. Despite these comparisons and despite the shared knowledge they typically stuck to their preferred solutions. As far as I am aware, the Americans never convinced the British of the need for the large, exponential horn, though (according to contemporary British sources) they may have convinced the Japanese. Similarly, the British did not, like the French, ever adopt the multiple horn solution, though, it appears, the Poles did (see AVIA 7/2810). Such systematic exercises of judgement are not illuminated by the random variation model. At least one contemporary, expert observer of these developments in the inter-war years noticed and expressed some surprise. 'Es ist interessant,' said Hunke (1935, p. 88), 'dass alle diese Staaten nach dem Krieg an den frueheren Schallempfaengern festgehalten haben.' I should like to thank Dr. Jonathan Miller for reminding me, in a rather striking way, of the need to address the null-hypothesis. He said that the photographs, especially those of the Perrin and Goerz locators, reminded him of some the profusion of exotic marine organisms thrown up in the course of evolution—as they were described, for example, in Gould's *Wonderful Life* (1991). So why was it necessary to go for a social rather than a biological and evolutionary mechanism based on random variation? The considerations given previously, about the preferences that were sustained even when alternatives were known about, bring with them the need to go beyond the analogy with evolution. Such preferences have a normative character and must be actively sustained as conventions within the relevant groups. I cannot resist one further observation arising out of this discussion. While Dr. Miller looks at the Goerz machine and sees, perhaps, some arthropod from the Burgess Shale, or looks at the Telesitemetre and imagines a sea anemone, others comment on the 'modern' look of the Goerz and mention the art-deco iron-work of a Paris Metro station in connection with Perrin's device. 'It looks as if it is made out of café tables' reported one observer. These constructive and projective processes are just those that Bartlett himself studied in chaps. II and III of *Remembering*. They involve what he called the 'effort after meaning' (1932, p. 20).

27 Could it be of any significance that it was the practice in Germany to refer to the 'Hornbostel–Horchgeraet' and the 'Waetzmann–Horchgeraet', that is, to designate them with an individual's name? From Hill et al. (1922) I suspect this was also a French practice. Of course, the British also made references to 'Bennett mountings' (and 'Sutton harnesses', 'Sidcot suits' and the like) but it is possible that this was, or was more frequently, an informal rather than an officially sanctioned practice. The issue needs proper investigation.

28 For a comparative study contrasting French and American engineering traditions see Kranakis (1989) and (1997). For further case studies in the sociology of technology see MacKenzie and Wajcman (1985) and MacKenzie (1990, 1996). Vincenti's (1990) *What Engineers Know and How They Know It*, provides case studies that not only deal with Bartlettian themes, such as conventionalisation, (see in particular chap. 4 on control-volume analysis) but do so in a rather Bartlettian style. Another striking example of different national styles in engineering is the switch to all-metal aeroplanes in the United States. This resulted in their manufacturers' effectively 'forgetting' how

to build wooden aircraft, something not true of the British, as witness the remarkable de Havilland Mosquito (see Schatzberg (1994, in press)).

29 See Bloor (1997). The sophisticated reception study I discuss is by Warwick (1992–93) who describes the divergent readings of Einstein's famous 1905 paper on relativity by Cambridge experimentalists and mathematicians. They selectively absorbed what was significant to them in the light of their goals and interests. Another recent study of the history of relativity theory can also be read as an identification of Bartlettian processes. Staley (1998) describes the role of what he calls participants' histories. These are historical commentaries provided by scientists themselves in the course of exposition and criticism of the theory during the time of its creative development. They are not to be looked on as merely amateur histories, to be contrasted with those produced by professionals, nor are they merely reflections on what has happened: They are part of the process by which the theory is constructed. They are constitutive of the reality on which they comment. We can think of these participant histories as rather like Bartlett's folk stories, which, he said, following Boas, present the 'autobiography of the tribe' (1923, p. 72). It is sad that Bartlett never pursued this self-referential aspect of the matter to any great depth.

30 Another pioneer was the associationist G.E. Mueller of Goettingen (see Kusch, 1999).

31 In his book *Thinking*, Bartlett (1958) gave a clear statement of methodological symmetry when he said, 'There is no psychological sense in saying that thinking takes place only if a "right" issue is reached. There is thinking whatever issue is reached so long as an attempt is made to carry further the evidence, or information, that has been made available' (p. 50). It is unfortunate that by this stage, despite the subtitle of the book ('An experimental and social study') and occasional references to the social character of knowledge, the approach was largely focused on individual psychological mechanisms.

32 What about the 'reflexivity' that is also characteristic of today's sociology of knowledge? Here is Bartlett in reflexive mode: 'for a large part of my own life,' he said, 'I have been watching experimentalists at work . . . all of this watching and working can be regarded as a sort of prolonged experiment on experimental thinking' (1958, p. 115). Bartlett was always highly aware of the extent to which his own experiments were themselves sites for the operation of the very processes under study. This was why he was sensitive to the problems created by placing a subject in an artificial and contrived laboratory environment. It would lead to the production of *ad hoc* responses that would say nothing about what might happen under more realistic and natural circumstances. He was always keen to proceed in ways that were as close to real circumstances as possible, and he knew that that meant taking into account the social dimension of a process. There is also a more poignant side to reflexivity as it impinged on Bartlett's work. The social constructiveness of *Remembering* (1932) has been forgotten because of exactly those mechanisms Bartlett himself identified. The message of his book has been conventionalised to make it fit the culture of current psychology; so these parts have dropped from awareness. Bartlett has been the victim of the very conventionalisation he made visible. Nevertheless, his theory certainly applies to itself and, at least, formally and logically, does so in a way that confirms rather than refutes it.

33 Today the approach known as social constructivism is highly controversial and is often dismissed as anti-scientific. This misunderstanding and mischaracterisation of

the field as a whole has wide circulation and has become something of a convention in academic discourse. It dominates the perceptions and memories of critics quite regardless of what is actually said. For some Bartlettian reflections on this deplorable state of affairs see my 'Remember the Strong Programme?' (Bloor, 1997). In Bartlett's day it was possible to be both a respected member of the Royal Society of London *and* a social constructivist.

Bibliography

The papers of Frederic Charles Bartlett

Hugh Frederic Bartlett

INTRODUCTORY NOTE

My father died in Cambridge, England, in September 1969 aged 82. He was born in the small Cotswold town of Stow-on-the-Wold. During his career he received honorary membership or fellowship of many professional societies and institutions throughout the world, honorary doctorates from seven universities, the Royal Medal of the Royal Society, the Gold Medal of the International Academy of Aviation and Space Medicine, the Baly Medal of the Royal College of Physicians and the Huxley Medal of the Royal Anthropological Society. He was knighted in 1948. His career is summarised in the obituaries and biographical notes that form part of this collection of papers.

The sections that follow, though incomplete in some respects, are probably the most complete listing of my father's academic work in existence. All of my father's published papers are, or should be, available to a determined reader through the world's libraries.

Papers deposited in the University Library, Cambridge

A list of papers sent by my mother to the Royal Society after my father's death is contained in CSAC 36/13/75 *Papers of Sir Frederic Bartlett CBE FRS 1886–1969*, prepared by Jeannine Alton and Harriot Weiskittel at The Contemporary Scientific Archives Centre, Joint Committee on Scientific and Technological Records, The Royal Commission on Historical Manuscripts, The Royal Society. In 1975 these papers were deposited in the University Library, Cambridge. This list has the following contents:

Notebooks	(A.1–A.42)
Lectures, Addresses, Reports	(B.1–B.88)
Publications	(C.1–C.32)
University of Cambridge	(D.1–D.5)

How complete are the lists?

My original intention was simply to make a fair copy of a catalogue of some papers (no longer available) sent to me after my father's death. This has now extended to include other papers. In this Bibliography Sections A, B, C and D are as complete as I can make them at this time. I believe that Section A is close to being complete and comprehensive. Section B is certainly incomplete but I know of no more complete list. Section C is probably fairly complete in the years that are covered, but years 1924 to 1941 are missing. Section D has an obvious omission; nearly all the papers are sourced in the UK and there are no foreign-language papers. Section E lists only the first four Sir Frederic Bartlett lectures. I do not know whether the series continued after the last of those I have listed.

Section F includes a representative choice of honours and awards. It is intended to supplement rather than replace the information provided in other sections.

A personal note

My father's powers of leadership and of constructive thought will be evident from the public record of his working life. Not shown in this record is the fact that he maintained a balance between his working life and his family life. He spent a part of each day with his family—my mother, my brother and myself. I have often considered myself fortunate to have been brought up in such a family.

SECTION A: THE PUBLISHED PAPERS OF FREDERIC CHARLES BARTLETT

This bibliography is based on A.O. Harris and O.L. Zangwill (1973), 'The Writings of Sir Frederic Bartlett CBE, FRS: An annotated handlist', *British Journal of Psychology* 64: 493–510, which lists 150 published papers. I have added more than 40 additional items that have come to me from various sources. My aim has been to produce as complete a list of Bartlett's published papers as possible.

Comments are based on the handlist of Harris and Zangwill.

Entries are in chronological order, as in Harris and Zangwill's paper, and are numbered sequentially. Foreign language translations are given the same number as the English version. Because of this and because items have been added the numbering differs from that of Harris and Zangwill.

1914

(1) *Exercises in Logic.* London: W.B. Clive, University Tutorial Press (pp. 136). (Reprinted 1926, 1948, 1955.)
    Exercises and *Key to Exercises* were designed to be used with J. Welton and A.J. Monahan (1911) *An Intermediate Logic*, London: W.B. Clive, University Tutorial Press (pp. xviii, 513), 'though this will not prevent the book being used with any other textbook'. Similar Keys were produced for other volumes in the University Tutorial Series.

(2) *Key to Exercises in Logic.* London: W.B. Clive, University Tutorial Press (pp. iv, 130). (2nd ed. 1930, London: University Tutorial Press.)

1916

(3) 'Transformations arising from repeated representation: A contribution towards an experimental study of the process of conventionalisation', Fellowship Dissertation, St. John's College, Cambridge.
    Although not in the public domain, Harris and Zangwill included this dissertation in their list of published papers, perhaps because of its importance to Bartlett's career. It contains the kernel of many ideas Bartlett expanded in his subsequent work.

The thesis is discussed in Zangwill's (1972) third Bartlett Memorial Lecture entitled '*Remembering* Revisited', *Quarterly Journal of Experimental Psychology* 24: 123–138, and also in R.C. Oldfield's Obituary Notice (Section D, 22).

(4) Symposium: 'The implications of recognition, Part II', *Proceedings of the Aristotelian Society* 16: 189–201. (Part I was by B. Edgell, Part III by G.E. Moore and Part IV by H. Willdon Carr.)

All four papers were read at a meeting of the Aristotelian Society on 20 March 1916, with the President, Dr. H. Willdon Carr, in the Chair. The minutes of the 37th session (1915–16) record that among those taking part in the debate were Professor G. Dawes Hicks, Professor T. Percy Nunn, Arthur Lynch, MP and Professor J. Brough. Miss Edgell replied to the discussion. Bartlett had been elected to the Society in the previous year together with Mr. T. Stearns Eliot and Professor A.N. Whitehead.

(5) 'An experimental study of some problems of perceiving and imaging', *British Journal of Psychology* 8: 222–266.

This is Bartlett's first published paper in experimental psychology. He described several related experiments on perceiving forms, patterns and representational designs under conditions of short exposure, together with some experiments on the interpretation of ink-blots. These experiments are reported in more condensed form in *Remembering* (see 53).

1917

(6) 'Valuation and existence', *Proceedings of the Aristotelian Society* 17: 117–138.

This paper was read at a meeting of the Aristotelian Society on 5 February 1917, with the President, Dr. H. Willdon Carr, in the Chair. According to the minutes of the 38th session (1916–17) the discussion was opened by the Chairman, and Mr. Douglas Ainslie, Professor G. Dawes Hicks, Miss Beatrice Edgell, Mr. W.A. Pickard-Cambridge, Miss F. Rosamond Shields, Rev. A.E. Davies, Rev. John Drake and Mr. Morris Ginsberg participated in the discussion. 'Mr. Bartlett replied to the criticisms that had been made.'

1918

(7) 'The development of criticism', *Proceedings of the Aristotelian Society* 18: 75–100.

Read to the Aristotelian Society on 3 December 1917, with the President, Dr. H. Willdon Carr, in the Chair. The minutes record that the Chairman opened the discussion, and the following members took part: Professor G. Dawes Hicks, Mr. St. George Lane Fox Pitt, Miss Beatrice Edgell, Mr. W.E. Urwick and Rev. S.E. Hooper. Mr. Bartlett replied.

(8)   'Critical notice of *Studies in Psychology*', *Mind* 27: 361–366.
       Referring to *Studies in Psychology: Contributed by colleagues and former students of Edward Bradford Titchener* (1917), Worcester, MA: L.N. Wilson (337pp.).

1919

(9)   [With E.M. Smith] 'On listening to sounds of weak intensity', pre-printed summary of lecture given to British Psychological Society on 31 May 1919.

1920

(10)   [With E.M. Smith] 'On listening to sounds of weak intensity, Part I', *British Journal of Psychology* 10: 101–129.
(11)   [With E.M. Smith] 'On listening to sounds of weak intensity, Part II', *British Journal of Psychology* 10: 133–165.
       These papers, written in association with E.M. Smith (later Lady Bartlett), constitute a highly interesting introspective study of auditory perception under conditions of near-threshold stimulation. They are the first of Bartlett's several publications in the psycho-acoustic field (see also 18, 50, 54, 57, 152).
(12)   [With E.M. Smith] 'Is thinking merely the action of language mechanisms? Part I', *British Journal of Psychology* 11: 55–62.
       This was a contribution to the symposium presented at the Congress of Philosophy in Oxford on 24–27 September 1920. Part II was by Godfrey H. Thomson, Part III by T.H. Pear, Part IV by Arthur Robinson and Part V by John B. Watson.
(13)   'Adventure', *The Eagle, St. John's College Cambridge* 41: 194–196.
(14)   'Some experiments on the reproduction of folk stories', *Folk-Lore* 31: 30–47.
(15)   'Psychology in relation to the popular story', *Folk-Lore* 31: 264–293.

1921

(16)   'The functions of images', *British Journal of Psychology* 11: 320–337.
(17)   'Critical notice of *The group mind: A sketch of the principles of collective psychology with some attempt to apply them to the interpretation of national life and character* by William McDougall', *British Journal of Psychology* 11: 3.

1922

(18)   [With H. Mark] 'A note on local fatigue in the auditory system', *British Journal of Psychology* 13: 215–218.
(19)   [With A.C. Haddon] 'Obituary notice: W.H.R. Rivers', *Man* 22: 97–104.

1923

(20) 'Williams Halse Rivers Rivers, 1864–1922', *American Journal of Psychology* 34: 275–277.
A touching personal tribute to W.H.R. Rivers and an indication of the influence which Rivers had upon Bartlett's interests and thoughts.
(21) 'W.H.R. Rivers', *The Eagle, St. John's College Cambridge* 43: 2–14.
(22) *Psychology and Primitive Culture*, Cambridge, UK: Cambridge University Press and New York: Macmillan (pp. ix, 294). Reprinted 1924, and in 1970 by Greenwood Press, CT.
Based on lectures delivered in 1922 at Bedford College for Women, in the University of London. A short and clearly written book in which Bartlett endeavours to apply psychological principles to our understanding of primitive culture. Although in some sense a reflection of Bartlett's unrealised anthropological vocation, the book merits attention as an early contribution towards what is nowadays called cross-cultural psychology. It is particularly noteworthy for its refutation of L. Lévy-Bruhl's conception of the 'pre-logical' character of primitive thought.

1924

(23) 'Symbolism in folk-lore', in *Proceedings of the VIIth International Congress of Psychology*, Cambridge, UK: Cambridge University Press (pp. 278–289).
The Congress was held at Oxford from 26 July to 2 August 1923, under the Presidency of Charles S. Myers. An interesting though difficult paper in which Bartlett discusses the psychological nature of symbols and their role in folk-lore. He returns to some of the problems discussed here in the second part of *Remembering* (see 53).

1925

(24) 'Group organisation and social behaviour', *International Journal of Ethics* 35: 346–367.
(25) 'Feeling, imaging and thinking', *British Journal of Psychology* 16: 16–28.
A short paper in which Bartlett advances the view that the term 'feeling' is commonly used to denote unclear or insufficiently analysed sensory or cognitive content.
(26) 'James Ward. 1843–1925 [obituary]', *American Journal of Psychology* 36: 449–453.
(27) 'The social functions of symbols', *Australasian Journal of Psychology and Philosophy* 3: 1–11.
(28) [With C.S. Myers] *A Text-book of Experimental Psychology with Laboratory Exercises: Pt. II. Laboratory exercises* (3rd ed.), Cambridge, UK: Cambridge University Press (pp. viii, 121). (Pt. I. Textbook, 3rd ed., Cambridge, UK: Cambridge University Press was by C.S. Myers.)

The first edition, in one volume, 1909, and the second edition, in two parts, 1911, were by Myers alone. First edition C.S. Myers, 1909, *A Text-book of Experimental Psychology*, London: Arnold (pp. viii, 432). Second edition C.S. Myers (1911), *A Text-book of Experimental Psychology with Laboratory Exercises: Pt. I. Textbook* (pp. vi, 344, 1 plate, 24 figures and diagrams), *Pt. II: Laboratory exercises* (42 figures and diagrams), Cambridge, UK: Cambridge University Press.

Bartlett contributed a number of new experiments to the *Laboratory Exercises*, in particular those concerned with the perception and reproduction of forms, recognition and recall, and processes of construction. In the main, however, the book continues to represent the German psychological tradition.

1926

(29) 'Psychology of culture contact', *Encyclopaedia Britannica, Vol. I* (13th ed.), London and New York: Encyclopaedia Britannica Co. Ltd (pp. 765–771).

(30) 'Critical notice of Head's *Aphasia*', *British Journal of Psychology* 17: 154–161.

(31) 'Critical notice of Head's *Aphasia*', *Brain* 49: 581–587.

Referring to Head, H. (1926) *Aphasia and Kindred Disorders of Speech*, 2 vols., Cambridge, UK: Cambridge University Press (pp. xvi, 549; xxiii, 430). Reprinted New York and London, Hafner Publishing Company (1963).

This review clearly reflects the powerful impact made on Bartlett by Head's thinking, which had an important influence on his own theory of memory (see 53). Bartlett's interpretation of Head's view has been examined in R.C. Oldfield and O.L. Zangwill (1942) 'Head's concept of the Schema and its Application in Contemporary British Psychology: Pt. II. Critical examination of Head's theory', *British Journal of Psychology* 33: 58–64.

(32) 'The social psychology of leadership', *Journal of the National Institute of Industrial Psychology* 3: 188–193.

This article is part of a paper read before Section J (Psychology) at the British Association Meeting in Oxford in 1926.

1927

(33) 'Temperament and social status', *Journal of the National Institute of Industrial Psychology* 3: 401–405.

A paper read before Section J (Psychology) of the British Association Meeting in Leeds in 1927, as part of a discussion with Dr. Morris Ginsberg and Professor Godfrey Thomson on 'Inheritance and Social Status'.

(34)   'The relevance of visual imagery to the process of thinking: Pt. III',
        British Journal of Psychology 18: 23–29.
        Contribution to a symposium at a joint meeting of the British Psy-
        chological Society and the Cambridge Psychological Society, held in
        Cambridge on 30 April 1927. Part I was by T.H. Pear and Part II
        by F. Aveling. This article is of particular interest in that Bartlett
        adumbrates certain of the views about schemata and the theory of mem-
        ory later developed in *Remembering* (see 53). He also presents interesting
        views on the functions of visualising and vocalising in recall.

(35)   'Critical notice of Watson's *Behaviorism*', *Mind* 36: 77–83.
        Referring to Watson, J.B. (1925) *Behaviorism*, London: Kegan Paul
        (251pp.).
        Although this review shows clearly that Bartlett was very sceptical
        of the tenets of Behaviourism, he none the less adopted certain of the
        Behaviourist conventions, not least that of stimulus and response, in his
        general psychological thinking (see 45).

(36)   'The psychology of the lower races', in *Proceedings of the VIIIth
        International Congress of Psychology*, Gröningen, The Netherlands:
        P. Noordhoff (pp. 198–202).

(37)   *Psychology and the Soldier*, Cambridge, UK: Cambridge University Press
        (pp. viii, 224).
        This is a selection from a course of lectures, on psychology in relation
        to military problems, for which Bartlett was responsible in Cambridge
        during the years which followed World War I.

(38)   'Psychological qualities in leadership and management', in *Report of the
        25th Lecture Conference for Works Directors, Managers, Foremen, and
        Forewomen*. Balliol College, Oxford, 29 September to 3 October 1927
        (pp. 21–25).

1928

(39)   'Social constructiveness: Pt. I', *British Journal of Psychology* 18: 388–
        391.
        Contributed to a joint psychological and anthropological discussion
        held at Cambridge in March 1928. Part II was by J.T. McCurdy, Part
        III by W.E. Armstrong and Part IV by A.C. Haddon.

(40)   'Temperament and social class', *Eugenics Review* 20: 25–28.

(41)   'An experiment upon repeated reproduction', *Journal of General Psy-
        chology* 1: 54–63.

(42)   'Types of imagination', *Journal of Philosophical Studies* 3: 78–85.

(43)   'Review of *Common Principles in Psychology and Physiology* by John T.
        McCurdy', *The Hibbert Journal* 4: 765–767.

(44)   'The psychological process of sublimation', *Scientia* 43: 89–98.

1929

(45) 'Experimental method in psychology', *Report of the British Association for the Advancement of Science* 97: 187–198. (Also in *Journal of General Psychology* 1930, 4: 49–66, and a shortened version in *Nature* 124: 341–345.)

> Presidential address to Section J of the British Association, delivered at the 97th meeting at Capetown on 26 July 1929. This address gives a good idea of Bartlett's earlier views on method in experimental psychology and includes shrewd comments on Gestalt psychology, behaviourism, and the work of C.E. Spearman and E.R. Jaensch.

(46) 'Psychology and the fighting services', *Royal Engineers' Journal* 43: 234–242.

(47) 'Experimental psychology', *Encyclopaedia Britannica, Vol. 8* (14th ed.), London and New York: Encyclopaedia Britannica (pp. 980–983).

(48) [With J.H. Parsons and C.B. Goulden] 'Vision or sight', in Vol. 23 of *Encyclopaedia Britannica* (14th ed.) London and New York: Encyclopaedia Britannica (pp. 199–214).

(49) [C. Murchison in co-operation with F.C. Bartlett, S. Blachowski and K. Bühler et al.] *The Psychological Register, Vol. II (International University Series in Psychology)*, Worcester, MA: Clark University Press.

1931

(50) 'On certain general conditions of auditory experiments', in *Report of a Discussion on Audition*, London: Physical Society (pp. 128–134).

> Discussion was held on 19 June 1931 at the Imperial College of Science, London.

(51) 'Maintenance of morale in war', *Royal Engineers' Journal* 45: 215–225.

1932

(52) 'A note on the visual perception of depth', in *Report of a Joint Discussion on Vision*, London: Physical Society (pp. 236–241; discussion with author's reply pp. 242–243).

> Discussion was held on 3 June 1932, at the Imperial College of Science, London, by the Physical and Optical Societies.

(53) *Remembering: A Study in Experimental and Social Psychology*, Cambridge, UK: Cambridge University Press (pp. x, 317, 3 plates). Reprinted 1950, 1954, 1961, 1964 and 1967. Reissued 1995, Paperback edition: Cambridge University Press, 1967. American edition: New York, Macmillan, 1932. Italian edition: *La Memoria* (1974) (trans. Viviana Poli Velicogna), Milan: Angeli Editore. Hungarian edition: *Az emlékezés: Kísérleti és szociálpszichológiai tanulmány* (1985) (trans. and foreword Pléh Csaba), Budapest: Gondolat. Spanish edition: *Recordar: Estudio de psicología*

experimental y social (1995) (trans. Pilar Soto and Cristina del Barrio, with Introduction by Alberto Rosa, which includes a 12-page academic biography of Bartlett), Madrid: Alianza.

This is Bartlett's most important book. Part I embodies the results and analysis of the early experiments on perception and imaging (see 5) together with those on the recall of pictures and stories first recorded in his unpublished *Fellowship Dissertation* (see 3) and mentioned in two earlier papers (see 14 and 41). He also puts forward a theory of memory based on Head's concept of schemata. Part II deals with the influence of social and cultural factors on memory and includes critical examination of Jung's concept of archetypes.

(54)   [With K.G. Pollock, H.C. Weston and S. Adams] 'Two studies of the psychological effects of noise: I. Psychological experiments on the effect of noise. II. The effect of noise on the performance of weavers', *Industrial Health Research Board Report No. 65*, London: HMSO (pp. iv, 70). (Part I, pp. 1–37 is by Pollock and Bartlett. Part II by Weston and Adams.)

1933

(55)   'Adaptation et fatigue', *Journale de Psychologie Normale et Pathologique* 30: 673–694.

1934

(56)   [With M.L. Harbinson] 'An investigation of the relation between discomfort and disability resulting from glaring light', *British Journal of Psychology* 24: 313–319.

(57)   *The Problem of Noise* (preface by C.S. Myers) [Cambridge Miscellany, 15], Cambridge, UK: Cambridge University Press (pp. x, 87).

A short, semi-popular account of its subject based upon what was reliably known at the time regarding the nature of noise and its allegedly harmful effects. It was an expansion of two Heath Clark lectures delivered at the invitation of the National Institute of Industrial Psychology.

1935

(58)   'Remembering', *Scientia* 57: 221–226.
(59)   'Dr. Shepherd Dawson, 1880–1935 [obituary]', *British Journal of Psychology* 26: 117–119.

1936

(60)   'Frederic Charles Bartlett [autobiography]', in C. Murchison (ed.) *A History of Psychology in Autobiography, Vol. III*, Worcester, MA: Clark University Press (pp. 39–52).

(61)   'The Future of Marriage in Western Civilisation by Edward Westermont [book review]', Folk-Lore (Sept.).

1937

(62)   'Cambridge, England, 1887–1937', American Journal of Psychology 50: 97–110.
       A short account of the development of experimental psychology in Cambridge and of the earlier work of the Psychological Laboratory.
(63)   'Psychological methods and anthropological problems', Africa 10: 401–420.
       A review of psychological methods applicable in anthropology. It contains a strong criticism of intelligence testing on the ground that such tests fail to take cultural differences sufficiently into account.
(64)   'Some observations on recent psychological experiments on visual and tactile judgements of wool fibres', Journal of the Textile Institute (Proceedings) 28: P94–P95.
(65)   'Psychology and the Royal Air Force: I. A general survey', Royal Air Force Quarterly 8: 270–276.
(66)   'Psychology and the Royal Air Force: II. Interests, temperament, character', Royal Air Force Quarterly 8: 375–387.

1938

(67)   'Psychology and the Royal Air Force: III. Interviewing and some remarks on training', Royal Air Force Quarterly 9: 60–68.
(68)   'The co-operation of social groups', Occupational Psychology 12: 30–42.
       In this paper Bartlett outlines the relations between remembering and constructive thinking, which he was later to develop in his book on Thinking (see 155, and also 109).
(69)   'Friendliness and unfriendliness between different social groups.' (Sectional Trans.) British Association for the Advancement of Science (August 1938).
(70)   'Prof. William McDougall, F.R.S. [obituary]', Nature 142: 1107–1108.

1939

(71)   [With M. Ginsberg, E.J. Lindgren and R.H. Thouless (eds)] The Study of Society: Methods and problems, London: Kegan Paul, Trench, Trubner & Co. (pp. xii, 498). Reprinted 1949. American edition: New York, Macmillan, 1939. Chapter II 'Suggestions for Research in Social Psychology' (pp. 24–45) is by Bartlett.

This is a collection of essays prepared by a group of British psychologists, anthropologists, psychiatrists and others, which was intended to stimulate systematic inquiry into social aspects of psychology. Bartlett was one of the main organisers of the group.

(72)   'Thinking', in *Centenaire de Th. Ribot: Jubilé de la Psychologie Scientifique Française, 1839–1889–1939*, Paris: Imprimerie Moderne (pp. 281–285).

(73)   'A psychologist looks at crime', *Police Journal* 13: 53–60.

(74)   *Political Propaganda*, Cambridge, UK: Cambridge University Press (pp. x, 158). Reprinted 1942. American edition: New York, Octagon Books, 1973. Mexican edition: *La Propaganda Politica* (1943) (trans. Francisco Giner de los Rios) Mexico D.F.: Fondo de Cultura Economica (148pp.).

1941

(75)   'Fatigue following highly skilled work', *Nature* 147: 717–718.
       This is an abbreviated version of 77.

1943

(76)   'Anthropology in reconstruction', *The Huxley Memorial Lecture for 1943*. London: The Royal Anthropological Institute (8pp.). (Also published in *Journal of the Royal Anthropological Institute* 72: 9–16, and summarised with additions in *Nature*, 152: 710–714. A further brief summary was published in *Man* (1944) 44: 25–26.)
       This noteworthy lecture delivered in London on 23 November 1943 summarises Bartlett's mature views on the relations between psychology and the social sciences, and on the future of anthropology.

(77)   'Fatigue following highly skilled work', *Proceedings of the Royal Society*, B131: 247–257. Reprinted in D. Legge (ed.) (1970) *Skills*, Harmondsworth, UK: Penguin Education.
       The Ferrier Lecture of the Royal Society, delivered 29 May 1941. An important paper based on the wartime work of the Cambridge Psychological Laboratory, in particular experiments conducted by K.J.W. Craik, G.C. Drew and D. Russell Davis on the effects of long spells of simulated operational duty using the 'Cambridge Cockpit' devised by Craik. Some of the findings were published later in D. Russell Davis (1948) *Pilot Error: Some laboratory experiments* (Air Ministry Publication 3139A), London: HMSO.

(78)   'Current problems in visual function and visual perception', *Proceedings of the Physical Society of London* 55: 417–425.
       The 13th Thomas Young Oration, delivered 4 June 1943.

1944

(79)   'Psychology after the war', *Agenda* 3: 1–11.

1945

(80)   'Dr. K.J.W. Craik [obituary]', *Nature* 155: 720.
(81)   'Some growing-points in experimental psychology', *Endeavour* 4: 43–52.

1946

(82)   'Kenneth J.W. Craik, 1914–45 [obituary]', *British Journal of Psychology* 36: 109–116. Reprinted in S.L. Sherwood (ed.) (1966) *The Nature of Psychology: A selection of papers, essays, and other writings by Kenneth J.W. Craik*, Cambridge, UK: Cambridge University Press (pp. xiii–xx).
       Contains portrait and bibliography of Craik. A remarkably frank personal memoir of K.J.W. Craik, who was killed in a road accident just before the end of World War II.
(83)   'Dr. Charles S. Myers, CBE, FRS [obituary]', *Nature* 158: 657–658.
(84)   'Psychological methods for the study of "hard" and "soft" features of culture', *Africa* 16: 145–155.

1947

(85)   'Visitor to America', *American Psychologist* 2: 372–374.
(86)   'Intelligence as a social problem', *Journal of Mental Science* 93: 1–8.
       The 20th Maudsley Lecture, delivered before the Royal Medico-Psychological Association on 27 November 1946. Bartlett gives his views on intelligence and intelligence testing, with special reference to the demands likely to be made on human capacity by an increasingly technological society.
(87)   'The task of the operator in machine work', *Bulletin for Industrial Psychology and Personnel Practice* 3(1): 3–12.
       Modified version of FPRC report 565, December 1943 and APU report 30, 1945 (see Section B, 27 and 28).
(88)   'Some problems of "display" and "control"', in Universitas Catholica Lovaniensis, *Miscellanea Psychologica Albert Michotte: études de psychologie offertes à M.A. Michotte à l'occasion de son jubilé professoral*, Paris: Librairie Philosophique (pp. 440–452).
(89)   'The embryology of behaviour', *British Medical Bulletin* 5: 232–233.
       Critical review of A. Gesell and C.S. Amatruda (1945) *The Embryology of Behaviour*, New York and London: Harper (pp. xix, 289).
(90)   'The measurement of human skill: (1) The nature of skill', *British Medical Journal* 1: 835–838. Also published in *Occupational Psychology* (1948) 22: 31–38.

This is the first of two Oliver-Sharpey lectures, given at the Royal College of Physicians of London on 21 January 1947.

(91) 'The measurement of human skill: (2) The grouping and stability of the constituent items in skill performance', *British Medical Journal* 1: 877–880. Also published in *Occupational Psychology* 22: 83–91.

This was the second of two Oliver-Sharpey lectures given at the Royal College of Physicians of London on 23 January 1947. The two lectures draw together Bartlett's ideas on the nature of high-level human skill and the changes which it may undergo in adverse environmental circumstances. Based on experimental work carried out in Cambridge during and after World War II by members of the MRC Applied Psychology Unit, of which Bartlett became Honorary Director after Craik's death.

(92) 'Group contact in contemporary society [report]', *The Daily Princetonian* 71(26th February): 36.

The first of a series of Vanuxen lectures at Princeton.

(93) 'The third Vanuxen lecture at Princeton [report]', *The Princeton Herald* 23(7th March): 19.

(94) 'Social factors in recall', in Committee on the Teaching of Social Psychology of the Society for the Psychological Study of Social Issues (eds) *Readings in Social Psychology*, New York: Henry Holt.

1948

(95) 'Fatigue in flying [abstract]', *British Medical Journal* 1: 166.

This paper was read in the Section of Occupational Health at the 116th meeting of the British Medical Association in Cambridge on 2 July 1948.

(96) 'Men, machines, and productivity', *Occupational Psychology* 22: 190–196.

(97) 'The first eighteen months of the Cambridge Nuffield Research Unit on Ageing', *Journal of Gerontology* 3: 294–295.

(98) 'Charles Samuel Myers. 1873–1946 [obituary]', *Obituary Notices of Fellows of the Royal Society of London* 5: 767–777.

(99) Foreword to J. Blackburn's pamphlet 'Intelligence'.

1949

(100) 'William McDougall. (1871–1938)', in L.G. Wickham Legg (ed.) *The Dictionary of National Biography, 1931–40*, London: Oxford University Press (pp. 570–572).

(101) 'What is industrial psychology?', *Occupational Psychology* 23: 212–218.

(102) 'Psychology and mental health, current trends and their implications', *British Medical Bulletin* 6: 7–10.

(103) 'Psychological research in industry', *Journal of the Textile Industry (Proceedings)* 40: P419–P425.
This was the Annual Mather Lecture of the Mather Institute.

(104) 'Incentives in industry', *Spectator* (23rd December): 878–879.

1950

(105) 'Challenge to experimental psychology', in *Proceedings and Papers of the Twelfth International Congress of Psychology*, Edinburgh and London: Oliver & Boyd (pp. 23–30).
The Congress was held at the University of Edinburgh from 23 to 29 July 1948, under the Presidency of Professor (Emeritus) James Drever. Bartlett's paper was given as an evening discourse on 27 July. In this address, Bartlett expresses his firm faith in the value of applied work in psychology as a basis for fundamental scientific advance.

(106) 'Incentives', *British Journal of Psychology* 41: 122–128.
The Henry Sidgwick Memorial Lecture delivered at Newnham College, Cambridge, on 19 November 1949. A defence of the view that incentives have rational and not merely emotional significance in human behaviour.

(107) 'Human tolerance limits', *Acta psychologica* 7: 133–141.
Special issue in honour of Géza Révész on his 70th birthday.

(108) [Unsigned] 'Psychology at University College, London. Sir Cyril L. Burt', *Nature* 165: 711.

(109) 'Programme for experiments on thinking', *Quarterly Journal of Experimental Psychology* 2: 145–152.
A version of a paper read on 22 July 1950 to a meeting of the Experimental Psychology Group in Cambridge. Bartlett outlines his views on the nature of thinking and proposes a coherent series of experiments designed to elucidate it. This programme was partly fulfilled in his book on *Thinking: An experimental and social study* published in 1958 (see 155).

(110) *Religion as Experience, Belief, Action*, London: Oxford University Press (38pp.).
The Riddell Memorial Lectures, 22nd series, University of Durham.

(111) [With N.H. Mackworth] *Planned Seeing: Some psychological experiments: 1. Visibility in the control rooms at Fighter Command. 2. The synthetic training of Pathfinder air bombers in visual centring on target indicators.* (Air Ministry Publications 3139B), London: HMSO (with plates. pp. vi, 76).
This report testifies to Bartlett's long-standing interest in aviation psychology (see also 65, 66, 67, 77). Although the experiments were carried out by the junior author, Bartlett contributed several of the guiding ideas and was responsible for the overall direction of the work.

(112)   'Subjective judgements', *Nature* 166: 984–985.
        Report of privately arranged discussion at University College, London, on 14 October 1950, in which Bartlett took the Chair.
(113)   'New light on old problems: psychology in modern society', *Times Review of the Progress of Science* (April): 18.
(114)   'Selection of leaders in war-time', *Nature* 166: 166.
        Review of book by H. Harris *The Group Approach to Leadership-testing*.

1951

(115)   'Thinking', *Memoirs of the Manchester Literary and Philosophical Society* 93: 31–44.
        The Clayton Memorial Lecture for 1951.
(116)   'The effects of flying upon human performance', *Année psychologique* 50: 629–638. (See also Section B, 38.)
        Volume Jubilaire Offert en Hommage à Henri Piéron.
(117)   'The experimental study of skill', *Research, Lond.* 4: 217–221.
(118)   *The Mind at Work and Play*, London: George Allen & Unwin (143pp. 7 plates and 26 figs). American edition: Boston, Beacon Press (1951). German edition: *Denken und Begreifen: Experimente der Praktischen Psychologie* (1952) (trans. Carl Friedrich Graumann and Edeltrud Seeger), Köln, Berlin: Kiepenheuer & Witsch (155pp.). Dutch edition: *Ernst en Spel Rondom Ons Brein* (1953) (trans. Walter Yzerdraat), The Hague: H.P. Leopold (167pp.). Swedish edition: *Rolig Psychologi* (1953) (trans. Karl Hylander), Stockholm: Natur och Kultur (155pp.). Spanish edition: *La Mente Trabaja Y Juega* (1954) (trans. Ignacio Bolivar Izquierdo), Madrid: Alhambra (142pp.). Italian edition: *La Mente Nel Lavora e Nel Gioco* (1957) (trans. Lionello Torossi), Milan: Valentino Bompiani (173pp.). Russian edition: *Psihika Celoveka V Trude I Igre* (1959) (trans. O.S. Vinogradova), Moscow: Izd-vo Akad (144pp.).
        The substance of lectures 'adapted to a juvenile audience' delivered at the Royal Institution during the Christmas season of 1948. Although intended for schoolchildren, this book embodies much of Bartlett's thinking on psychological issues and is delightfully written.
(119)   'The laboratory analysis of human activities', *The Applications of Scientific Methods to Industrial and Service Medicine*. Proceedings of a conference held 29–31 March 1950. London: HMSO (pp. 77–82).
(120)   'The bearing of experimental psychology upon human skilled performance', *British Journal of Industrial Medicine* 8: 209–217.
(121)   'Human control systems', *Transactions of the Society of Instrument Technology* 3: 134–142.
(122)   'Psychology of behaviour: Critical review of Parsons' *Springs of Conduct*', *Nature* 167: 574–575.

(123)   Foreword in A.T. Welford *Skill and Age: An experimental approach*, London, New York & Toronto: Oxford University Press (pp. iii–v).
(124)   Foreword in R.W. Pickford *Individual Differences in Colour Vision*, London: Routledge & Kegan Paul (pp. xii–xiii).
(125)   'The measurement of skill', *Times Review of the Progress of Science* 1: 6.
(126)   'Anticipation in human performance', in G. Ekman, T. Husén, G. Johansson and C.I. Sandström (eds) *Essays on Psychology: Dedicated to David Katz*, Uppsala: Almqvist & Wiksell (pp. 1–17).

1952

(127)   'Review of *Thinking: An introduction to its experimental psychology* by George Humphrey' (1951), *Quarterly Journal of Experimental Psychology* 4(1): 87–90.
(128)   'The employment of the older worker', *The Worker in Industry*, London: HMSO (pp. 80–87).
         A contribution to Ministry of Labour and National Service Centenary Lectures, 1951.
(129)   'Psychological medicine' and 'Psychology' in P.O. Williams (ed.) *Careers in Medicine*, London: Hodder & Stoughton (pp. 66–69).
(130)   'The experimental study of human skilled performance', *Report of the Medical Research Council for the Year 1950–51*, London: HMSO (pp. 25–27).

1953

(131)   'Psychological criteria of fatigue', in W.F. Floyd and A.T. Welford (eds) *Symposium on Fatigue*, London: H.K. Lewis (pp. 1–5).
(132)   'The nature and place of thinking in medicine', *British Medical Journal* (11th April, pp. 795–798).
(133)   'Challenge to experimental psychology—1953'
         [I have no further details on this paper. The title appears in a card file of Bartlett's published papers. It may have been published under a different name. HFB.]

1954

(134)   'Intelligence tests: Assumptions, uses, and limitations', *Times Science Review* 12: 9.
(135)   'Use and value of intelligence and aptitude tests', *Proceedings of the First World Conference on Medical Education*, London: Oxford University Press (pp. 198–210).
         The Conference was held in London, 24–31 August 1953.

(136)   'The transfer of training', *Bulletin of the Cambridge Institute of Education* (June 1954). Also in *Bulletin de l'Association Internationale de Psychotechnique* 2(1): 31–41.

(137)   'Psychological aspects of ageing', *Ciba Foundation Colloquia on Ageing* 1: 209–213.

(138)   'Psychology in medicine', *The Eagle, St. John's College Cambridge* 61(244): 6–13.
        Based on the Linacre Lecture for 1953.

(139)   'Review of *Faces in the Crowd: Individual studies in character and politics* by David Riesman', *International Affairs* (January).

(140)   'Review of *The Ultimate Weapon* by Oleg Anisimov', *International Affairs* (January).

1955

(141)   'Timing: La regulación del factor tiempo como característica fundamental de la actividad humana [Timing: Control of the time factor as a fundamental characteristic of human activity]', *Revista Psicología General y Aplicada* 10: 521–533. Also 'Timing—A fundamental character in human skill', *Proceedings of the XII Congress of the International Association of Applied Psychology*. London: IAAP.

(142)   'Fifty years of psychology', *Occupational Psychology* 19: 203–216.
        Based on two lectures given at Oxford in 1955. Two earlier versions of this were entitled 'Experimental psychology in the 20th century' and 'Psychology today'.

(143)   'Thinking: An experimental approach', *Proceedings of the Royal Institution of Great Britain* (pp. 1–10).
        Weekly evening meeting of the Royal Institution of Great Britain, 4 March 1955.

(144)   'Contact of cultures in the present social world', *Twentieth Century* 158(943): 269–278.

(145)   'The teacher of the deaf'.
        Presidential address to the National College of Teachers of the Deaf, Doncaster, February.

1956

(146)   'Changing scene', *British Journal of Psychology* 47: 81–87.
        Presidential Address to the British Psychological Society, March 1951.

(147)   'Training older people: An experimental approach to a social problem', *Revista Psicología Normal y Patológica* 50: 45–54.

(148)   'Some experiments about thinking', *Proceedings of the Royal Society* B145: 443–451.
        The Croonian Lecture, delivered 31 May 1956.

1957

(149)   *Some Recent Developments of Psychology in Great Britain*, Istanbul: Baha Mathaasi (pp. viii, 92).

>   Six lectures delivered at Istanbul University in 1956, and two others also given in Turkey. The pamphlet contains a Turkish edition (pp. 1–44), introduced by M. Turhan, and the English version (pp. 45–92), introduced by W.R. Miles.

(150)   'Review of *Ciba Foundation Symposium on Extrasensory Perception*, edited by G.E.W. Wolstenholme and E.C.P. Millar'.

(151)   'Review of *Sense and Nonsense in Psychology*, by H.J. Eysenck'.

>   Book reviews 150 and 151 were in a list of Bartlett's published papers but without any indication of the journal in which they were published.

1958

(152)   'Recent advances in knowledge about hearing', *New Scientist* 4(90, 7 August 1958): 557–559.

(153)   'Review of *Figural Alter-effects* by P. McEwen', *Science Progress* (Oct. Review).

(154)   'Laboratory work on fatigue', *Royal Society of Health Journal* 78: 510–513.

>   Contributed to a Symposium on Fatigue, and read to the Occupational Health Section at the Eastbourne Health Congress on 1 March 1958.

(155)   *Thinking: An experimental and social study*, London: George Allen & Unwin. (203pp.). Second impression 1964. Paperback edition: London, Unwin University Books (1962). American edition: New York, Basic Books (1958). Italian edition: *Il Pensiero: Ricerche Sperimentale e Aspetti Sociali* (1975) with Introduction by Fulvio Sceparto, Milan: Franco Angeli Editore (239pp.). Spanish edition: *Pensamiento: Un Estudio De Psicología Experimental Y Social* (1988) (trans. Cristina Simón Cordero, prologue by J.L. Zaccagnini Sancho), Madrid: S.A. Zurbano.

>   Bartlett's last book represents in some ways a sequel to *Remembering* (see 53), and in others a development of his ideas about sensorimotor skills developed during and after World War II (see 77, 90, 91, 111, 117, 141).

(156)   'Herbert Sidney Langfeld: 1879–1958 [obituary]', *American Journal of Psychology* 71: 616–619.

(157)   'Anticipation in flying', *Congrès Mondial de Medicine Aeronautique, III.* Louvain, Belgium: Congrès Européen (pp. 356–358).

1959

(158) 'Some problems of scientific thinking', *Ergonomics* 2: 229–238.
Based on the Huxley Lecture delivered at the University of Birmingham on 13 March 1958.

(159) 'Charles Samuel Myers (1873–1946)', in L.G. Wickham Legg and E.T. Williams (eds) *The Dictionary of National Biography, 1941–50*, London: Oxford University Press (pp. 613–614).

(160) 'A reply to Dr. Kristof', *Zeitschrift für experiment und angeswandte Psychologie* 7/8: 165–167.

(161) 'Review of *Psychology: A Study of a Science*, edited by Sigmund Koch', *Experimental Psychology* 1959: 1059.

1960

(162) 'Karl Spencer Lashley: 1890–1958', *Biographical Memoirs of Fellows of the Royal Society* 5: 107–118.

(163) 'Review of *The Anatomy of Judgements: An investigation into the processes of perception and reasoning* by M.L. Johnson Abercrombie', *The New Scientist* (31 March).

(164) Opening Address to the *1960 Conference on the Care of the Deaf* (pp. 5–9).
Held at Church House, Westminster, 5–7 October 1960.

(165) 'The teacher as an investigator', *The Teacher of the Deaf* 58(347): 300–303.

(166) 'La cinéma et la transmission de la culture', *Journal de Filmologie* 10(32/33): 3–12.

1961

(167) 'The bearing of medicine and psychology on engineering', *The Chartered Mechanical Engineer* 8(5): 297–299.

1962

(168) 'The future of ergonomics', *Ergonomics* 5: 505–511.
Ergonomics Research Society Lecture for 1962. Given at Loughborough on 9 April 1962.

(169) 'The way we think now', *Psychologische Beiträge* 6: 387–394.
Essays presented to Professor Wolfgang Köhler on the occasion of his 75th birthday, 21 January 1962.

(170) 'Alucinación', *Revista Psicología General y Aplicada* 17: 235–246.
Communication presented to the Seventh Annual Meeting of the Sociedad Española de Psicología, Madrid, May 1961.

(171) 'The outlook for flying personnel research', in A.B. Barbour and
       H.E. Whittingham (eds) *Human Problems of Supersonic and Hypersonic
       Flight*, London: Pergamon (pp. 3–8).
       Proceedings of the Fifth European Congress of Aviation Medicine,
       London, 29 August to 6 September 1960.
(172) [With S.M. Nandé, A.B. Van der Merwe and C. Murchison] 'Simon
       Biesheuvel', *Psychologia Africana* 19: 3–13.
(173) 'On getting and using information', in N. Mitchison (ed.) *What the
       Human Race is Up To*, London: Victor Gollancz (pp. 145–155).
(174) 'Review of *Psychologist at Large: An autobiography and selected
       essays* by E.G. Boring', *Perceptual and Motor Skills* 14: 347.

1963

(175) 'Propaganda and technique of mass persuasion', *Financial Times*
       (11 February, 75th Anniversary Issue): 69–70.

1964

(176) 'The evaluation of sensory experience', *Laboratory Practice* 13(2):
       596–598.

1965

(177) 'Thinking', in J.O. Whitaker (ed.) *Introduction to Psychology*, Philadel-
       phia: W.B. Saunders (pp. 319–349).
       Contributors include: Frederic Bartlett, S.M. Luria, Russell Sergeant,
       Robert D. Meade, Muzafer Sherif and Carolyn Sherif.
(178) 'Remembering Dr. Myers', *Bulletin of the British Psychological Society*
       18: 1–10.
       The first Myers Memorial Lecture, delivered in Cambridge on
       8 November 1964. A perceptive memoir of C.S. Myers and his varied
       contributions to psychology in Cambridge and further afield.
(179) 'Review of *Thinking: From association to Gestalt* by Jean and George
       Handler', *Quarterly Journal of Experimental Psychology* 17(3).

1966

(180) 'Baron Michotte Van Den Berck (1881–1965) [obituary]' *Bulletin of the
       British Psychological Society* 19: 35–37.
(181) 'Some remarks about skill', *Manpower and Applied Psychology* 1: 3–7.
(182) 'George Humphrey. 1889–1966 [obituary]', *American Journal of Psy-
       chology* 79(4): 657–658.
(183) 'La Destreza en la Acción en la Dirección de Personas', *XI Annual
       Reunion of the National Congress of Psychology of Spain.*

1968

(184) 'W.H.R. Rivers', *The Eagle, St. John's College Cambridge* 62(269): 156–160.

SECTION B: REPORTS TO GOVERNMENT BODIES

This catalogue is based on A.O. Harris and O.L. Zangwill (1973) 'The Writings of Sir Frederic Bartlett CBE, FRS: An annotated handlist', *British Journal of Psychology* 64: 493–510, which I have supplemented with some additional items that have come to me from various sources. Following Harris and Zangwill I have included a few items which are not strictly reports but contain material relevant to listed reports.

The following abbreviations have been used:

APU   Applied Psychology Unit, Medical Research Council, Cambridge (UK)
FPRC Flying Personnel Research Committee (UK)
HPS   Department of Defense (USA) Panel on Human Engineering and Psychophysiology of the Committee on Human Resources
MRC   Medical Research Council (UK)

1939

(1) 'Psychology, war and post-war research in the Royal Air Force', FPRC 7(a).
(2) 'Temperamental characteristics and flying ability', FPRC 7(b).
(3) 'Medical examination of flying personnel' (Report by sub-committee), FPRC 17 (Restricted).
(4) 'Pre-selection of air crews', FPRC 58.
(5) 'The Reid apparatus for testing ability to learn to fly (evaluation)', FPRC 59.

1940

(6) 'Progress report, experiments in psychological testing', FPRC 118.
(7) 'Sources of error in plotting and telling map information', FPRC 124(a).
(8) 'Note on Morse training in signalling', FPRC 124(b).
(9) 'Experiment on flying fatigue', FPRC 126.
(10) 'Proposed revised procedure for Selection Board' FPRC 139.
(11) 'Elementary Flying Training Schools, Instructors' assessment (attempt to obtain uniformity)', FPRC 140.
(12) 'Pre-selection tests developed at the Psychological Laboratory, Cambridge', FPRC 191.
(13) 'Comments on the auditory tests proposed by the R.A.F. Acoustics Laboratory', FPRC 216.
(14) 'R.A.F. flying accidents, notes', FPRC 226 (Restricted).

1941

(15) 'Selection of radio and wireless operators', FPRC 281.
(16) 'Benzedrine conclusions and recommendations', FPRC 308.
(17) 'Progress report (psychological) of work undertaken on behalf of the R.A.F.', FPRC 325.

1942

(18) 'Recruitment, selection and training of sector controllers', FPRC 403.
(19) 'Pre-selection tests in the R.A.F.', FPRC 429.
(20) 'Note on investigation of flying accidents', FPRC 447.
(21) 'Selection of filterers', FPRC 480.
(22) 'Fatigue in the air pilot', FPRC 488.

1943

(23) 'Progress report, psychological, on work for the R.A.F. by Cambridge Psychological Laboratory', FPRC 423(p).
(24) 'Sub-committee on assessment of temperament in connection with air crew selection', FPRC 529.
(25) 'Preliminary note on promising procedure for assessment of temperament', FPRC 529(a).
(26) 'Scheme for testing of temperament in the R.A.F.', FPRC 529(e).
(27) 'Instrument controls and display—efficient manipulation', FPRC 565.
(28) 'Task of the operator in machine work', APU 30 (Postdated 1945).
        Also in *Industrial Psychology and Personnel Practice.* 8 October 1943 (see also 87 in Section A, and items 27 and 28 in this section are related reports).
(29) 'The future of industrial psychology', MRC (Confidential report, 8 October 1943).

1944

(30) 'Synthesis in education', Address to the Institute of Sociology Summer Conference, Cambridge, August 1944.

1945

(31) 'Synthetic training of Path Finder Air Bombers in visual centring on target indicators', FPRC 423(w).
(32) 'The relation of "thresholds" of sensory acuity to perceptual efficiency', FPRC 636.

1946

(33) 'The after-contraction of muscle: a possible fresh approach to the study of transport accidents', APU 42.

1948

(34) 'A note on early signs of skill fatigue', FPRC 703.

1949

(35) 'The Industrial Health Research Board and operational research', MRC 49/494.

1950

(36) 'Principles of synthetic equipment and training', APU 143.
(37) 'Comments on *Some aspects of fatigue* by Dr. W.S. Henderby', FPRC 723(c).

1951

(38) 'The effects of flying upon human performance', FPRC 765 (see also Section A, 116).

1952

(39) 'Hail and Farewell', Lecture to the Cambridge Psychological Society March, 1952.

1953

(40) 'What human factors research will contribute most to systems design', HPS 206/1.

1955

(41) 'The man and the weapons', and 'Attack and defence', FPRC 1008.
(42) 'Introduction to *Effects on human performance of various stress conditions*', APU, February 1956.
(43) 'Delays in the industrial application of the results of research', MRC 55/205.

SECTION C: BOOK REVIEWS

Book reviews for which I have a full reference to the journal in which they were published are included in Section A: Published Papers. The following list is of book reviews prepared by my father for which I do not have such a reference (some will have been published in the *British Journal of Psychology* of which my father was Editor from 1924 until 1948 and some perhaps were never published). The list is arranged chronologically by the publication year of the book being reviewed. That it is only a partial list will be seen by the many years (1924–41 in particular) for which I have no information.

1919

(1)   S. Kent *Strategic Intelligence for American World Police*, Princeton, NJ: Princeton University Press.

1920

(2)   E. Claparède *Psychologie de l'Enfant et Pedagogie Expérimentale* (8th ed.), Geneva, Switzerland: Kundig.

(3)   W. McDougall *The Group Mind: A sketch of the principles of collective psychology with some attempt to apply these to the interpretation of national life and character*, Cambridge, UK: Cambridge University Press (see Section A, 17 for a different version of this review).

1921

(4)   C. Read *The Origin of Man and of his Superstitions*, Cambridge, UK: Cambridge University Press.

1922/23

(5)   M. Hamblin Smith (1922) *The Psychology of the Criminal*, London: Methuen & Co. *and* G.G. Campion (1923) *Elements in Thought and Emotion*, London: University of London Press.

1942

(6)   W.E. Agar *A Contribution to the Theory of the Living Organism*, Melbourne, Australia: Melbourne University Press in association with Oxford University Press.

1944

(7)   E.L. Thorndike *Man and his Works*, Cambridge, MA: Harvard University Press and London: H. Milford.

1945/46

(8)   J. Hadamard (1945) *The Psychology of Invention in the Mathematical Field*, Princeton, NJ: Princeton University Press and London: Humphrey Milford *and* M. Wertheimer (1946) *Productive Thinking*, New York: Harper Brothers.

1948

(9)   K. Lewin *Resolving Social Conflicts*, New York: Harper & Row.

(10)   *Quarterly Journal of Experimental Psychology*, Vol. 1, Pt. 1, Cambridge, UK: Heffer & Sons.

(11)   J.H. Gerald *The Press and the Constitution 1931–47*, Minnesota, MN: University of Minnesota Press and London: Oxford University Press.

(12)   Otto Pollak *Social Adjustment in Old Age*, Social Science Research Council (Bulletin 59), New York: SSRC.

(13)   L.W. Deeb *Public Opinion and Propaganda*, London: The Cresset Press.

(14)   H. Sachs *Masks of Love and Life* (with an Introduction, Memoir and Glossary by A.A. Roback), Cambridge, MA: Science Art Publishers *and* A.A. Roback (ed.) *The Albert Schweitzer Jubilee Book*, Cambridge, MA: Science Art Publishers. (Reviewed for *British Journal of Psychology.*)

1949

(15)   C. Kluckhohn and H.A. Murray (eds) *Personality: In nature, society, and culture*, London: Jonathan Cape.

(16)   G. Saldes *The People Don't Know: The American Press and the Cold War*, New York: Gaer Associates.

(17)   *Culture and Personality.* Proceedings of an Interdisciplinary Conference held under the auspices of the Viking Fund.

(18)   G.S. Counts and N. Lodge *The Country of the Blind: The Soviet system of mind control*, Boston: Houghton Mifflin Co. (Reviewed for *International Affairs.*)

1950

(19)   O. Klinsberg *Tension Affecting International Understanding: A survey of research* (Bulletin 62), New York: Social Science Research Council.

(20)   *Freedom of Information: A compilation: Vol. 1. Comments of governments*, London: HMSO for the United Nations.

(21)   G. Révéss *Psychology and Art of the Blind* (trans. from the German by H.A. Wolff), London: Longman, Green & Co.

(22)   J. Parsons *The Springs of Conduct*, London: Churchill.

(23)   F.S. Dunn *War and the Mind of Man*, New York: Harper & Brothers. (Reviewed for *International Affairs.*)

(24)   H. Cantril (ed.) *Tensions that Cause Wars: Common statement and individual papers by a group of social scientists brought together by UNESCO.* Urbana, IL: University of Illinois Press. (Reviewed for *International Affairs.*)

(25)   F. Lens *Meinungsforschung in Deutschland*, Stuttgart, Germany: Carl Ernst Poeschel.

(26)   D. Reisman *The Lonely Crowd*, New Haven, CT: Yale University Press.

(27) J.J. Gibson *The Perception of the Visual World*, Boston and New York: Houghton Mifflin Co.

(28) F. Heitman *Psychotic Art: A study of the art products of the mentally ill*, London: Routledge & Kegan Paul.

1951

(29) F.C. Bartlett *The Mind at Work and Play*, London: George Allen & Unwin and Boston: The Beacon Press. (Reviewed for *Psychological Previews.*) Here Bartlett reviews his own book.

(30) S.D. Hobbins *A Dictionary of Speech Pathology and Therapy*, Cambridge, MA: Science Art Publishers.

(31) J. Drièncourt *Propaganda* (no publisher stated).

(32) M. Abrams *Social Survey and Social Actions*, London: William Heinemann.

(33) D. Lerner (ed.) *Propaganda in War and Crisis*, New York: G.W. Stewart.

(34) S.S. Stevens (ed.) *Handbook of Experimental Psychology*, New York: John Wiley and London: Chapman & Hall.

(35) H. Cantril and M. Strunk (eds) *Public Opinion 1935–46*, Princeton, NJ: Princeton University Press.

(36) D. Lerner, H.D. Lasswell et al. (eds) *The Policy Sciences: Recent developments in scope and method*, Stanford: Stanford University Press.

(37) H.J. Morgenthau (ed.) *Germany and the Future of Europe*, Chicago: University of Chicago Press.

(38) N. Tinbergen *The Study of Instinct*, Oxford, UK: Clarendon Press.

(39) J.A.R. Pimlott *Public Relations and American Democracy*, Princeton, NJ: Princeton University Press.

(40) E. Jacques *The Changing Culture of a Factory: A study of authority and participation in an industrial society*, London: Tavistock Publications.

1953

(41) The International Press Institute, Zurich *The Flow of News: A study by the International Press Institute.*

(42) E. Montecou *The Federal Loyalty-Security Program*, New York: Cornell University Press. (Reviewed for the Royal Institute of International Affairs.)

1954

(43) H.S. Commager *Freedom, Loyalty, Dissent*, London: Oxford University Press. (Reviewed for the Royal Institute of International Affairs.)

(44) J.P. Roche and M.S. Shedman *The Dynamics of Democratic Government*, New York, Toronto and London: McGraw-Hill.

(45) W. Ebenstein *Modern Political Thought: The great issues*. (Revised edition of *Man and the State: Modern political ideas*), New York: Rinehart.

(46) H.J. Eysenck *The Psychology of Politics*, London: Routledge & Kegan Paul.

(47) A.A. Roback *Destiny and Motivation in Language: Studies in psycho-linguistics and glossodynamics*, Cambridge, MA: Sci-Art Publishers.

(48) T. Grygier *Oppression: A study in social and criminal psychology*, London: Routledge & Kegan Paul.

(49) A. Huxley *The Doors of Perception*, London: Chatto & Windus.

(50) Panel on Psychology and Physiology, National Research Council in America *A Survey Report on Human Factors in Undersea Warfare*. (Reviewed for *Nature*.)

1955

(51) S. Chase and M.T. Chase *Power of Words*, London: Phoenix House. (Reviewed for the Royal Institute of International Affairs.)

(52) W. Esslinger *Politics and Science*, New York: Philosophical Library. (Reviewed for the Royal Institute of International Affairs.)

(53) G. Skard (trans. A.G. Jayne) *Ideological Strategy*, London: Blandford Press. (Reviewed for the Royal Institute of International Affairs.)

(54) H. Wiener *The Human Use of Human Beings, Cybernation and Society*, London: Eyre & Spottiswoode.

(55) J. Scott *Political Warfare: A guide to competitive coexistence*, New York: The John Day Company. (Reviewed for the Royal Institute of International Affairs.)

1956

(56) J.E. Gerald *The British Press Under Government Economic Controls*, Minneapolis, MN: University of Minnesota Press and London: Oxford University Press. (Reviewed for the Royal Institute of International Affairs.)

(57) W. Albig *Modern Public Opinion*, New York: McGraw-Hill. (Reviewed for the Royal Institute of International Affairs.)

(58) M. Mégret *La Guerre Psychologique*, Paris: Presses Universitaires de France. (Reviewed for the Royal Institute of International Affairs.)

(59) R. Hillman *Strategic Intelligence and National Decisions*, Glencoe, IL: The Free Press. (Reviewed for the Royal Institute of International Affairs.)

1957

(60) Å. Hultkrantz *The North American Indian Orpheus Tradition: A contribution to comparative religion*, Stockholm: Ethnological Museum of Sweden. (Reviewed for the Royal Anthropological Institute of Great Britain and Ireland.)

1958

(61) I.R. Ewing and A.W.G. Ewing *New Opportunities for Deaf Children*, London: London University Press. (Reviewed for *The New Scientist.*)
(62) M. Polanyi *Personal Knowledge: Towards a Post-critical Philosophy*, London: Routledge & Kegan Paul.
(63) J. Cohen *Humanistic Psychology*, London: George Allen & Unwin. (Review sent to A. Rodger, Birkbeck College, London, WC1.)

1959

(64) S. Schacter *The Psychology of Affiliations: Experimental studies of the sources of gregariousness*, Stanford: Stanford University Press.
(65) R. Thomson *The Psychology of Thinking*, London: Pelican. (Reviewed for *The New Scientist.*)
(66) B.N. Mukherjee *A Laboratory Guide to Psychology* (publisher's details not stated). (Reviewed for Pustak-Bhandar, Patna, India.)

1960

(67) G. Visud (English translation by A.K. Pomerans) *Intelligence: Its evolution and forms*, London: Hutchinson & Co.

SECTION D: BIOGRAPHIES AND OBITUARIES

(1) F.C. Bartlett (1936) 'Frederic Charles Bartlett', in C. Murchison *A History of Psychology in Autobiography, Vol. III*, Worcester, MA: Clark University Press.
(2) The North Carolina Chapter of the Society of Sigma Xi (1947) 'announces a public lecture by Sir Frederic C. Bartlett, 3 April 1947 "Experimental Psychology in England during the War"'. (Biographical Sketch).
(3) Edgell, B., Knight, R. and Mitchell, F.W. 'The British Psychological Society 1901–61', *Supplement to Bulletin of the British Psychological Society.*
   Records Bartlett's Honorary Fellowship of the Society 1954, Presidency of the Society 1950–51 and Editorship of the Society's Bulletin 1924–48.
(4) Hearnshaw, L.S. (1964) 'Sir Frederic Bartlett (b. 1886)', in L.S. Hearnshaw *A Short History of British Psychology, 1810–1910*, London: Methuen.
(5) International Academy of Aviation and Space Medicine (1964). Biographical notes and portrait in programme for presentation of Gold Medal, 14 September 1964, Dublin.
(6) Zangwill, O.L. (1968) 'Bartlett, F.C.', in *International Encyclopedia of the Social Sciences*, New York: Macmillan and the Free Press (pp. 19–21).

(7)   Drew, G.C. (1969) 'British Psychology', *Presidential Address to the XIX International Congress of Psychology, London, 27 July to 2 August 1969*. This paper sets the scene in British psychology for the arrival of Cyril Burt and then Bartlett, and discusses the career and work of each of them.

(8)   [Obituary] (1969) *Cambridge Daily News*, 1 October.

(9)   [Obituary] (1969) *The Times*, 1 October.

(10)   [Obituary] (1969) *The Guardian*, 2 October.

(11)   [Obituary] (1969) *The Daily Telegraph*, 2 October.

(12)   [Obituary] (1969) *The Times*, 3 October (by D.E. Broadbent).

(13)   [Obituary] (1969) *British Medical Journal* 4: 175 (18 October). Contains notes by DRD [D. Russell Davis] and HJE.

(14)   [Obituary] (1969) *The Lancet* 2: 855–856 (18 October). Contains a note by Zangwill.

(15)   Chapel of the College of St. John the Evangelist (1969) *Order of Memorial Service for Sir Frederic Charles Bartlett CBE, MA, FRS*, 22 November. A Notice of this Service appeared in *The Times*, 24 November 1969 and contains a note 'among those present were . . .'.

(16)   Broadbent, D.E. (1970) 'Sir Frederic Bartlett: An appreciation', *Bulletin of the British Psychological Society* 23: 1–3.

(17)   Broadbent, D.E. (1970) 'Frederic Charles Bartlett, 1886–1969', *Biographical Memoirs of Fellows of the Royal Society* 16: 1–313. Contains bibliography and portrait.

(18)   Conrad, R. (1970) 'Sir Frederic Bartlett, 1886–1969: A personal homage', *Ergonomics* 13: 159–161.

(19)   Zangwill, O.L. (1970) 'Sir Frederic Bartlett (1886–1969) [obituary]', *Quarterly Journal of Experimental Psychology* 22: 77–84 (with portrait).

(20)   Welford, A.T. (1970) 'Sir Frederic Charles Bartlett (1886–1969)', *Year Book of the American Philosophical Society* 1970: 109–114.

(21)   Buzzard, R.B. (1971) 'Sir Frederic Bartlett, CBE, MA, LLD, DSc, DPhil, DPsych, FRS, 1886–1969', *Occupational Psychology* 45: 1–11. Contains bibliography, list of appointments and awards, portrait and notes by Alice Heim, Tom Singleton and others.

(22)   Oldfield, R.C. (1972) 'Frederic Charles Bartlett (1886–1969)', *American Journal of Psychology* 85: 132–140 (with portrait).

(23)   Zangwill, O.L. (1972) '*Remembering* Revisited', *Quarterly Journal of Experimental Psychology* 24: 123–138. Based on the Third Sir Frederic Bartlett Lecture, Cambridge, 9 July 1971.

(24)   Rosa, A. (1995) 'Una biografía intelectual de Sir Frederic Charles Bartlett (1886–1969)', in *Recordar: Estudio de psicología experimental y social* (Spanish edition of *Remembering*, see Section A, 53) (pp. 14–27).

SECTION E: THE SIR FREDERIC BARTLETT LECTURES

The Sir Frederic Bartlett lectures were given every two or three years. The first two lectures occurred during my father's lifetime. Lecturers and the titles of the first four lectures were as follows:

Professor R.C. Oldfield, 'Things, Words, and the Brain', 12 July 1966.

Professor R.A. Hinde, 'The Control of Movement Patterns in Animals', 7 January 1969.

Professor O.L. Zangwill, '*Remembering* Revisited', 9 July 1971.

Dr. Saul Sternberg, 'Memory Scanning: New Findings and Current Controversies', 5 January 1973.

SECTION F: EVENTS, HONOURS AND AWARDS

I have used Biographies and Obituaries in Section D to supplement my personal knowledge in preparing this list.

1886   Born, Stow-on-the-Wold, Gloucestershire.

1909   BA First Class Honours in Philosophy, London. University Correspondence College (Cambridge).

1909   Tutorship in all Philosophical subjects, University Correspondence College. Move to Cambridge.

1911   MA with special distinction in Sociology and Ethics, London.

1912   Accepted as undergraduate by St. John's College, Cambridge.

1914   BA First Class Honours, Moral Science Tripos, Logic Section, Cambridge.

1914   *Exercises in Logic*, University Tutorial Press.

1914–18   During the 1914–18 war Bartlett, who was rejected thrice by the armed forces because of a weak heart following an earlier serious illness, worked with shell-shocked victims at the First Eastern General Hospital in Cambridge as well as continuing his academic work including pioneering experiments in memory described in his Fellowship Dissertation and in his book *Remembering*.

1915–22   Assistant Director in Experimental Psychology, University of Cambridge.

1917–19   Working with E.M. Smith and others, Bartlett carried out experimental work on listening to sounds of weak intensity, existing testing methods having proved unsatisfactory, and as a result was asked to set up a Unit in Crystal Palace to carry out work for the Lancashire Anti-Submarine Committee (LASC) on the selection of personnel for hydrophone work in detection and identification of enemy submarines.

1917   MA, Cambridge.
1917   Elected Fellow, St. John's College, Cambridge. He remained a Fellow until his death in 1969.
1920   Married Emily Mary Smith (Fellow of Newnham College, Cambridge).
1922–31   Reader in Experimental Psychology, Cambridge.
1922–52   Director, Psychological Laboratory, Cambridge.
1923   *Psychology and Primitive Culture*, Cambridge University Press.
1923   Son Hugh born.
1924–48   Editor, *Journal of the British Psychological Society.*
1925   *Textbook of Experimental Psychology* (with C.S. Myers), Cambridge University Press.
1925   Son Denis born.
1927   *Psychology and the Soldier*, Cambridge University Press.
1929   President, Section J, British Association. Attended British Association meeting in Capetown. Visited Swaziland on anthropological study as part of return journey.
1930   Membre associé de la Société Française de Psychologie.
1931–52   Professor in Experimental Psychology, Cambridge.
1932   Fellow of the Royal Society.
1932   *Remembering*, Cambridge University Press.
1934   *The Problem of Noise*, Cambridge University Press.
1937   Hon. DPhil, Athens.
1938–63   Member of the Royal Air Force Flying Personnel Research Committee (FPRC).
1939   *The Study of Society* (with others), Kegan Paul.
1939   *Political Propaganda*, Cambridge University Press.
1941–47   and 1949–52   Member of the Medical Research Council (MRC).
1939–45   Cambridge Psychological Laboratory was involved in wartime projects for FPRC and MRC, some of which continued after the war.
1941   Made Companion of the British Empire (CBE).
1943   Baly Medal of the Royal College of Physicians.
1943   Huxley Medal of the Royal Anthropological Society.
1944   MRC set up an Applied Psychology Unit (APU) in Cambridge. On the accidental death of K.J.W. Craik in 1945, Bartlett was made Hon. Director of the Unit.
1946   Member, Foreign, American Philosophical Society, Philadelphia.
1946   Nuffield Unit for Research into Problems of Ageing established in Cambridge under the Directorship of A.T. Welford.
1947   Hon. DSc Princeton. Visited many establishments in USA and Canada.
1947   Foreign Associate, National Academy of Sciences.
1948   Knighted.
1949   Hon. DPsych, Louvain.

1949	Hon. DSc, London.
1951	*The Mind at Work and Play*, George Allen & Unwin.
1950–51	President, British Psychological Society.
1952	As required by then current Cambridge University Statutes, at age 65 he retired from the Chair of Experimental Psychology and the Directorship of the Psychological Laboratory. He retained his interest and involvement in the MRC and Nuffield Units.
1952–69	Professor Emeritus.
1952	Hon. Member, Swedish Psychological Society.
1952	Royal Medal of the Royal Society.
1952	Longacre Award of the Aeromedical Association.
1954	Hon. Fellow, British Psychological Society.
1955	Hon. Member, Spanish Psychological Society.
1956	Hon. Member, Swiss Psychological Society.
1957	Hon. Member, Turkish Psychological Society.
1958	*Thinking*, George Allen & Unwin.
1958	Hon. Member, Belgian Psychological Society.
1958	Hon. Member, International Association for Applied Psychology.
1959	Hon. Member, Foreign, American Academy of Arts and Sciences.
1960	Hon. Member, Ergonomics Society.
1960	Hon. Member, Experimental Psychological Society.
1961	Hon. LLD, Edinburgh.
1962	Hon. DSc, Oxford.
1964	Gold Medal of the International Academy of Aviation and Space Medicine.
1965	Hon. DEd, Padua.
1969	Died in Cambridge.

References

Abric, J.-C. and Kahan, J.P. (1972) 'The effects of representations and behaviour in experimental games', *European Journal of Social Psychology* 2: 129–144.

Ackernecht, E.H. (1942) 'In memory of William H.R. Rivers (1864–1922)', *Bulletin of the History of Medicine* 11: 478–481.

Ackil, J.K. and Zaragoza, M.S. (1998) 'Memorial consequences of forced confabulation', *Developmental Psychology* 34: 1358–1372.

Alba, J.W. and Hasher, L. (1983) 'Is memory schematic?', *Psychological Bulletin* 93: 203–231.

Allansdottir, A., Jovchelovitch, S. and Stathopoulou, A. (1993) 'Social representations: The versatility of a concept', *Papers on Social Representations* 2: 3–10.

Allport, F.H. (1924a) 'The group fallacy in relation to culture', *Journal of Abnormal and Social Psychology* 19: 60–73.

Allport, F.H. (1924b) 'The group fallacy in relation to social science', *Journal of Abnormal and Social Psychology* 19: 185–191.

Allport, G.W. and Postman, L. (1947) *The psychology of rumour*, New York: Holt.

Anderson, S.J. and Conway, M.A. (1993) 'Investigating the structure of autobiographical memories', *Journal of Experimental Psychology: Learning, Memory, and Cognition* 19: 1178–1196.

Asch, S.E. (1956) 'Studies in independence and conformity: A minority of one against a unanimous majority', *Psychological Monographs* 70(9, Whole No. 416).

Augoustinos, M. (1990) 'The mediating role of representations on causal attributions in the social world', *Social Behaviour* 5: 49–62.

Ayers, M.S. and Reder, L.M. (1998) 'A theoretical review of the misinformation effect: Predictions from an activation-based memory model', *Psychonomic Bulletin and Review* 5(1): 1–21.

Azmitia, M. (1996) 'Peer interactive minds: Developmental, theoretical, and methodological issues', in P.B. Baltes and U.M. Staudinger (eds) *Interactive minds* (pp. 133–162), Cambridge, UK: Cambridge University Press.

Baddeley, A. and Gathercole, S. (1999) 'Individual differences in learning and memory: Psychometrics and the single case', in P.L. Ackerman, P.C. Kyllonen and R.D. Roberts (eds) *Learning and Individual Differences: Process, traits and content determinants* (pp. 31–54), Washington DC: American Psychological Association.

Bakhtin, M.M. (1981) *The dialogical imagination: Four essays by M.M. Bakhtin*, Austin, TX: University of Texas Press.

Ballard, P.B. (1913) 'Oblivescence and reminiscence', *British Journal of Psychology Monograph Supplements* 1: 1–82.

Bangerter, A. and Lehmann, K. (1997) 'Serial reproduction as a method for studying social representations', an expanded version of a paper presented at the 3rd International Conference on Social Representations, Aix-en-Provence, France, 27–30 September 1996.

Barclay, C.R. (1996) 'Autobiographical remembering: Narrative constraints on objectified selves', in D.C. Rubin (ed.) *Remembering our past: Studies in autobiographical memory* (pp. 94–125), New York: Cambridge University Press.

Barclay, C.R. and Smith, T.S. (1992) 'Autobiographical remembering: Creating personal culture', in M.A. Conway, D.C. Rubin, H. Spinnler and W.A. Wagenaar (eds) *Theoretical perspectives on autobiographical memory* (pp. 75–97), Dordrecht, The Netherlands: Kluwer.

Barker, P. (1991) *Regeneration*, London: Viking.

Barker, P. (1993) *The eye in the door*, London: Viking.

Barker, P. (1995) *The ghost road*, London: Viking.

Barnes, B. (1983) 'Social life as bootstrapped induction', *Sociology* 4: 524–545.

Barnes, J.A. (1967) *Politics in a changing society*, Manchester, UK: Manchester University Press.

Barsalou, L.W. (1988) 'The content and organisation of autobiographical memories', in U. Neisser and E. Winograd (eds) *Remembering reconsidered: Ecological and traditional approaches to the study of memory* (pp. 193–243), New York: Cambridge University Press.

Barsalou, L.W. (1990) 'On the indistinguishability of exemplar memory and abstraction in category representation', in T.K. Srull and R.S. Wyer Jr. (eds) *Advances in social cognition: Vol. 3* (pp. 61–88). *Content and process specificity in the effects of prior experiences*, Hillsdale, NJ: Lawrence Erlbaum Associates Inc.

Bartlett, F.C. (1916a) 'An experimental study of some problems of perceiving and imaging', *British Journal of Psychology* 8: 222–266.

Bartlett, F.C. (1916b) 'Symposium: The implications of recognition (Part II)', *Proceedings of the Aristotelian Society* 16: 189–201.

Bartlett, F.C. (1916c) *Transformations arising from repeated representation: A contribution towards an experimental study of the process of conventionalisation*, Fellowship dissertation, St. John's College, Cambridge, UK.

Bartlett, F.C. (1920a) 'Some experiments on the reproduction of folk-stories', *Folk-Lore* 31: 30–47.

Bartlett, F.C. (1920b) 'Psychology in relation to the popular story', *Folk-Lore* 31: 264–293.

Bartlett, F.C. (1921) 'The functions of images', *British Journal of Psychology* 11: 320–337.

Bartlett, F.C. (1923) *Psychology and primitive culture*, Cambridge, UK: Cambridge University Press.

Bartlett, F.C. (1923a) 'Obituary notice of W.H.R. Rivers', *The Eagle, St. John's College Cambridge*, 43: 2–14.

Bartlett, F.C. (1924) 'Symbolism in folk lore', in *Proceedings of the VIIth International Congress of Psychology* (pp. 278–289), Cambridge, UK: Cambridge University Press.

Bartlett, F.C. (1925) Feeling, imaging and thinking, *British Journal of Psychology* 16: 16–28.

Bartlett, F.C. (1926a) 'Critical notice of Head's *Aphasia*', *British Journal of Psychology* 17: 154–161.

Bartlett, F.C. (1926b) 'Critical review of Head's *Aphasia*', *Brain* 49: 581–587.

Bartlett, F.C. (1927) *Psychology and the soldier*, Cambridge, UK: Cambridge University Press.

Bartlett, F.C. (1928a) 'An experiment upon repeated reproduction', *Journal of General Psychology* 1: 54–63.

Bartlett, F.C. (1928b) 'Social constructiveness Pt. I', *British Journal of Psychology* 18: 388–391.

Bartlett, F.C. (1929) 'Psychology and the fighting services', *The Royal Engineers Journal* 43: 234–242.

Bartlett, F.C. (1931) 'On certain general conditions of auditory experiments', in *Report on a discussion on audition* (pp. 128–134), London: The Physical Society.

Bartlett, F.C. (1932) *Remembering: A study in experimental and social psychology*, Cambridge, UK: Cambridge University Press.

Bartlett, F.C. (1936) 'Frederic Charles Bartlett', in C. Murchison (ed.) *A history of psychology in autobiography* (Vol. 3, pp. 39–52), Worcester, MA: Clark University Press.

Bartlett, F.C. (1937) 'Cambridge, England 1887–1937', *American Journal of Psychology* 50: 97–110.

Bartlett, F.C. (1939b) 'Suggestions for research in social psychology', in F.C. Bartlett, M. Ginsberg, E.J. Lindgren and R.H. Thouless (eds) *The study of society: Methods and problems* (pp. 24–45), London: Kegan Paul/Trench, Trubner.

Bartlett, F.C. (1940) *Political propaganda*, Cambridge, UK: Cambridge University Press.

Bartlett, F.C. (1943) 'Fatigue following highly skilled work', *Proceedings of the Royal Society*, B131: 247–257.

Bartlett, F.C. (1947) 'The measurement of human skill: 1. The nature of skill', *British Medical Journal* 1: 835–877. [Reprinted in *Occupational Psychology* (1948), 22: 31–38.]

Bartlett, F.C. (1950) 'Programme for experiments on thinking', *Quarterly Journal of Experimental Psychology*, 2: 145–152.

Bartlett, F.C. (1951) *The mind at work and play*, London: George Allen & Unwin.

Bartlett, F.C. (1956) 'Changing scene', *British Journal of Psychology* 47: 81–87.

Bartlett, F.C. (1958) *Thinking: An experimental and social study*, London: George Allen & Unwin.

Bartlett, F.C. (1968) 'W.H.R. Rivers', *The Eagle, St. John's College Cambridge*: 156–160.

Bartlett, F.C., Ginsberg, M., Lindgren, E.J., & Thouless, R.H. (1939a) *The study of society: Methods and problems*, London: Kegan Paul.

Bartlett, F.C. and Mark, H. (1922) 'A note on local fatigue in the auditory system', *British Journal of Psychology* 13: 215–218.

Bartlett, F.C. and Smith, E.M. (1920) 'Is thinking merely the action of language mechanisms? Part I', *British Journal of Psychology* 11: 55–62.

Benjamin, D. (1996) *The essential injustice*, Berlin, Germany: Springer.

Bergman, E.T. and Roediger, H.L. (in press) 'Can Bartlett's repeated reproduction experiments be replicated?', *Memory & Cognition.*

Berntsen, D. (1996) 'Involuntary autobiographical memories', *Applied Cognitive Psychology* 10: 435–454.

Berntsen, D. (1998) 'Voluntary and involuntary access to autobiographical memory', *Memory* 6: 113–141.

Berntsen, D. and Kennedy, J.M. (1994) 'Contradictions between metaphors: A means of expressing an attitude', *Metaphor and Symbolic Activity* 9: 193–209.

Berntsen, D. and Larsen, S.F. (1996) 'Personal and non-personal narrativity in reading', in M.S. MacNealy and R. Kreuz (eds) *Advances in discourse processes Vol. 52: Empirical approaches to literature and aesthetics* (pp. 615–631), Norwood, NJ: Ablex.

Betz, A.L., Skowrowski, J.J. and Ostrom, T.M. (1996) 'Shared realities: Social influence and stimulus memory', *Social Cognition* 14: 113–140.

Betz, W. (1910) 'Vorstellung und Einstellung: I. Über Wiedererkennen', *Archiv für die gesamte Psychologie* 17: 266–296.

Betz, W. (1928) 'Zur Psychologie der Tiere und Menschen', *Psychological Abstracts* 2: 65(No. 281). [Author's abstract in English]

Billig, M. (1987) *Arguing and thinking: A rhetorical approach to social psychology*, Cambridge, UK: Cambridge University Press.

Bloor, D. (1997) 'Remember the strong programme?', *Science, Technology and Human Values* 22: 373–385.

Bohannan, L. (1952) 'A genealogical charter', *Africa* 22(4): 301–315.

Boring, E. (1942) *Sensation and perception in the history of experimental psychology*, New York: Appleton-Century-Crofts.

Boring, E. (1950) *A history of experimental psychology* (2nd ed.), New York: Appleton-Century-Crofts.

Boring, E., Langfeld, H.S. and Weld, H.P. (1948) *Foundations of psychology*, London: Chapman & Hall.

Bourdieu, P. (1977) *Outline of a theory of practice*, Cambridge: Cambridge University Press.

Bourdieu, P. (1991) *Language and symbolic power*, Cambridge, MA: Harvard University Press.

Bower, G.H., Black, J.B. and Turner, T.J. (1979) 'Scripts in memory for text', *Cognitive Psychology* 11: 177–220.

Boyd, R. and Richerson, P.J. (1985) *Culture and the evolutionary process*, Chicago: University of Chicago Press.

Breuer, J. and Freud, S. (1895) *Studien über Hysterie*, Leipzig and Vienna: Deuticke.

Brewer, W.F. (1977) 'Memory for the pragmatic implications of sentences', *Memory & Cognition* 5: 673–678.

Brewer, W.F. (1986) 'What is autobiographical memory?', in D.C. Rubin (ed.), *Autobiographical memory* (pp. 25–49), New York: Cambridge University Press.

Brewer, W.F. (1987) 'Schemas versus mental models in human memory', in P. Morris (ed.) *Modelling cognition* (pp. 187–197), Chichester, UK: Wiley.

Brewer, W.F. (1993) 'What are concepts? Issues of representation and ontology', in G.V. Nakamura, R. Taraban and D.L. Medin (eds) *The psychology of learning and motivation: Vol. 29. Categorization by humans and machines* (pp. 495–533), San Diego, CA: Academic Press.

Brewer, W.F. (1996) 'What is recollective memory?', in D.C. Rubin (ed.) *Remembering our past: Studies in autobiographical memory* (pp. 19–66), Cambridge, UK: Cambridge University Press.

Brewer, W.F. (in press a) 'Bartlett', in F.C. Keil and R.A. Wilson (eds) *Encyclopedia of the cognitive sciences*, Cambridge, MA: MIT Press.

Brewer, W.F. (in press b) 'Schemata', in F.C. Keil and R.A. Wilson (eds) *Encyclopedia of the cognitive sciences*, Cambridge, MA: MIT Press.

Brewer, W.F. (in press c) 'Scientific theories and naïve theories as forms of mental representation: Psychologism revived', *Science and Education*.

Brewer, W.F. and Hay, A.E. (1984) 'Reconstructive recall of linguistic style', *Journal of Verbal Learning and Verbal Behavior* 23: 237–249.

Brewer, W.F. and Nakamura, G.V. (1984) 'The nature and functions of schemas', in R.S. Wyer Jr. and T.K. Srull (eds) *Handbook of social cognition* (*Vol. 1*, pp. 119–160), Hillsdale, NJ: Lawrence Erlbaum Associates Inc.

Brewer, W.F. and Tenpenny, L. (1998) *The role of schemata in the recall and recognition of episodic information*, unpublished manuscript, Department of Psychology, University of Illinois at Urbana-Champaign.

Brewer, W.F. and Treyens, J.C. (1981) 'Role of schemata in memory for places', *Cognitive Psychology* 13: 207–230.

Broadbent, D.E. (1958) *Perception and communication*, Oxford, UK: Pergamon Press.

Broadbent, D.E. (1970) 'Frederic Charles Bartlett, 1886–1969', *Biographical memoirs of Fellows of the Royal Society* 16: pp. 1–13.

Broadbent, D. (1973) *In defence of empirical psychology*, London: Methuen.

Brown, W. (1923) 'To what extent is memory measured by a single recall trial?', *Journal of Experimental Psychology* 6: 377–382.

Bruner, J. (1958) 'Review of "Thinking" by F.C. Bartlett (1958)', *British Journal of Psychology* 49: 160–163.

Bruner, J. (1990) *Acts of meaning*, Cambridge, MA: Harvard University Press.

Bruner, J. (1996) *Culture and education*, Cambridge, MA: Harvard University Press.

Buchmann, M. (1989) *The script of life in modern society*, Chicago: University of Chicago Press.

Buck, N.C. (1963) Note in the St. John's College archive (for which Paul Whittle is indebted to Dr. Paul Ries).

Burt, C. (1933) Review of F.C. Bartlett, *Remembering, British Journal of Educational Psychology* 3: 187–192.

Cairns, R.B., Elder, G.H. and Costello, E.J. (eds) (1996) *Developmental science*, Cambridge: Cambridge University Press.

Cambridge University Reporter, 9 June 1891.

Campos, G.P. (1998) 'Social representation and the ontology of the social world: Bringing another signification into the dialogue', *Culture & Psychology* 4(3): 297–330.

Carr, H.W. (1916) 'Symposium: The implications of recognition (Part IV)', *Proceedings of the Aristotelian Society* 16: 224–233.

Chapman, M. (1988) *Constructive evolution: Origins and development of Piaget's thought*, Cambridge, UK: Cambridge University Press.

Chombart de Lauwe, M.-J. (1971) *Un monde autre: L'enfance, de ses représentations à son mythe*, Paris: Payot. (Second edition 1978.)

Christianson, S.-Å. (ed.) (1992) *The handbook of emotion and memory: Research and theory*, Hillsdale, NJ: Lawrence Erlbaum Associates Inc.

Claparède, E. (1951) 'Recognition and "me-ness"', in D. Rapaport (ed.), *Organization and pathology of thought* (pp. 58–75), New York: Columbia University Press. (Original work published in French 1911.)

Codol, J.-P. (1974) 'On the systems of representations in a group situation', *European Journal of Social Psychology* 4: 343–365.

Cole, J. (1997) 'Sacrifice, narratives and experience in East Madagascar', *Journal of Religion in Africa* 27(4): 401–425.

Cole, J. (1998) 'The uses of defeat: Memory and political morality in East Madagascar', in R. Werbner (ed.) *Memory in the post-colony* (pp. 104–125), London: Zed Books.

Cole, J. & Middleton, K. (unpublished). *Ancestors and colonial power in Madagascar.*

Cole, M. (1990) 'Cultural psychology: A once and future discipline?', in J.J. Berman (ed.) *Cross-cultural perspectives: Nebraska symposium on motivation, 1989* (pp. 279–335), London/Lincoln, NE: University of Nebraska Press.

Cole, M. (1996) *Cultural psychology: A once and future discipline*, Cambridge, MA: Harvard University Press.

Collins, H. (1985) *Changing order: Replication and induction in scientific practice*, London: Sage.

Comaroff, J. and Comaroff, J. (1991) *Of revelation and revolution, Vol. 1*, Chicago: University of Chicago Press.

Conrad, R. (1955) 'Some effects on performance of changes in perceptual load', *Journal of Experimental Psychology* 49: 313–322.

Conrad, R. (1964) 'Acoustic confusion in immediate memory', *British Journal of Psychology* 55: 75–84.

Conway, M.A. (1996) 'Autobiographical knowledge and autobiographical memory', in D.C. Rubin (ed.) *Remembering our past: Studies in autobiographical memory* (pp. 67–93), New York: Cambridge University Press.

Conway, M.A. and Rubin, D.C. (1993) 'The structure of autobiographical memory', in A.C. Collins, S.E. Gathercole, M.A. Conway and P.E.M. Morris (eds) *Theories of memory* (pp. 103–137), Hove, UK: Psychology Press.

Cooper, F. and Stoler, A.L. (eds) (1997) *Tensions of empire: Colonial cultures in a bourgeois world*, Berkeley, CA: University of California Press.

Costall, A. (1991) 'Frederic Bartlett and the rise of prehistoric psychology', in A. Still and A. Costall (eds) *Against cognitivism* (pp. 39–54), London: Harvester Wheatsheaf.

Costall, A. (1992) 'Why British psychology is not social: Frederic Bartlett's promotion of the new academic discipline', *Canadian Psychology* 33(3): 633–639.

Costall, A. (1996) *Pear and his peers: The beginnings of psychology at Manchester*, unpublished manuscript.

Costall, A. (1998) 'Dire straits? Relations between psychology and anthropology *and* medicine after the 1898 expedition', paper presented at the conference on

Anthropology and Psychology: The Legacy of the Torres Strait Expedition (1898–1998), at St. John's College, Cambridge, UK, 10–12 August.

Craik, K. (1943) *The nature of explanation*, Cambridge, UK: Cambridge University Press.

Craik, K. (1948) 'Theory of the human operator in control systems: 2. Man as an element in a control system', *British Journal of Psychology* 38: 142–148.

Crane, T. (1995) *The mechanical mind: A philosophical introduction to minds, machines and mental representation*, Harmondsworth, UK: Penguin.

Cunnison, I.G. (1959) *The Luapula peoples of Northern Rhodesia*, Manchester, UK: Manchester University Press.

Damasio, A. (1994) *Descartes' error: Emotion, reason and the human brain*, London: Picador.

Damon, W. (1996) 'The lifelong transformation of moral goals through social influence', in P.B. Baltes and U.M. Staudinger (eds) *Interactive minds*, Cambridge, UK: Cambridge University Press.

Danziger, K. (1985) 'The origins of the psychological experiment as a social institution', *American Psychologist* February: 133–139.

Danziger, K. (1997) 'The varieties of social construction', *Theory & Psychology* 7: 399–416.

Davidson, D. and Hoe, S. (1993) 'Children's recall and recognition memory for typical and atypical actions in script-based stories', *Journal of Experimental Child Psychology* 55: 104–126.

Davis, M. (1996) 'Bartlett, F.C. (1932) Hendersen (1903)', *History and Philosophy of Psychology Newsletter* 23: 21–30.

Dirks, N. (ed.) (1992) *Colonialism and culture*, Ann Arbor, MI: University of Michigan Press.

Doise, W. (1985) Les représentations sociales: Définition d'un concept. *Connexions* 45: 243–253.

Douglas, M. (1980) *Evans-Pritchard*, London: Fontana.

Douglas, M. (1987) *How institutions think*, London: Routledge & Kegan Paul.

Douglas, M. (1992) *Risk and blame: Essays in cultural theory*, London: Routledge.

Douglas, M. (1996) *Thought styles*, London: Sage.

Douglas, M. and Ney, S. (1998) *Missing persons: A critique of the social sciences*, Berkeley, CA: California University Press.

Drever, J. (1952) *A dictionary of psychology*, Harmondsworth, UK: Penguin.

Driver, R., Guesne, E. and Tiberghien, A. (eds) (1985) *Children's ideas in science*, Milton Keynes, UK: Open University Press.

Dugatkin, A.L. (1998) *Cooperation among animals*, Oxford, UK: Oxford University Press.

Durkheim, E. (1898) 'Représentations individuelles et représentations collectives', *Revue de Metaphysique et de Morale* 6: 273–302.

Duveen, G. and Lloyd, B. (1990) 'Introduction', in G. Duveen and B. Lloyd (eds) *Social representations and the development of knowledge* (pp. 1–10), Cambridge, UK: Cambridge University Press.

Dyer, M., Cullingford, R. and Alvarado, S. (1990) 'Scripts', in S.C. Shapiro (ed.) *Encyclopedia of artificial intelligence* (Vol. 2, pp. 980–994), New York: Wiley.

Ebbinghaus, H. (1913/1964) *Memory: A contribution to experimental psychology*, New York: Dover. (Original work published 1885.)

Edelman, G. (1992) *Bright air, brilliant fire: On the matter of the mind*, New York: Basic Books.

Edelman, G. (1998) 'Building a picture of the brain', *Daedalus* 127(2): 37–69.

Edwards, D. and Middleton, D. (1986) 'Conversation with Bartlett', *Quarterly Newsletter of the Laboratory of Comparative Human Cognition* 8(3): 79–89.

Edwards, D. and Middleton, D. (1987) 'Conversation and remembering: Bartlett revisited', *Applied Cognitive Psychology* 1: 77–92.

Ellenberger, H.F. (1970) *The discovery of the unconscious*, London: Allen Lane.

Ellis, R. and Thompson, M. (eds) (1997) *Culture matters*, Boulder, CO: Westview Press.

Ellis, R., Thompson, M. and Wildavsky, A. (1990) *Cultural theory*, Boulder, CO: Westview Press.

Erdelyi, M.H. (1996) *The recovery of unconscious memories: Hypermnesia and reminiscence*, Chicago/London: University of Chicago Press.

Erdelyi, M.H. and Becker, J. (1974) 'Hypermnesia for pictures: Incremental memory for pictures but not for words in multiple recall trials', *Cognitive Psychology* 6: 159–171.

Evans-Pritchard, E. (1934) 'Lévy-Bruhl's theory of primitive mentality', *Bulletin of the Faculty of Arts (Cairo)* 2: 1–36.

Evans-Pritchard, E. (1940) *The Nuer: A description of the modes of livelihood and political institutions of a Nilotic people*, Oxford, UK: Clarendon Press.

Evans-Pritchard, E. (1950) 'Social anthropology: Past and present (the Maret lecture)', *Man* 198: 118–124.

Evans-Pritchard, E. (1951) *Social anthropology (the broadcast lectures)*, London: Cohen & West.

Farr, R.M. (1996) *The roots of modern social psychology*, Oxford, UK: Blackwell.

Farr, R.M. (1998) 'From collective to social representations: *Aller et Retour*', *Culture & Psychology* 4(3): 275–296.

Farr, R.M. and Moscovici, S. (eds) (1984) *Social representations*, Cambridge, UK: Cambridge University Press.

Flugel, J.C. (1919) 'On local fatigue in the auditory system', *British Journal of Psychology* 11: 105–134.

Foley, R.A. (1995) *Humans before humanity*, Oxford, UK: Blackwell.

Foley, R.A. and Lee, P.E. (1989) 'Finite social space, evolutionary pathways and reconstructing hominid behaviour', *Science* 243: 901–906.

Foucault, M. (1964) 'L'ordre du discours', *Archéologie du Savoir*, Paris: Gallimard.

Frank, S.A. (1998) *Foundations of social evolution*, Princeton, NJ: Princeton University Press.

Fremigacci, J. (1977) 'Le colonisé, une création du colonisateur? *Omaly sy anio* 5–6: 233–243.

Gardiner, J.M. and Java, R.I. (1993) 'Recognising and remembering', in A.F. Collins, S.E. Gathercole, M.A. Conway and P.E. Morris (eds) *Theories of memory* (pp. 163–188), Hove, UK: Psychology Press.

Gardner, H. (1985) *The mind's new science: A history of the cognitive revolution*, New York: Basic Books.

Gauld, A. and Stephenson, G.M. (1967) 'Some experiments related to Bartlett's theory of remembering', *British Journal of Psychology* 58: 39–49.

Geertz, C. (1988). *Works and lives: The anthropologist as author*, Stanford: Stanford University Press.

Gergen, K. (1989) 'Social psychology and the wrong revolution', *European Journal of Social Psychology* 19: 463–484.

Gibson, J.J. (1950) *Perception of the visual world*, Cambridge, MA: The Riverside Press.

Goodnow, J.J. (1996) 'Collaborative rules: How are people supposed to work with one another?', in P.B. Baltes and U.M. Staudinger (eds) *Interactive minds* (pp. 163–197), Cambridge, UK: Cambridge University Press.

Gopnik, A. and Wellman, H.M. (1992) 'Why the child's theory of mind really *is* a theory', *Mind and Language* 7: 145–171.

Gould, S.J. (1991) *Wonderful life: The Burgess Shale and the nature of history*, Harmondworth, UK: Penguin.

Graesser, A.C. (1981) *Prose comprehension beyond the word*, New York: Springer-Verlag.

Grande, P. and Rosa, A. (1993) 'Antecedentes y aparición de la psicología del procesamiento de la información', *Estudios de Psicología* 50: 107–124.

Graumann, C.F. (1988) 'Introduction to a history of social psychology', in M. Hewstone, W. Stroebe, J.-P. Codol and G.M. Stephenson (eds) *Introduction to social psychology* (pp. 3–19), Oxford, UK: Blackwell.

Gregory, R.L. (1964) 'A technique for minimizing the effects of atmospheric disturbance on photographic telescopes', *Nature* 203: 274.

Gregory, R.L. (1974) 'A technique for minimizing the effects of atmospheric disturbance on photographic telescopes', in R.L. Gregory (ed.) *Concepts and mechanisms of perception* (pp. 501–518), London: Duckworth.

Gregory, R.L. (1980) 'Perceptions as hypotheses', *Philosophical Transactions of the Royal Society of London* B290: 181–197.

Gregory, R.L. (1997) 'Knowledge in perception and illusion', *Philosophical Transactions of the Royal Society of London* B352: 1121–1128.

Gregory R.L. and Wallace J.G. (1963) *Recovery from early blindness: A case study.* (Experimental Society Monograph No. 2), Cambridge, UK: Heffers.

Grendstad, G. and Selle, P. (eds) (1996) *Kultur som levemate, Hierarki, Egalitarianisme, Individualisme, Fatalisme*, Bergen, Norway: Samlaget.

Gross, J. and Rayner, S. (1985) *Measuring culture*, New York: Columbia University Press.

Gruber, H.E. (1989) 'Networks of enterprise in creative scientific work', in B. Gholson, W.R. Shadish, R.A. Niemeyer & A.C. Houts (eds) *Psychology of science: Contributions to metascience*, Cambridge, UK: Cambridge University Press. pp. 246–265.

Haddon, A.C. (1894) *The decorative art of New Guinea: A study in Papuan ethnography*, Dublin, Eire: The Academic House.

Haddon, A.C. (1895) *Evolution in art as illustrated by the life histories of designs*, London: Scott.

Haddon, A.C. (ed.) (1901) *Reports of the Cambridge Anthropological Expedition to Torres Straits, Vol. II, Physiology and Psychology, Part I*, Cambridge: Cambridge University Press.

Haddon, A.C. (ed.) (1901–35) *Reports of the Cambridge Anthropological Expedition to Torres Straits, Vols. I–VI*, Cambridge: Cambridge University Press. (1901) Vol. II, Physiology and Psychology, Part I; (1903) Vol. II, Physiology and Psychology, Part II; (1904) Vol. V, Sociology, Magic and Religion of the Western Islanders; (1907) Vol. III, Linguistics; (1908) Vol. VI, Sociology, Magic and Religion of the Eastern Islanders; (1912) Vol. IV, Arts and Crafts; (1935) Vol. I, General Ethnography.

Haddon, A.C. (ed.) (1935) *Reports of the Cambridge Anthropological Expedition to Torres Straits, Vol. I, General Ethnography*, Cambridge: Cambridge University Press.

Halbwachs, M. (1925) *Les cadres sociaux de la mémoire*, Paris: Alcan.

Halbwachs, M. (1939) 'La mémoire collective chez les musiciens', *Revue Philosophique* 1939: 136–165.

Harré, R. (1984) 'Some reflections on the concept of "social representation"', *Social Research* 51(4): 927–938.

Harré, R. (1985) Review of Farr, R. and Moscovici, M. (eds) (1984), Social representations, *British Journal of Psychology* 76(1): 138–140.

Harré, R. (1998) 'The epistemology of social representations', in U. Flick (ed.) *The psychology of the social* (pp. 129–137), Cambridge, UK: Cambridge University Press.

Harris, A.D. and Zangwill, O.L. (1973) 'The writings of Sir Frederic Bartlett, CBE, FRS: An annotated handlist', *British Journal of Psychology* 64(4): 493–510.

Hartcup, G. (1988) *The war of invention*, London: Brassey.

Head, H. (1920) *Studies in neurology*, London: Hodder & Stoughton/Oxford University Press.

Head, H. (1923) 'William Halse Rivers Rivers, 1864–1922', *Proceedings of the Royal Society of London* B95: xlii–xlvii.

Head, H. (1926) *Aphasia and kindred disorders of speech* (2 vols.), Cambridge, UK: Cambridge University Press.

Hearnshaw, L.S. (1964) *A short history of British psychology 1840–1940*, London: Methuen.

Hebb, D.O. (1949) *Organization of behaviour*, New York: Wiley.

Helmholtz, H. von (1867) *Handbuch der Physiologischen Optik*, Leipzig: Voss.

Henderson, E.N. (1903) 'A study of memory for connected trains of thought', *Psychological Review Monograph Supplements* 5(Whole No. 23).

Herle, A. and Rouse, S. (1998) *Cambridge and the Torres Strait*, Cambridge, UK: Cambridge University Press.

Herzlich, C. (1973) *Health and illness*, London: Academic Press.

Hesse, M. (1974) *The structure of scientific inference*, London: Macmillan.

Hewstone, M., Stroebe, W., Codol, J.-P. and Stephenson, G.M. (eds) (1988) *Introduction to social psychology*, Oxford, UK: Blackwell.

Hewstone, M., Stroebe, W. and Stephenson, G.M. (eds) (1996) *Introduction to social psychology* 2nd ed., Oxford, UK: Blackwell.

Hick, W.E. (1952) 'On the rate of gain of information', *Quarterly Journal of Experimental Psychology* 4: 67.

Hill, A.V., Jakeman, C., Ward, A., Milne, E.A., Monkhouse, S.E. and Tucker, W.S. (1922) *Theory and use of anti-aircraft sound-locators*, London: HMSO.

Hintzman, D.L. (1986) '"Schema abstraction" in a multiple-trace memory model', *Psychological Review* 93: 411–428.

Ho, D.Y.-F. and Chiu, C.-Y. (1998) 'Collective representations as a metaconstruct: An analysis based on methodological relationalism', *Culture & Psychology* 4(3): 331–348.

Høffding, H. (1889) 'Umiddelbar genkendelse [Immediate recognition]', *Det Kongelige Danske Videnskabernes Selskabs Skrifter*, 6(Whole no. 3). (Also published in German in 1889.)

Høffding, H. (1891) *Outlines of psychology*, London: Macmillan. (Original work published in Danish 1885.)

Hogg, M.A. and Vaughan, G.M. (1995) *Social psychology: An introduction*, London: Prentice-Hall.

Hornbostel, E.M. von (1931) 'The time theory of sound-localization: A restatement', *Report on a Discussion of Audition*, London: The Physical Society, pp. 120–127.

Horowitz, M.J. (1988) *Introduction to psychodynamics: A new synthesis*, London: Routledge.

Humphrey, N. (1976) 'The social function of intellect', in P.P.G. Bateson and R.A. Hinde (eds) *Growing points in ethology*, Cambridge, UK: Cambridge University Press.

Hunke, H. (1935) *Luftgefahr und Luftschutz*, Berlin, Germany: Mittler.

Hutchins, E. (1995) *Cognition in the wild*, Cambridge, MA: MIT Press.

Jacoby, L.L. (1988) 'Memory observed and memory unobserved', in U. Neisser and E. Winograd (eds) *Remembering reconsidered: Ecological and traditional approaches to the study of memory* (pp. 145–177), New York: Cambridge University Press.

Jahoda, G. (1982) *Psychology and anthropology: A psychological perspective*, London: Academic Press.

Jahoda, G. (1988) 'Critical notes and reflections on "social representations"', *European Journal of Social Psychology* 18: 195–209.

Jahoda, G. (1992) *Crossroads between culture and mind: Continuities and change in theories of human nature*, New York: Harvester Wheatsheaf.

James, H. (ed.) (1920) *The letters of William James* (2 vols.), Boston: Atlantic Monthly.

James, H. (1936) *The localisation of sound* (Medical Research Council, Special Report Series, No. 207), London: HMSO.

James, H. and Massey, M. (1932) *Some factors in auditory localisation* (Medical Research Council, Special Report Series, No. 166 B), London: HMSO.

James, W. (1890) *The principles of psychology*, Vol. 1, New York: Holt.

Jenkins, J.G. (1935) Review of F.C. Bartlett, *Remembering*, *American Journal of Psychology* 47: 712–715.

Johnson, M. (1987) *The body in the mind: The bodily basis of meaning, imagination, and reason*, Chicago: University of Chicago Press.

Johnson, M.K. (1988) 'Reality monitoring: An experimental phenomenological approach', *Journal of Experimental Psychology General* 117: 390–394.

Johnson, R.E. (1962) 'The retention of qualitative changes in learning', *Journal of Verbal Learning and Verbal Behavior* 1: 218–223.

Johnson-Laird, N. (1980) 'Mental models in cognitive science', *Cognitive Science* 4: 71–115.

Johnson-Laird, N. (1983) *Mental models*, Cambridge, MA: Harvard University Press.

Jones, E. (1920) Review of *Instinct and the unconscious*, by W.H.R. Rivers, MD, DSC, FRS, *International Journal of Psychoanalysis* 1: 470–476.

Jones, E.E. (1985) History of social psychology, in G.A. Kimble and K. Schlesinger (eds) *Topics in the history of psychology* (pp. 371–407), Hillsdale, NJ: Lawrence Erlbaum Associates Inc.

Jones, H.A. (1935) *The war in the air*, Oxford, UK: Clarendon.

Kahlbaugh, P.E. (1993) 'James Mark Baldwin: A bridge between social and cognitive theories of development', *Journal for the Theory of Social Behaviour* 23(1): 79–103.

Karmasin, H. and Karmasin, M. (1997) *Cultural Theory, ein neuer Ansatz fur Kommunikation, Marketing und Management*, Vienna: Linde.

Kashima, Y. (1997) *Recovering Bartlett's social psychology of cultural dynamics*, unpublished manuscript.

Katz, B. (1978) 'Archibald Vivian Hill, 1886–1977', *Biographical Memoirs of Fellows of the Royal Society* 24: 71–149.

Keller, L. and Genoud, M. (1997) 'Extraordinary lifespans in ants: A test of evolutionary theories of ageing', *Nature* 389: 958–960.

Kim, U. (1997) 'Social representation of success and failure experience: Indigenous analysis of Korean and American responses', paper presented at the 2nd Meeting of Asian Association of Social Psychology, Kyoto, Japan, 4–6 August.

Kintsch, W. (1995) 'Introduction', in F.C. Bartlett (1932, reissued 1995) *Remembering: A study in experimental and social psychology* (pp. xi–xv), Cambridge, UK: Cambridge University Press.

Koffka, K. (1936) *Principles of Gestalt psychology*, London: Kegan Paul, Trench & Trubner.

Kohli, M. (1986) 'Social organization and subjective construction of the life course', in A.B. Sørensen, F.E. Weiner and L.R. Sherrod (eds) *Human development and the life course* (pp. 271–292), Hillsdale, NJ: Lawrence Erlbaum Associates Inc.

Koriat, A. and Goldsmith, M. (1996) 'Memory metaphors and the real-life/laboratory controversy: Correspondence versus storehouse conceptions of memory', *Behavioral and Brain Sciences* 19: 167–228.

Kosslyn, S.M., Pinker, S., Smith, G.E. and Shwartz, S.P. (1979) 'On the demystification of mental imagery', *Behavioral and Brain Sciences* 2: 535–581.

Kranakis, E. (1989) 'Social determinants of engineering practice: A comparative view of France and America in the nineteenth century', *Social Studies of Science* 19: 5–70.

Kranakis, E. (1997) *Constructing a bridge: An exploration of engineering culture, design, and research in nineteenth-century France and America*, Cambridge, MA: MIT Press.

Kuhn, T.S. (1962) *The structure of scientific revolutions*, Chicago: University of Chicago Press.

Kuper, A. and Kuper, J. (1985) *The social science encyclopedia*, London: Routledge & Kegan Paul.

Kusch, M. (1999) *Psychological knowledge: A social history and philosophy*, London: Routledge.

Lachman, R., Lachman, J.L. and Butterfield, E.C. (1979) *Cognitive psychology and information-processing: An introduction*, Hillsdale, NJ: Lawrence Erlbaum Associates Inc.

Lakoff, G. (1987) *Women, fire, and dangerous things: What categories reveal about the mind*, Chicago: University of Chicago Press.

Langdon-Brown, W. (1936) 'To a very wise man', *St. Bartholomew's Hospital Journal*, Nov: 29–30.

Larsen, S.F. (1996) 'Memorable books: Recall of reading and its personal context', in M.S. MacNealy and R. Kreuz (eds) *Advances in discourse processes: Vol. 52. Empirical approaches to literature and aesthetics* (pp. 583–600), Norwood, NJ: Ablex.

Larsen, S.F. (1998) 'What is it like to remember? On phenomenal qualities of memory', in C.P. Thompson, D.J. Herrmann, D. Bruce, D.J. Read, D.G. Payne and M.P. Toglia (eds) *Autobiographical memory: Theoretical and applied perspectives* (pp. 163–190), Mahwah, NJ: Lawrence Erlbaum Associates Inc.

Latour, B. (1987) *Science in action*, Cambridge, MA: Harvard University Press.

Lave, J. (1988) *Cognition in practice*, Cambridge: Cambridge University Press.

Lave, J. (1993) 'The practice of learning', in S. Chaiklin and J. Lave (eds) *Understanding practice: Perspectives on activity and context* (pp. 3–32), New York: Cambridge University Press.

Lazarus, R.S. (1991) 'Cognition and motivation in emotion', *American Psychologist* 46: 352–367.

Lévy-Bruhl, L. (1910) *Les founctions mentales dans les sociétés inférieures*, Paris: Presses Universitaires de France.

Lévy-Bruhl, L. (1922) *La mentalité primitive*, Paris: Alcan.

Lévy-Bruhl, L. (1966) *How natives think*, New York: Washington Square Press.

Leyens, J.-P. and Codol, J.-P. (1988) 'Social cognition', in M. Hewstone, W. Stroebe, J.-P. Codol and G.M. Stephenson (eds) *Introduction to social psychology* (pp. 89–110), Oxford, UK: Blackwell.

Leyens, J.-P. and Dardenne, B. (1996) 'Basic concepts and approaches in social cognition', in M. Hewstone, W. Stroebe and G.M. Stephenson (eds) *Introduction to social psychology* 2nd ed. (pp. 109–134), Oxford, UK: Blackwell.

Lindsay, H. and Norman, D.A. (1977) *Human information processing: An introduction to psychology* (2nd ed.), New York: Academic Press.

Loftus, E.F. (1991) 'Made in memory: Distortions of recollection after misleading information', in Bower (ed.) *Psychology of learning and motivation* (pp. 187–215), New York: Academic Press.

Loftus, E.F., Miller, D.G. and Burns, H. (1978) 'Semantic integration of verbal information into a visual memory', *Journal of Experimental Psychology: Human Learning and Memory* 4: 19–31.

Loftus, E.F. and Palmer, J.C. (1974) 'Reconstruction of automobile destruction: An example of the interaction between language and memory', *Journal of Verbal Learning and Verbal Behavior* 13: 585–589.

Luria, A.R. (1932) *The nature of human conflicts*, New York: Liveright.

MacKenzie, D. (1990) *Inventing accuracy: A historical sociology of nuclear missile guidance*, Cambridge, MA: MIT Press.

MacKenzie, D. (1996) *Knowing machines: Essays on technological change*, Cambridge, MA: MIT Press.

MacKenzie, D. and Wajcman, J. (eds) (1985) *The social shaping of technology*, Milton Keynes, UK: Open University Press.

Magnusson, D. (ed.) (1996) *The lifespan development of individuals: Behavioural, neurobiological and psychosocial perspectives*, Cambridge, UK: Cambridge University Press.

Maida, A.S. (1990) 'Frame theory', in S.C. Shapiro (ed.) *Encyclopedia of artificial intelligence* (Vol. 1, pp. 302–312), New York: Wiley.

Mandelbaum, D.G. (1980) 'The Todas in time perspective', *Reviews in Anthropology* 1: 279–302.

Mandler, J.M. and Johnson, N.S. (1977) 'Remembrance of things parsed: Story structure and recall', *Cognitive Psychology* 9: 111–151.

Marková, I. (1982) *Paradigms, thought, and language*, Chichester, UK: John Wiley.

Martin, K. (1966) *Father figures: A first volume of autobiography, 1897–1931*, London: Hutchinson.

McClelland, C.E. (1980) *State, society and university in Germany, 1700–1914*, Cambridge, UK: Cambridge University Press.

McCrea, W. (1951) 'Edward Arthur Milne, 1896–1950', *Obituary Notices of Fellows of the Royal Society* 7: 420–443.

McDermott, K.B. (1996) 'The persistence of false memories in list recall', *Journal of Memory and Language* 35: 212–230.

McDougall, W. (1908) *Introduction to social psychology*, London: Methuen.

McDougall, W. (1920) *The group mind*, Cambridge, UK: Cambridge University Press.

McDougall, W. (1930) William McDougall, in Murchison C. (ed.) *A history of psychology in autobiography* (Vol. I, pp. 191–223). Worcester, MA: Clark University Press.

McKinlay, A. and Potter, J. (1987) 'Social representations: A conceptual critique', *Journal for the Theory of Social Behaviour* 17(4): 471–487.

Medin, D.L. and Ross, B.H. (1989) 'The specific character of abstract thought: Categorization, problem solving, and induction', in R.J. Sternberg (ed.) *Advances in the psychology of human intelligence* (Vol. 5, pp. 189–223), Hillsdale, NJ: Lawrence Erlbaum Associates Inc.

Middleton, D. and Crook, C. (1996) 'Bartlett and socially ordered consciousness: A discursive perspective. Comments on Rosa (1996)', *Culture & Psychology* 2(3): 379–396.

Middleton, D. and Edwards, D. (eds) (1990a) *Collective remembering*, London: Sage.

Middleton, D. and Edwards, D. (1990b) 'Introduction', in D. Middleton and D. Edwards (eds) *Collective remembering* (pp. 1–22), London: Sage.

Minsky, M. (1975) 'A framework for representing knowledge', in P.H. Wiston (ed.) *The psychology of computer vision*, New York: McGraw-Hill.

Mishra, P. and Brewer, W.F. (1998) 'The role of theories in the recall of text information', unpublished manuscript, Department of Psychology, University of Illinois at Urbana-Champaign.

Mitchell, T. (1988) *Colonizing Egypt*, Cambridge, UK: Cambridge University Press.

Mollon, J.D. and Perkins, A.J. (1996) 'Errors of judgement at Greenwich in 1796', *Nature* 380: 101–102.

Monk, R. (1990) *Ludwig Wittgenstein*, London: Jonathan Cape.

Moscovici, S. (1961) *La Psychanalyse: son image et son public*. Paris: Presses Universitaires de France. (Second edition 1976.)

Moscovici, S. (1972) 'Society and theory in social psychology', in J. Israel and H. Tajfel (eds) *The context of social psychology* (pp. 17–68), London: Academic Press.

Moscovici, S. (1981) 'On social representations', in J.P. Forgas (ed.) *Social cognition* (pp. 181–209), London: Academic Press.

Moscovici, S. (1984) 'The phenomenon of social representations', in R. Farr and S. Moscovici (eds) *Social representations*, Cambridge, UK: Cambridge University Press.

Moscovici, S. (1985) 'Comment on Potter and Litton', *British Journal of Social Psychology* 24: 91–92.

Moscovici, S. (1988) 'Notes towards a description of social representations', *European Journal of Social Psychology* 18: 211–250.

Moscovici, S. (1990) 'Social psychology and developmental psychology: Extending the conversation', in G. Duveen and B. Lloyd (eds) *Social representations and the development of knowledge* (pp. 164–185), Cambridge, UK: Cambridge University Press.

Moscovici, S. (1998a) 'Social consciousness and its history', *Culture & Psychology* 4(3): 411–429.

Moscovici, S. (1998b) 'The history and actuality of social representations', in U. Flick (ed.) *The psychology of the social*, Cambridge, UK: Cambridge University Press.

Moscovici, S. and Hewstone, M. (1983) 'Social representations and social explanations: From the "naïve" to the "amateur" scientist', in M. Hewstone (ed.) *Attribution theory* (pp. 98–125), Oxford, UK: Blackwell.

Moscovici, S. and Marková, I. (1998) 'Presenting social representations: A conversation', *Culture & Psychology* 4(3): 371–410.

Murphy, R.F. (1967) 'Tuary kinship', *American Anthropologist* 69: 167–170.

Myers, C.S. (1923) 'The influence of the late W.H.R. Rivers', presidential address to the Psychology Section of the British Association, 1922, in W.H.R. Rivers *Psychology and politics and other essays*, London: Kegan Paul/Trench, Trubner.

Myers, C.S. (1936) 'Autobiography', in C. Murchison (ed.) *A history of psychology in autobiography* (Vol. III, pp. 215–230), Worcester, MA: Clark University Press.

Neisser, U. (1967) *Cognitive psychology*, New York: Appleton-Century-Crofts.

Neisser, U. (1976) *Cognition and reality*, San Francisco: Freeman.

Neisser, U. (1978) 'Memory: What are the important questions?', in M.M. Gruneberg, E. Morris and R.N. Sykes (eds) *Practical aspects of memory* (pp. 3–14), London: Academic Press.

Neisser, U. (1984) 'Interpreting Harry Bahrick's discovery: What confers immunity against forgetting?', *Journal of Experimental Psychology: General* 113: 32–35.

Neisser, U. (1986) 'Nested structure in autobiographical memory', in D.C. Rubin (ed.) *Autobiographical memory* (pp. 71–82), Cambridge, UK: Cambridge University Press.

Neisser, U. (1988) 'What is ordinary memory the memory of?', in U. Neisser and E. Winograd (eds) *Remembering reconsidered: Ecological and traditional approaches to the study of memory* (pp. 356–373), New York: Cambridge University Press.

Nelson, K. (ed.) (1989) *Narratives from the crib*, Cambridge, MA: Harvard University Press.

Nelson, K. (1993a) 'Explaining the emergence of autobiographical memory in early childhood', in A.F. Collins, S.E. Gathercole, M.A. Conway and P.E. Morris (eds) *Theories of memory* (pp. 355–385), Hove, UK: Psychology Press.

Nelson, K. (1993b) 'The psychological and social origins of autobiographical memory', *Psychological Science* 4: 1–8.

Norman, D.A. (1991) 'Cognitive artefacts', in J.M. Carroll (ed.), *Designing interaction: Psychology at the human–computer interface*, Cambridge, UK: Cambridge University Press.

Oldfield, R.C. (1972) 'Frederic Charles Bartlett: 1886–1969', *American Journal of Psychology* 85: 133–140.

Oldfield, R.C. and Zangwill, O.L. (1942a) 'Head's concept of the schema and its application in contemporary British psychology: Part I. Head's concept of the schema', *British Journal of Psychology* 32: 267–286.

Oldfield, R.C. and Zangwill, O.L. (1942b) 'Head's concept of the schema and its application in contemporary British psychology: Part II. Critical analysis of Head's theory', *British Journal of Psychology* 33: 58–64.

Oldfield, R.C. and Zangwill, O.L. (1943) 'Head's concept of the schema and its application in contemporary British psychology: Part III. Bartlett's theory of memory', *British Journal of Psychology* 33: 113–129.

Olson, D. (1995) 'Writing and the mind', in J.V. Wertsch, P. del Río and A. Alvarez (eds) *Sociocultural studies of mind* (pp. 95–123), Cambridge, UK: Cambridge University Press.

Osgood, C.E. (1953) *Method and theory in experimental psychology*, New York: Oxford University Press.

Oyserman, D. and Markus, H. (1998) 'Self as social representation', in U. Flick (ed.) *The psychology of the social* (pp. 107–125), Cambridge, UK: Cambridge University Press.

Palmer, S.E. (1975) 'Visual perception and world knowledge: Notes on a model of sensory-cognitive interaction', in D.A. Norman and D.E. Rumelhart (eds) *Explorations in cognition* (pp. 279–307), San Francisco: W.H. Freeman.

Paris, E.T. (1933) 'Binaural sound-locators', *Science Progress* 27: 457–469.

Parker, I. (1987) '"Social representations": Social psychology's (mis)use of sociology', *Journal for the Theory of Social Behaviour* 17(4): 447–469.

Parot, F. (ed.) (1996) *Pour une psychologie historique: Ecrits en hommage à Ignace Meyerson*, Paris: Presses Universitaires de France.

Pattison, M. (1983) 'Scientists, inventors and the military in Britain, 1915–19: The munitions inventions department', *Social Studies of Science* 13: 521–568.

Paul, I.H. (1959) 'Studies in remembering: The reproduction of connected and extended verbal material', *Psychological Issues* 1(Monograph 2).

Payne, D.G. (1987) 'Hypermnesia and reminiscence in recall: A historical and empirical review', *Psychological Bulletin* 101: 5–27.

Payne, D.G., Toglia, M.P. and Anastasi, J.S. (1994) 'Recognition performance level and the magnitude of the misinformation effect in eyewitness memory', *Psychonomic Bulletin and Review* 1: 376–382.

Perrig, W. and Kintsch, W. (1985) 'Propositional and situational representations of text', *Journal of Memory and Language* 24: 503–518.

Philippe, J. (1897) 'Sur les transformations de nos images mentales', *Review of Philosophy* 43: 481–493.

Plotkin, H. (1998) *Evolution in mind*, Cambridge, MA: Harvard University Press.

Potter, J. and Litton, I. (1985) 'Some problems underlying the theory of social representations', *British Journal of Social Psychology* 24: 81–90.

Potter, J. and Wetherell, M. (1998) 'Social representations, discourse analysis, and racism', in U. Flick (ed.) *The psychology of the social* (pp. 138–155), Cambridge, UK: Cambridge University Press.

Rapaport, D. (1971) *Emotions and memory* (5th. ed.), New York: International Universities Press. (1st ed. published 1941.)

Rayner, S. and Malone, E. (1998) *Human choice and global climate change*, Columbus, OH: Battelle Institute.

Richards, G. (1998) 'Getting a result: The expedition's psychological research 1898–1913', in A. Herle and S. Rouse (eds) *Cambridge and the Torres Strait: Centenary essays on the 1898 expedition* (pp. 136–157), Cambridge, UK: Cambridge University Press.

Ridley, M. (1996) *The origins of virtue*, London: Viking.

Rignano, E. (1920) *The psychology of reasoning*, London: Routledge & Kegan Paul.

Rivers, W.H.R. (1900) 'Vision', in E.A. Schäfer (ed.) *Textbook of physiology*, Vol. 2 (pp. 1026–1148), Edinburgh, UK: Young J. Pentland.

Rivers, W.H.R. (1901a) 'Introduction', in A.C. Haddon (ed.) *Reports of the Cambridge Anthropological Expedition to Torres Strait, Vol. II: Physiology and psychology, Part I* (pp. 1–7), Cambridge, UK: Cambridge University Press.

Rivers, W.H.R. (1901b) 'Vision', in A.C. Haddon (ed.) *Reports of the Cambridge Anthropological Expedition to Torres Strait, Vol. II: Physiology and psychology, Part I* (pp. 8–132), Cambridge, UK: Cambridge University Press.

Rivers, W.H.R. (1906) *The Todas*, London: Macmillan.

Rivers, W.H.R. (1912) 'Conventionalism in primitive art', *Reports of the British Association for the Advancement of Science* (Section H): 599.

Rivers, W.H.R. (1914a, b) 'Kinship and social organisation', London: Constable.

Rivers, W.H.R. (1914c) 'Psychology and medicine', *British Journal of Psychology* 10: 183–193.

Rivers, W.H.R. (1914d) *The history of Melanesian society*, Cambridge, UK: Cambridge University Press.

Rivers, W.H.R. (1920) *Instinct and the unconscious*, Cambridge, UK: Cambridge University Press.

Rivers, W.H.R. (1923a) *Conflict and dream*, London: Kegan Paul/Trench, Trubner.

Rivers, W.H.R. (1923b) *Psychology and politics and other essays*, London: Kegan Paul/ Trench, Trubner.

Rivers, W.H.R. (1926) *Psychology and ethnology*, London: Kegan Paul/Trench, Trubner.

Rivers, W.H.R. and Head, H. (1908) 'A human experiment in nerve division', *Brain* 31: 323–450.

Robinson, J.A. (1996) 'Perspective, meaning, and remembering', in D.C. Rubin (ed.) *Remembering our past: Studies in autobiographical memory*, New York: Cambridge University Press.

Rodger, A. (1971) 'C.S. Myers in retrospect', *Bulletin of the British Psychological Society* 24: 177–185.

Roediger, H.L. (1996) 'Memory illusions', *Journal of Memory and Language* 35: 76–100.

Roediger, H.L. (1997) 'Two views of *Remembering*', *Contemporary Psychology* 42: 488–492.

Roediger, H.L. and Challis, B.H. (1989) 'Hypermnesia: Increased recall with repeated tests', in C. Izawa (ed.) *Current issues in cognitive processes*: *The Tulane Floweree symposium on cognition* (pp. 175–199), Hillsdale, NJ: Lawrence Erlbaum Associates Inc.

Roediger, H.L., Jacoby, D. and McDermott, K.B. (1996) 'Misinformation effects in recall: Creating false memories through repeated retrieval', *Journal of Memory and Language* 35: 300–318.

Roediger, H.L. and McDermott, K.B. (1995) 'Creating false memories: Remembering words that were not presented in lists', *Journal of Experimental Psychology: Learning, Memory and Cognition* 21: 803–814.

Roediger, H.L. and McDermott, K.B. (in press) 'Distortions of memory', in E. Tulving and F.I.M. Craik (eds) *Oxford handbook of memory*. Oxford, UK: Oxford University Press.

Roediger, H.L., Payne, D., Gillespie, G.L. and Lean, D.S. (1982) 'Hypermnesia as determined by level of recall', *Journal of Verbal Learning and Verbal Behavior* 21: 635–665.

Roediger, H.L., Wheeler, M.A. and Rajaram, S. (1993) 'Remembering, knowing and reconstructing the past', in D.L. Medin (ed.) *The psychology of learning and motivation: Advances in research and theory* (pp. 97–134), New York: Academic Press.

Rogoff, B. and Lave, J. (eds) (1984) *Everyday cognition: Its development in social context*, Cambridge, MA: Harvard University Press.

Rokeach, M. (1968) 'Attitudes: I. The nature of attitudes', in D.L. Sills (ed.) *International encyclopedia of the social sciences* (Vol. 1, pp. 449–458), New York: Collier & Macmillan.

Rosa, A. (1995a) 'Emoción y afecto en la obra temprana de Bartlett, Comunicación presentada in el IV Symposium de la Sociedad Española de Historia de la Psicología', *Revista de Historia de la Psicología* 15(3–4): 79–91.

Rosa, A. (1995b) 'Introducción: *El Recuerdo* y la obra de Frederic Charles Bartlett', in F.C. Bartlett *El Recuerdo* (1932, Spanish edition 1995, pp. 9–43), Madrid, Spain: Alianza.

Rosa, A. (1996) 'Bartlett's psycho-anthropological project', *Culture & Psychology* 2(4): 355–378.

Rubin, E. (1921) *Visuell wahrgenommene Figuren*, Copenhagen, Denmark: Gyldendal.

Rumelhart, D.E. (1980) 'Schemata: The building blocks of cognition', in R.J. Spiro, B.C. Bruce and W.F. Brewer (eds) *Theoretical issues in reading comprehension* (pp. 33–58), Hillsdale, NJ: Lawrence Erlbaum Associates Inc.

Rumelhart, D.E. and Ortony, A. (1977) 'The representation of knowledge in memory', in R.C. Anderson and R.J. Spiro (eds) *Schooling and the acquisition of knowledge* (pp. 99–135), Hillsdale, NJ: Lawrence Erlbaum Associates Inc.

Rumelhart, D.E., Smolensky, P., McClelland, J.L. and Hinton, G.E. (1986) 'Schemata and sequential thought processes in PDP models', in D.E. Rumelhart and J.L. McClelland (eds) *Parallel distributed processing*, Cambridge, MA: MIT Press.

Russell, B. (1921) *The analysis of mind*, London: George Allen & Unwin.

Saito, A. (1994) 'Bartlett's social psychology', paper presented at the British Psychological Society Social Psychology Section Annual Conference, Cambridge, September 1994. *Proceedings of the British Psychological Society* 3(1): 65.

Saito, A. (1996a) '"Bartlett's way" and social representations: The case of Zen transmitted across cultures', *Japanese Journal of Experimental Social Psychology* 35(3): 263–277.

Saito, A. (1996b) 'Social origins of cognition: Bartlett, evolutionary perspective and embodied mind approach', *Journal for the Theory of Social Behaviour* 26(4): 399–421.

Saito, A. (1998) 'Lifespan development and phylogeny of interactive minds', *Culture & Psychology* 4(2): 245–258.

Salomon, G. (ed.) (1993) *Distributed cognitions: Psychological and educational considerations*, Cambridge, UK: Cambridge University Press.

Schacter, D.L. (1995) 'Memory distortion: History and current status', in D.L. Schacter, J.T. Coyle, G.D. Fischback, M.M. Mesulam and L.E. Sullivan (eds) *Memory distortion* (pp. 1–43), Cambridge, MA: Harvard University Press.

Schank, R.C. (1982) *Dynamic memory*, New York: Cambridge University Press.

Schank, R.C. and Abelson, R. (1977) *Scripts, plans, goals, and understanding*, Hillsdale, NJ: Lawrence Erlbaum Associates Inc.

Schatzberg, E. (1994) 'Ideology and technical choice: The decline of the wooden airplane in the United States, 1920–45', *Technology and Culture* 35: 34–69.

Schatzberg, E. (in press) 'Nationalism, resource endowments, and technical choice: Wooden airplanes in the United States, Canada and Great Britain during WWII', in P. Galison and A. Rowland (eds) *The evolution of atmospheric flight in the twentieth century*, Cambridge, MA: MIT Press.

Schneider, D.M. and Watkins, M.J. (1996) 'Response conformity in recognition testing', *Psychonomic Bulletin and Review* 3(4): 481–485.

Shapin, S. (1982) 'History of science and its sociological reconstructions', *History of Science* 20: 157–211.

Shaxby, J. and Gage, F. (1932) *The localisation of sounds in the median plane* (Medical Research Council, Special Reports, No. 166 A), London: HMSO.

Sherif, M. (1936) *The psychology of social norms*, New York: Harper.

Sherrick, C.E. and Cholewiak, R.W. (1986) 'Cutaneous sensitivity', in K.R. Boff, L. Kaufman and J.P. Thomans (eds) *Handbook of perception and human performance*, New York: Wiley.

Sherrington, C.S. (1953) *Man and his nature*, Cambridge, UK: Cambridge University Press.

Shotter, J. (1990) 'The social construction of remembering and forgetting', in D. Middleton and D. Edwards (eds) *Collective remembering* (pp. 120–138), London: Sage.

Showalter, E. (1985) *The female malady*, London: Virago.

Shweder, R.A., Goodnow, J., Hatano, G., LeVine, R.A., Markus, H. and Miller, P. (1998) 'The cultural psychology of development', in W. Damon and R.M. Lerner (eds), *Handbook of child psychology, Vol. 1* (5th ed., pp. 865–937), New York: Wiley.

Slobodin, R. (1978) *W.H.R. Rivers*, New York: Columbia University Press. (Reprinted in 1997, Stroud, UK: Sutton.)

Smith, R. (1997) *The Fontana history of the human sciences*, London: Fontana Press.

Snow, C.P. (1959) *The Two Cultures*, Cambridge: Cambridge University Press.

Sober, E. and Wilson, D.S. (1998) *Unto others: The evolution and psychology of unselfish behavior*, Cambridge, MA: Harvard University Press.

Spiro, R.J. (1980) 'Constructive processes in prose comprehension and recall', in R.J. Spiro, B.C. Bruce and W.F. Brewer (eds) *Theoretical issues in reading comprehension* (pp. 245–278), Hillsdale, NJ: Lawrence Erlbaum Associates Inc.

Staley, R. (1998) 'On the histories of relativity: The propagation and elaboration of relativity theory in participant histories in Germany, 1905–11', *Isis* 89: 263–299.

Staudinger, U.M. (1996) 'Wisdom and the social-interactive foundation of the mind', in P.B. Baltes and U.M. Staudinger (eds) *Interactive minds* (pp. 276–315), Cambridge, UK: Cambridge University Press.

Stephen, K. (1933) *Psychoanalysis and medicine*, Cambridge, UK: Cambridge University Press.

Stone, M. (1985) 'Shellshock and the psychologists', in W.F. Bynum, R. Porter and M. Shepherd (eds) *The anatomy of madness II* (pp. 242–271), London: Routledge.

Stout, G.F. (1938) *A Manual of Psychology, 5th edition*, London: University Tutorial Press.

Thelen, E. and Smith, L. (1994) *A dynamic systems approach to the development of cognition and action*, Cambridge, MA: MIT Press.

Thompson, C.P., Hermann, D.J., Bruce, D., Read, J.D., Payne, D.G. and Toglia, M.P. (eds) (1998) *Autobiographical memory: Theoretical and applied perspective*, Mahwah, NJ: Lawrence Erlbaum Associates Inc.

Thorndyke, W. and Yekovich, F.R. (1980) 'A critique of schema-based theories of human story memory', *Poetics* 9: 23–49.

Tomkins, S.S. (1979) 'Script theory: Differential magnification of affects', in H.E. Howe, Jr. (ed.) *Nebraska symposium on motivation* (Vol. 26, pp. 201–236), Lincoln, NE: University of Nebraska Press.

Tucker, W.S. (1931) 'The localisation of sound by means of observations of intensity', in *Report on a Discussion of Audition*, London: The Physical Society, pp. 114–119.

Tucker, W.S. (1936) 'Direction finding by sound', *Proceedings of the Royal Institution* 29: 262–287.

Tulving, E. (1972) 'Episodic and semantic memory', in E. Tulving and W. Donaldson (eds) *Organization and memory* (pp. 381–403), New York: Academic Press.

Tulving, E. (1985) 'Memory and consciousness', *Canadian Psychologist* 26: 1–12.

Underwood, J. and Pezdek, K. (1998) 'Memory suggestibility as an example of the sleeper effect', *Psychonomic Bulletin and Review* 5(3): 449–453.

Urbach, P. (1980) 'Social propensities', *British Journal for the Philosophy of Science* 31: 317–328.

Valvo, A. (1971) *Sight restoration rehabilitation*, New York: American Foundation for the Blind.

Van der Veer, R. (1996) 'On some historical roots and present-day doubts: A reply to Niconopoulou and Weintraub (1996)', *Culture & Psychology* 2(4): 457–463.

Van der Veer, R. and Valsiner, J. (1991) *Understanding Vygotsky*, Oxford, UK: Blackwell.

Varela, F. (1992) 'Whence perceptual meaning? A cartography of current ideas', in F. Varela and J.-P. Dupuy (eds) *Understanding origins* (pp. 235–263), Dordrecht, The Netherlands: Kluwer.

Vincenti, W. (1990) *What engineers know and how they know it: Analytical studies from aeronautical history*, Baltimore: Johns Hopkins University Press.

Vygotsky, L.S. (1979) *Mind in society*, Cambridge, MA: Harvard University Press.

Waetzmann, H. and Heisig, H. (1931) 'The measurement of the threshold sensitivity of the ear by resonance telephone', *Report on a Discussion of Audition*, London: The Physical Society, pp. 101–103.

Wagner, W. (1996) 'The social representation paradigm', *Japanese Journal of Experimental Social Psychology* 35(3): 247–255.

Ward, J. (1875) *The Relation of Physiology and Psychology*, Fellowship dissertation, Trinity College, Cambridge.

Ward, J. (1886) 'Psychology', in *Encyclopaedia Britannica* (9th ed.), Chicago, IL: Encyclopaedia Britannica.

Warwick, A. (1992) 'Cambridge mathematics and Cavendish physics: Cunningham, Campbell and Einstein's relativity 1905–11: Part I. The uses of theory', *Studies in the History and Philosophy of Science* 23: 625–656.

Warwick, A. (1993) 'Cambridge mathematics and Cavendish physics: Cunningham, Campbell and Einstein's Relativity 1905–11: Part II. Comparing traditions in Cambridge physics', *Studies in the History and Philosophy of Science* 24: 1–25.

Watt, H.J. (1905) 'Experimentelle Beiträge zur eine Theorie des Denkens', *Archiv für die gesamte Psychologie* 4: 289–436.

Weingardt, K.R., Toland, H.K. and Loftus, E.F. (1994) 'Reports of suggested memories: Do people truly believe them?', in D.R. Ross, J.D. Read and M.P. Toglia (eds) *Adult eyewitness testimony: Current trends and developments* (pp. 3–26), Cambridge, UK: Cambridge University Press.

Wertsch, J.V. (1991) *Voices of the mind*, Cambridge, MA: Harvard University Press.

Wertsch, J.V. (1994) 'Struggling with the past: Some dynamics of historical representation', in M. Carretero and J. Voss (eds) *Cognitive and instructional processes in history and the social sciences* (pp. 333–338), Hillsdale, NJ: Lawrence Erlbaum Associates Inc.

Wheeler, M.A. and Roediger III, H.L. (1992) 'Disparate effects of repeated testing: Reconciling Ballard's (1913) and Bartlett's (1932) results', *Psychological Science* 3: 240–245.

White, M.J. (1983) 'Prominent publications in cognitive psychology', *Memory & Cognition* 11: 423–427.

Wiener, N. (1956) *I am a mathematician*, London: Victor Gollancz.

Williams, O. (1926) 'A study of the phenomenon of reminiscence', *Journal of Experimental Psychology* 9: 368–387.

Woodworth, R. (1939) *Experimental psychology*, London: Methuen.

Woodworth, R.S. and Schlosberg, H. (1954) *Experimental psychology, second edition*, New York: Holt, Rinehart & Winston.

Wynn, V.E. and Logie, R.H. (1998) 'The veracity of long-term memories: Did Bartlett get it right?' *Applied Cognitive Psychology* 12: 1–20.

Zangwill, O.L. (1970) 'Sir Frederic Bartlett (1886–1969)', *Quarterly Journal of Experimental Psychology* 22: 77–81.

Zangwill, O.L. (1972a) '*Remembering* revisited', *Bulletin de Psychologie* 41: 165–174.

Zangwill, O.L. (1972b) '*Remembering* revisited', *Quarterly Journal of Experimental Psychology* 24: 123–138.

Zangwill, O.L. (1987) Rivers, William Halse Rivers (1864–1922), in R.L. Gregory (ed.) *The Oxford companion to the mind* (p. 686), Oxford, UK: Oxford University Press.

Author index

As the works of Frederic Bartlett are cited frequently throughout the book, we have not included an entry to him in the Author index.

Subject index